Shojo Beat

We Were There

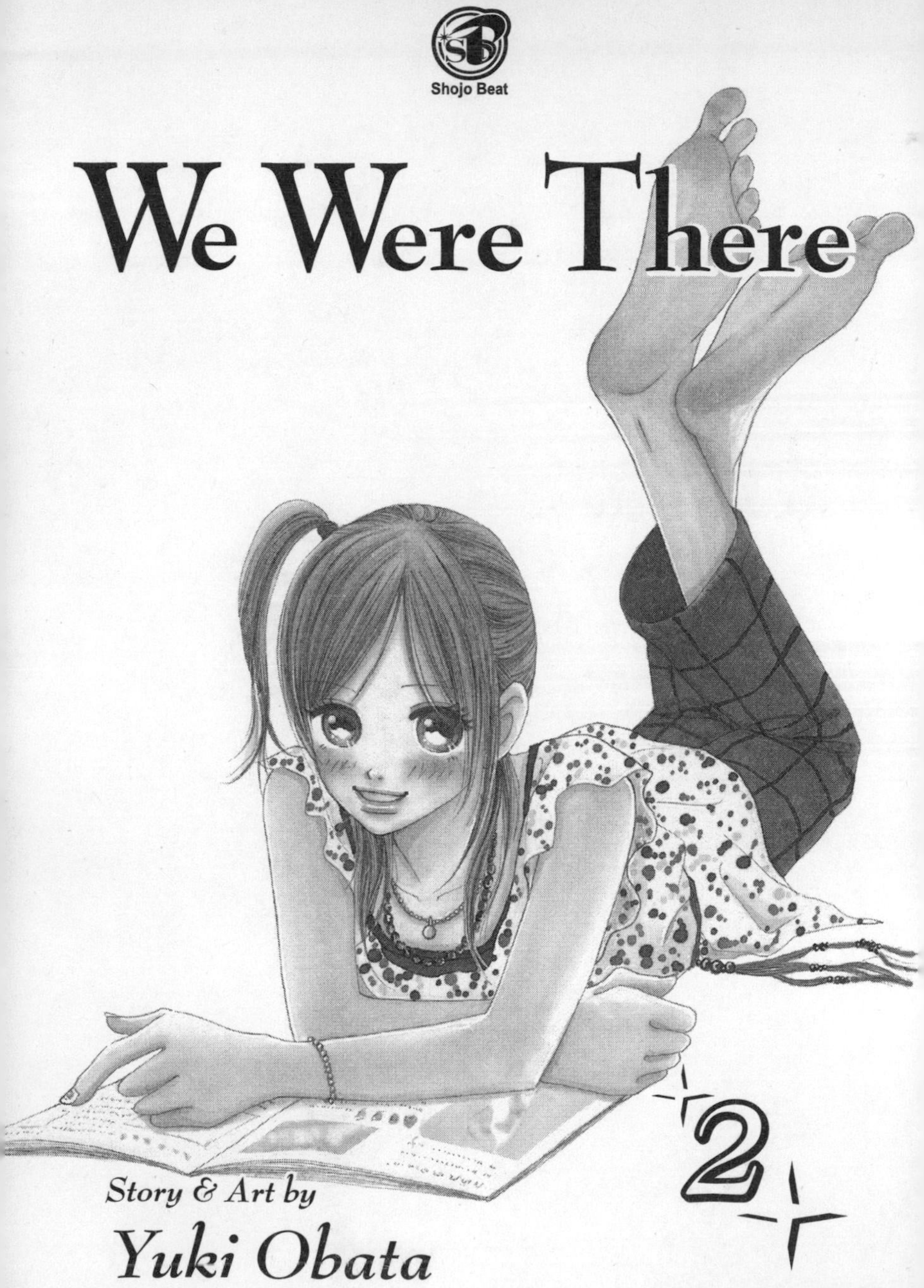

2

Story & Art by

Yuki Obata

Contents

Characters

Yuri Yamamoto
Nanami's classmate.
Nana-san, who dated Yano,
was her older sister.

Motoharu Yano
Nanami's classmate.
He's a popular guy who
gets good grades.

Nanami Takahashi
She's earnest but a bit
forgetful at times.

Story

Nanami enters high school with high hopes of making friends, only to meet Yano, who is extremely popular with the girls. Though Yano doesn't make a good impression on her at first, she is gradually drawn to his kindness. She finds out Yano's girlfriend died in an accident, but unable to hold back her feelings, she tells Yano she likes him...

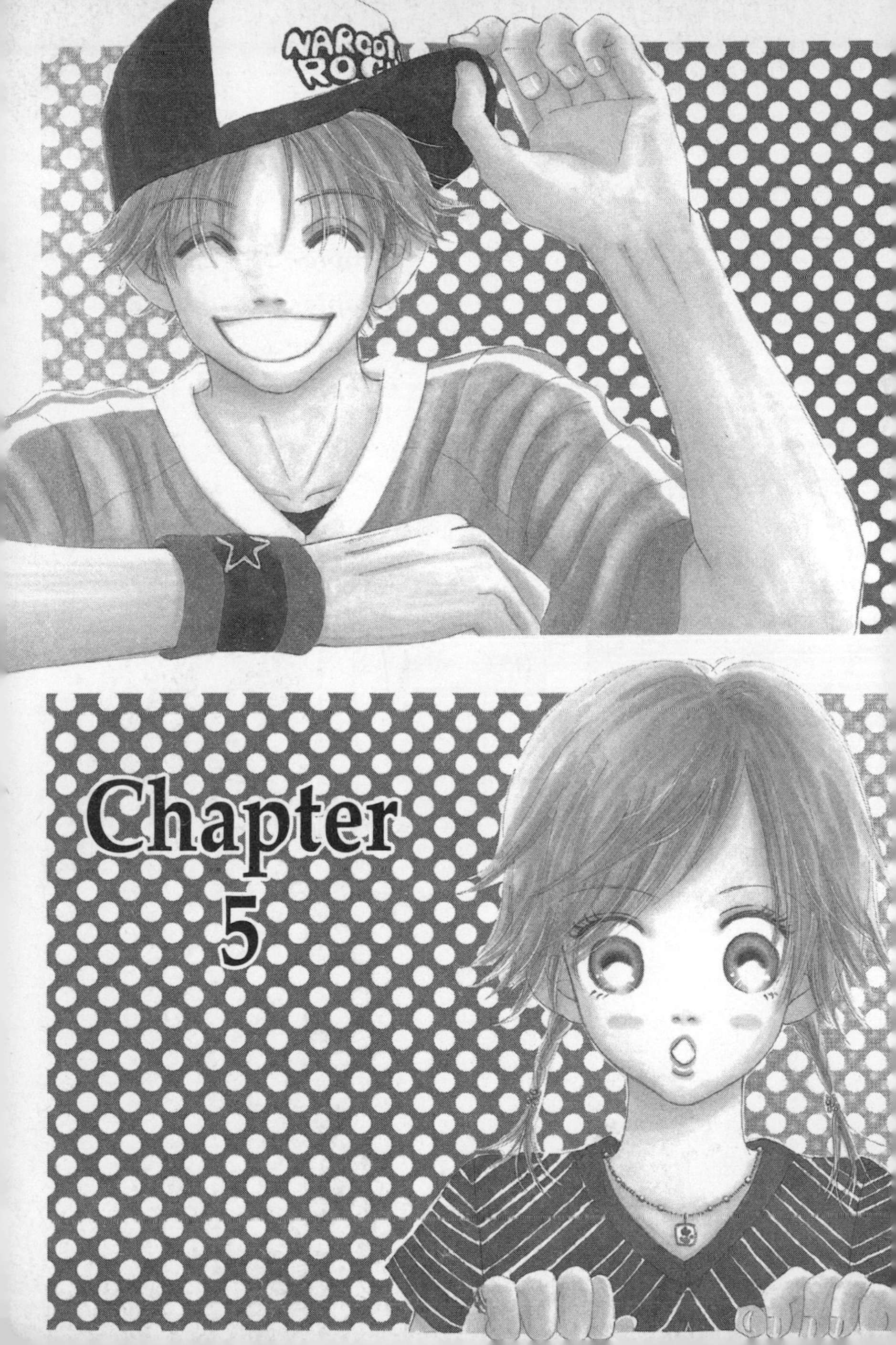
Chapter
5

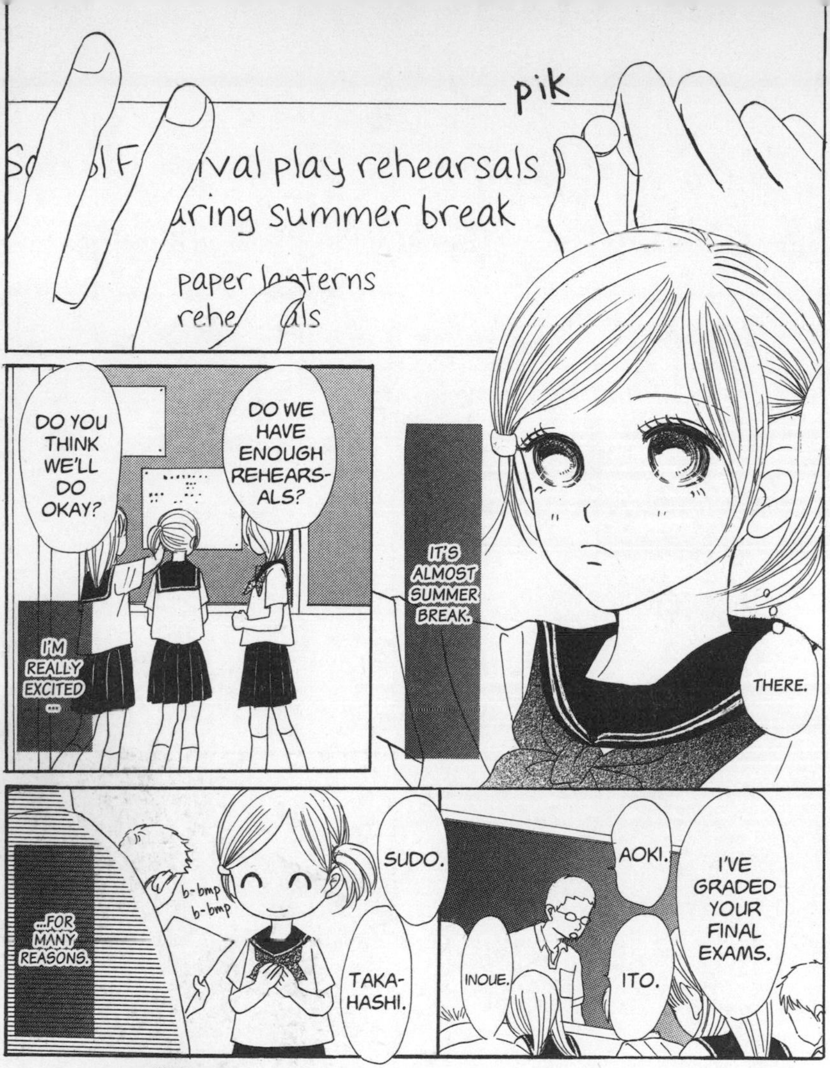
pik
ival play rehearsals
uring summer break
paper l nterns
rehe als
THERE.
IT'S ALMOST SUMMER BREAK.
DO WE HAVE ENOUGH REHEARSALS?
DO YOU THINK WE'LL DO OKAY?
I'M REALLY EXCITED...
I'VE GRADED YOUR FINAL EXAMS.
AOKI.
ITO.
INOUE.
SUDO.
TAKAHASHI.
b-bmp b-bmp
...FOR MANY REASONS.

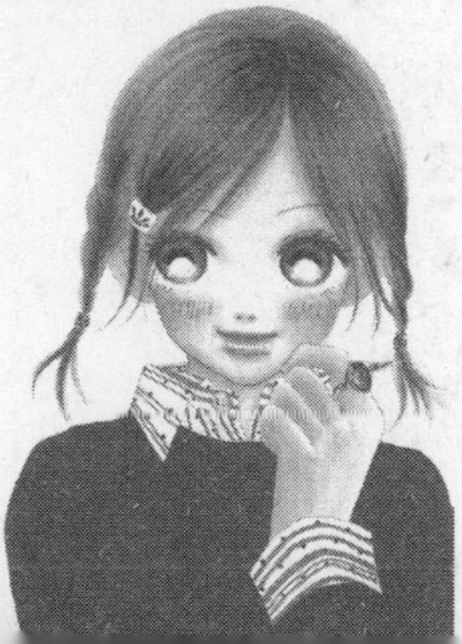

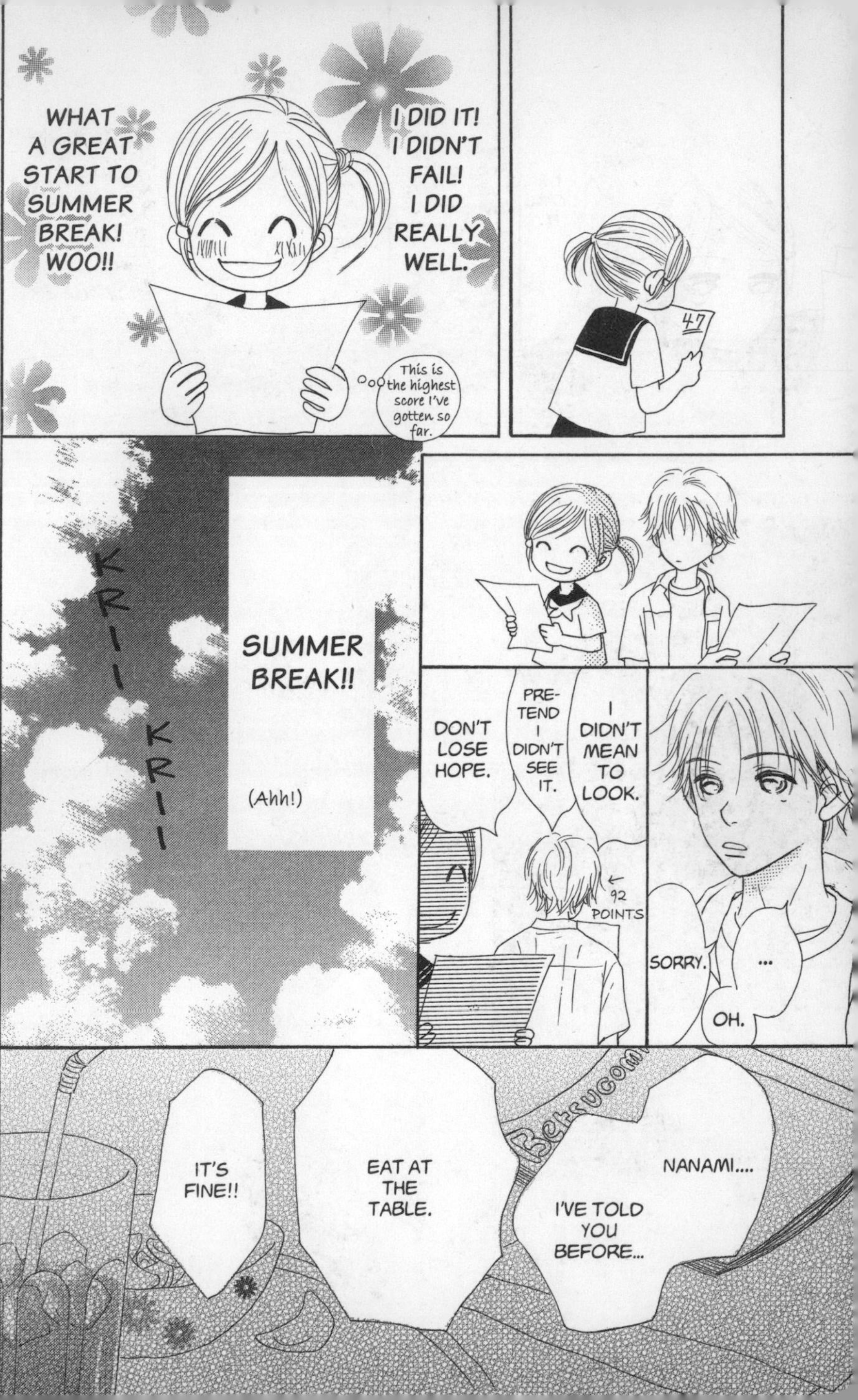
47
I DID IT! I DIDN'T FAIL! I DID REALLY WELL.
WHAT A GREAT START TO SUMMER BREAK! WOO!!
This is the highest score I've gotten so far.
...
SORRY.
OH.
I DIDN'T MEAN TO LOOK.
PRE-TEND I DIDN'T SEE IT.
DON'T LOSE HOPE.
← 92 POINTS
KRII
KRII
SUMMER BREAK!!
(Ahh!)
NANAMI....
I'VE TOLD YOU BEFORE...
EAT AT THE TABLE.
IT'S FINE!!

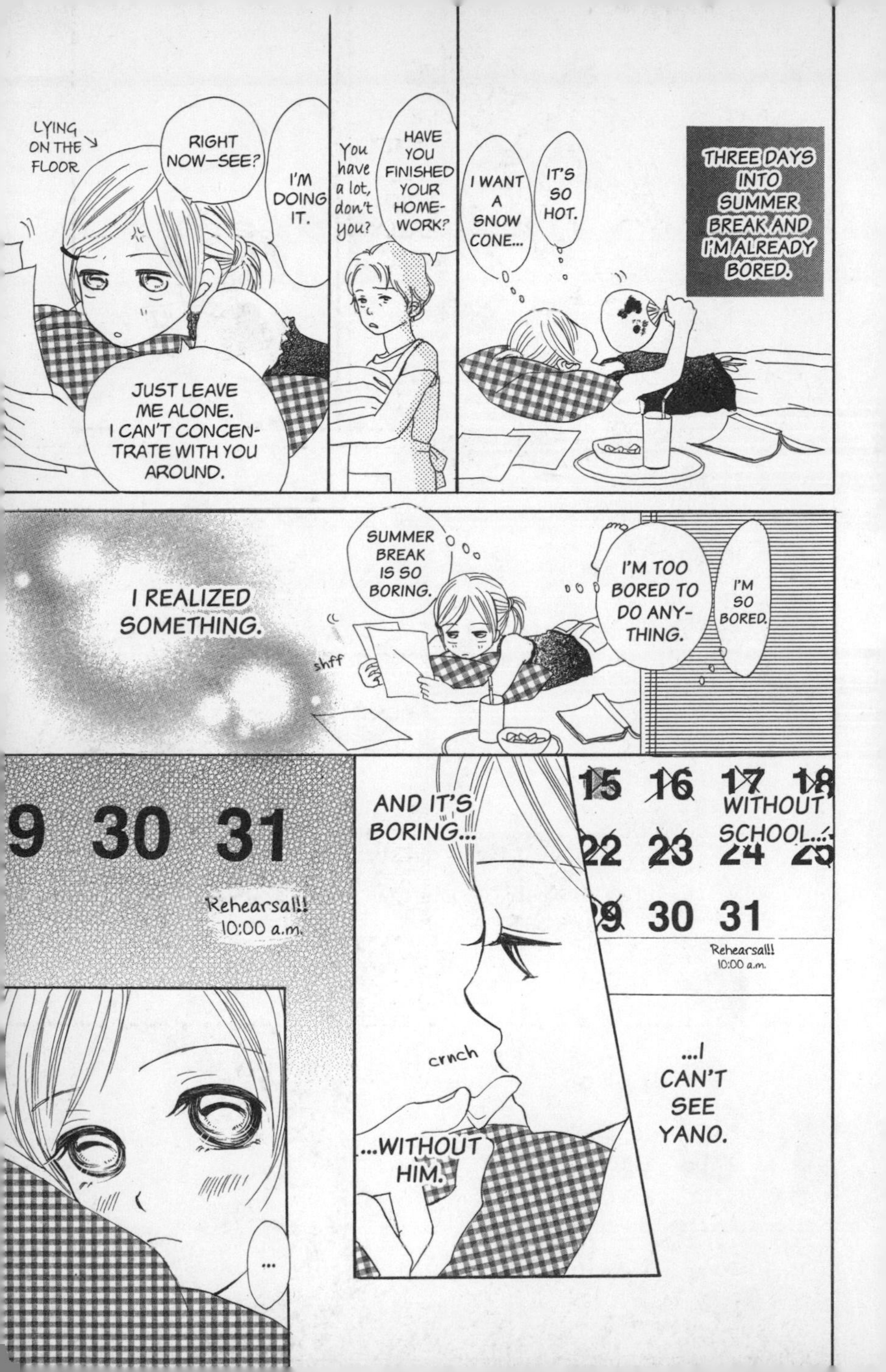
THREE DAYS INTO SUMMER BREAK AND I'M ALREADY BORED.
IT'S SO HOT.
I WANT A SNOW CONE...
HAVE YOU FINISHED YOUR HOMEWORK?
You have a lot, don't you?
I'M DOING IT.
RIGHT NOW—SEE?
LYING ON THE FLOOR
JUST LEAVE ME ALONE. I CAN'T CONCENTRATE WITH YOU AROUND.
I'M SO BORED.
I'M TOO BORED TO DO ANYTHING.
SUMMER BREAK IS SO BORING.
shff
I REALIZED SOMETHING.
15 16 17 18
WITHOUT SCHOOL...
22 23 24 25
29 30 31
Rehearsal!! 10:00 a.m.
...I CAN'T SEE YANO.
AND IT'S BORING...
crnch
...WITHOUT HIM.
9 30 31
Rehearsal!! 10:00 a.m.
...

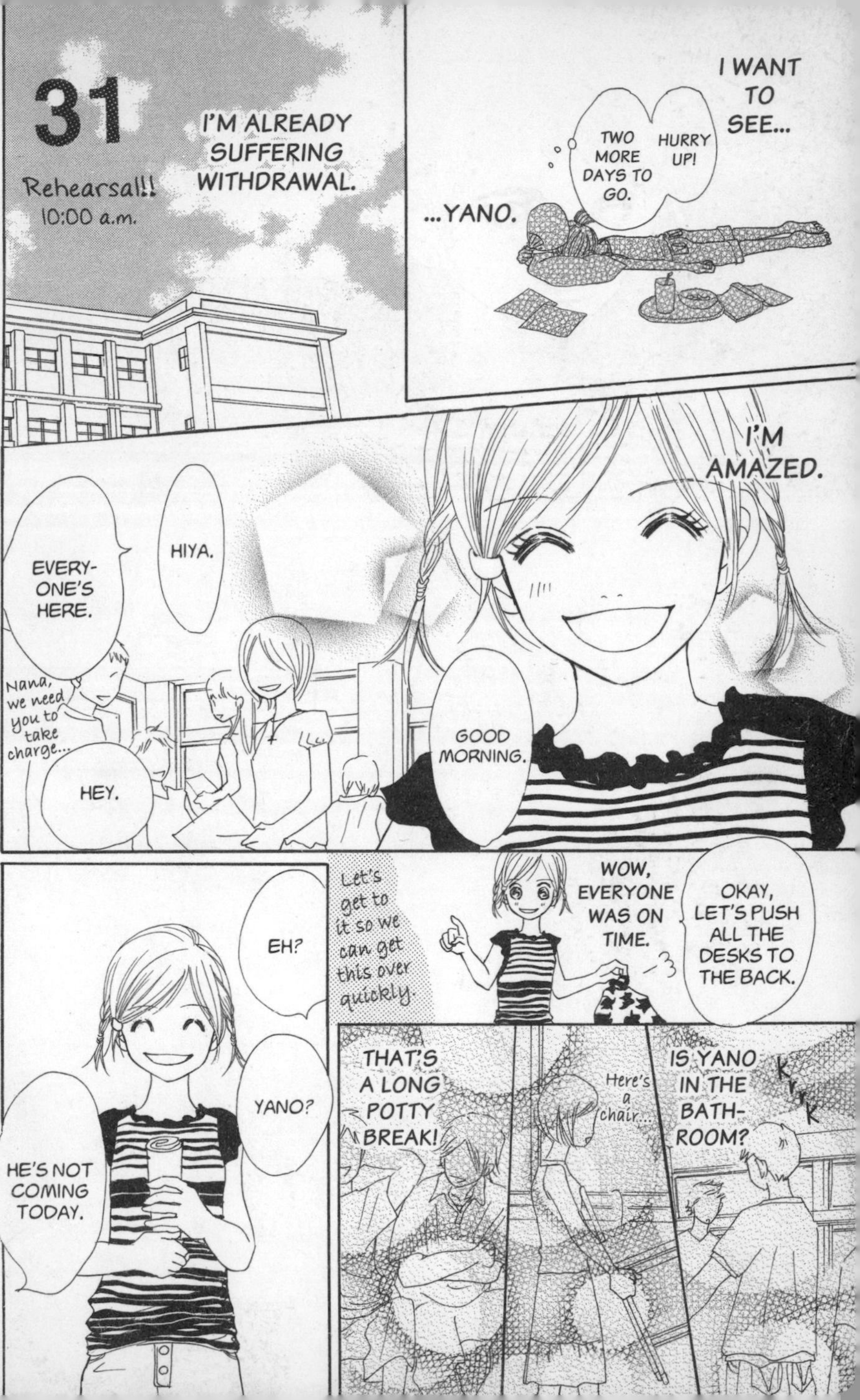

I WANT TO SEE...
HURRY UP!
TWO MORE DAYS TO GO.
...YANO.
I'M ALREADY SUFFERING WITHDRAWAL.
31
Rehearsal!!
10:00 a.m.
I'M AMAZED.
GOOD MORNING.
HIYA.
EVERY-ONE'S HERE.
Nana, we need you to take charge...
HEY.
OKAY, LET'S PUSH ALL THE DESKS TO THE BACK.
WOW, EVERYONE WAS ON TIME.
Let's get to it so we can get this over quickly.
IS YANO IN THE BATH-ROOM?
Krrk
Here's a chair...
THAT'S A LONG POTTY BREAK!
EH?
YANO?
HE'S NOT COMING TODAY.

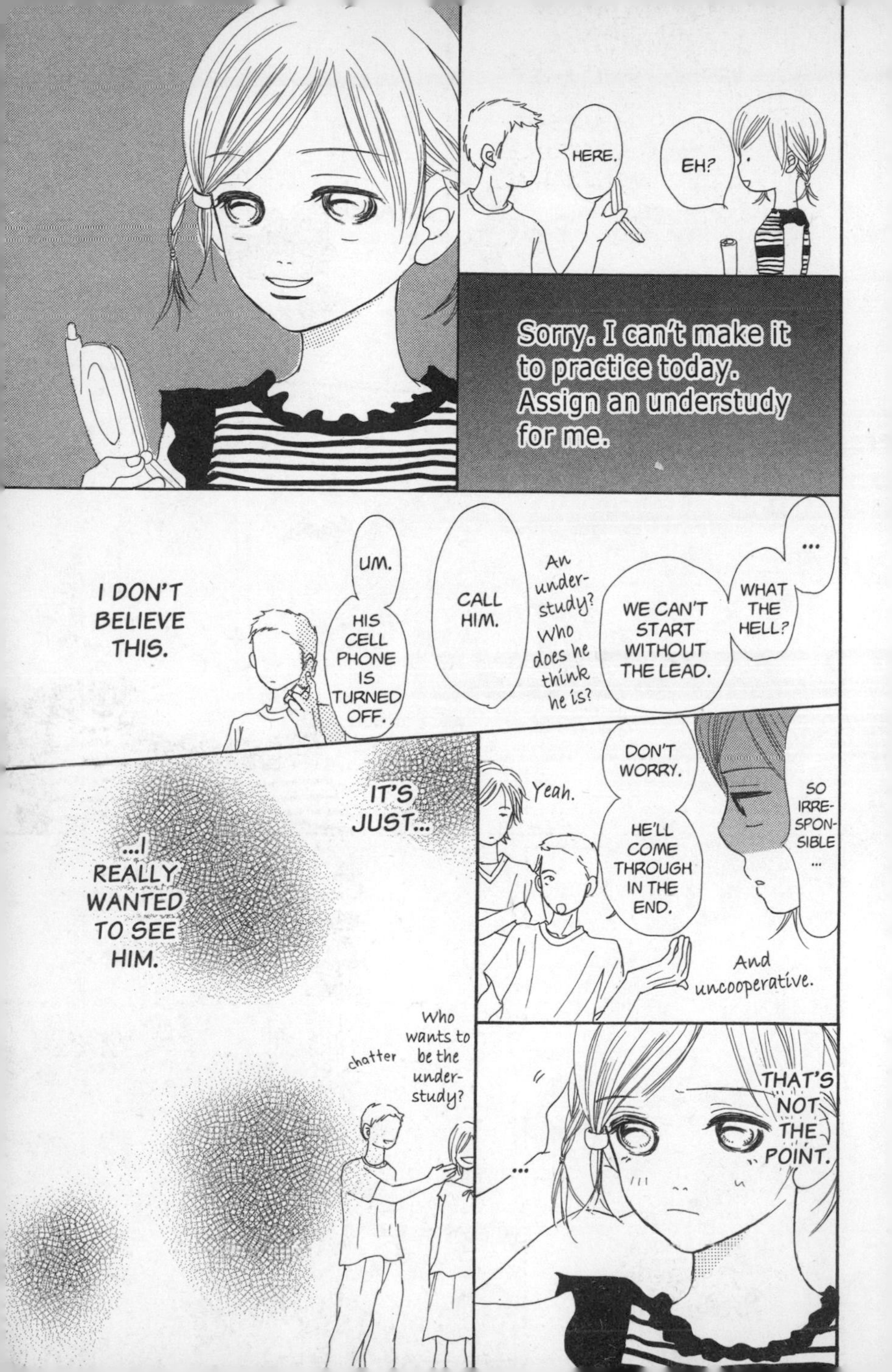

HERE.
EH?
Sorry. I can't make it to practice today. Assign an understudy for me.
...
WHAT THE HELL?
WE CAN'T START WITHOUT THE LEAD.
An understudy? Who does he think he is?
CALL HIM.
UM.
HIS CELL PHONE IS TURNED OFF.
I DON'T BELIEVE THIS.
SO IRRESPONSIBLE...
DON'T WORRY.
HE'LL COME THROUGH IN THE END.
Yeah.
And uncooperative.
THAT'S NOT THE POINT.
...
IT'S JUST...
...I REALLY WANTED TO SEE HIM.
Who wants to be the understudy?
chatter

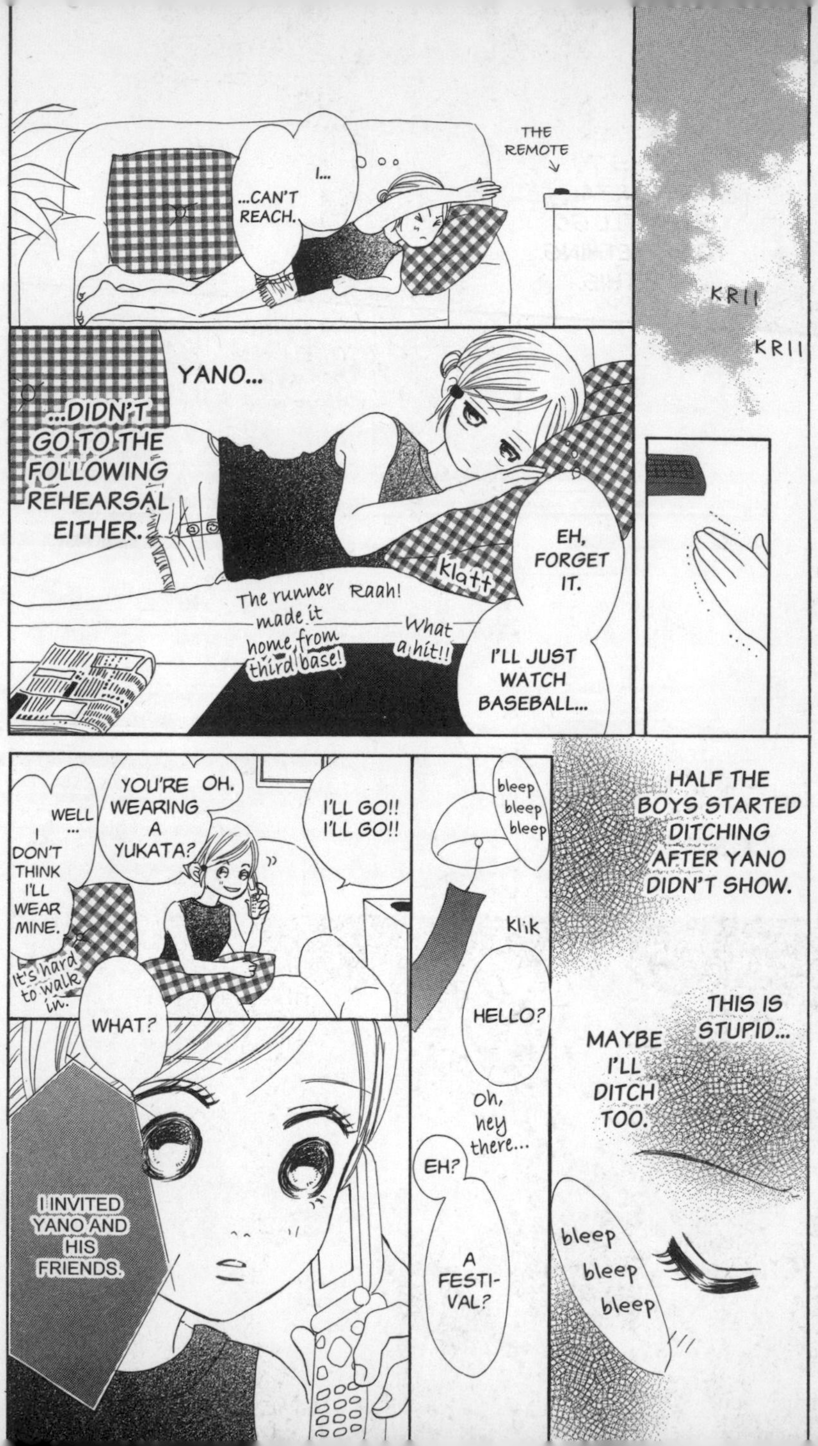
KRII
KRII
THE REMOTE
I...
...CAN'T REACH.
YANO...
...DIDN'T GO TO THE FOLLOWING REHEARSAL EITHER.
EH, FORGET IT.
I'LL JUST WATCH BASEBALL...
Klatt
Raah!
The runner made it home from third base!
What a hit!!
HALF THE BOYS STARTED DITCHING AFTER YANO DIDN'T SHOW.
THIS IS STUPID...
MAYBE I'LL DITCH TOO.
bleep bleep bleep
bleep bleep bleep
klik
HELLO?
Oh, hey there...
EH?
A FESTI-VAL?
I'LL GO!! I'LL GO!!
OH.
YOU'RE WEARING A YUKATA?
WELL... I DON'T THINK I'LL WEAR MINE.
It's hard to walk in.
WHAT?
I INVITED YANO AND HIS FRIENDS.

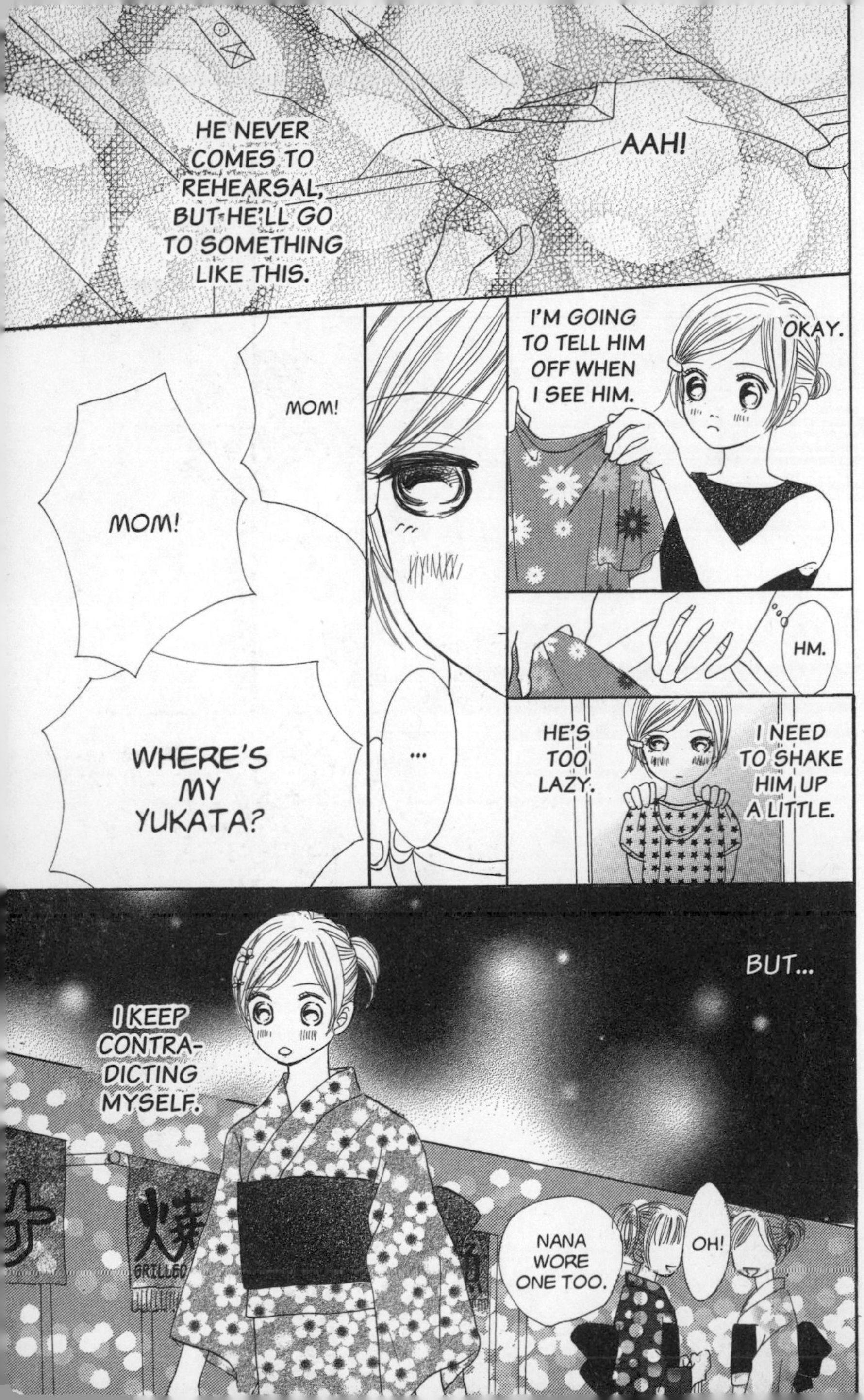
AAH!
HE NEVER COMES TO REHEARSAL, BUT HE'LL GO TO SOMETHING LIKE THIS.
OKAY.
I'M GOING TO TELL HIM OFF WHEN I SEE HIM.
HM.
I NEED TO SHAKE HIM UP A LITTLE.
HE'S TOO LAZY.
...
MOM!
MOM!
WHERE'S MY YUKATA?
BUT...
I KEEP CONTRA-DICTING MYSELF.
GRILLED
OH!
NANA WORE ONE TOO.

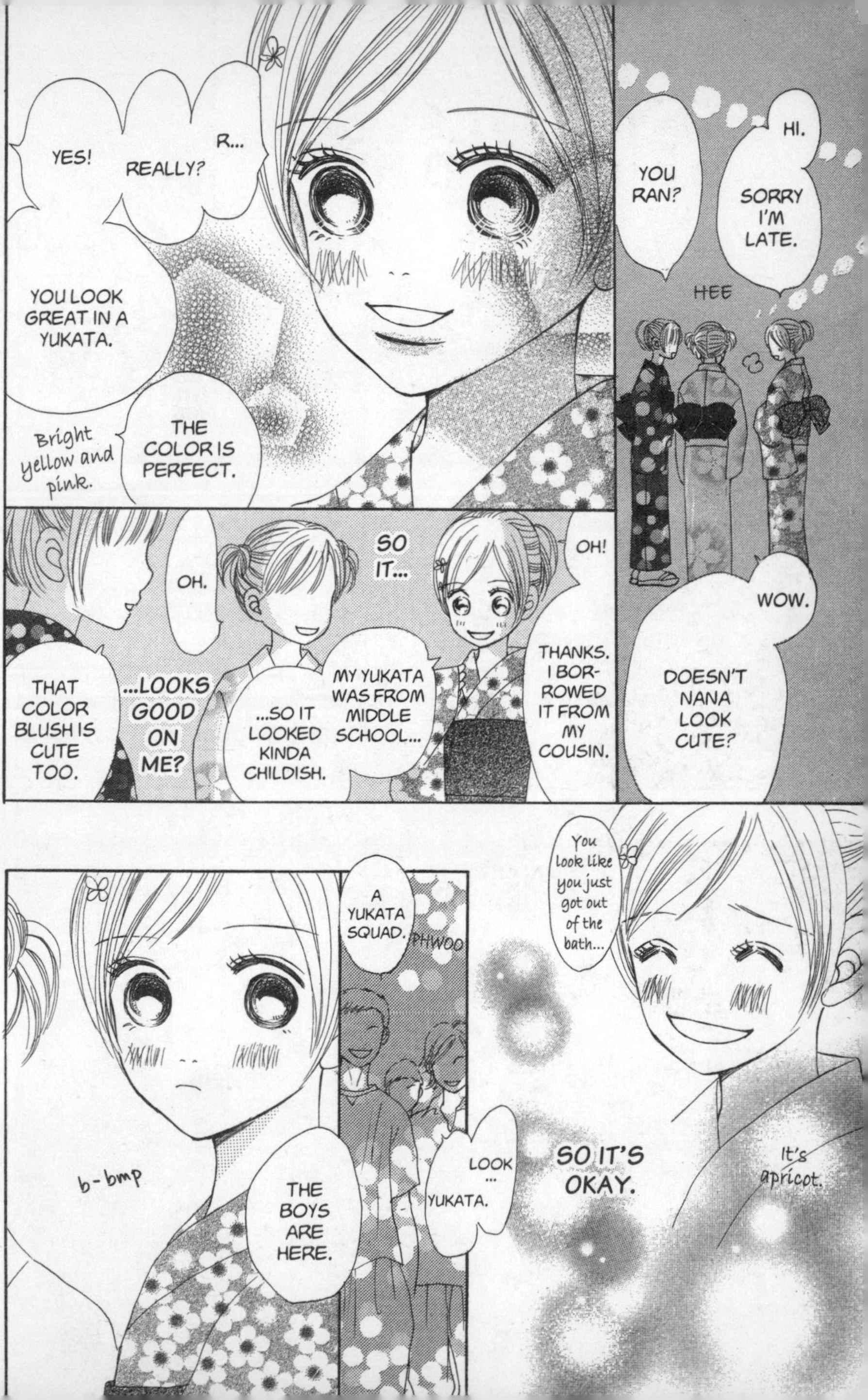
HI.
SORRY I'M LATE.
YOU RAN?
HEE
WOW.
DOESN'T NANA LOOK CUTE?
R... REALLY?
YES!
YOU LOOK GREAT IN A YUKATA.
THE COLOR IS PERFECT.
Bright yellow and pink.
OH!
THANKS. I BORROWED IT FROM MY COUSIN.
SO IT...
MY YUKATA WAS FROM MIDDLE SCHOOL...
...SO IT LOOKED KINDA CHILDISH.
OH.
...LOOKS GOOD ON ME?
THAT COLOR BLUSH IS CUTE TOO.
You look like you just got out of the bath...
It's apricot.
SO IT'S OKAY.
A YUKATA SQUAD.
PHWOO
LOOK ... YUKATA.
THE BOYS ARE HERE.
b-bmp

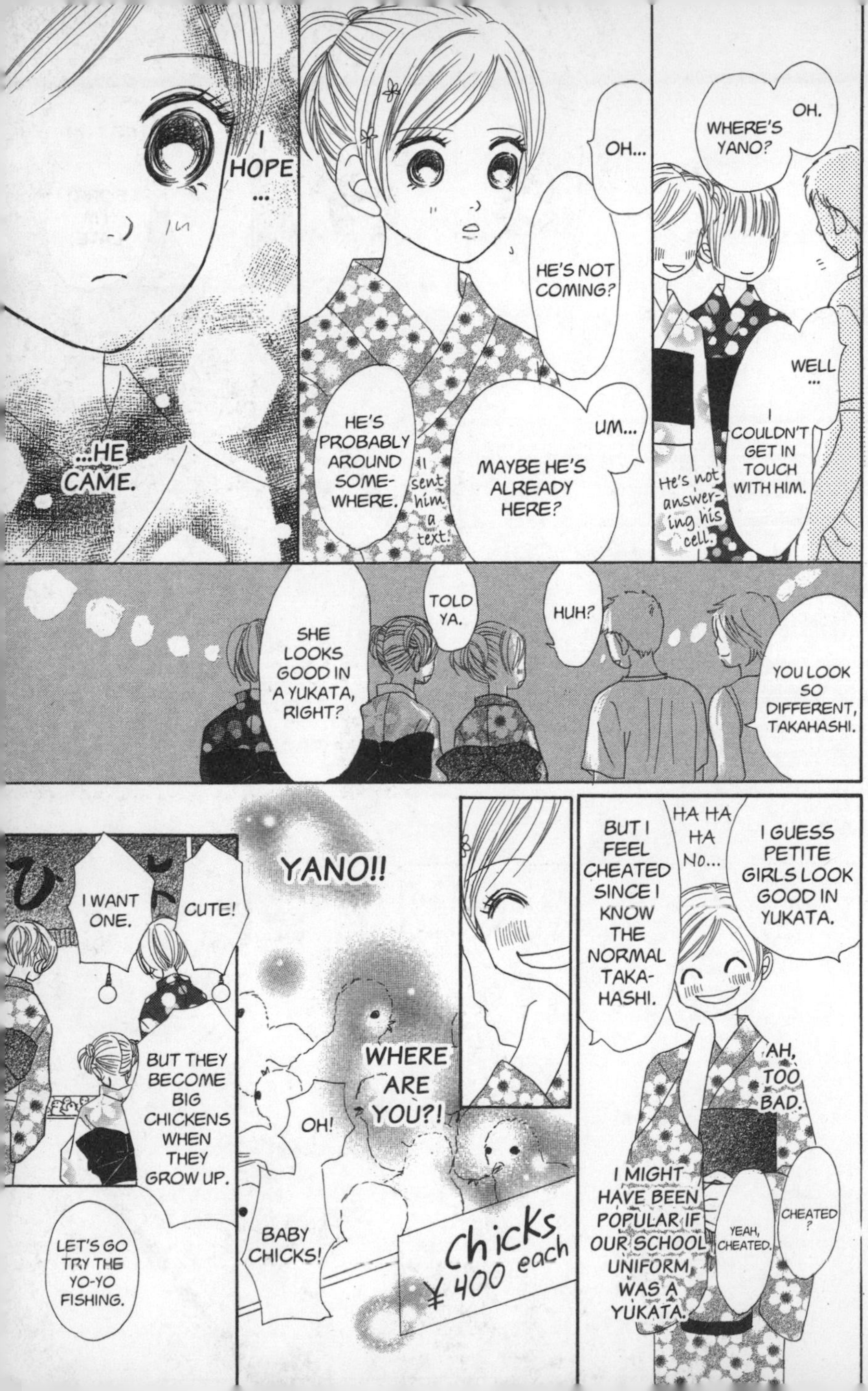
OH.
WHERE'S YANO?
WELL...
I COULDN'T GET IN TOUCH WITH HIM.
He's not answering his cell.
OH...
HE'S NOT COMING?
UM...
MAYBE HE'S ALREADY HERE?
HE'S PROBABLY AROUND SOME-WHERE.
I sent him a text!
I HOPE...
...HE CAME.
YOU LOOK SO DIFFERENT, TAKAHASHI.
HUH?
TOLD YA.
SHE LOOKS GOOD IN A YUKATA, RIGHT?
I GUESS PETITE GIRLS LOOK GOOD IN YUKATA.
HA HA HA No...
BUT I FEEL CHEATED SINCE I KNOW THE NORMAL TAKA-HASHI.
AH, TOO BAD.
CHEATED?
YEAH, CHEATED.
I MIGHT HAVE BEEN POPULAR IF OUR SCHOOL UNIFORM WAS A YUKATA.
YANO!!
WHERE ARE YOU?!
OH!
BABY CHICKS!
Chicks ¥400 each
CUTE!
I WANT ONE.
BUT THEY BECOME BIG CHICKENS WHEN THEY GROW UP.
LET'S GO TRY THE YO-YO FISHING.

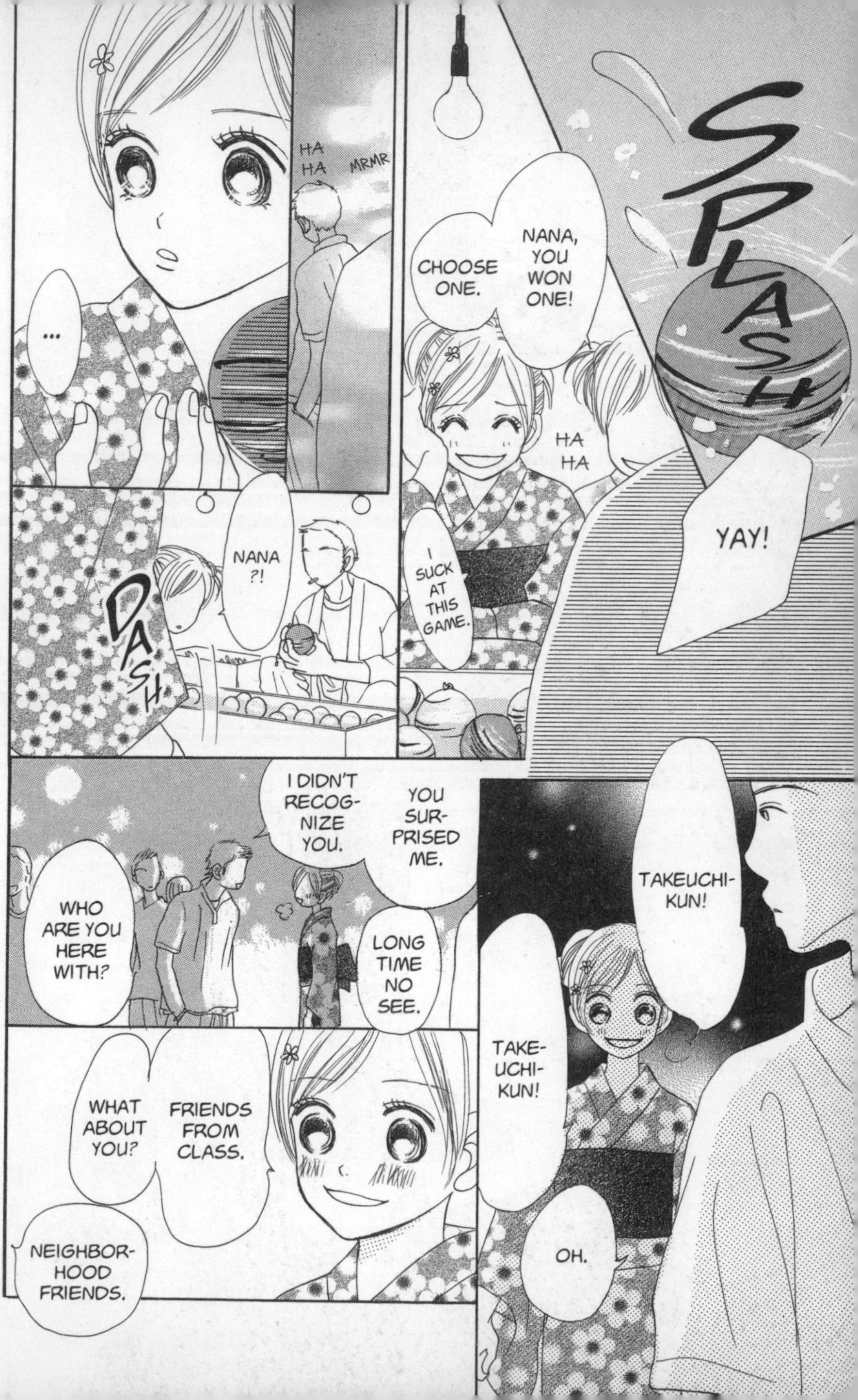
SPLASH
YAY!
NANA, YOU WON ONE!
CHOOSE ONE.
HA HA
I SUCK AT THIS GAME.
HA HA
MRMR
...
NANA ?!
DASH
TAKEUCHI-KUN!
TAKE-UCHI-KUN!
OH.
YOU SUR-PRISED ME.
I DIDN'T RECOG-NIZE YOU.
LONG TIME NO SEE.
WHO ARE YOU HERE WITH?
FRIENDS FROM CLASS.
WHAT ABOUT YOU?
NEIGHBOR-HOOD FRIENDS.

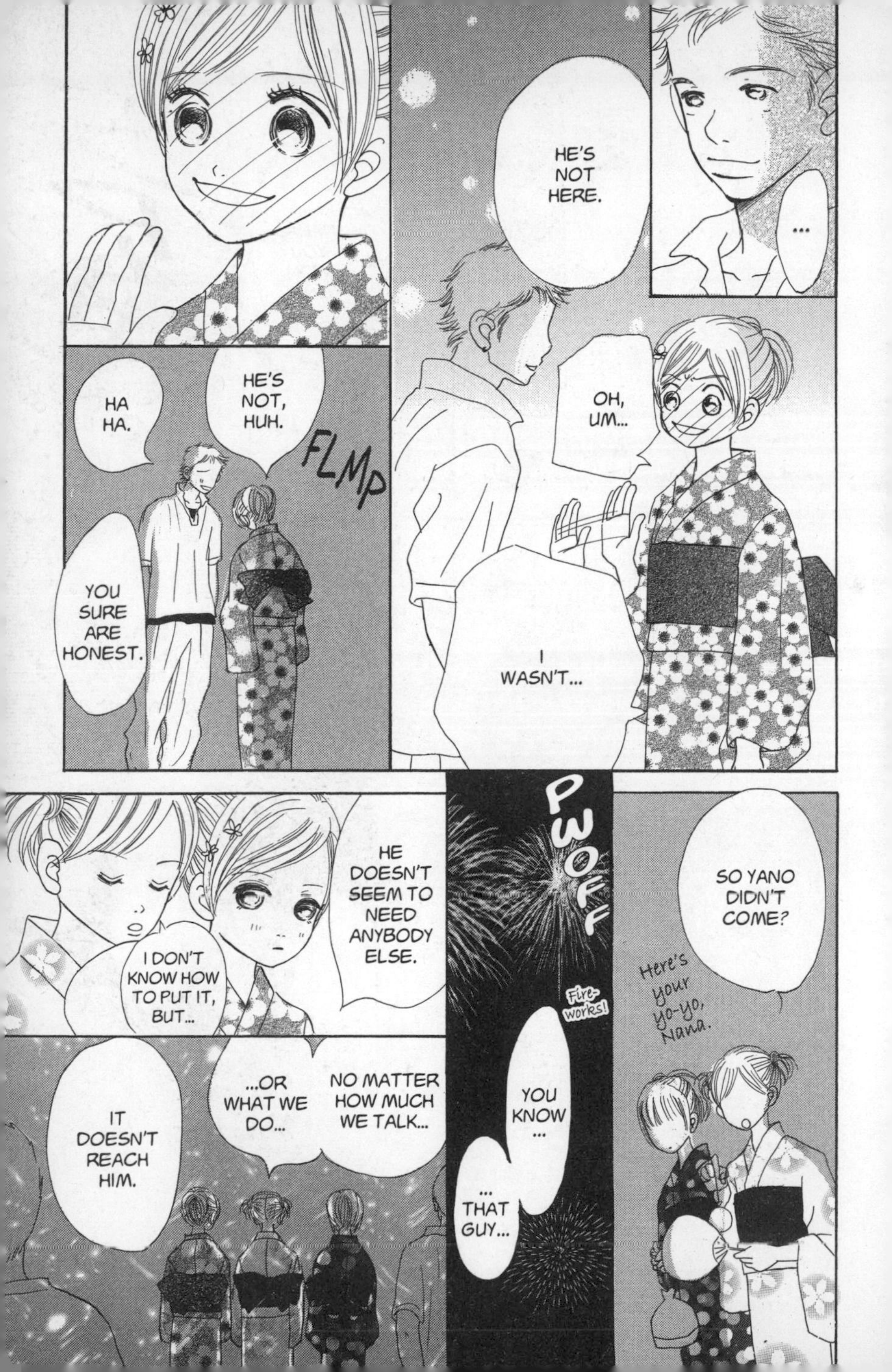
...
HE'S NOT HERE.
OH, UM...
I WASN'T...
HE'S NOT, HUH.
HA HA.
FLMP
YOU SURE ARE HONEST.
SO YANO DIDN'T COME?
Here's your yo-yo, Nana.
PWOFF
Fire-works!
YOU KNOW ...
... THAT GUY...
HE DOESN'T SEEM TO NEED ANYBODY ELSE.
I DON'T KNOW HOW TO PUT IT, BUT...
NO MATTER HOW MUCH WE TALK...
...OR WHAT WE DO...
IT DOESN'T REACH HIM.

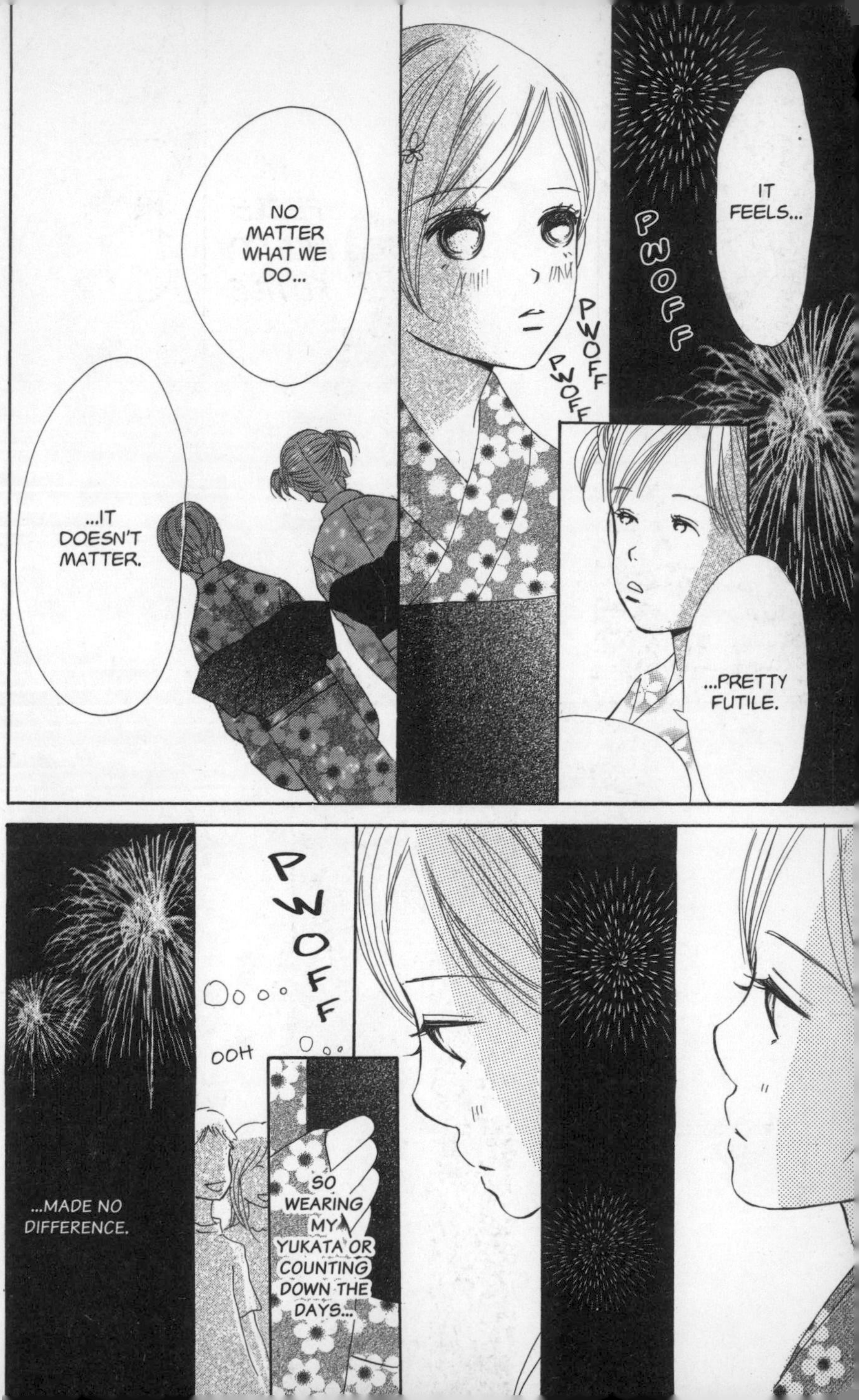
IT FEELS...
PWOFF
...PRETTY FUTILE.
PWOFF
PWOFF
NO MATTER WHAT WE DO...
...IT DOESN'T MATTER.
PWOFF
Oooo
OOH
Oo
SO WEARING MY YUKATA OR COUNTING DOWN THE DAYS...
...MADE NO DIFFERENCE.

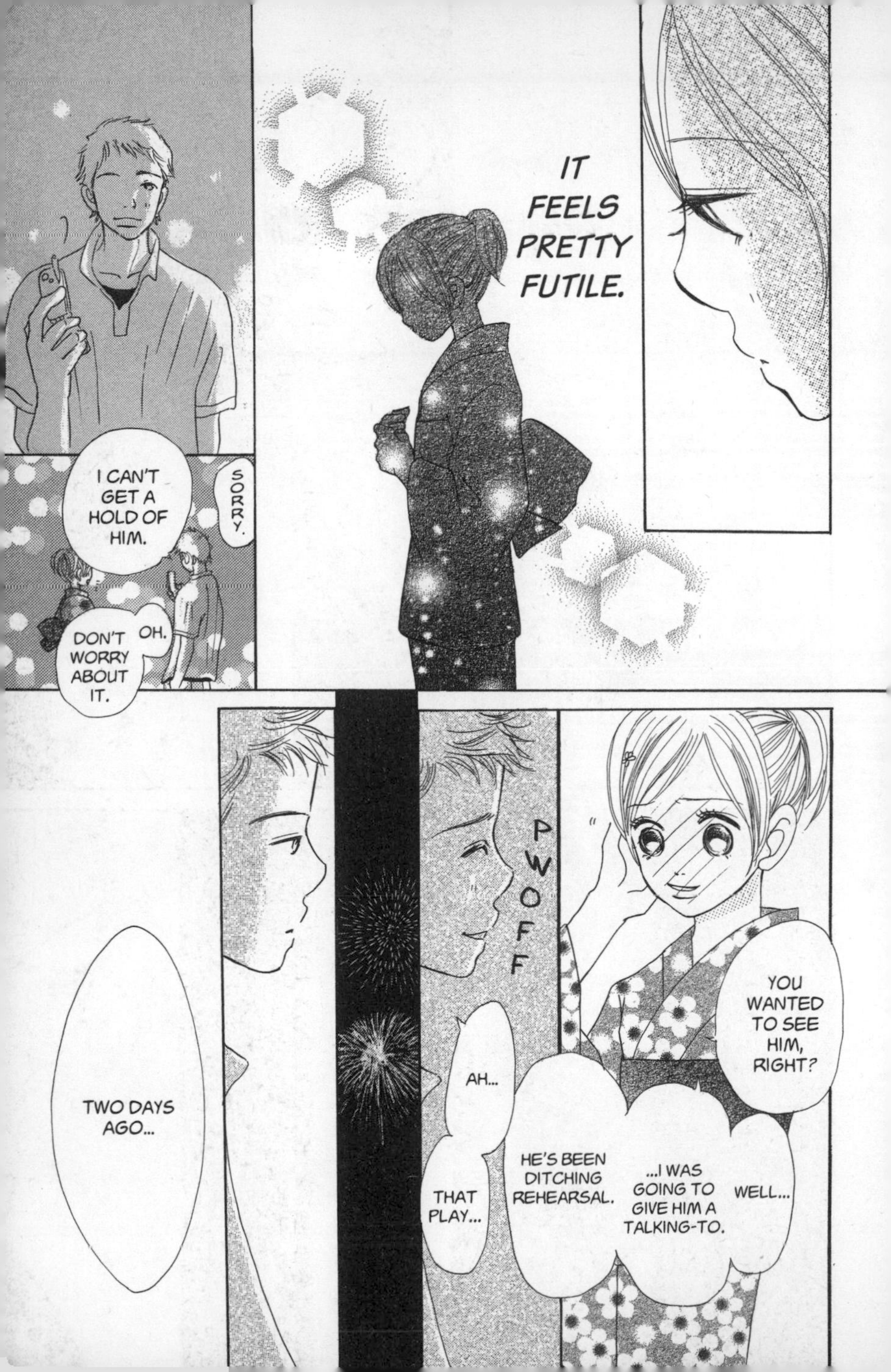
IT FEELS PRETTY FUTILE.
SORRY.
I CAN'T GET A HOLD OF HIM.
OH.
DON'T WORRY ABOUT IT.
YOU WANTED TO SEE HIM, RIGHT?
WELL...
...I WAS GOING TO GIVE HIM A TALKING-TO.
HE'S BEEN DITCHING REHEARSAL.
PWOFF
AH...
THAT PLAY...
TWO DAYS AGO...

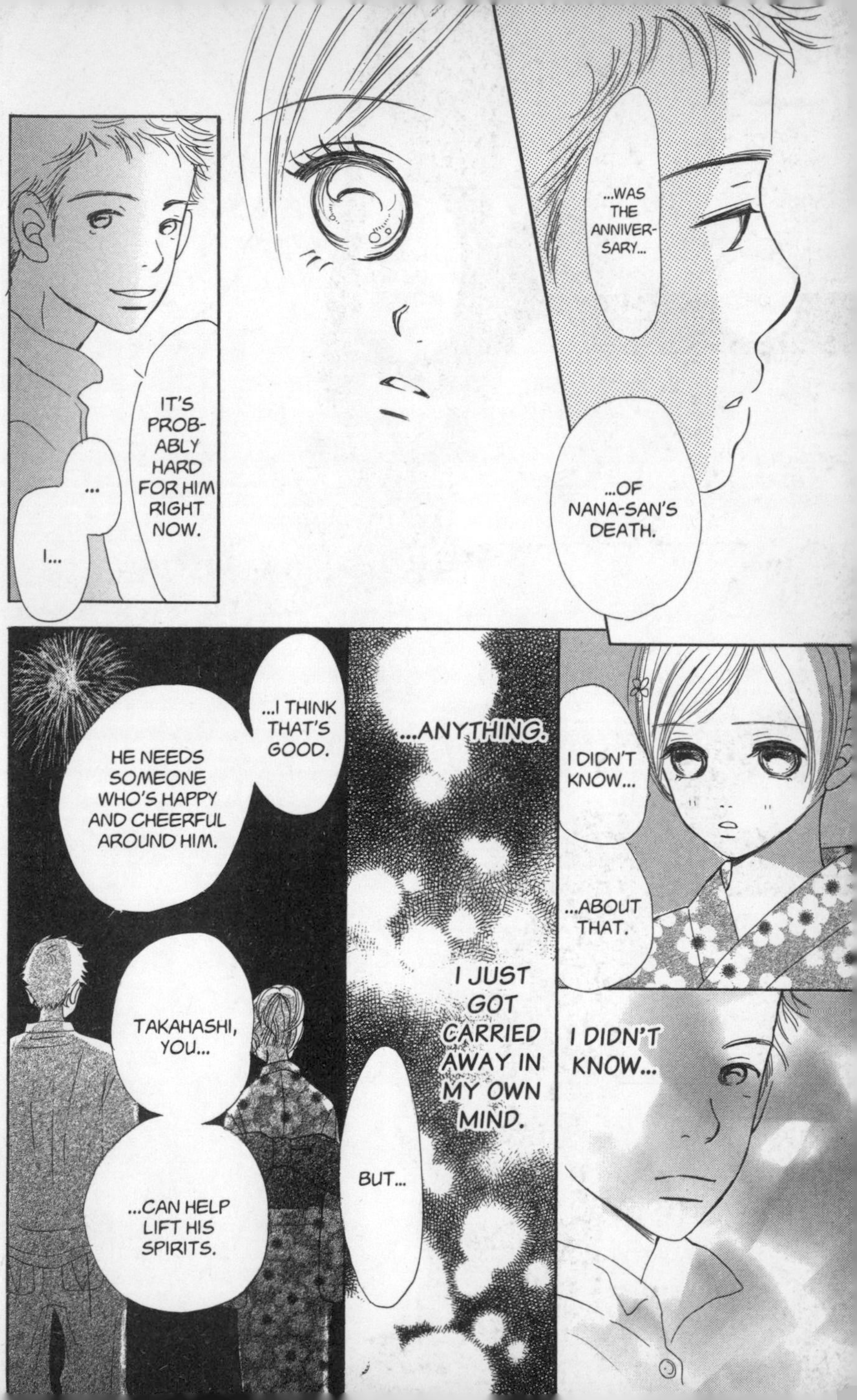
...WAS THE ANNIVERSARY...
...OF NANA-SAN'S DEATH.
IT'S PROBABLY HARD FOR HIM RIGHT NOW.
...
I...
I DIDN'T KNOW...
...ABOUT THAT.
I DIDN'T KNOW...
...ANYTHING.
I JUST GOT CARRIED AWAY IN MY OWN MIND.
BUT...
...I THINK THAT'S GOOD.
HE NEEDS SOMEONE WHO'S HAPPY AND CHEERFUL AROUND HIM.
TAKAHASHI, YOU...
...CAN HELP LIFT HIS SPIRITS.

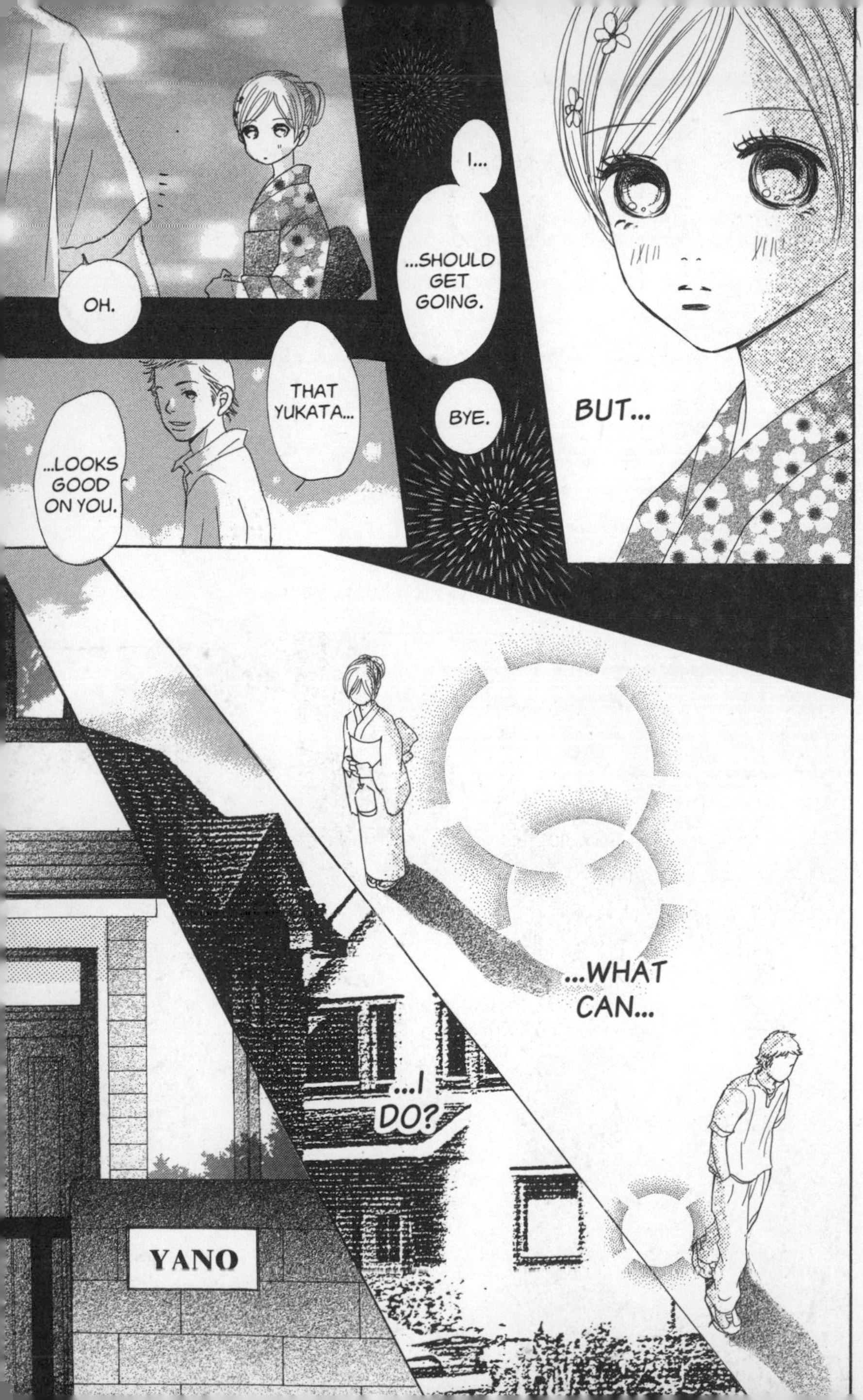
BUT...
I...
...SHOULD GET GOING.
BYE.
OH.
THAT YUKATA...
...LOOKS GOOD ON YOU.
...WHAT CAN...
...I DO?
YANO

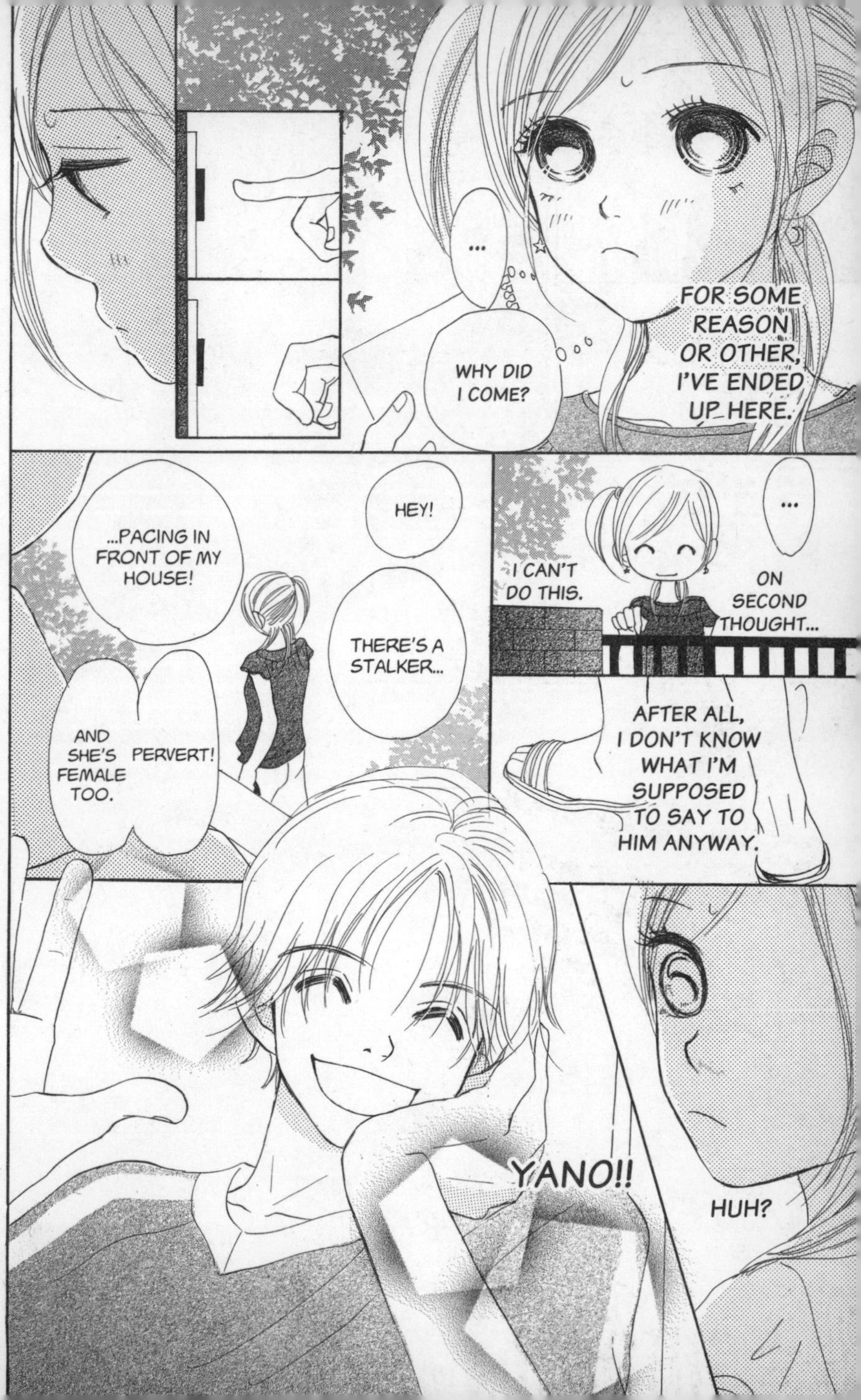
FOR SOME REASON OR OTHER, I'VE ENDED UP HERE.
...
WHY DID I COME?
...
ON SECOND THOUGHT...
I CAN'T DO THIS.
AFTER ALL, I DON'T KNOW WHAT I'M SUPPOSED TO SAY TO HIM ANYWAY.
HEY!
THERE'S A STALKER...
...PACING IN FRONT OF MY HOUSE!
PERVERT!
AND SHE'S FEMALE TOO.
HUH?
YANO!!

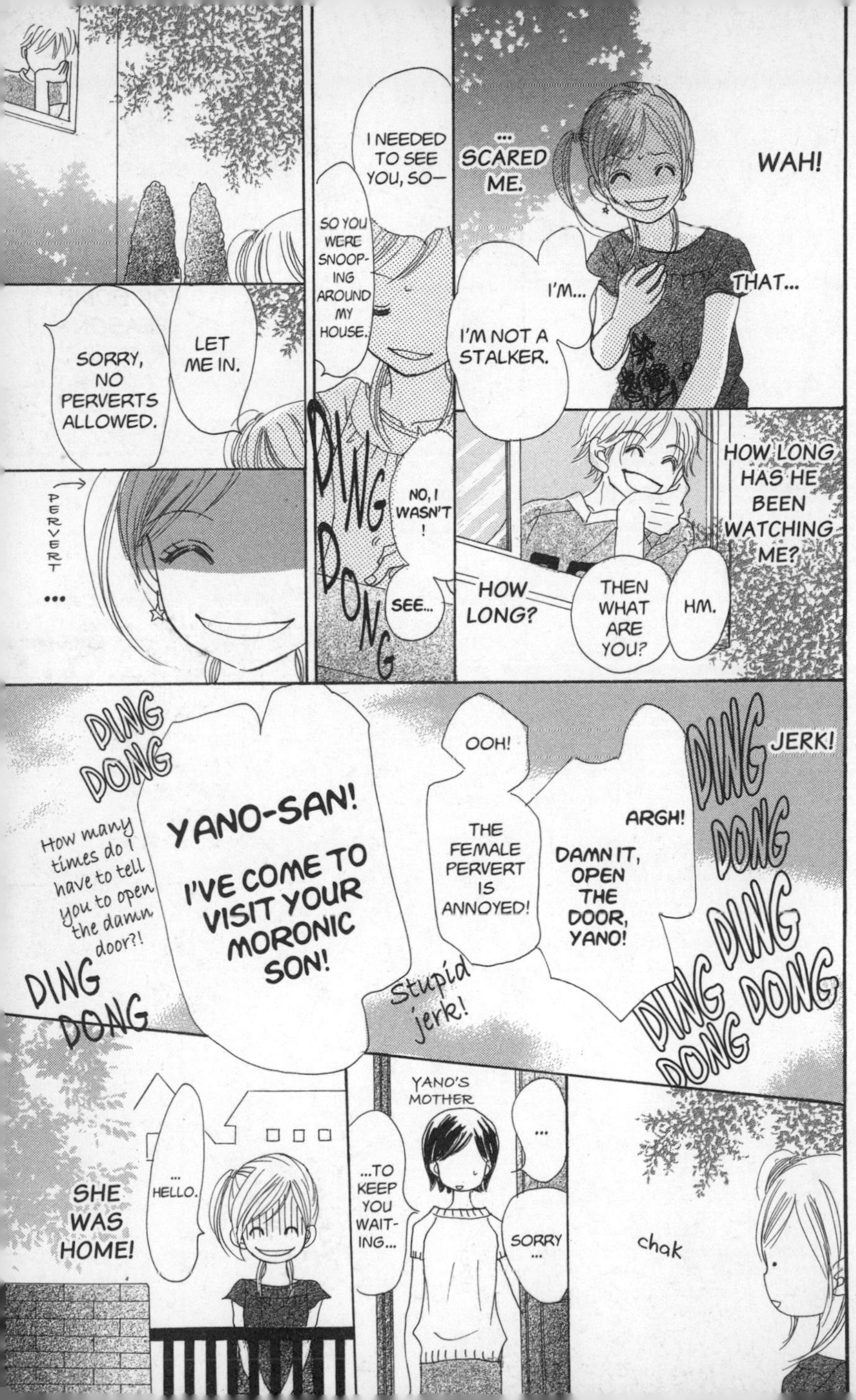
WAH!
... SCARED ME.
THAT...
I'M...
I'M NOT A STALKER.
HOW LONG HAS HE BEEN WATCHING ME?
HM.
THEN WHAT ARE YOU?
HOW LONG?
I NEEDED TO SEE YOU, SO—
SO YOU WERE SNOOPING AROUND MY HOUSE.
DING DONG
NO, I WASN'T!
SEE...
LET ME IN.
SORRY, NO PERVERTS ALLOWED.
PERVERT
...
JERK!
DING DONG
ARGH!
DAMN IT, OPEN THE DOOR, YANO!
OOH!
THE FEMALE PERVERT IS ANNOYED!
DING DING
DING DONG DONG DONG
Stupid jerk!
YANO-SAN!
I'VE COME TO VISIT YOUR MORONIC SON!
DING DONG
How many times do I have to tell you to open the damn door?!
DING DONG
chak
YANO'S MOTHER
...
SORRY ...
...TO KEEP YOU WAIT-ING...
... HELLO.
SHE WAS HOME!

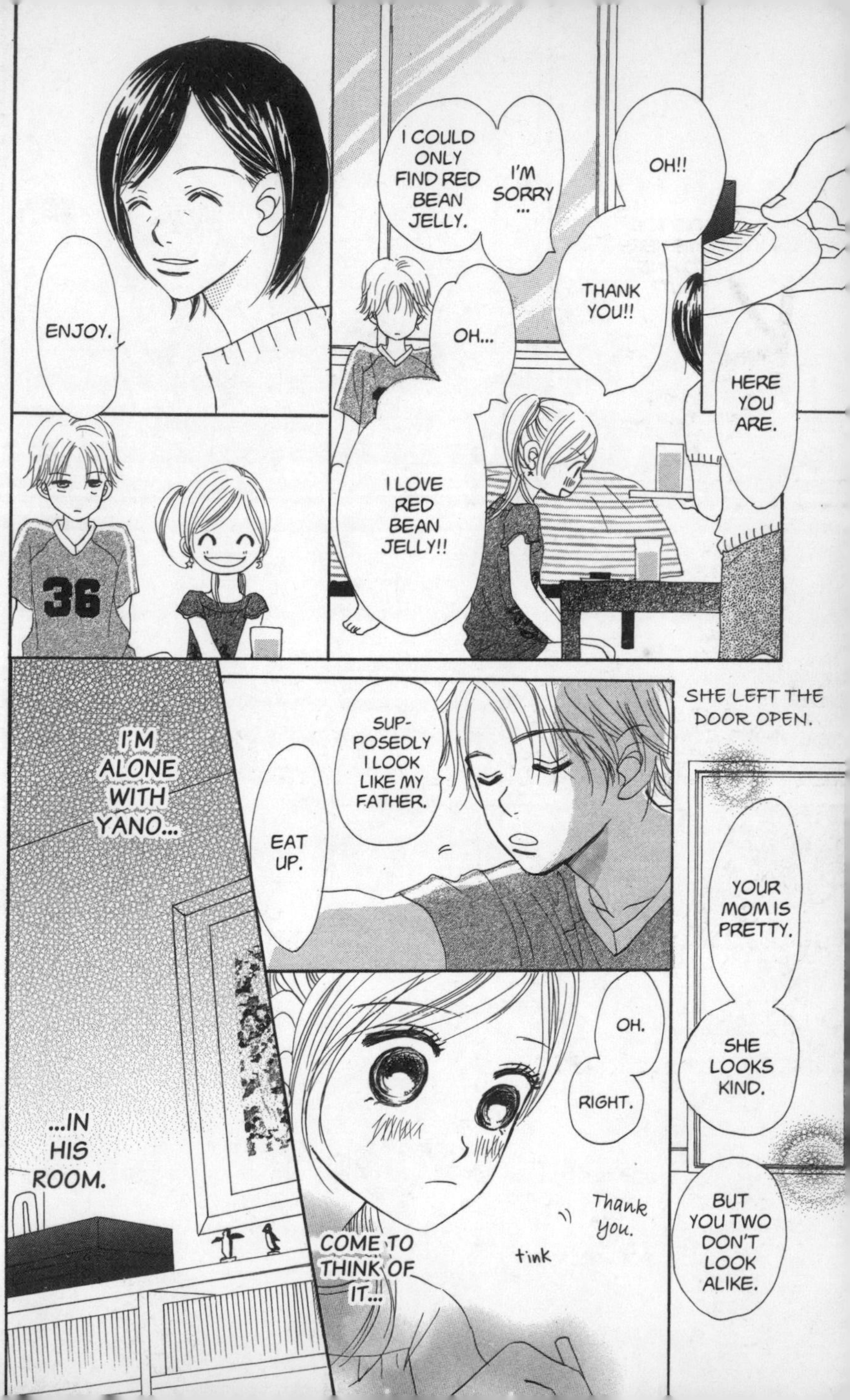
OH!!
THANK YOU!!
HERE YOU ARE.
I'M SORRY ...
I COULD ONLY FIND RED BEAN JELLY.
OH...
I LOVE RED BEAN JELLY!!
ENJOY.
SHE LEFT THE DOOR OPEN.
YOUR MOM IS PRETTY.
SHE LOOKS KIND.
BUT YOU TWO DON'T LOOK ALIKE.
SUP-POSEDLY I LOOK LIKE MY FATHER.
EAT UP.
OH.
RIGHT.
Thank you.
tink
COME TO THINK OF IT...
I'M ALONE WITH YANO...
...IN HIS ROOM.

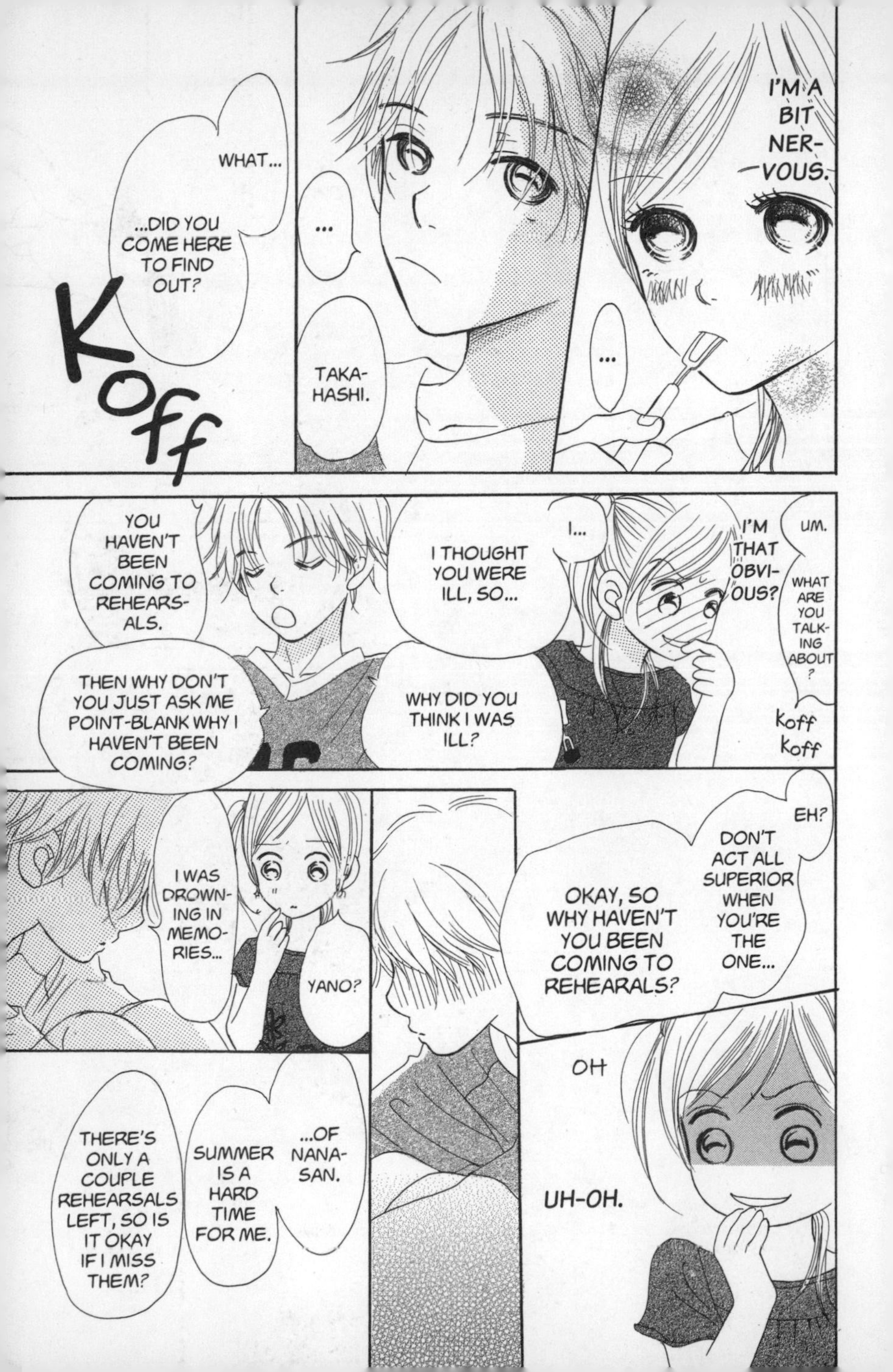
I'M A BIT NER-VOUS.
...
...
TAKA-HASHI.
WHAT...
...DID YOU COME HERE TO FIND OUT?
Koff
UM.
WHAT ARE YOU TALKING ABOUT?
I'M THAT OBVIOUS?
Koff Koff
I...
I THOUGHT YOU WERE ILL, SO...
WHY DID YOU THINK I WAS ILL?
YOU HAVEN'T BEEN COMING TO REHEARS-ALS.
THEN WHY DON'T YOU JUST ASK ME POINT-BLANK WHY I HAVEN'T BEEN COMING?
EH?
DON'T ACT ALL SUPERIOR WHEN YOU'RE THE ONE...
OKAY, SO WHY HAVEN'T YOU BEEN COMING TO REHEARALS?
OH
UH-OH.
YANO?
I WAS DROWN-ING IN MEMO-RIES...
...OF NANA-SAN.
SUMMER IS A HARD TIME FOR ME.
THERE'S ONLY A COUPLE REHEARSALS LEFT, SO IS IT OKAY IF I MISS THEM?

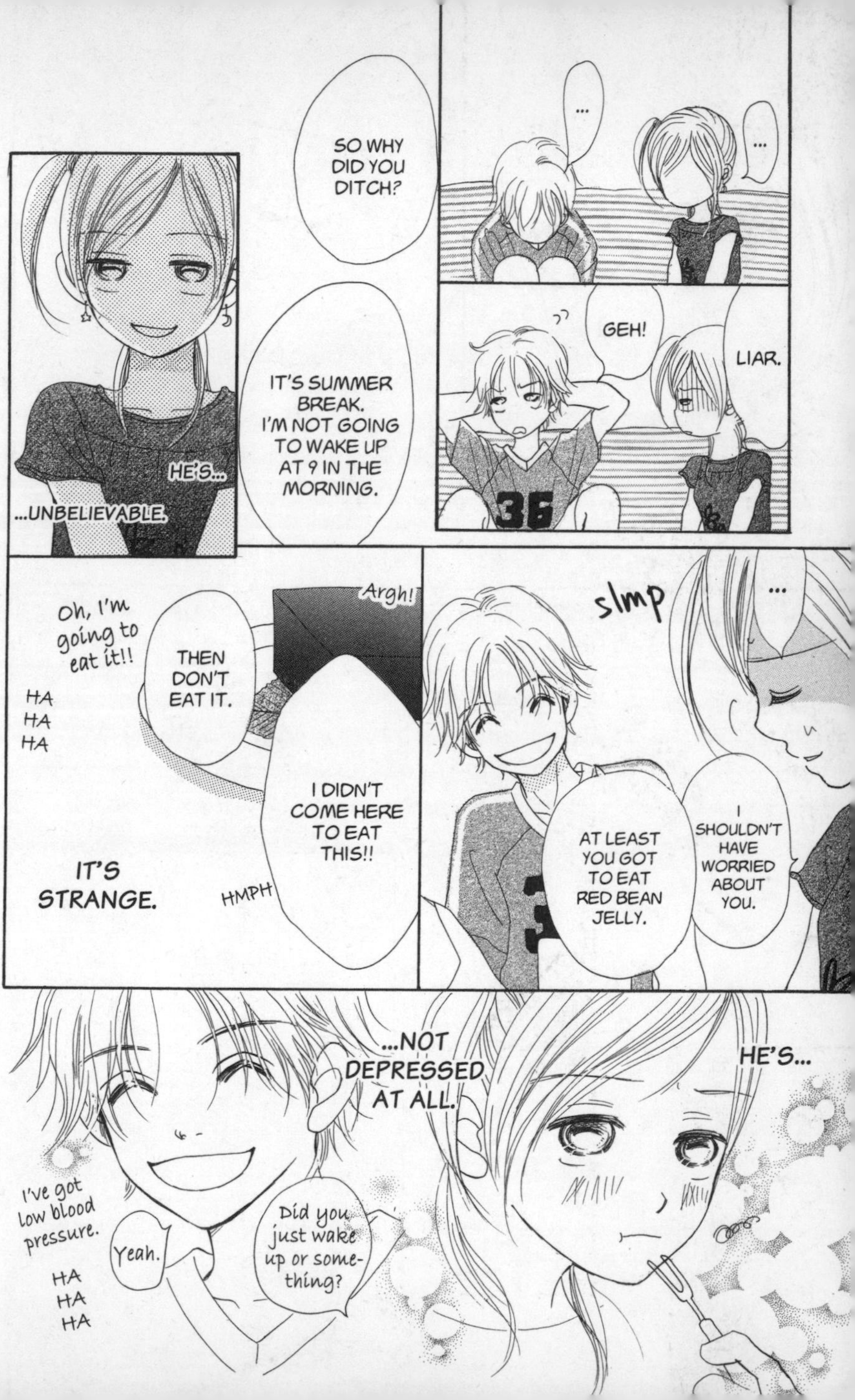
...
...
SO WHY DID YOU DITCH?
IT'S SUMMER BREAK. I'M NOT GOING TO WAKE UP AT 9 IN THE MORNING.
GEH!
LIAR.
HE'S...
...UNBELIEVABLE.
slmp
...
I SHOULDN'T HAVE WORRIED ABOUT YOU.
AT LEAST YOU GOT TO EAT RED BEAN JELLY.
Argh!
Oh, I'm going to eat it!!
THEN DON'T EAT IT.
HA HA HA
I DIDN'T COME HERE TO EAT THIS!!
HMPH
IT'S STRANGE.
HE'S...
...NOT DEPRESSED AT ALL.
Did you just wake up or something?
Yeah.
I've got low blood pressure.
HA HA HA

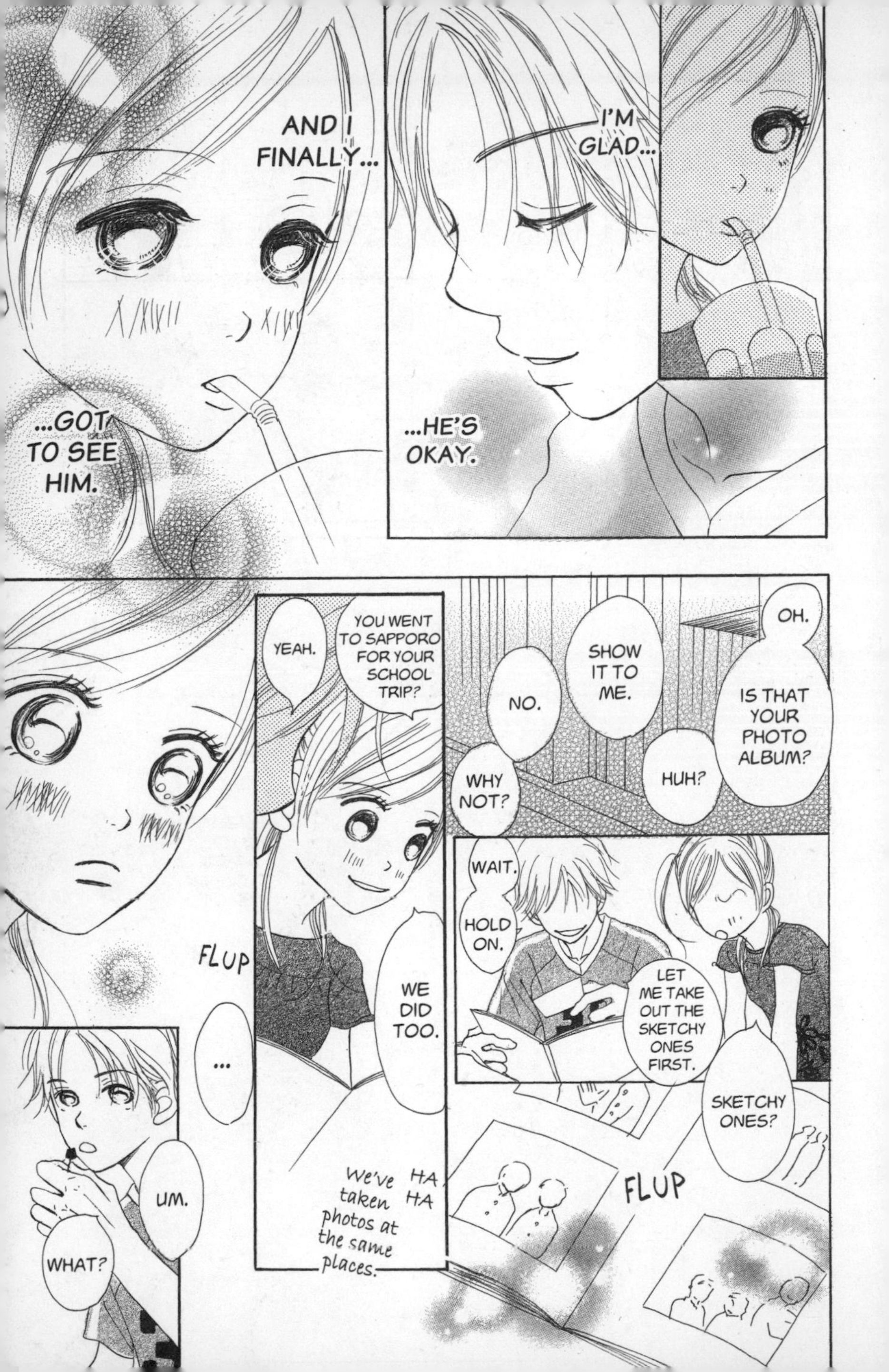
I'M GLAD...
...HE'S OKAY.
AND I FINALLY...
...GOT TO SEE HIM.
OH.
IS THAT YOUR PHOTO ALBUM?
HUH?
SHOW IT TO ME.
NO.
WHY NOT?
WAIT.
HOLD ON.
LET ME TAKE OUT THE SKETCHY ONES FIRST.
SKETCHY ONES?
FLUP
YOU WENT TO SAPPORO FOR YOUR SCHOOL TRIP?
YEAH.
WE DID TOO.
HA HA
We've taken photos at the same places.
FLUP
...
UM.
WHAT?

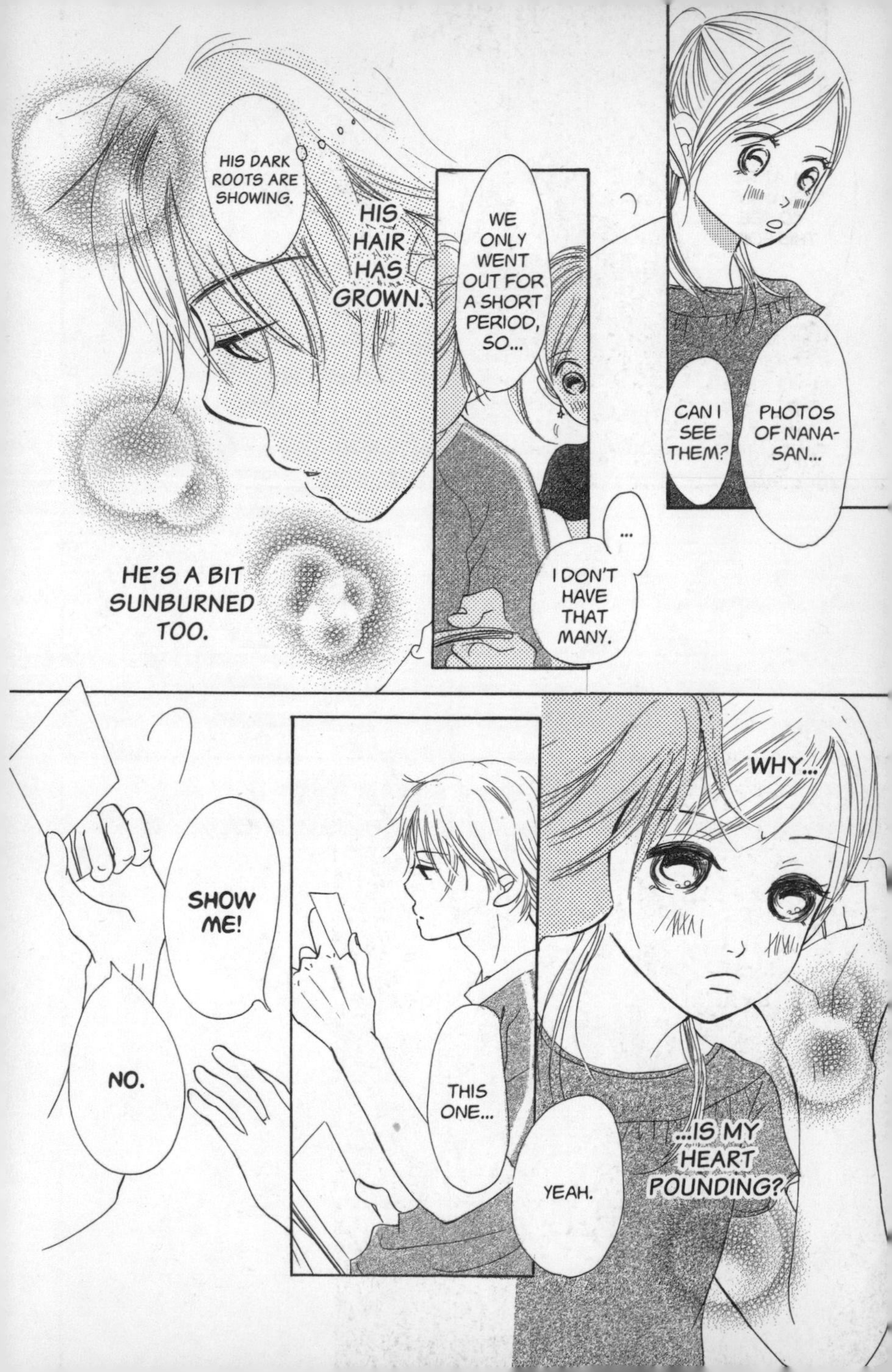
PHOTOS OF NANA-SAN...
CAN I SEE THEM?
...
I DON'T HAVE THAT MANY.
WE ONLY WENT OUT FOR A SHORT PERIOD, SO...
HIS DARK ROOTS ARE SHOWING.
HIS HAIR HAS GROWN.
HE'S A BIT SUNBURNED TOO.
WHY...
THIS ONE...
YEAH.
...IS MY HEART POUNDING?
SHOW ME!
NO.

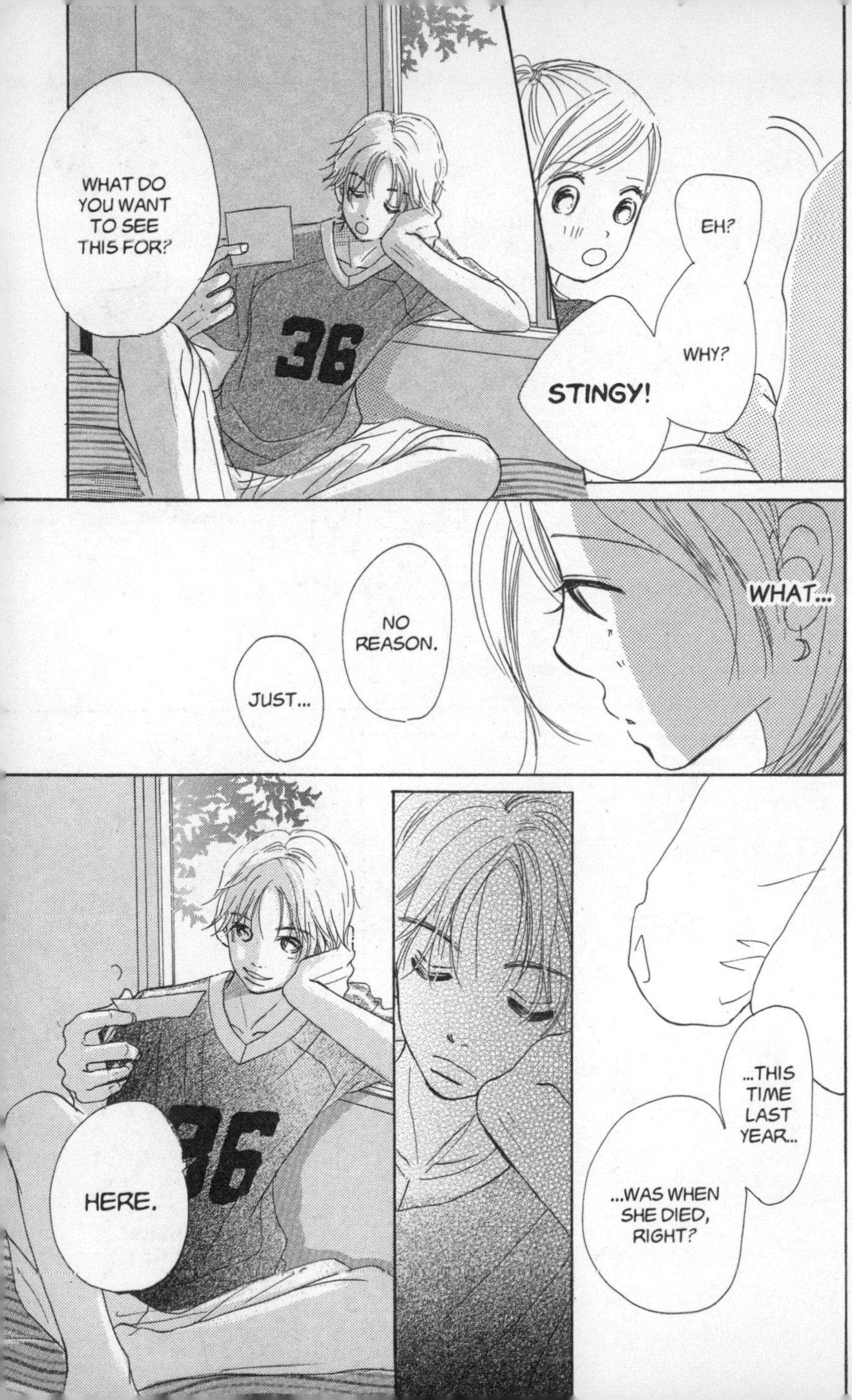
EH?
WHY?
STINGY!
WHAT DO YOU WANT TO SEE THIS FOR?
WHAT...
NO REASON.
JUST...
...THIS TIME LAST YEAR...
...WAS WHEN SHE DIED, RIGHT?
HERE.

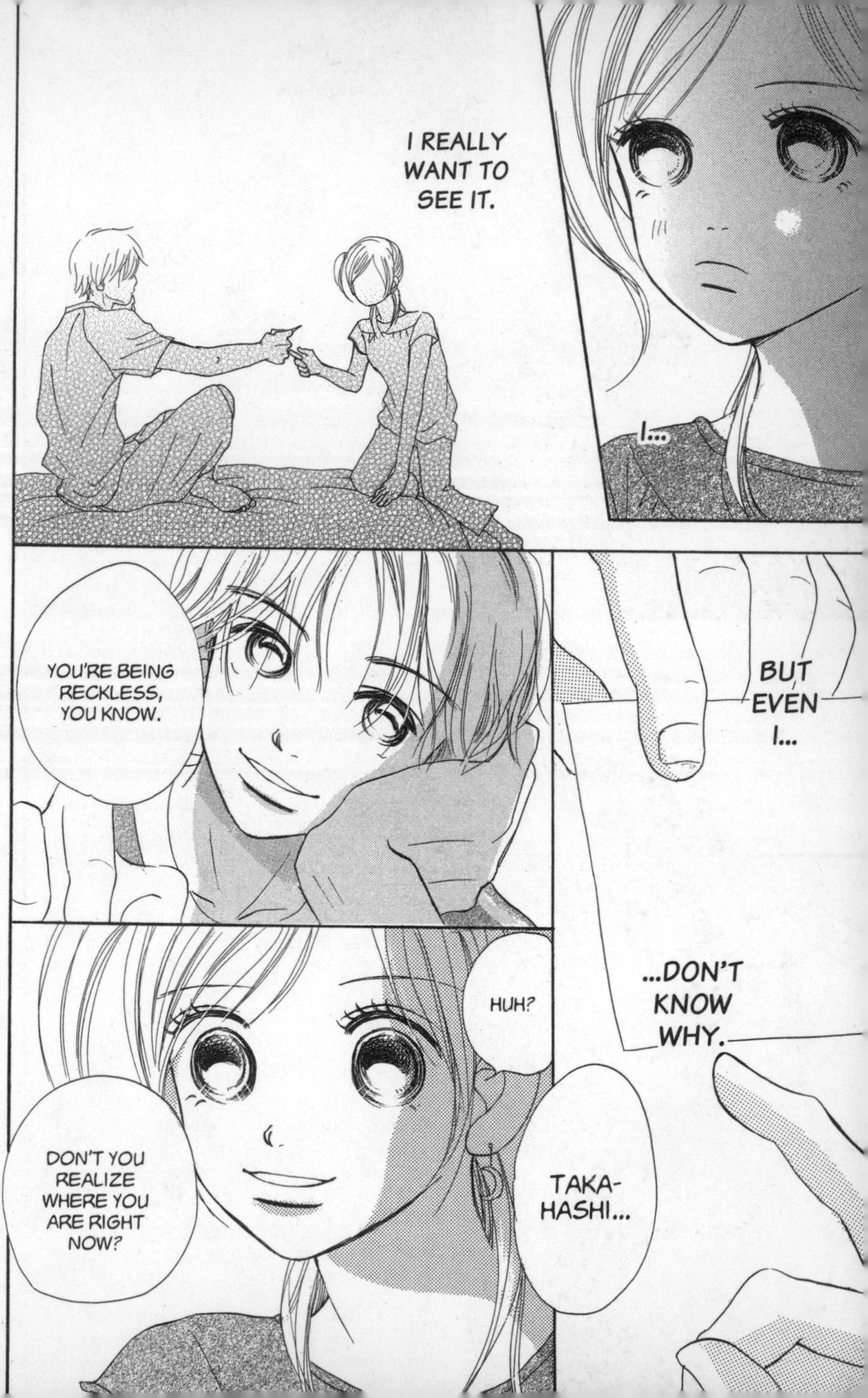

I...
I REALLY WANT TO SEE IT.
BUT EVEN I...
...DON'T KNOW WHY.
YOU'RE BEING RECKLESS, YOU KNOW.
HUH?
TAKA-HASHI...
DON'T YOU REALIZE WHERE YOU ARE RIGHT NOW?

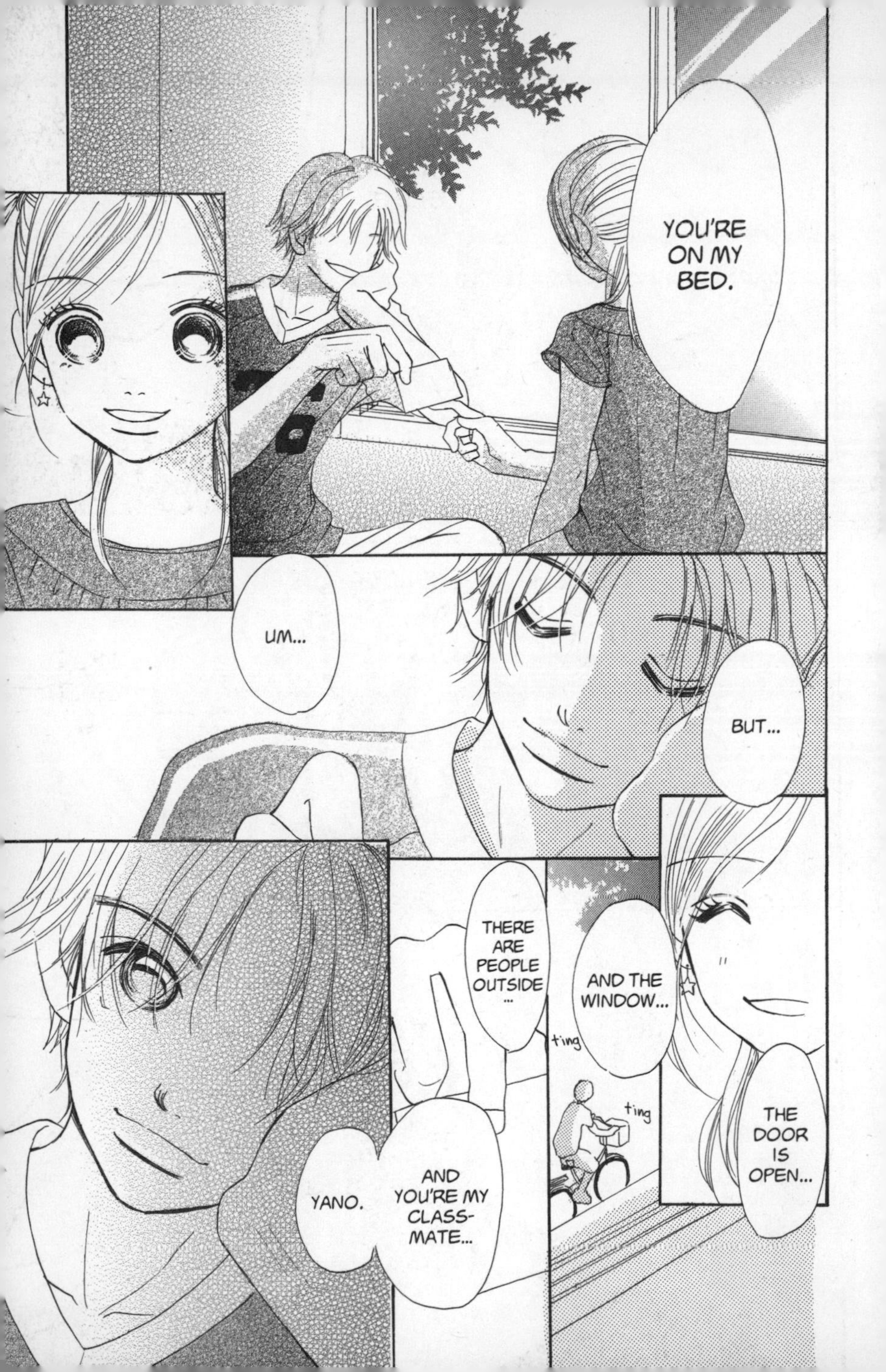
YOU'RE ON MY BED.
UM...
BUT...
THE DOOR IS OPEN...
AND THE WINDOW...
ting
ting
THERE ARE PEOPLE OUTSIDE...
AND YOU'RE MY CLASSMATE...
YANO.

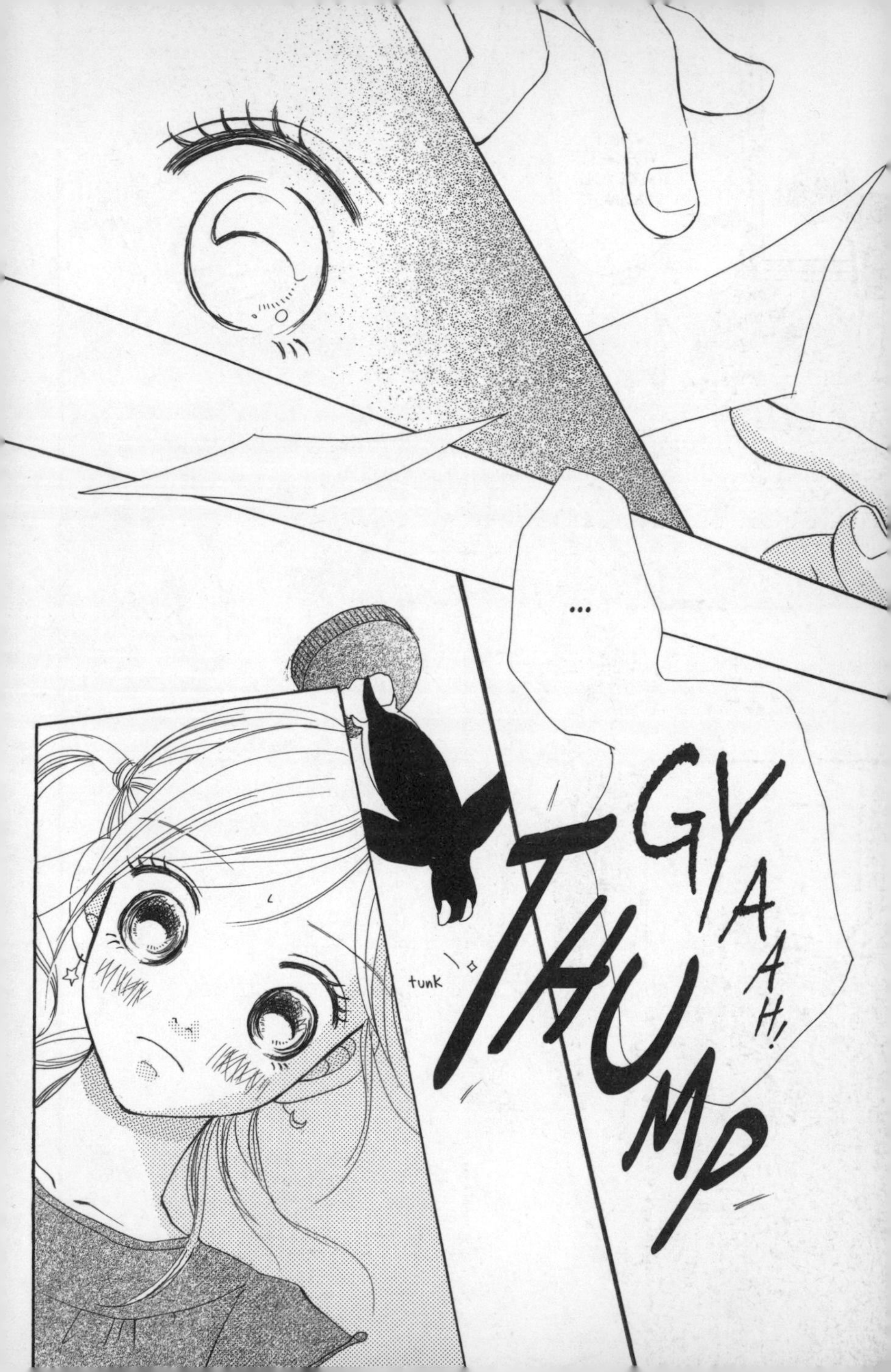
...
GYAAH!
THUMP
tunk

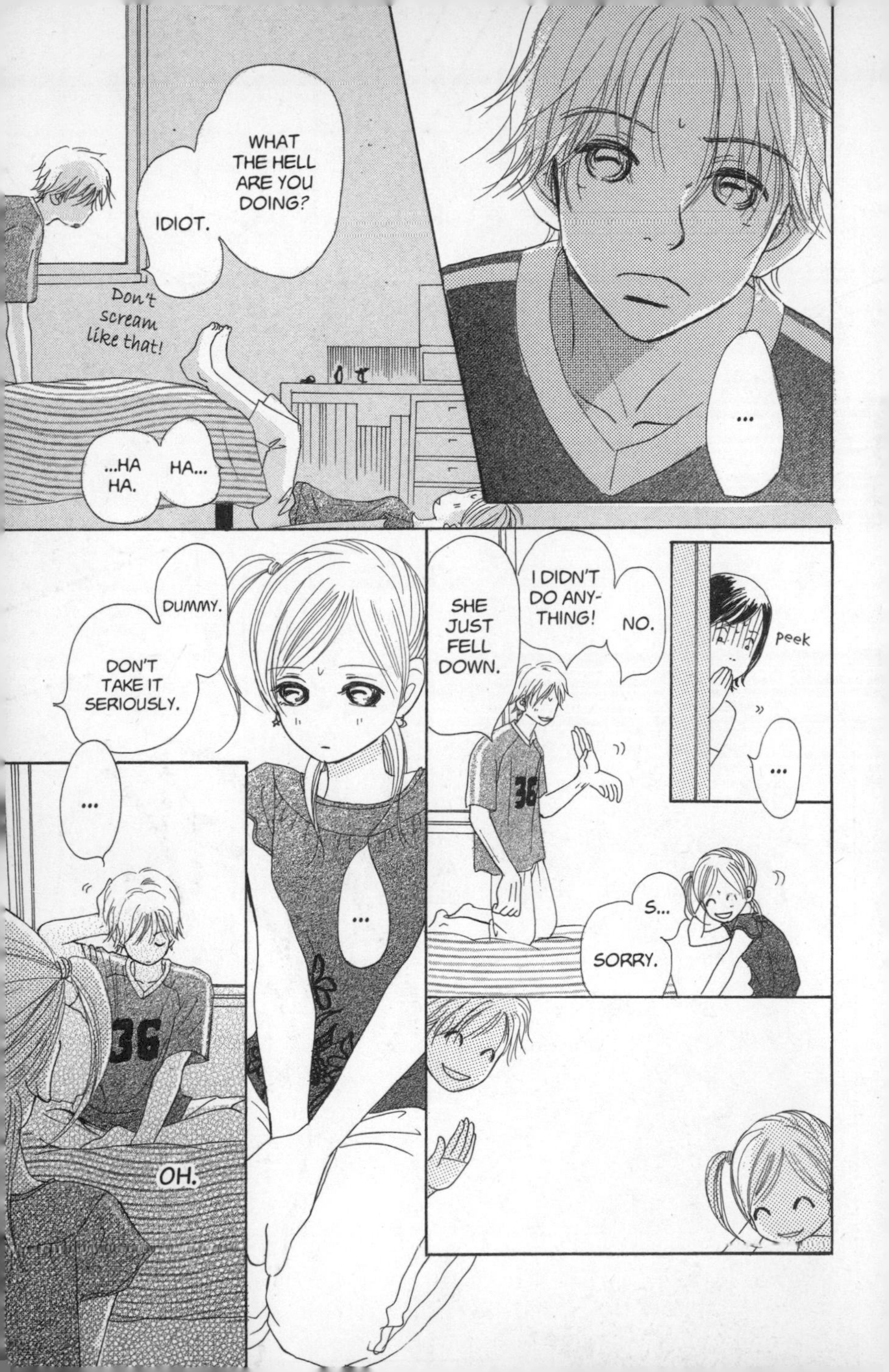
...
WHAT THE HELL ARE YOU DOING?
IDIOT.
Don't scream like that!
HA...
...HA HA.
peek
...
NO.
I DIDN'T DO ANY-THING!
SHE JUST FELL DOWN.
S...
SORRY.
DUMMY.
DON'T TAKE IT SERIOUSLY.
...
...
OH.

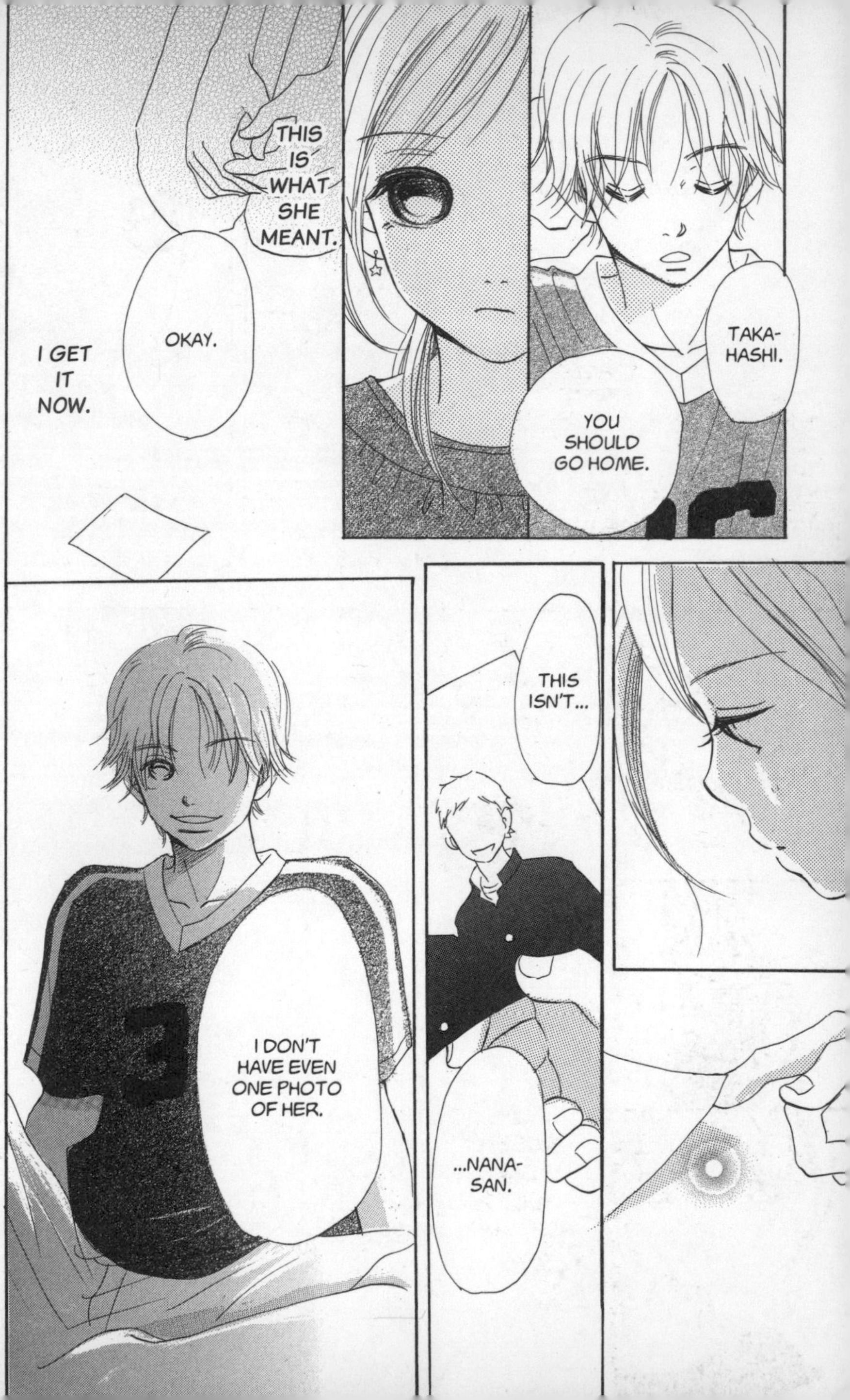
TAKA-HASHI.
YOU SHOULD GO HOME.
THIS IS WHAT SHE MEANT.
OKAY.
I GET IT NOW.
THIS ISN'T...
...NANA-SAN.
I DON'T HAVE EVEN ONE PHOTO OF HER.

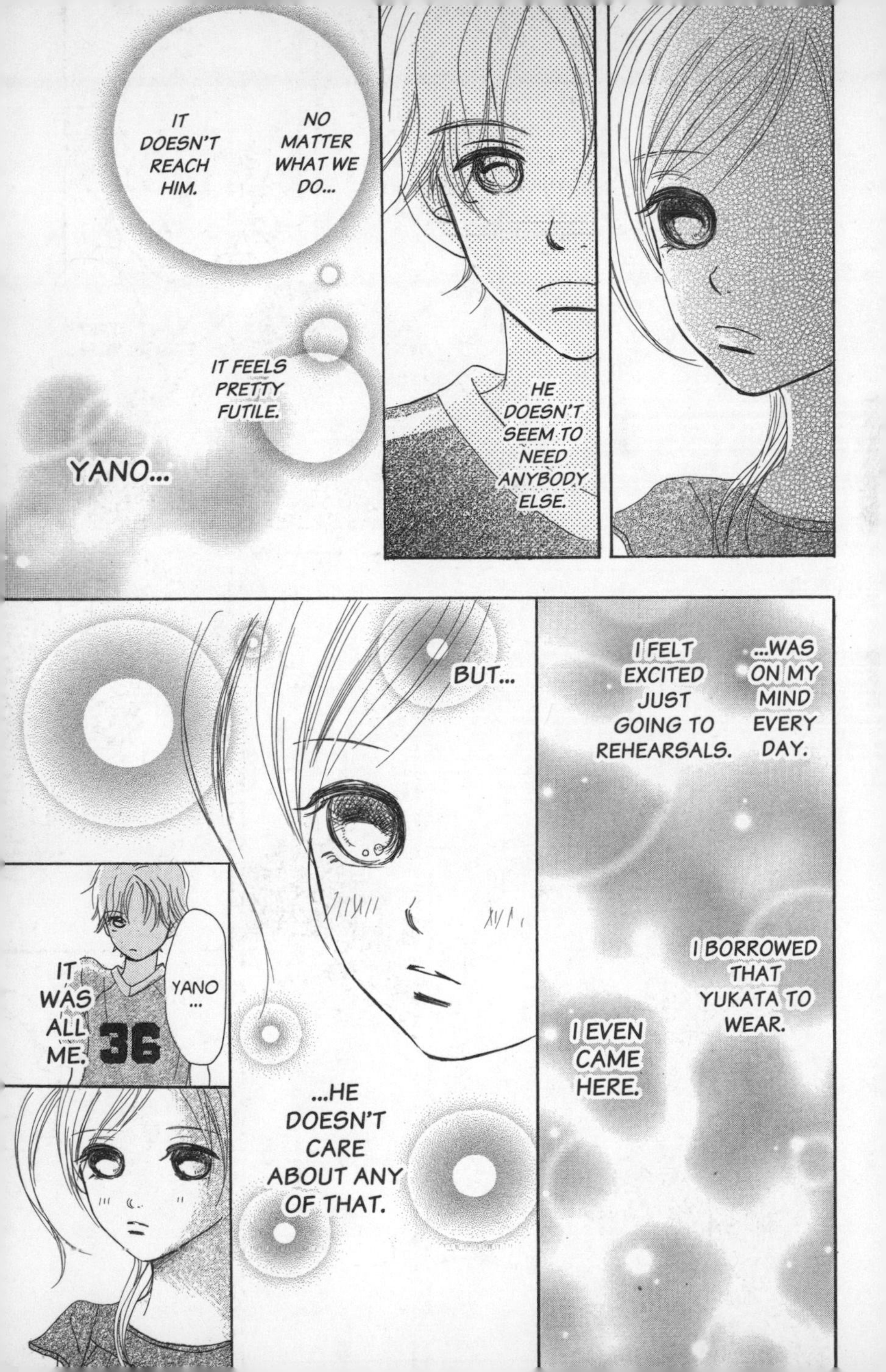
HE DOESN'T SEEM TO NEED ANYBODY ELSE.
NO MATTER WHAT WE DO...
IT DOESN'T REACH HIM.
IT FEELS PRETTY FUTILE.
YANO...
...WAS ON MY MIND EVERY DAY.
I FELT EXCITED JUST GOING TO REHEARSALS.
I BORROWED THAT YUKATA TO WEAR.
I EVEN CAME HERE.
BUT...
...HE DOESN'T CARE ABOUT ANY OF THAT.
YANO ...
IT WAS ALL ME.
36

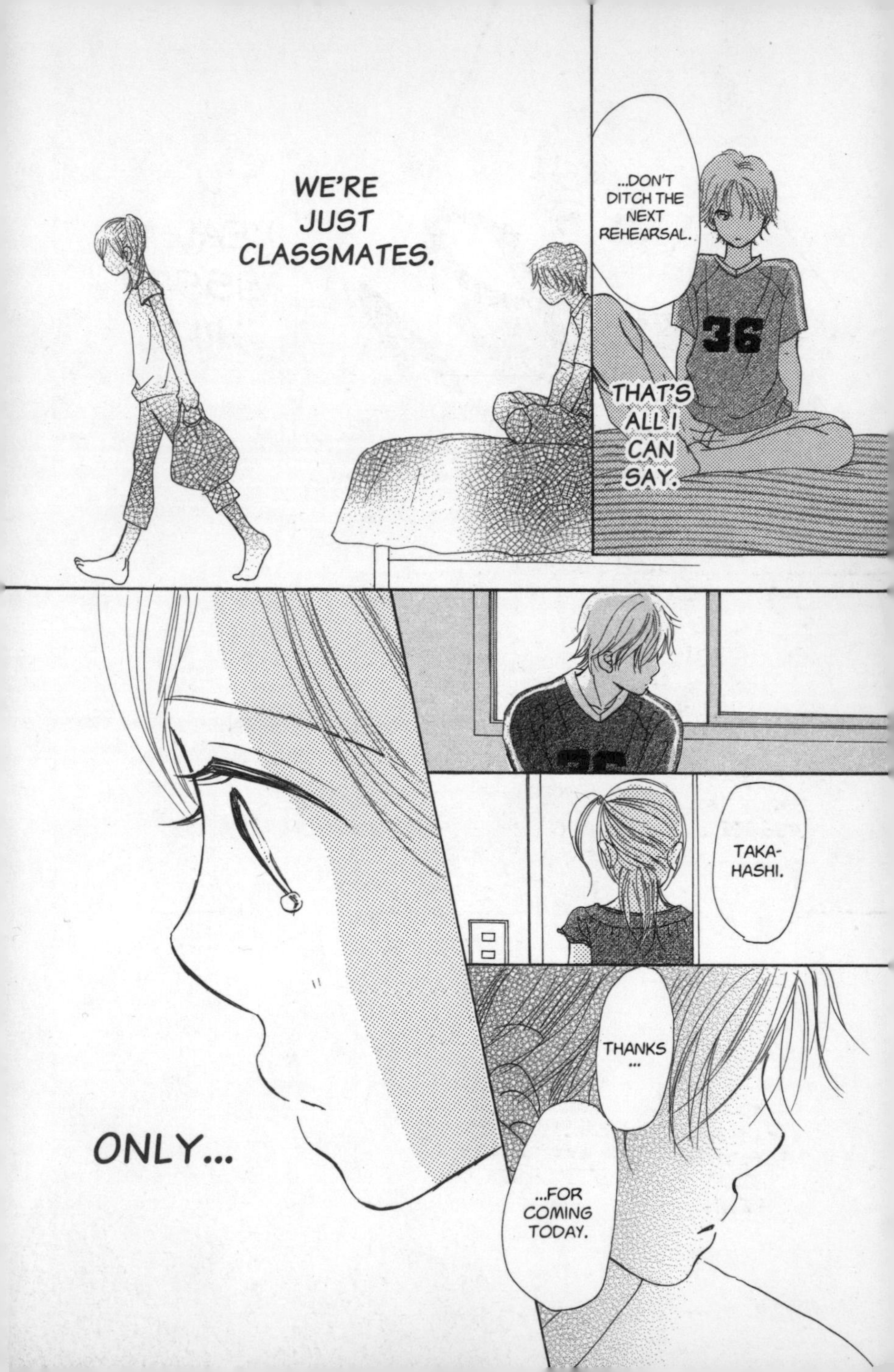
...DON'T DITCH THE NEXT REHEARSAL.
THAT'S ALL I CAN SAY.
WE'RE JUST CLASSMATES.
TAKA-HASHI.
THANKS ...
...FOR COMING TODAY.
ONLY...

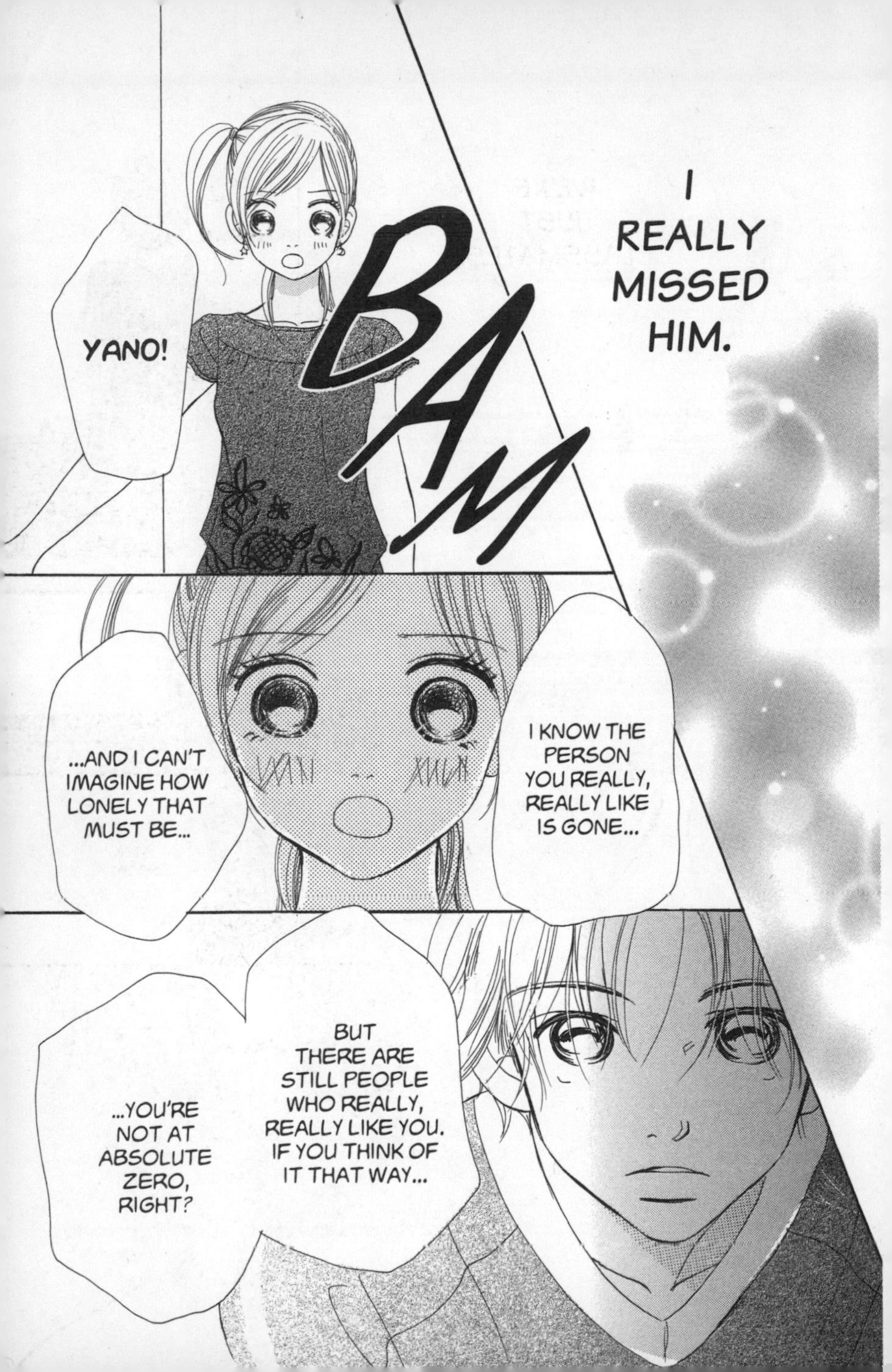
I REALLY MISSED HIM.
BAM
YANO!
I KNOW THE PERSON YOU REALLY, REALLY LIKE IS GONE...
...AND I CAN'T IMAGINE HOW LONELY THAT MUST BE...
BUT THERE ARE STILL PEOPLE WHO REALLY, REALLY LIKE YOU. IF YOU THINK OF IT THAT WAY...
...YOU'RE NOT AT ABSOLUTE ZERO, RIGHT?

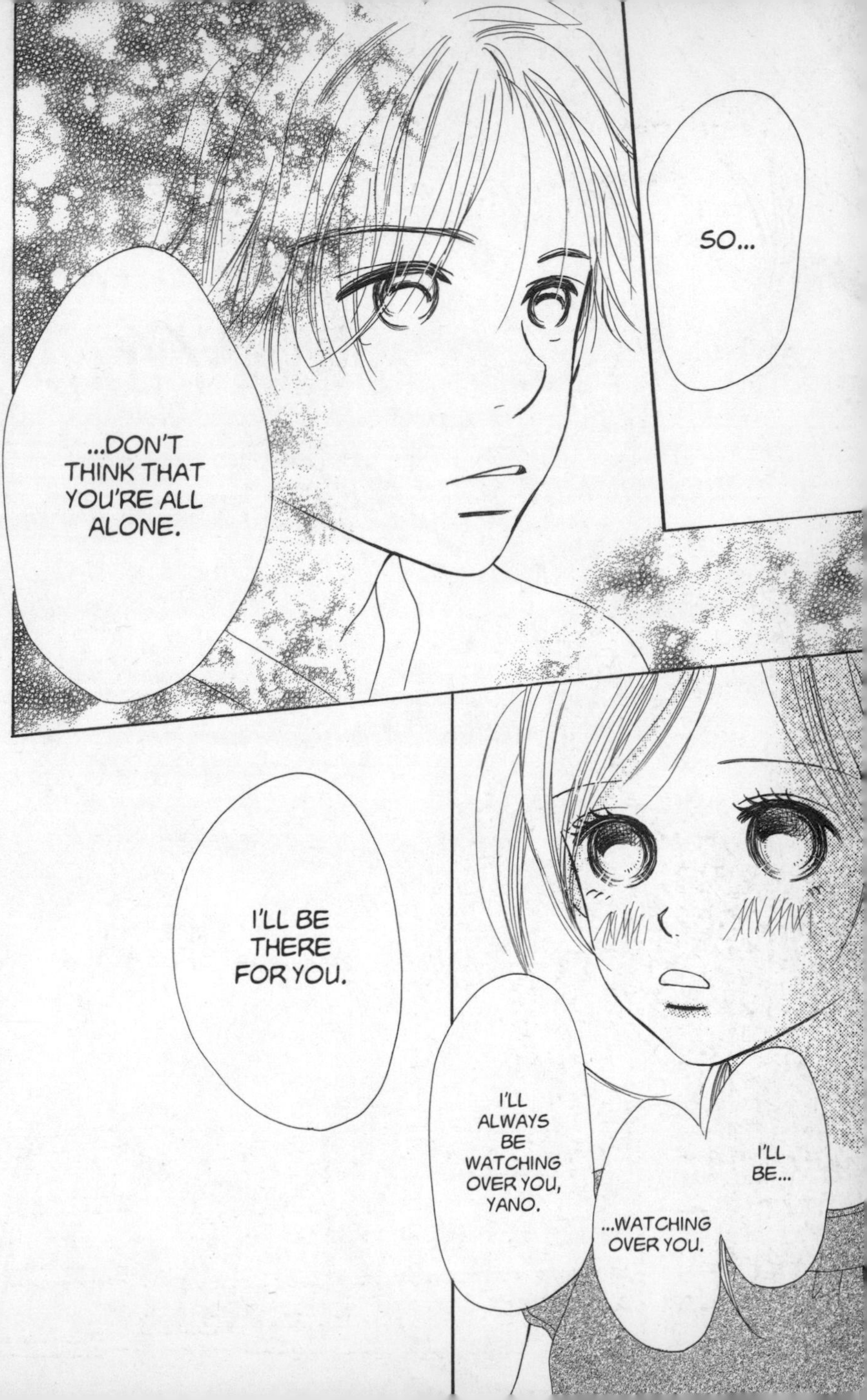
SO...
...DON'T THINK THAT YOU'RE ALL ALONE.
I'LL BE...
...WATCHING OVER YOU.
I'LL ALWAYS BE WATCHING OVER YOU, YANO.
I'LL BE THERE FOR YOU.

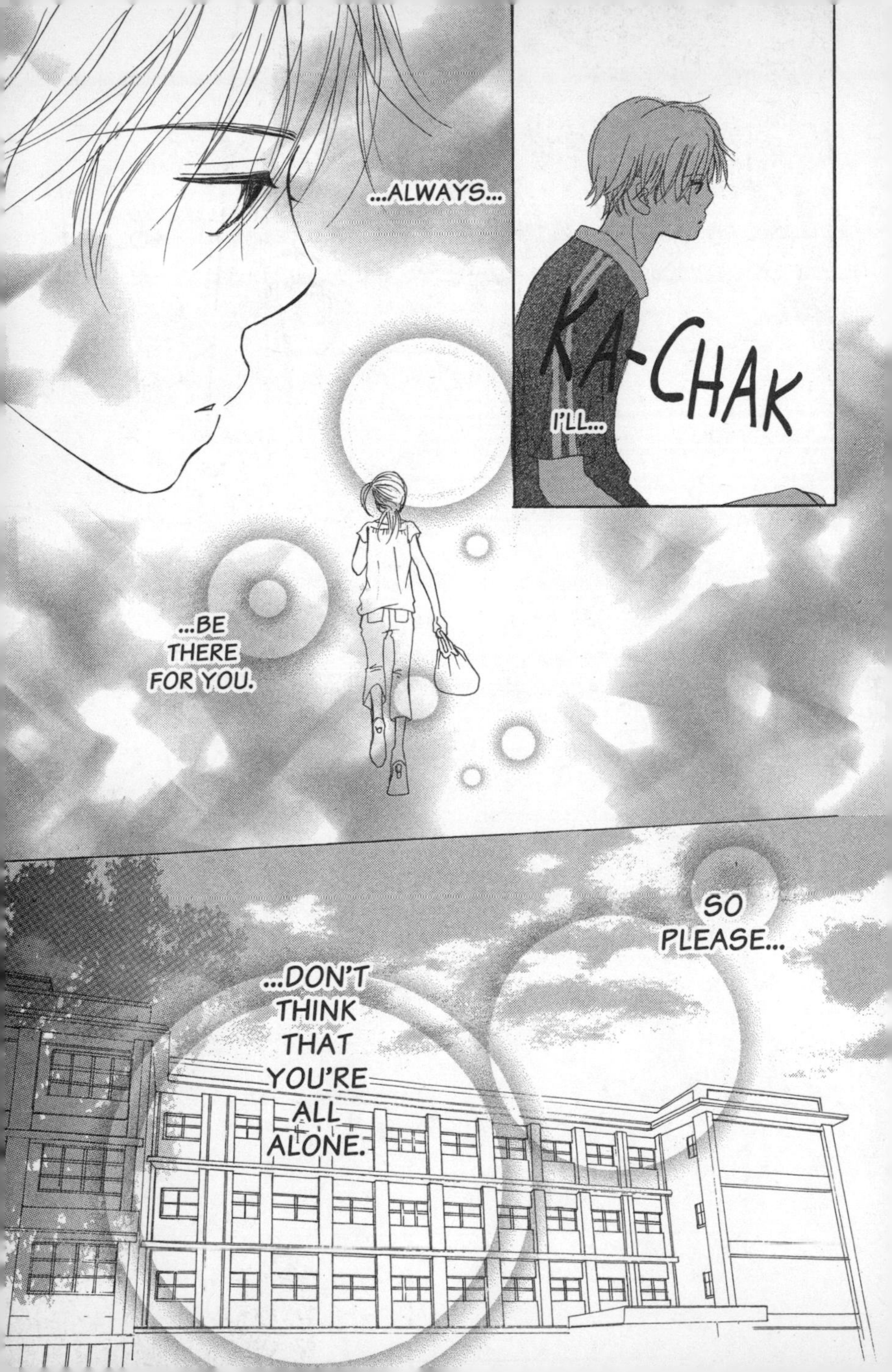
KA-CHAK
I'LL...
...ALWAYS...
...BE THERE FOR YOU.
SO PLEASE...
...DON'T THINK THAT YOU'RE ALL ALONE.

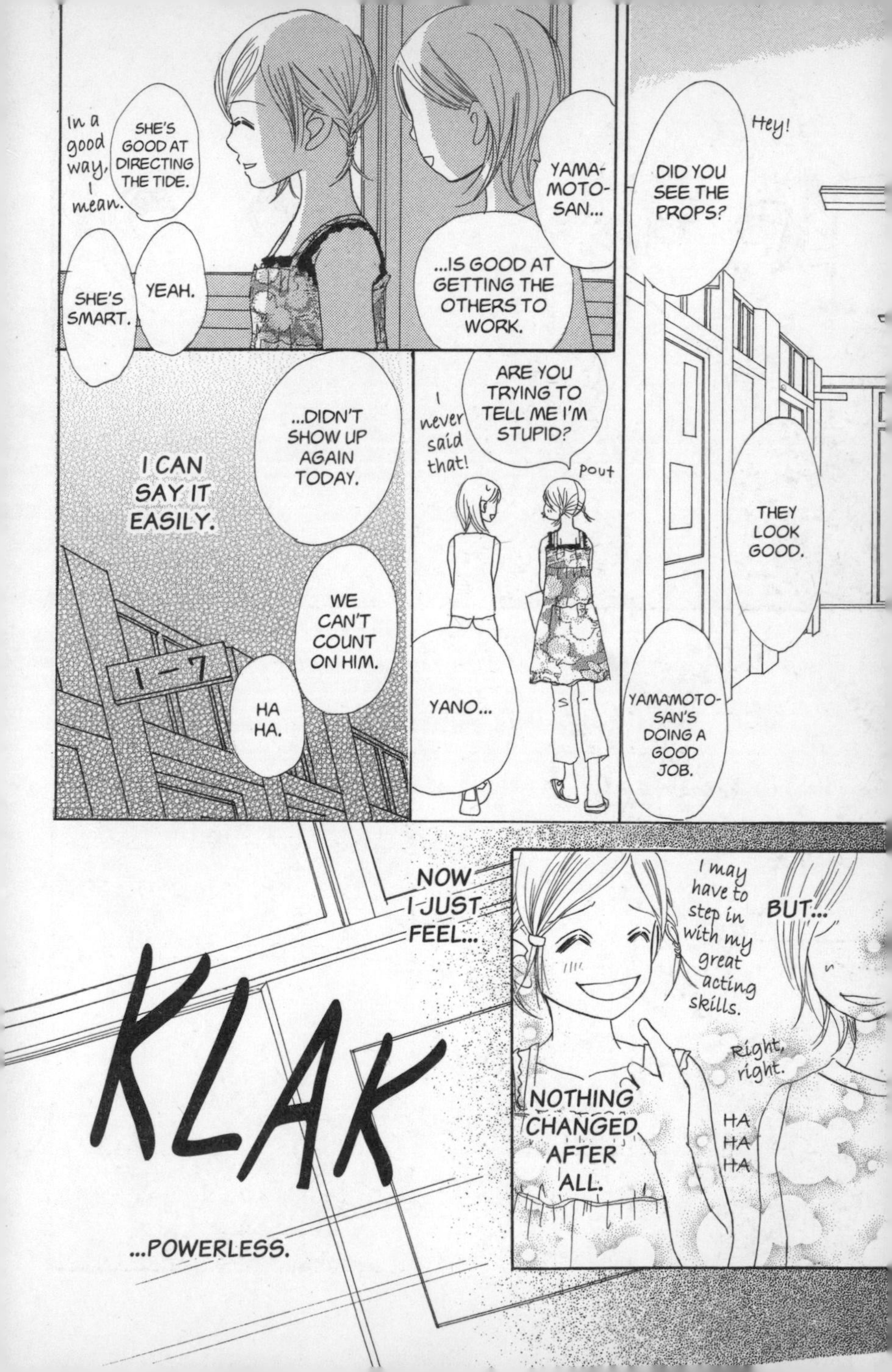
Hey!
DID YOU SEE THE PROPS?
THEY LOOK GOOD.
YAMAMOTO-SAN'S DOING A GOOD JOB.
YAMA-MOTO-SAN...
...IS GOOD AT GETTING THE OTHERS TO WORK.
SHE'S GOOD AT DIRECTING THE TIDE.
In a good way, I mean.
YEAH.
SHE'S SMART.
ARE YOU TRYING TO TELL ME I'M STUPID?
Pout
I never said that!
YANO...
...DIDN'T SHOW UP AGAIN TODAY.
WE CAN'T COUNT ON HIM.
HA HA.
I CAN SAY IT EASILY.
1-7
BUT...
I may have to step in with my great acting skills.
Right, right.
HA HA HA
NOTHING CHANGED AFTER ALL.
NOW I JUST FEEL...
KLAK
...POWERLESS.

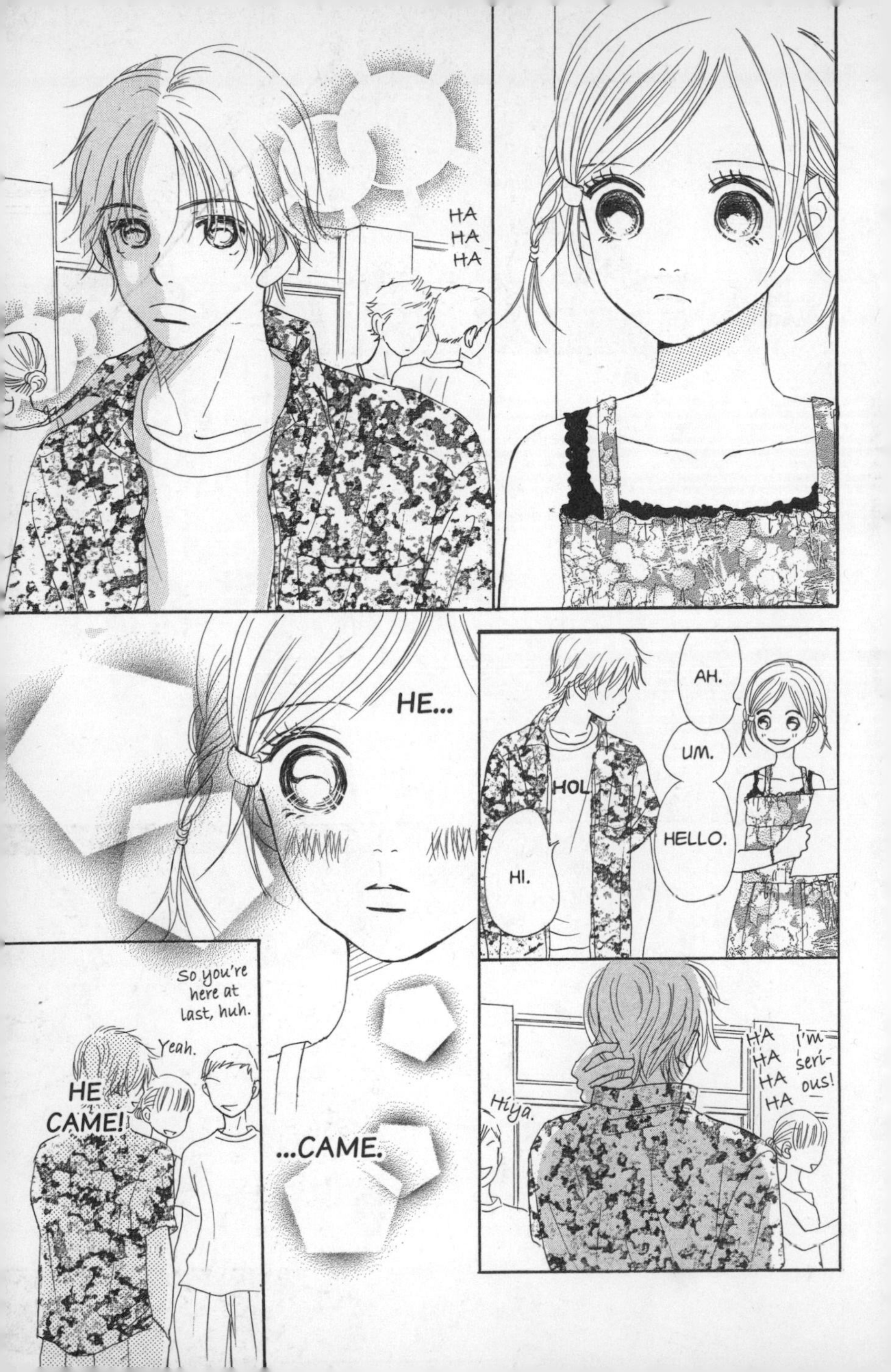
HA
HA
HA
AH.
UM.
HOL
HELLO.
HI.
HA
HA
HA
HA
I'm seri-ous!
Hiya.
HE...
...CAME.
So you're here at last, huh.
Yeah.
HE CAME!

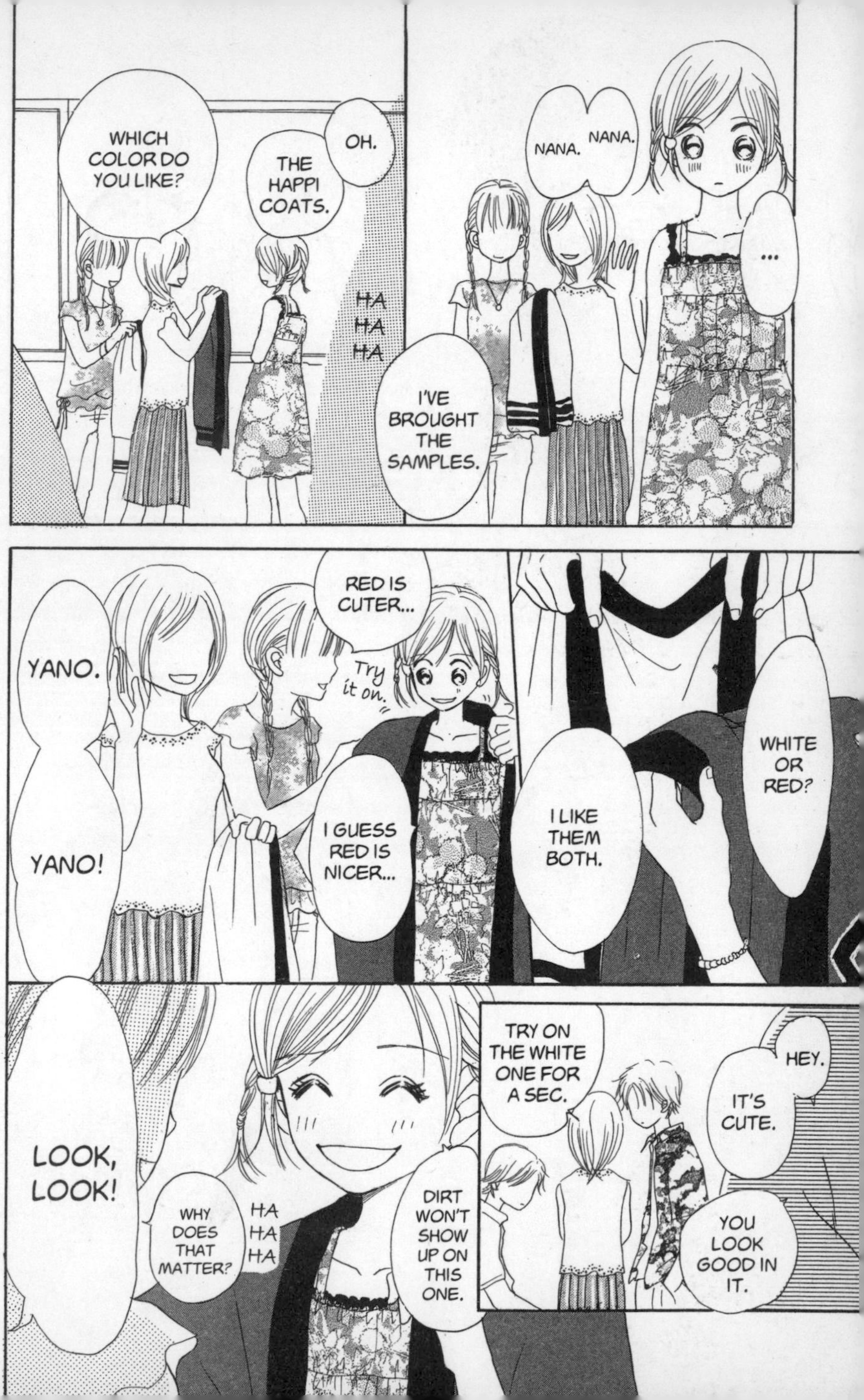
NANA.
NANA.
...
I'VE BROUGHT THE SAMPLES.
OH.
THE HAPPI COATS.
WHICH COLOR DO YOU LIKE?
HA HA HA
WHITE OR RED?
I LIKE THEM BOTH.
RED IS CUTER...
Try it on.
I GUESS RED IS NICER...
YANO.
YANO!
HEY.
IT'S CUTE.
TRY ON THE WHITE ONE FOR A SEC.
YOU LOOK GOOD IN IT.
DIRT WON'T SHOW UP ON THIS ONE.
HA HA HA
WHY DOES THAT MATTER?
LOOK, LOOK!

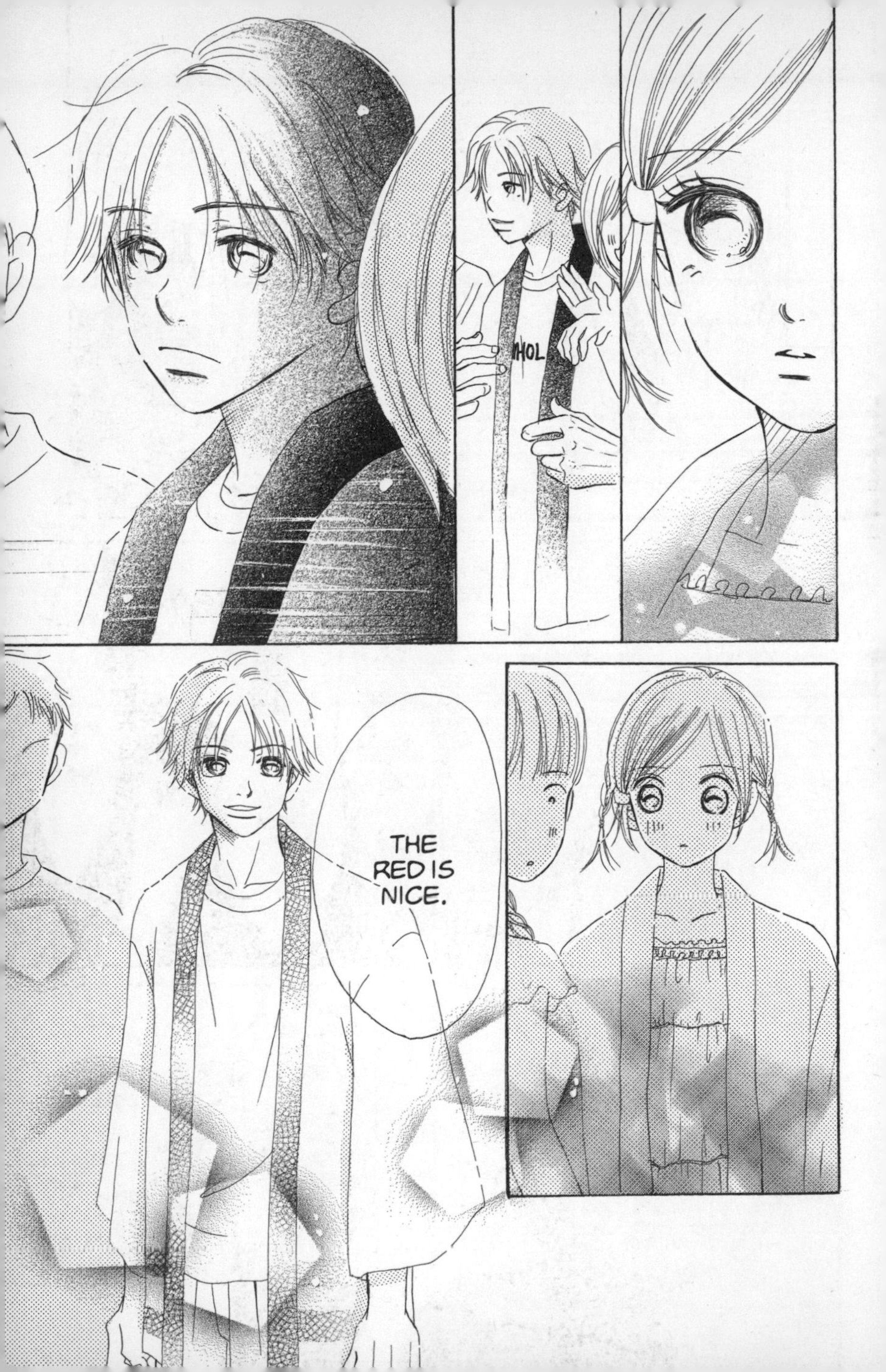
THE RED IS NICE.

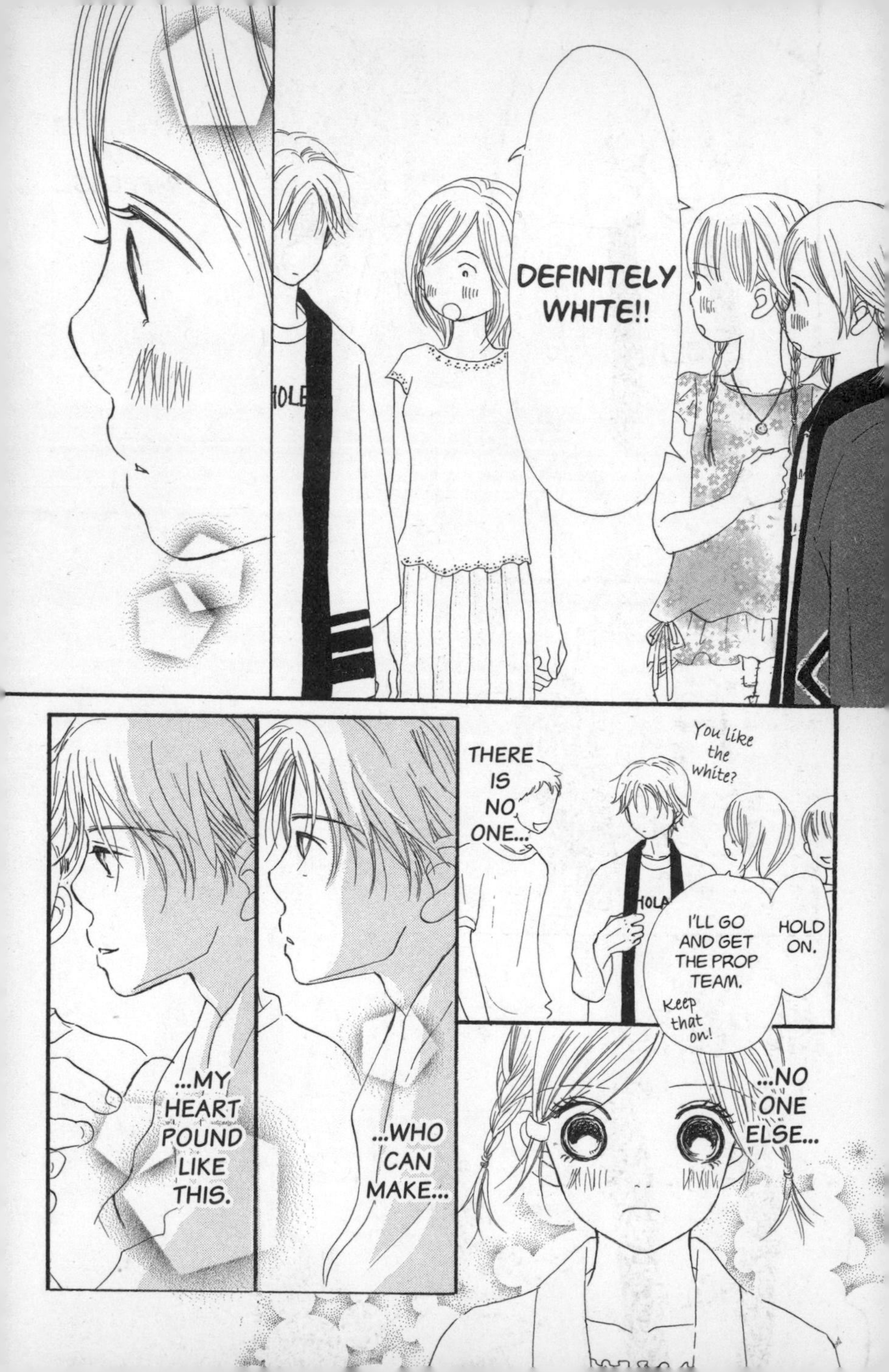
DEFINITELY WHITE!!
You like the white?
HOLD ON.
I'LL GO AND GET THE PROP TEAM.
Keep that on!
THERE IS NO ONE...
...NO ONE ELSE...
...WHO CAN MAKE...
...MY HEART POUND LIKE THIS.

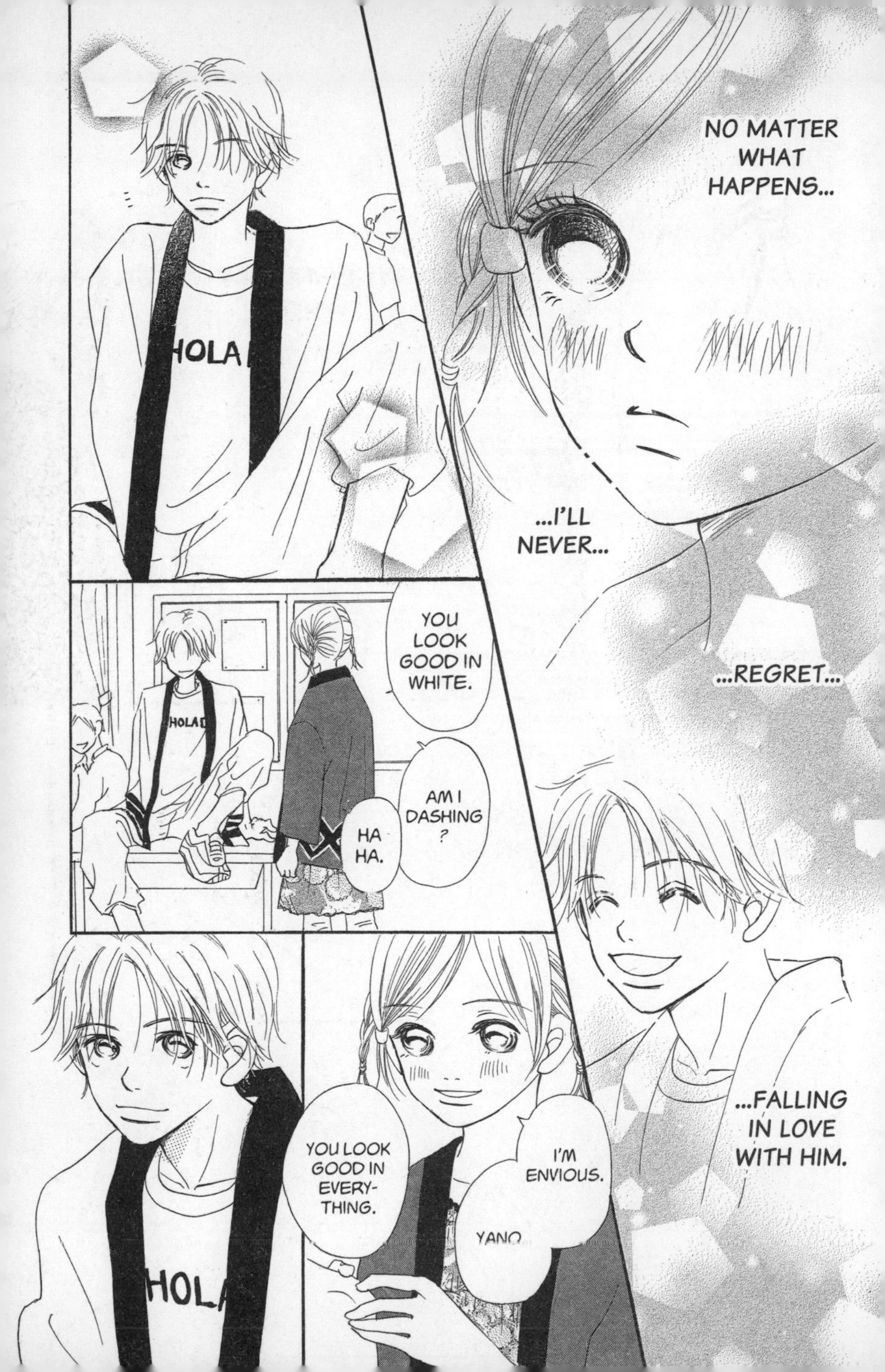
NO MATTER WHAT HAPPENS...
...I'LL NEVER...
...REGRET...
...FALLING IN LOVE WITH HIM.
YOU LOOK GOOD IN WHITE.
AM I DASHING?
HA HA.
I'M ENVIOUS.
YOU LOOK GOOD IN EVERYTHING.
YANO...

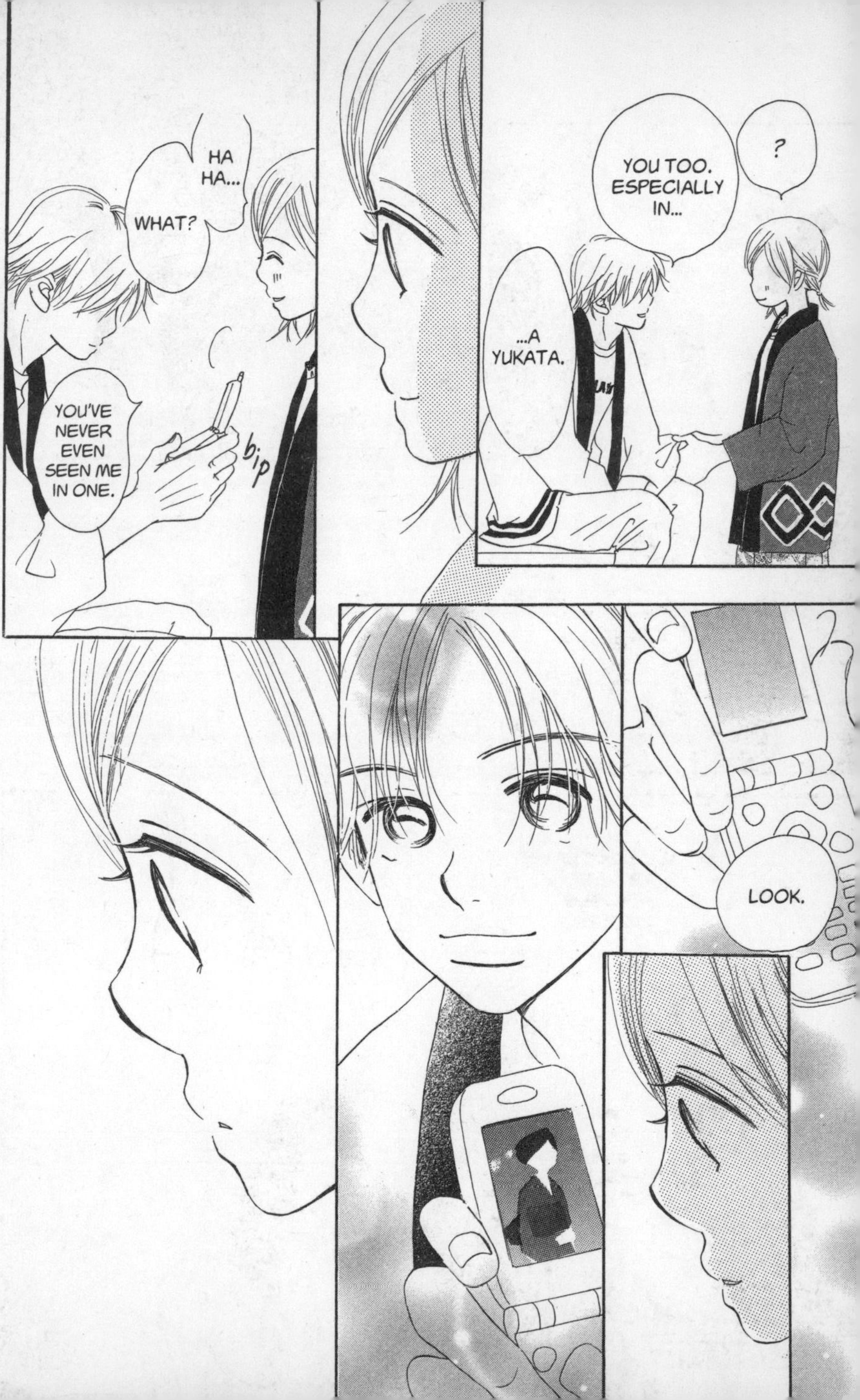
?
YOU TOO. ESPECIALLY IN...
...A YUKATA.
HA HA...
WHAT?
YOU'VE NEVER EVEN SEEN ME IN ONE.
bip
LOOK.

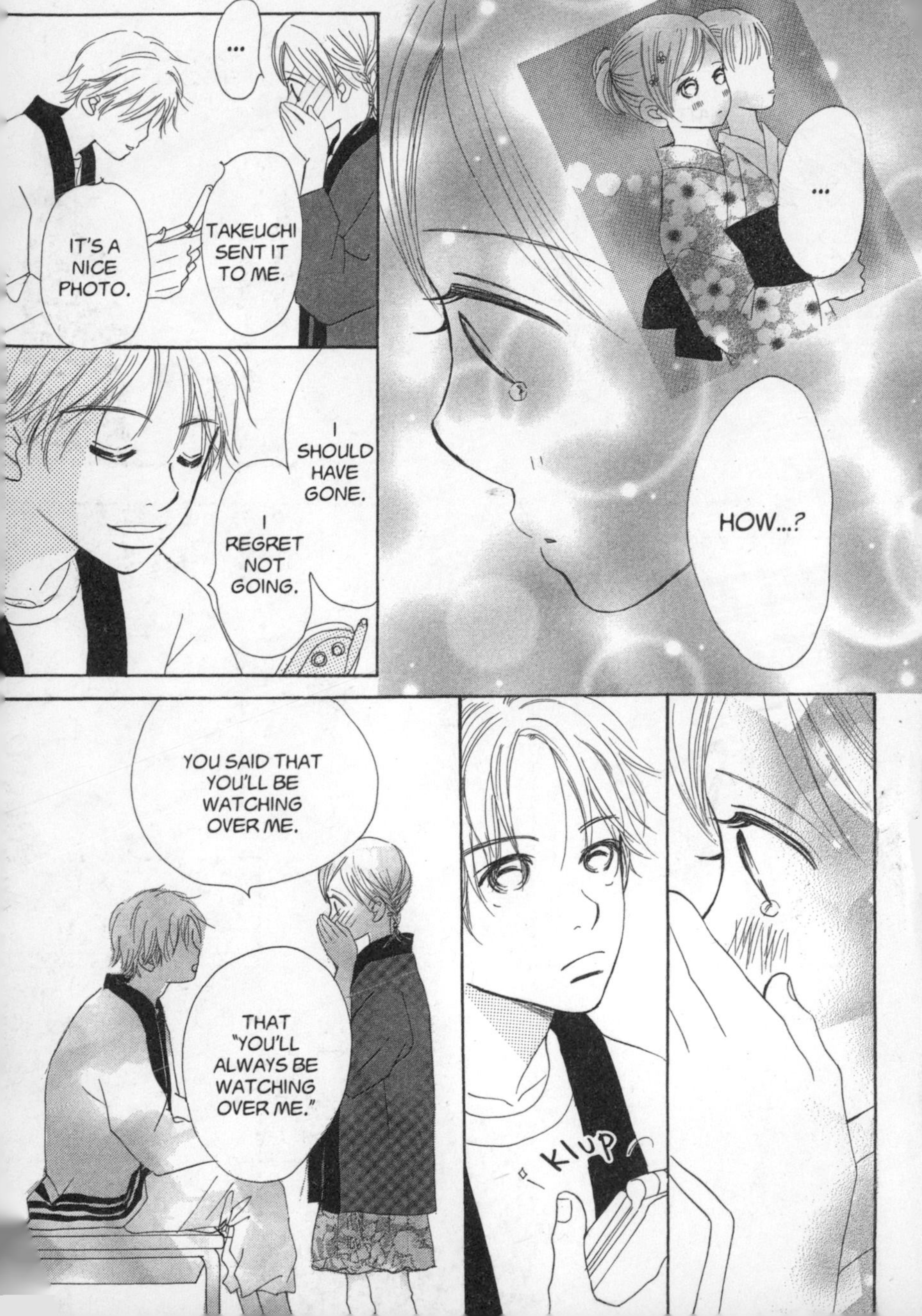
...
HOW...?
...
TAKEUCHI SENT IT TO ME.
IT'S A NICE PHOTO.
I SHOULD HAVE GONE.
I REGRET NOT GOING.
Klup
YOU SAID THAT YOU'LL BE WATCHING OVER ME.
THAT "YOU'LL ALWAYS BE WATCHING OVER ME."

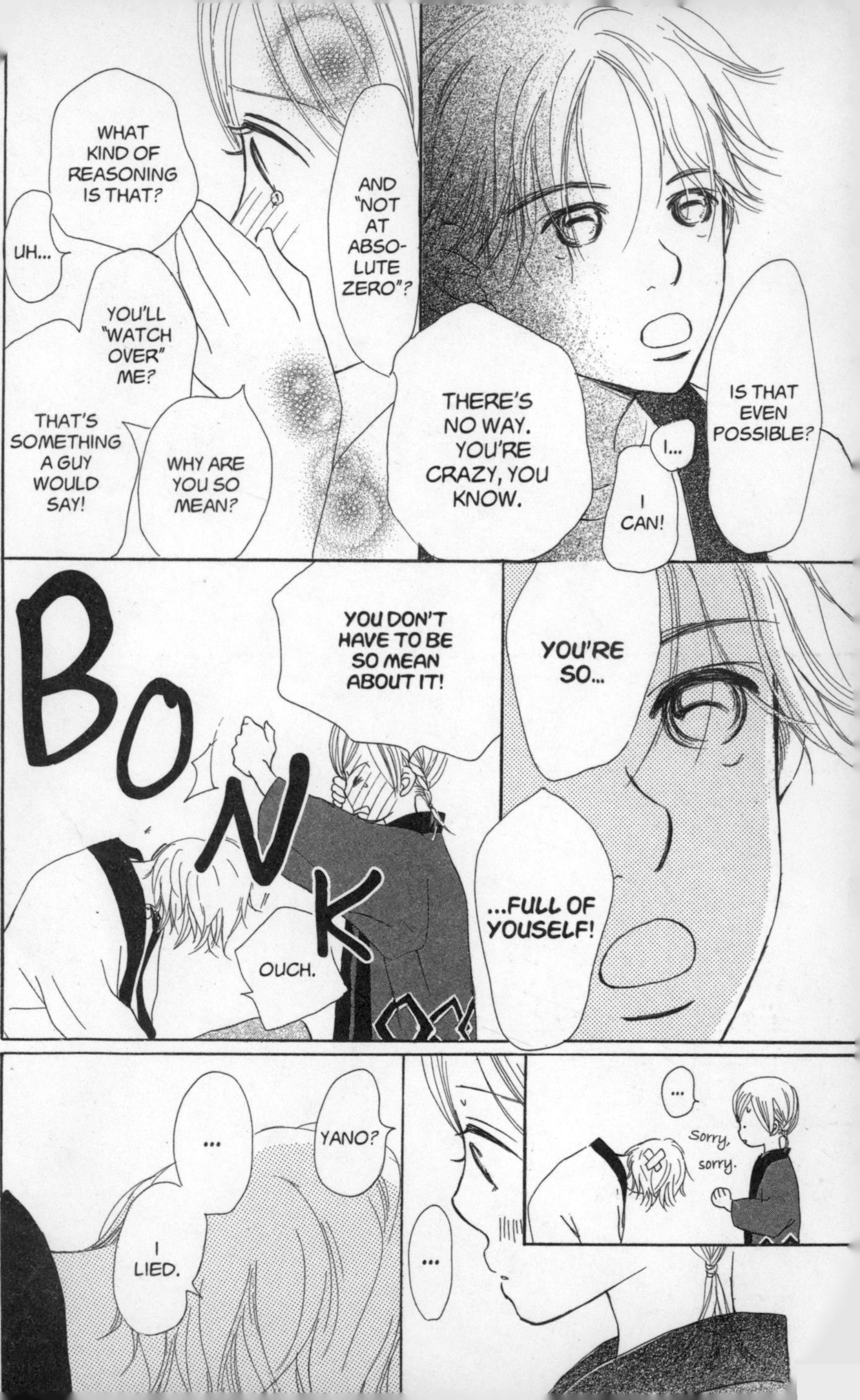
IS THAT EVEN POSSIBLE?
I...
I CAN!
THERE'S NO WAY. YOU'RE CRAZY, YOU KNOW.
AND "NOT AT ABSOLUTE ZERO"?
WHAT KIND OF REASONING IS THAT?
UH...
YOU'LL "WATCH OVER" ME?
WHY ARE YOU SO MEAN?
THAT'S SOMETHING A GUY WOULD SAY!
YOU'RE SO...
...FULL OF YOUSELF!
YOU DON'T HAVE TO BE SO MEAN ABOUT IT!
BONK
OUCH.
...
Sorry, sorry.
...
YANO?
...
I LIED.

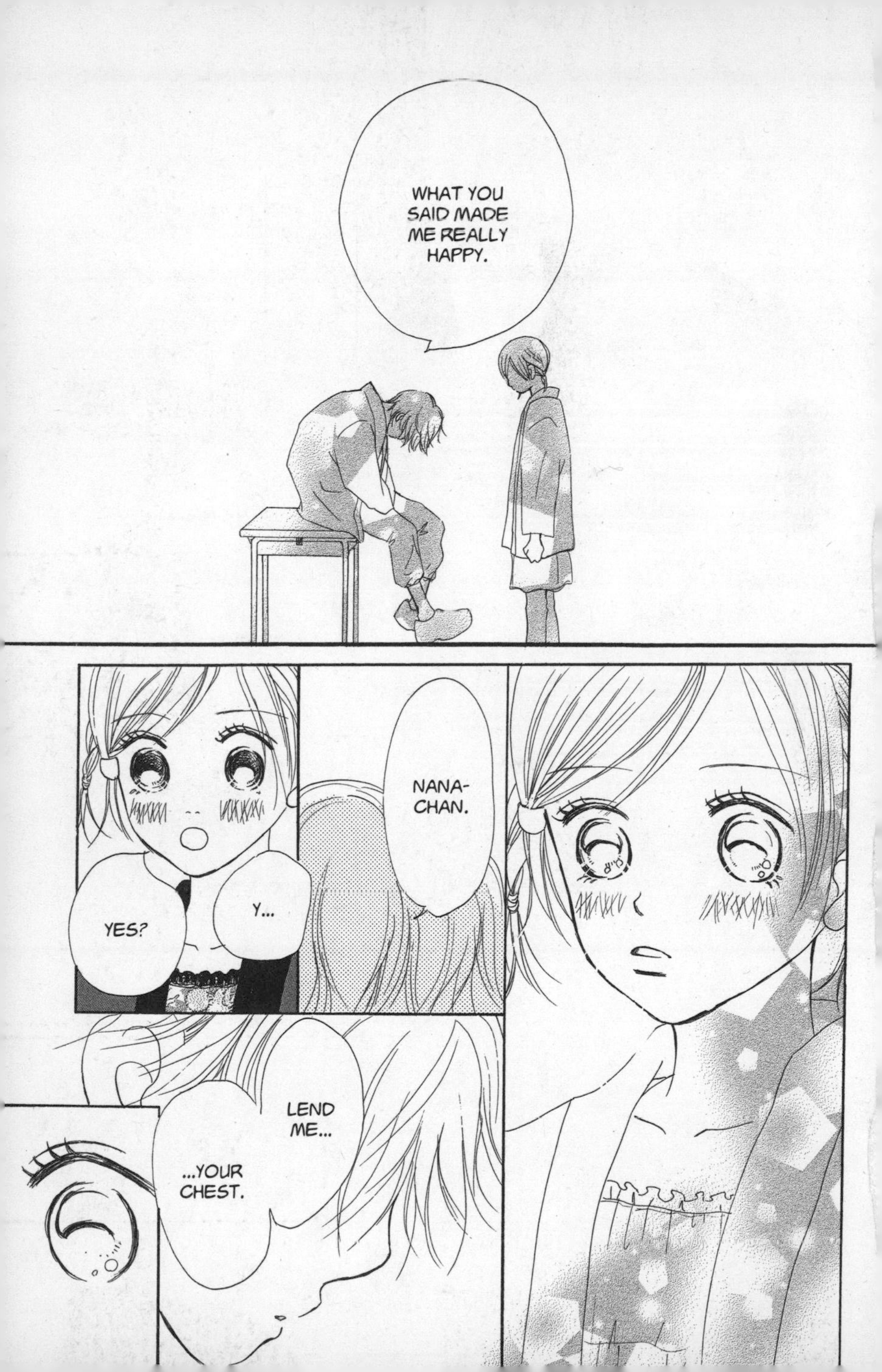
WHAT YOU SAID MADE ME REALLY HAPPY.
NANA-CHAN.
Y...
YES?
LEND ME...
...YOUR CHEST.

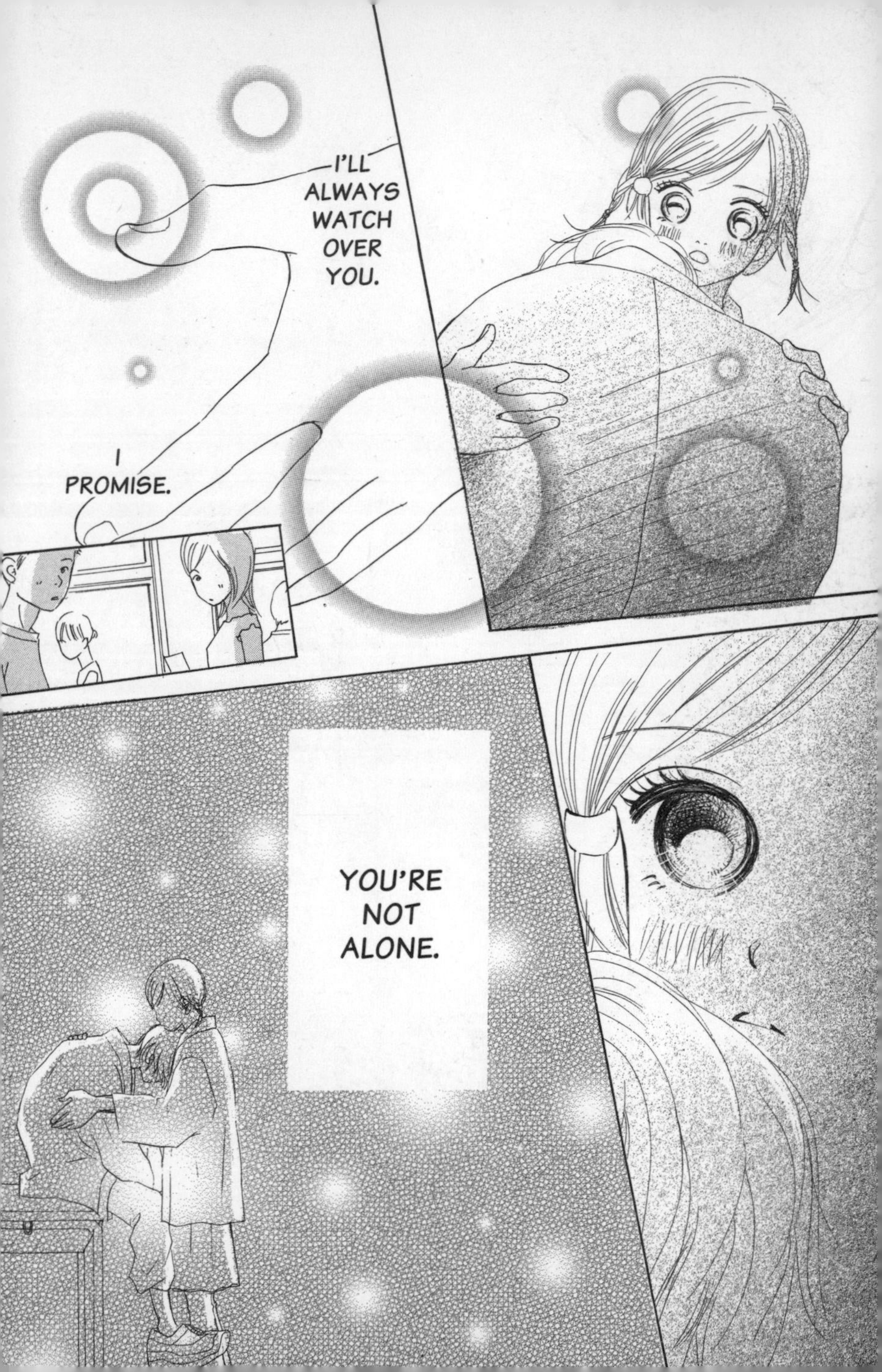
I'LL ALWAYS WATCH OVER YOU.
I PROMISE.
YOU'RE NOT ALONE.

IT'S NO USE.
HE'S DEAD TO THE WORLD.
I CAN'T BELIEVE HE CAN SLEEP SO WELL HERE.
HE'S USING MY BAG AS A PILLOW.
He's out.
I WONDER IF HE'S DREAMING?
He looks so peaceful.
BACK THEN...

Chapter 6

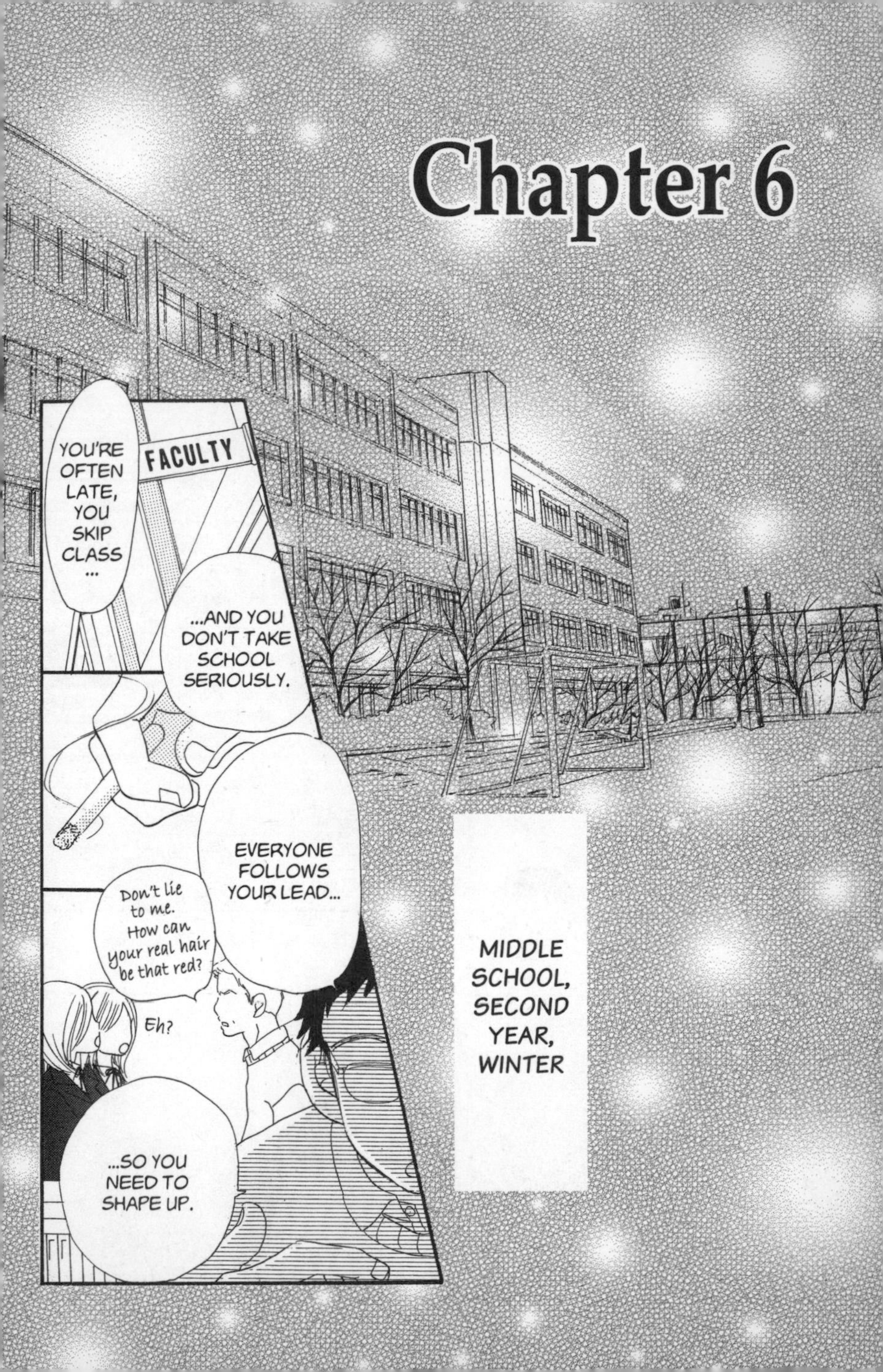
MIDDLE SCHOOL, SECOND YEAR, WINTER
FACULTY
YOU'RE OFTEN LATE, YOU SKIP CLASS ...
...AND YOU DON'T TAKE SCHOOL SERIOUSLY.
EVERYONE FOLLOWS YOUR LEAD...
Don't lie to me. How can your real hair be that red?
Eh?
...SO YOU NEED TO SHAPE UP.

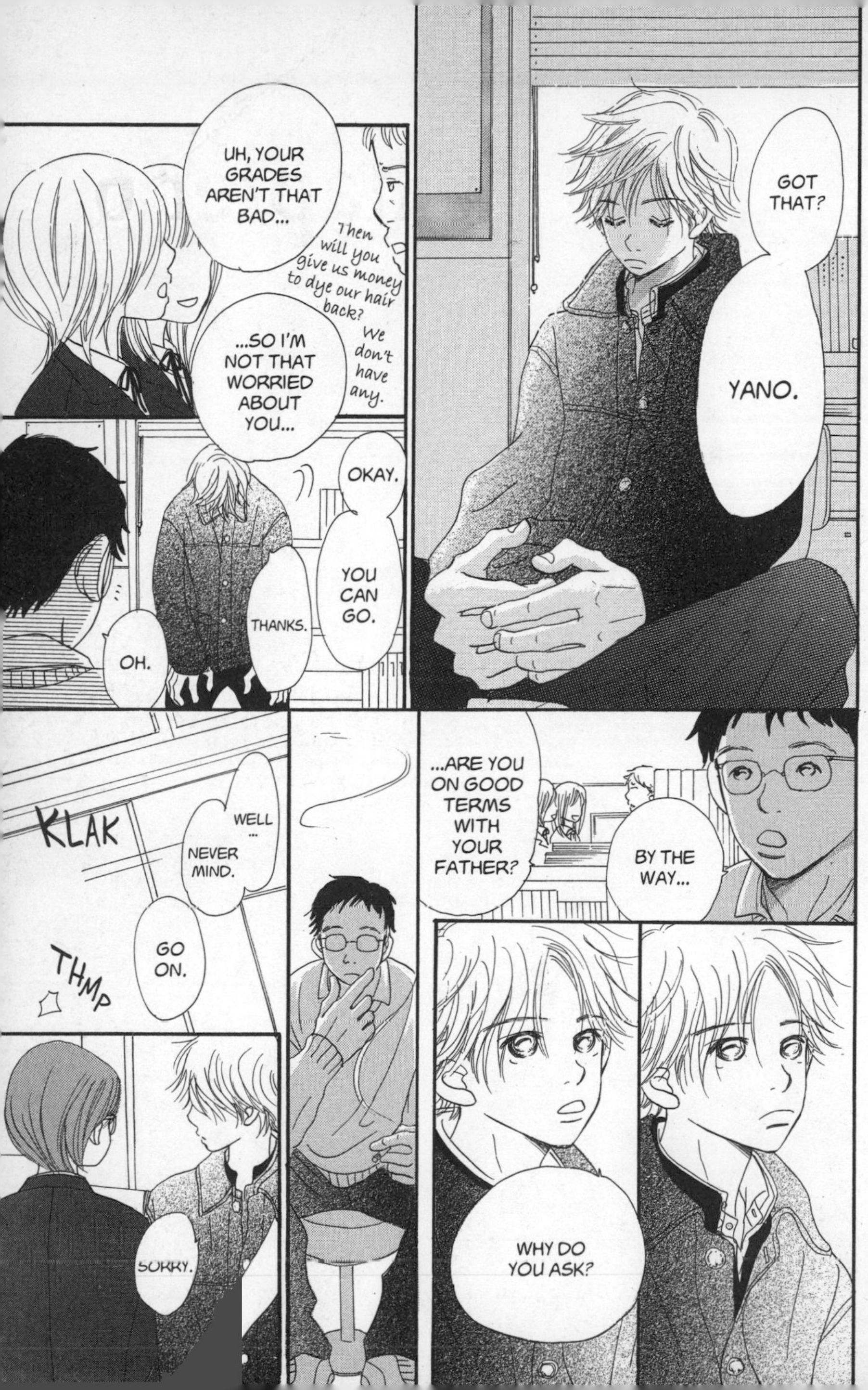
GOT THAT?
YANO.
UH, YOUR GRADES AREN'T THAT BAD...
Then will you give us money to dye our hair back?
...SO I'M NOT THAT WORRIED ABOUT YOU...
We don't have any.
OKAY.
YOU CAN GO.
THANKS.
OH.
BY THE WAY...
...ARE YOU ON GOOD TERMS WITH YOUR FATHER?
WHY DO YOU ASK?
WELL ...
NEVER MIND.
GO ON.
KLAK
THMP
SORRY.

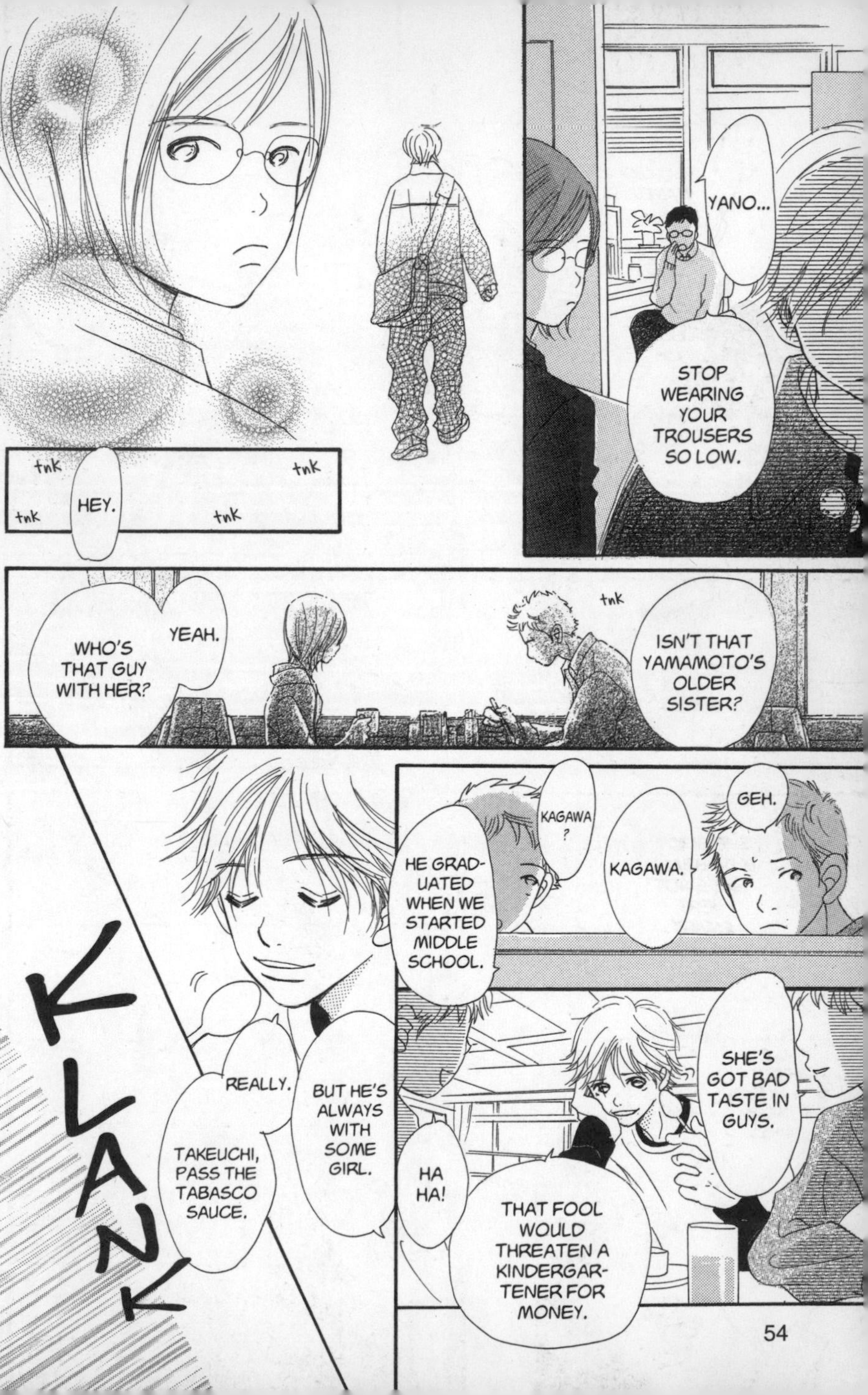
YANO...
STOP WEARING YOUR TROUSERS SO LOW.
tnk
HEY.
tnk
tnk
tnk
tnk
ISN'T THAT YAMAMOTO'S OLDER SISTER?
YEAH.
WHO'S THAT GUY WITH HER?
GEH.
KAGAWA.
KAGAWA ?
HE GRADUATED WHEN WE STARTED MIDDLE SCHOOL.
SHE'S GOT BAD TASTE IN GUYS.
THAT FOOL WOULD THREATEN A KINDERGARTENER FOR MONEY.
HA HA!
BUT HE'S ALWAYS WITH SOME GIRL.
REALLY.
TAKEUCHI, PASS THE TABASCO SAUCE.
KLANK

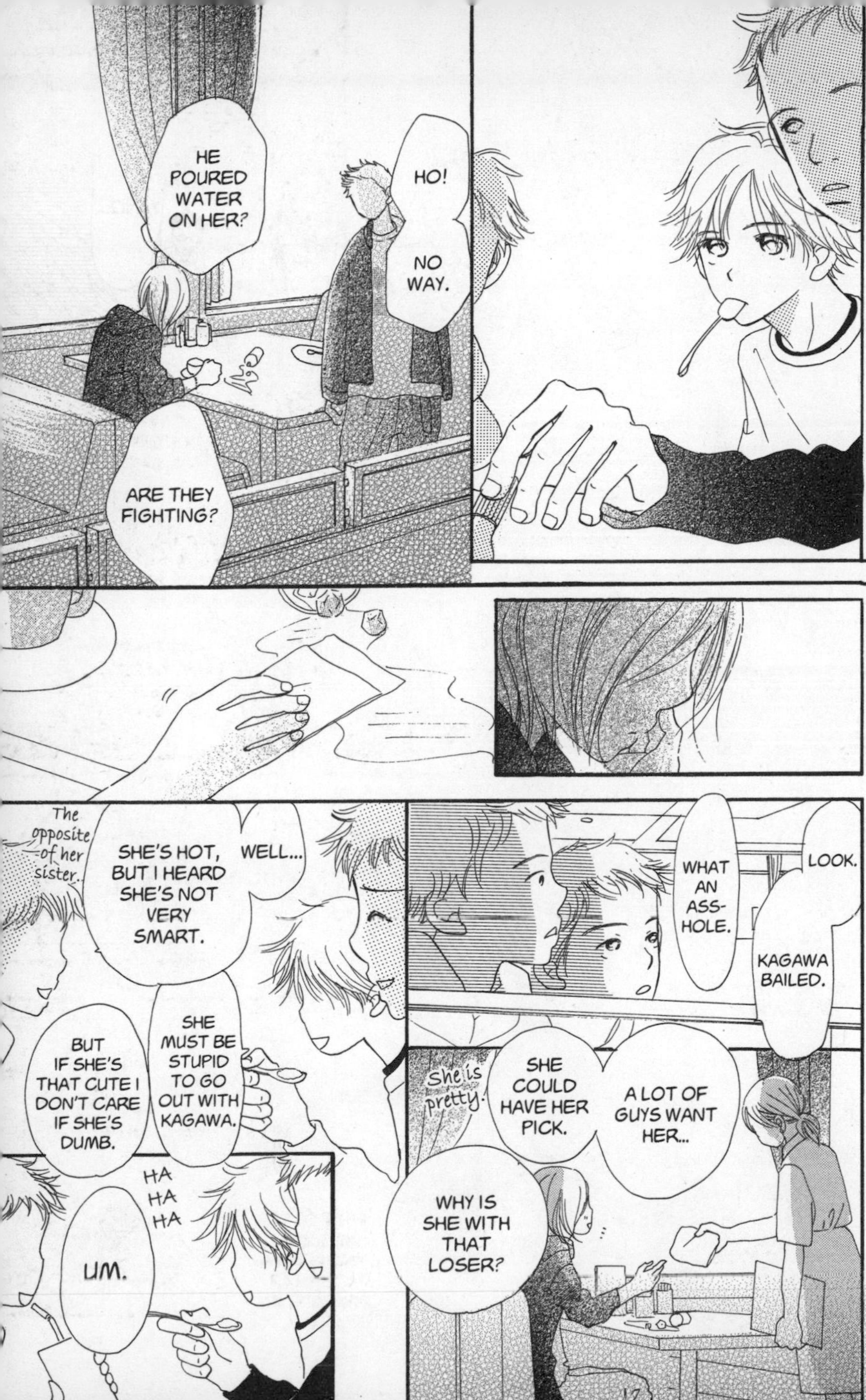
HO!
NO WAY.
HE POURED WATER ON HER?
ARE THEY FIGHTING?
LOOK.
KAGAWA BAILED.
WHAT AN ASS-HOLE.
A LOT OF GUYS WANT HER...
SHE COULD HAVE HER PICK.
She is pretty.
WHY IS SHE WITH THAT LOSER?
WELL...
SHE'S HOT, BUT I HEARD SHE'S NOT VERY SMART.
The opposite of her sister.
SHE MUST BE STUPID TO GO OUT WITH KAGAWA.
BUT IF SHE'S THAT CUTE I DON'T CARE IF SHE'S DUMB.
HA HA HA
UM.

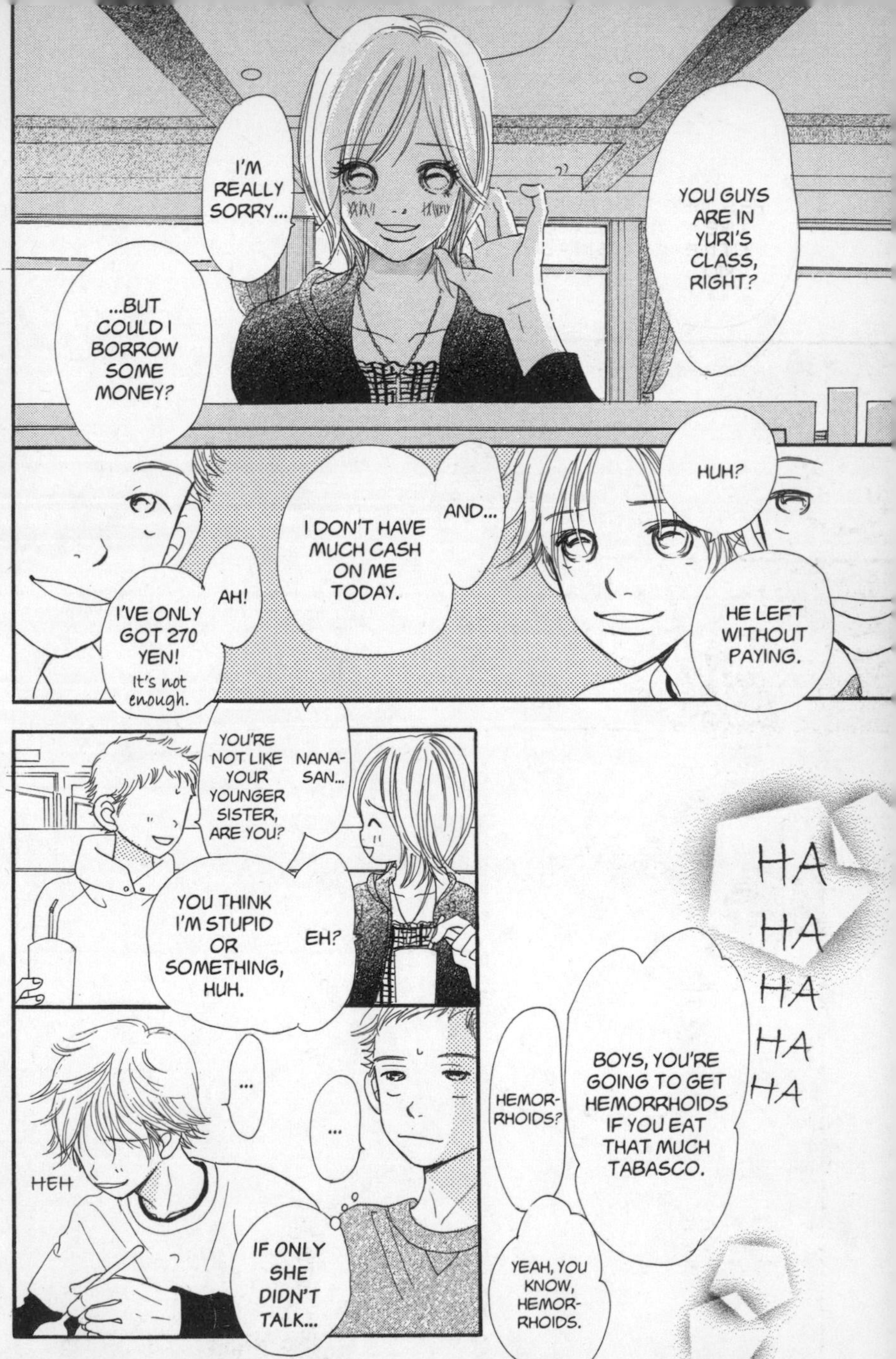
YOU GUYS ARE IN YURI'S CLASS, RIGHT?
I'M REALLY SORRY...
...BUT COULD I BORROW SOME MONEY?
HUH?
HE LEFT WITHOUT PAYING.
AND...
I DON'T HAVE MUCH CASH ON ME TODAY.
AH!
I'VE ONLY GOT 270 YEN!
It's not enough.
HA HA HA HA HA
BOYS, YOU'RE GOING TO GET HEMORRHOIDS IF YOU EAT THAT MUCH TABASCO.
HEMORRHOIDS?
YEAH, YOU KNOW, HEMORRHOIDS.
NANA-SAN...
YOU'RE NOT LIKE YOUR YOUNGER SISTER, ARE YOU?
EH?
YOU THINK I'M STUPID OR SOMETHING, HUH.
...
...
IF ONLY SHE DIDN'T TALK...
HEH

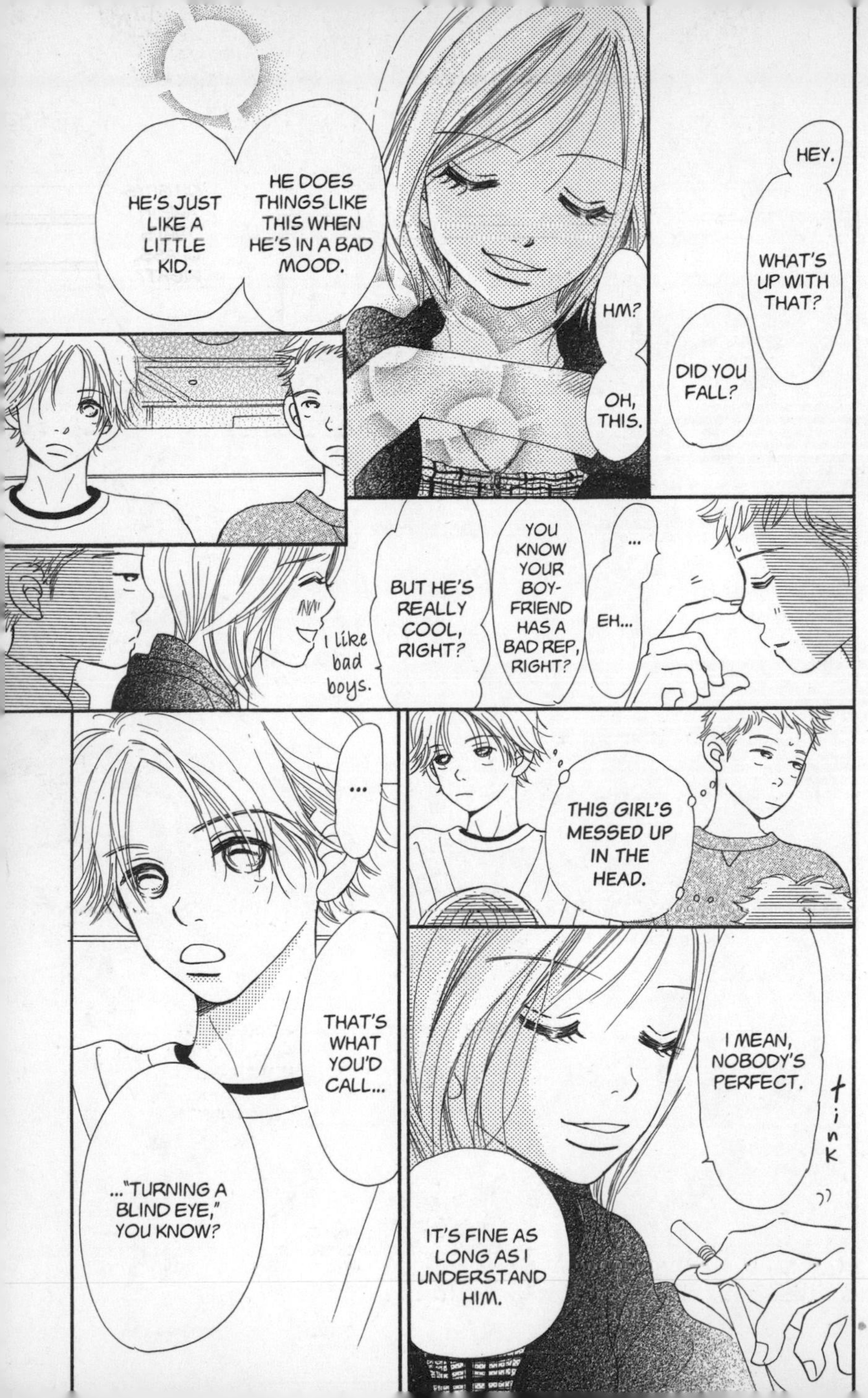
HEY.
WHAT'S UP WITH THAT?
DID YOU FALL?
HM?
OH, THIS.
HE DOES THINGS LIKE THIS WHEN HE'S IN A BAD MOOD.
HE'S JUST LIKE A LITTLE KID.
...
EH...
YOU KNOW YOUR BOY-FRIEND HAS A BAD REP, RIGHT?
BUT HE'S REALLY COOL, RIGHT?
I like bad boys.
THIS GIRL'S MESSED UP IN THE HEAD.
I MEAN, NOBODY'S PERFECT.
tink
IT'S FINE AS LONG AS I UNDERSTAND HIM.
...
THAT'S WHAT YOU'D CALL...
..."TURNING A BLIND EYE," YOU KNOW?

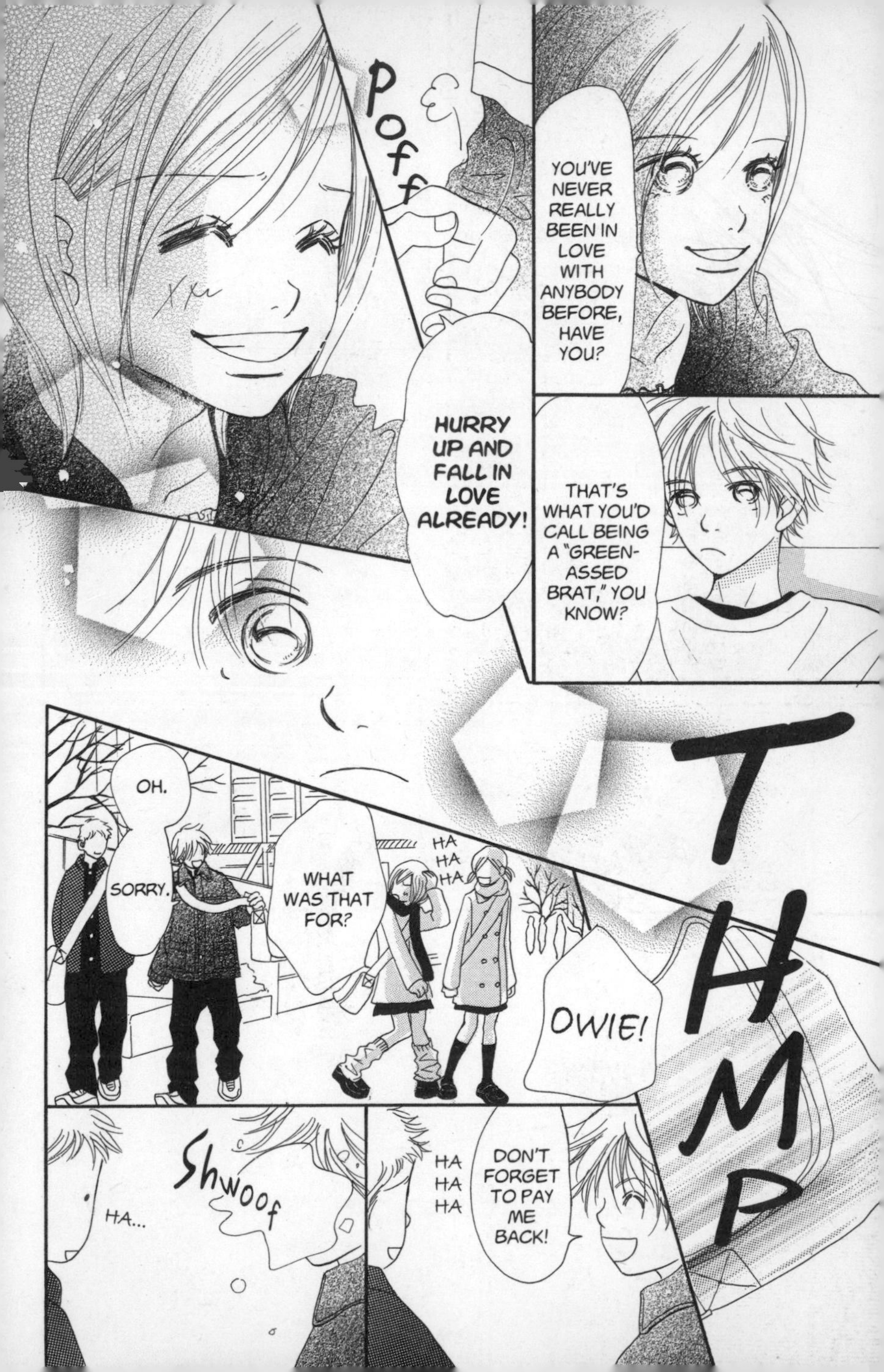
YOU'VE NEVER REALLY BEEN IN LOVE WITH ANYBODY BEFORE, HAVE YOU?
THAT'S WHAT YOU'D CALL BEING A "GREEN-ASSED BRAT," YOU KNOW?
Poff
HURRY UP AND FALL IN LOVE ALREADY!
THMP
OWIE!
HA HA HA
WHAT WAS THAT FOR?
OH.
SORRY.
DON'T FORGET TO PAY ME BACK!
HA HA HA
Shwoof
HA...

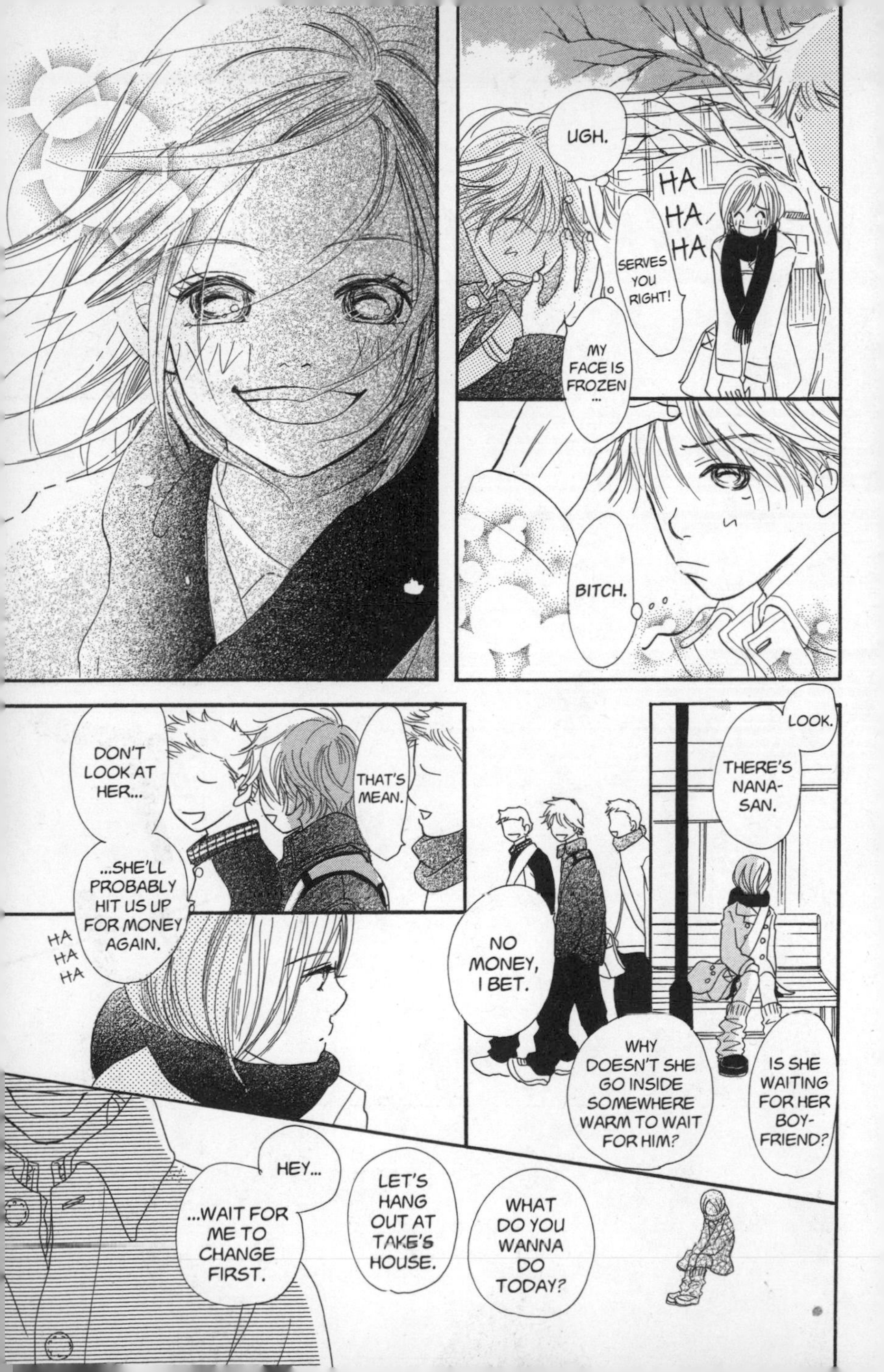
UGH.
HA HA HA
SERVES YOU RIGHT!
MY FACE IS FROZEN...
BITCH.
LOOK.
THERE'S NANA-SAN.
IS SHE WAITING FOR HER BOY-FRIEND?
WHY DOESN'T SHE GO INSIDE SOMEWHERE WARM TO WAIT FOR HIM?
NO MONEY, I BET.
THAT'S MEAN.
DON'T LOOK AT HER...
...SHE'LL PROBABLY HIT US UP FOR MONEY AGAIN.
HA HA HA
WHAT DO YOU WANNA DO TODAY?
LET'S HANG OUT AT TAKE'S HOUSE.
HEY...
...WAIT FOR ME TO CHANGE FIRST.

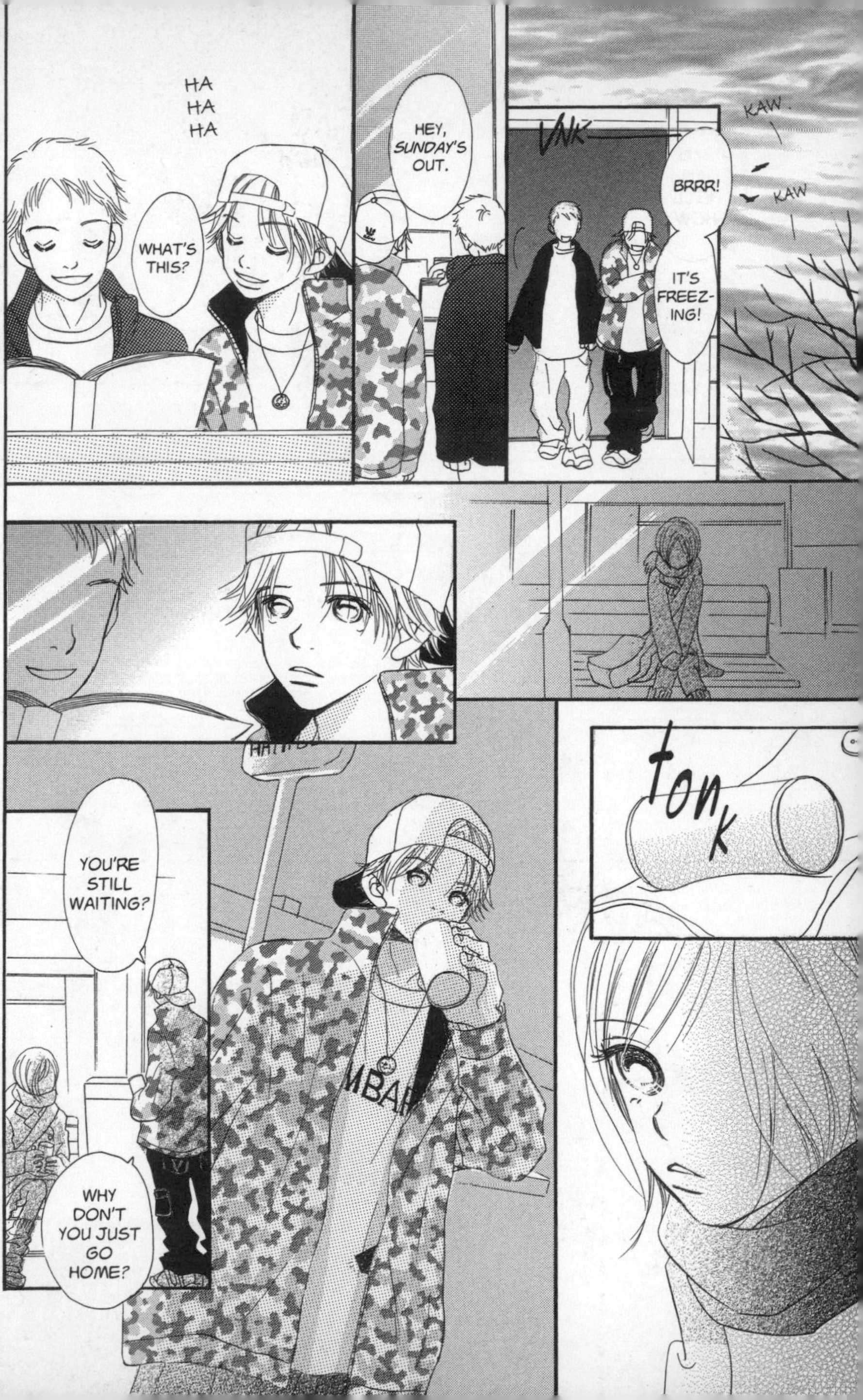
KAW
KAW
VNK
BRRR!
IT'S FREEZING!
HEY, SUNDAY'S OUT.
HA HA HA
WHAT'S THIS?
tonk
YOU'RE STILL WAITING?
WHY DON'T YOU JUST GO HOME?

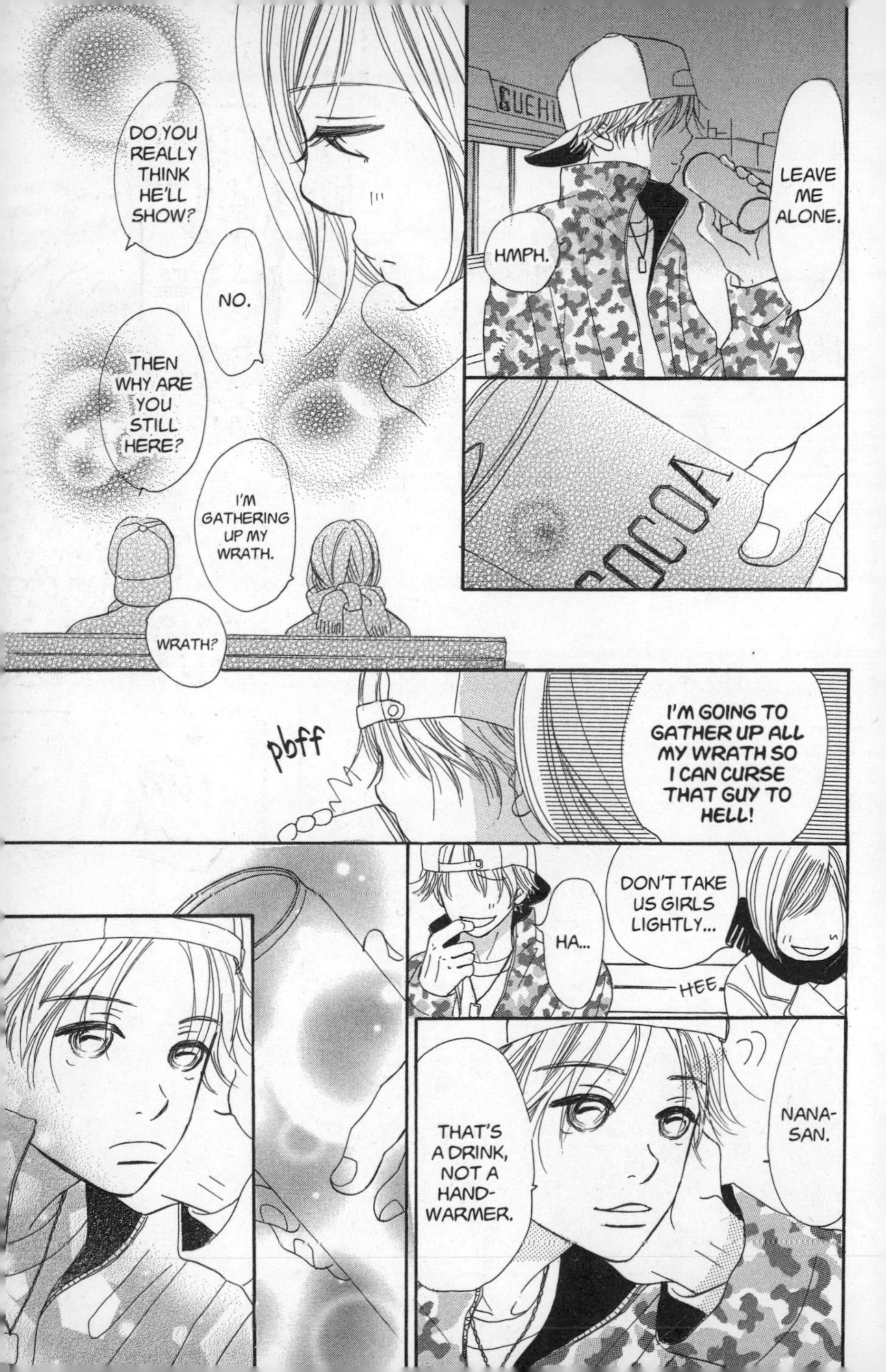
LEAVE ME ALONE.
HMPH.
DO YOU REALLY THINK HE'LL SHOW?
NO.
THEN WHY ARE YOU STILL HERE?
I'M GATHERING UP MY WRATH.
WRATH?
I'M GOING TO GATHER UP ALL MY WRATH SO I CAN CURSE THAT GUY TO HELL!
pbff
DON'T TAKE US GIRLS LIGHTLY...
HA...
HEE.
NANA-SAN.
THAT'S A DRINK, NOT A HAND-WARMER.

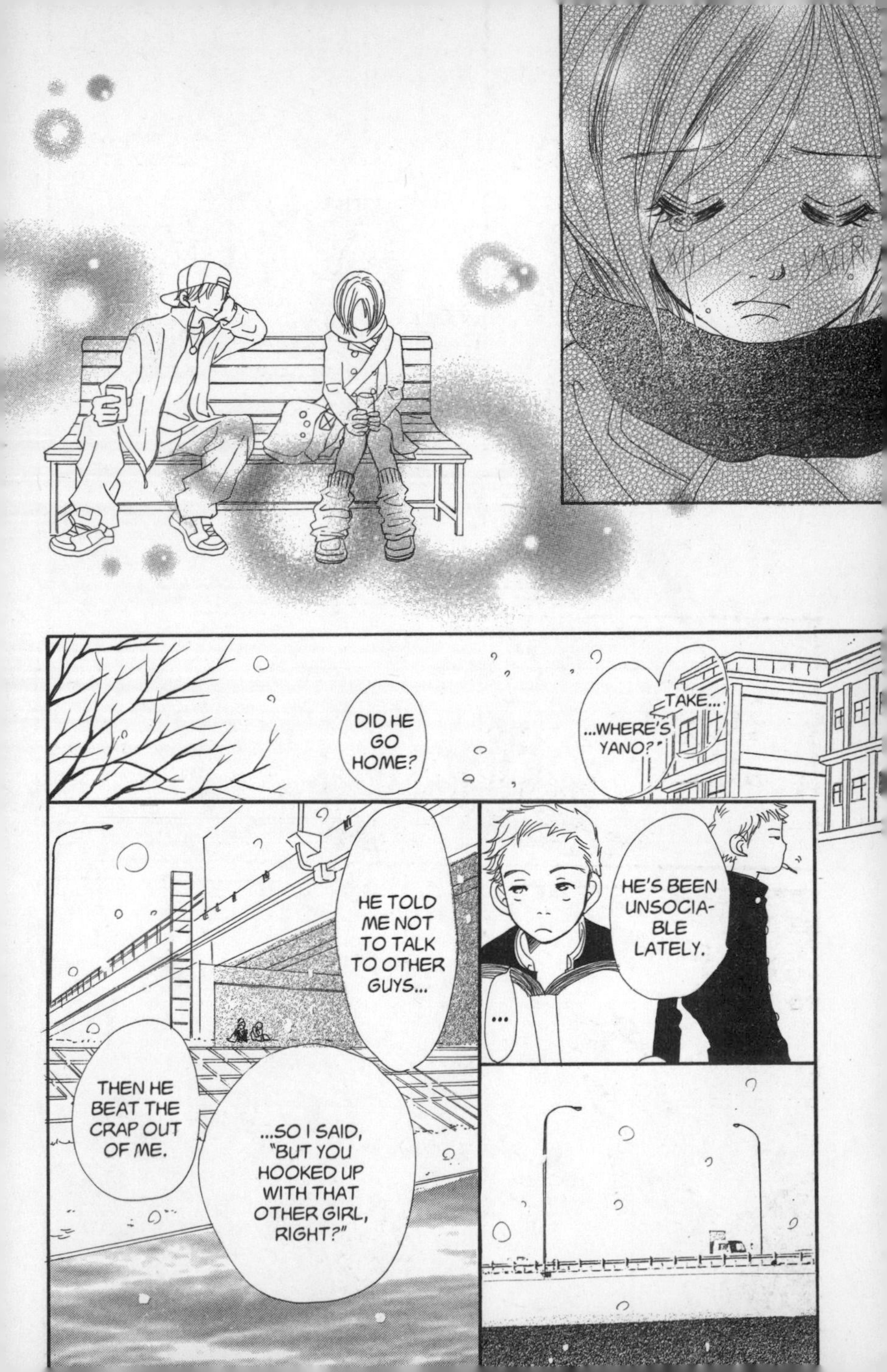
TAKE... ...WHERE'S YANO?
DID HE GO HOME?
HE'S BEEN UNSOCIABLE LATELY.
...
HE TOLD ME NOT TO TALK TO OTHER GUYS...
...SO I SAID, "BUT YOU HOOKED UP WITH THAT OTHER GIRL, RIGHT?"
THEN HE BEAT THE CRAP OUT OF ME.

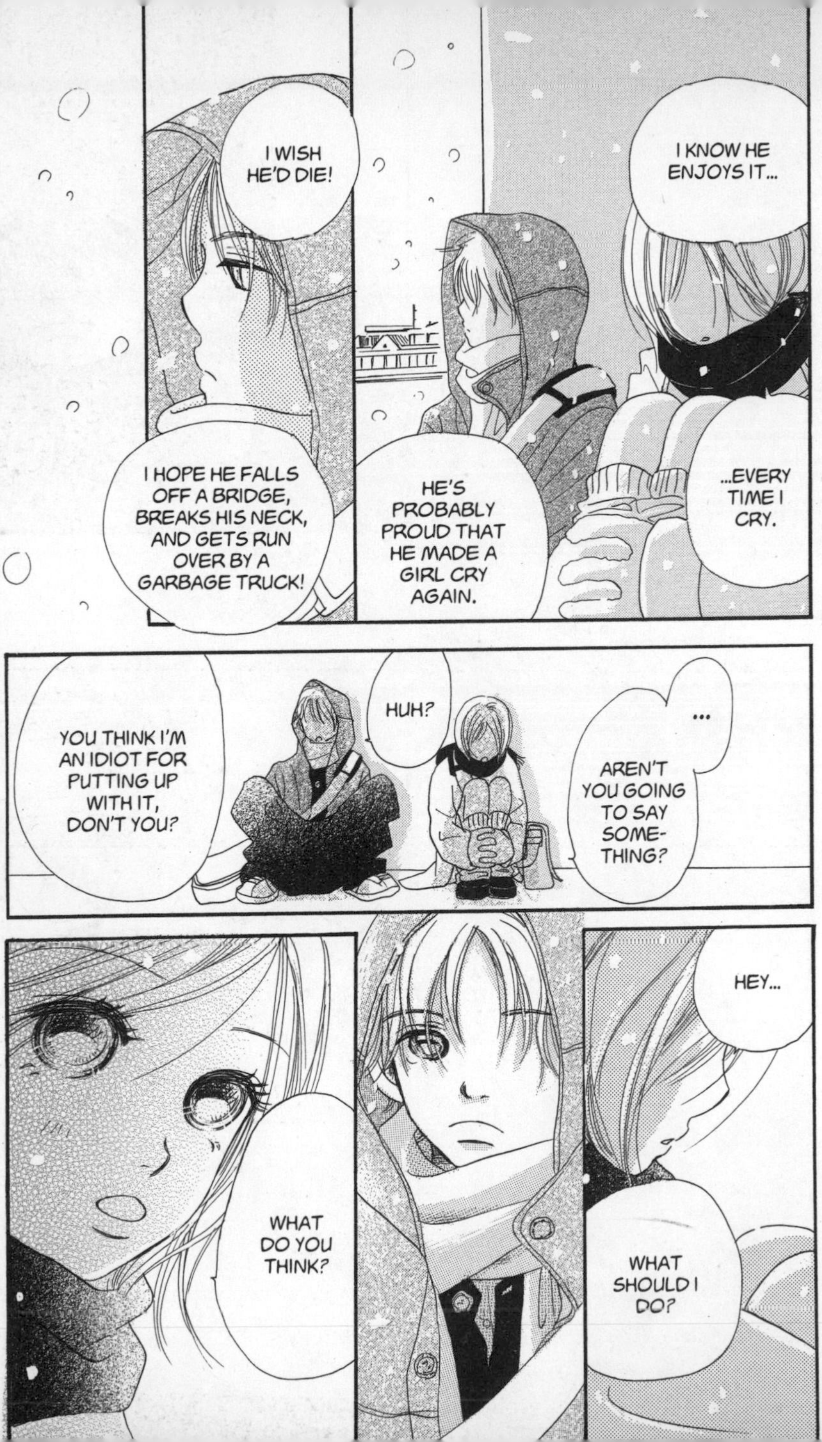
I KNOW HE ENJOYS IT...
...EVERY TIME I CRY.
HE'S PROBABLY PROUD THAT HE MADE A GIRL CRY AGAIN.
I WISH HE'D DIE!
I HOPE HE FALLS OFF A BRIDGE, BREAKS HIS NECK, AND GETS RUN OVER BY A GARBAGE TRUCK!
...
AREN'T YOU GOING TO SAY SOME-THING?
HUH?
YOU THINK I'M AN IDIOT FOR PUTTING UP WITH IT, DON'T YOU?
HEY...
WHAT SHOULD I DO?
WHAT DO YOU THINK?

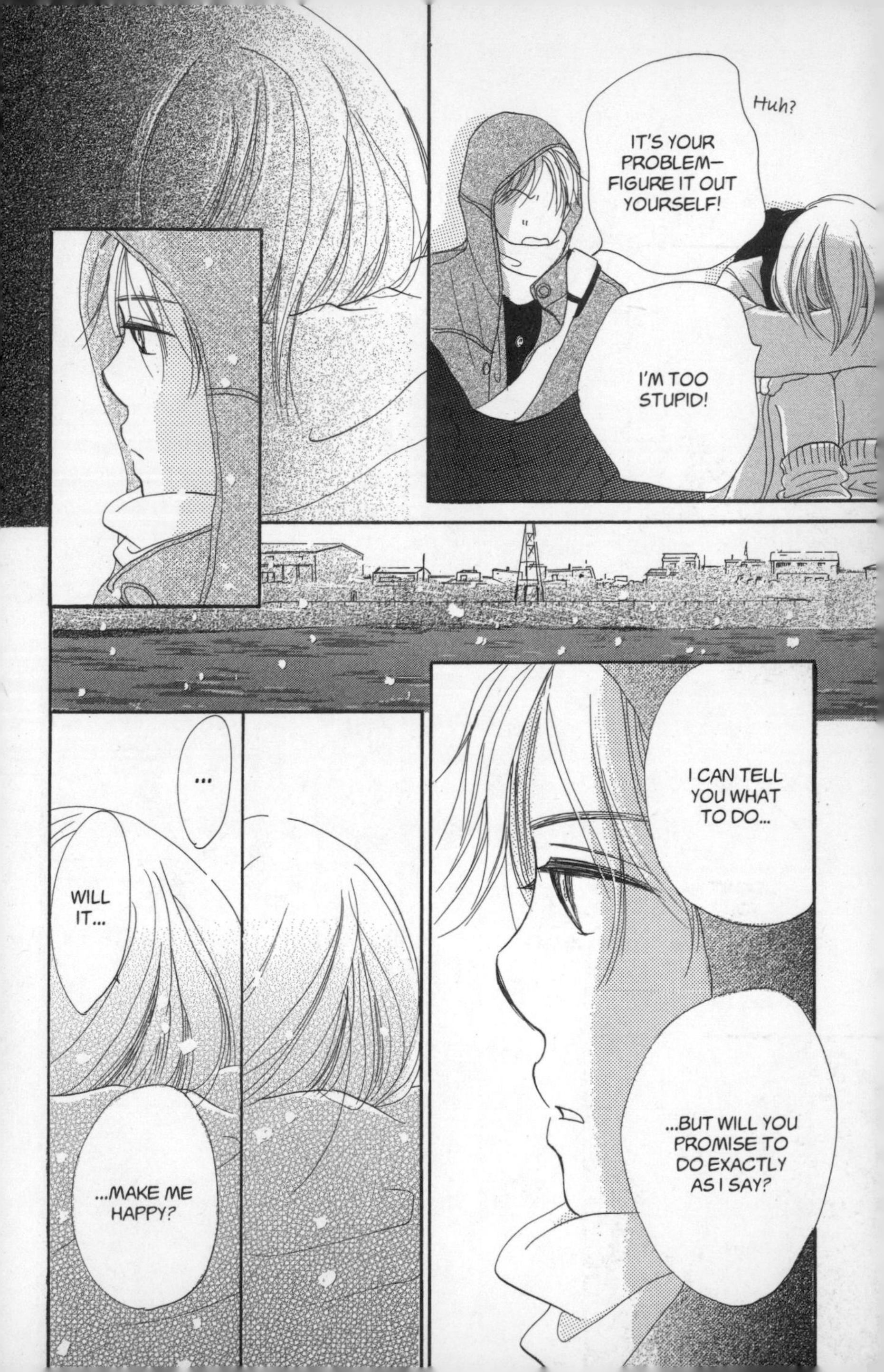
Huh?
IT'S YOUR PROBLEM—FIGURE IT OUT YOURSELF!
I'M TOO STUPID!
I CAN TELL YOU WHAT TO DO...
...BUT WILL YOU PROMISE TO DO EXACTLY AS I SAY?
...
WILL IT...
...MAKE ME HAPPY?

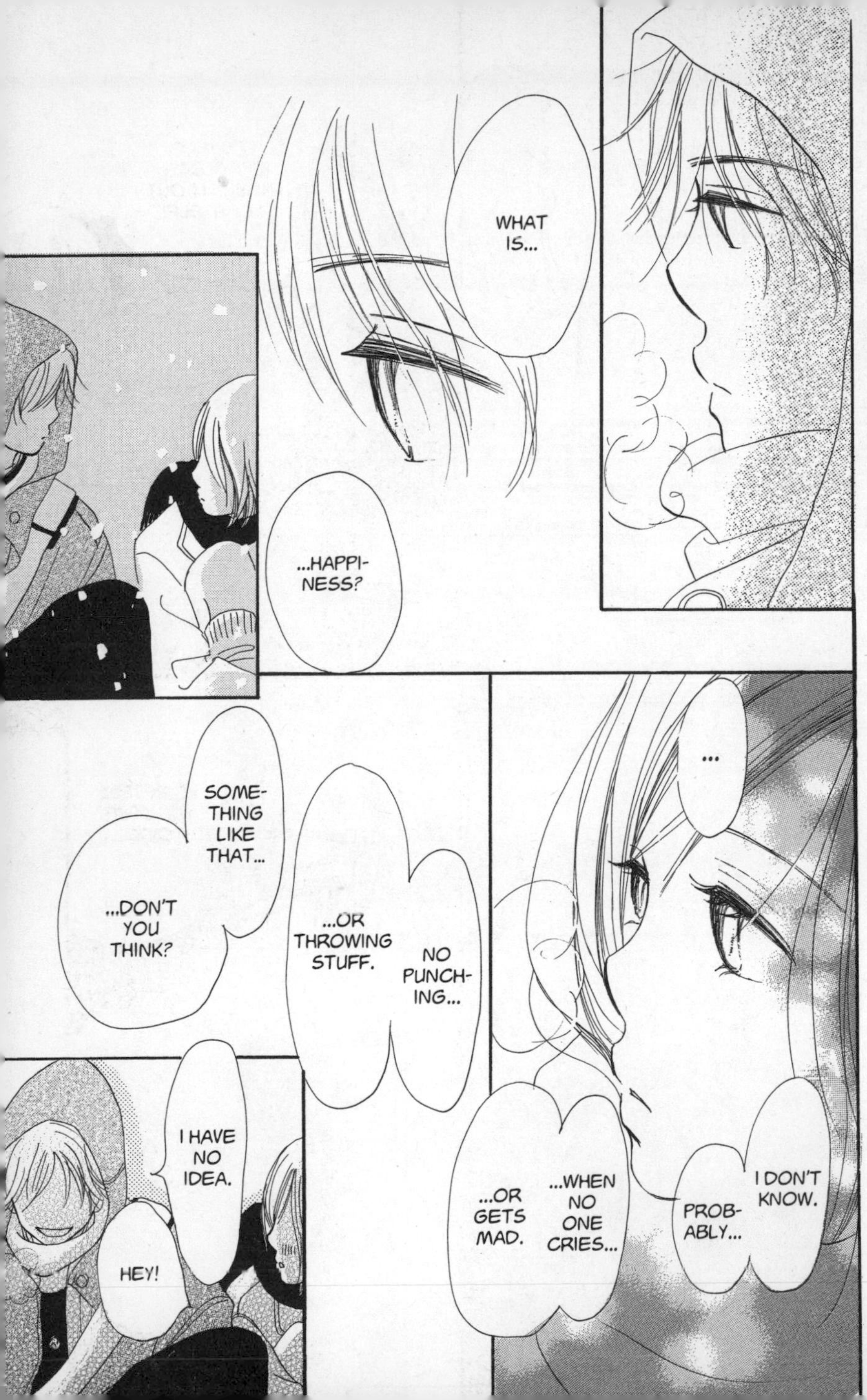
WHAT IS...
...HAPPINESS?
...
I DON'T KNOW.
PROBABLY...
...WHEN NO ONE CRIES...
...OR GETS MAD.
NO PUNCHING...
...OR THROWING STUFF.
SOMETHING LIKE THAT...
...DON'T YOU THINK?
I HAVE NO IDEA.
HEY!

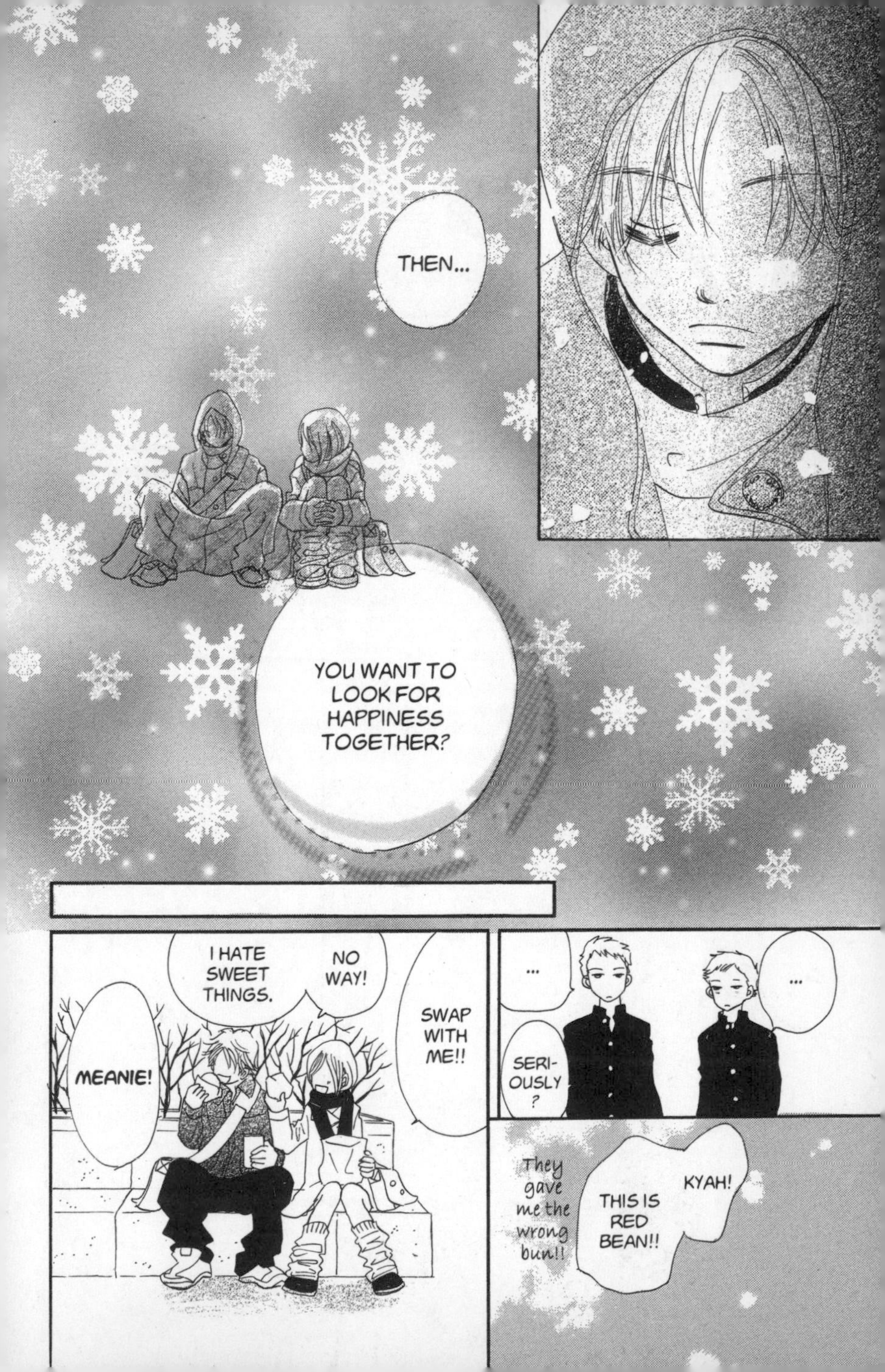
THEN...
YOU WANT TO LOOK FOR HAPPINESS TOGETHER?
...
...
SERIOUSLY?
KYAH!
THIS IS RED BEAN!!
They gave me the wrong bun!!
SWAP WITH ME!!
NO WAY!
I HATE SWEET THINGS.
MEANIE!

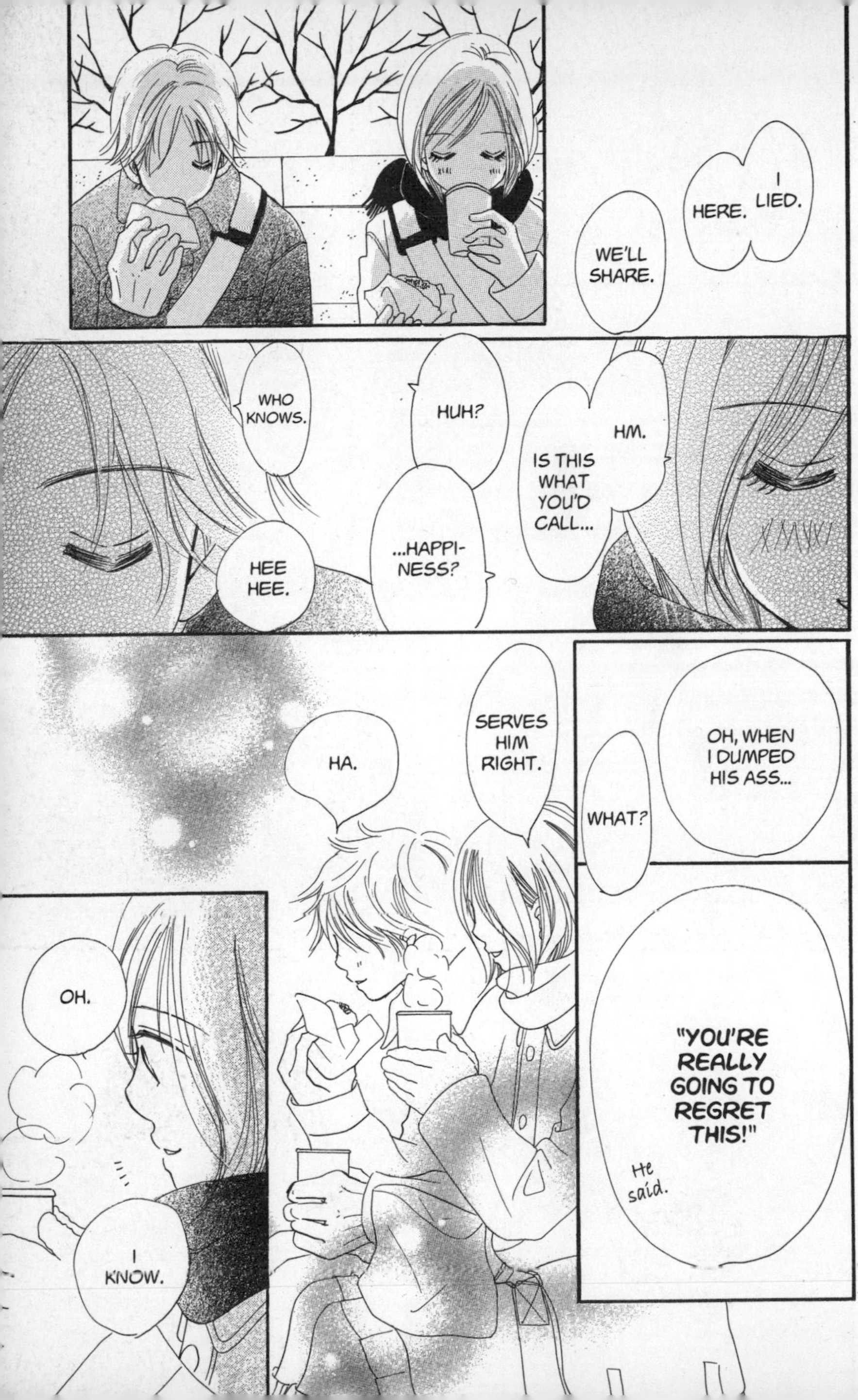
I LIED.
HERE.
WE'LL SHARE.
HM.
IS THIS WHAT YOU'D CALL...
HUH?
...HAPPINESS?
WHO KNOWS.
HEE HEE.
OH, WHEN I DUMPED HIS ASS...
WHAT?
"YOU'RE REALLY GOING TO REGRET THIS!"
He said.
SERVES HIM RIGHT.
HA.
OH.
I KNOW.

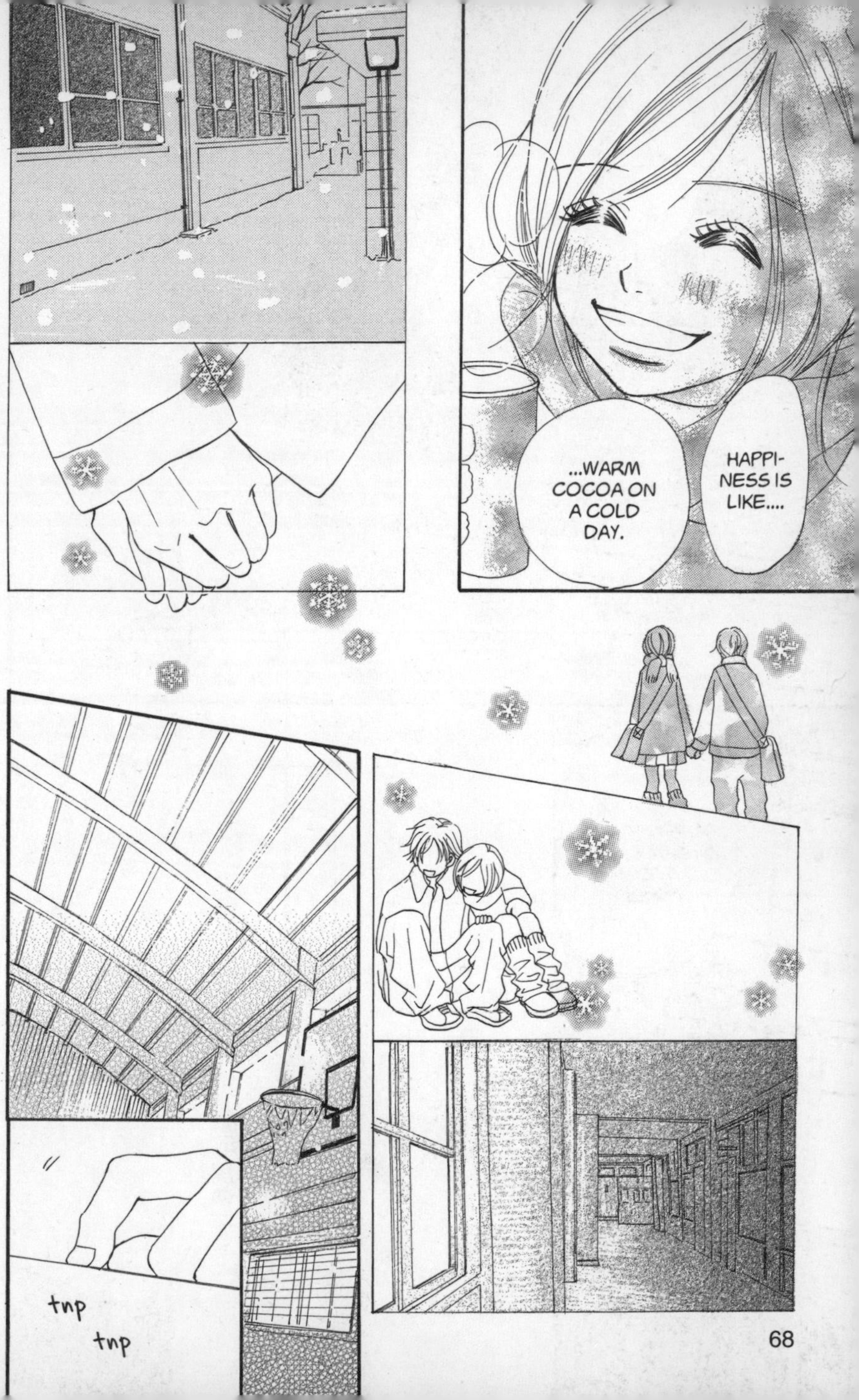
HAPPI-NESS IS LIKE....
...WARM COCOA ON A COLD DAY.
tnp
tnp

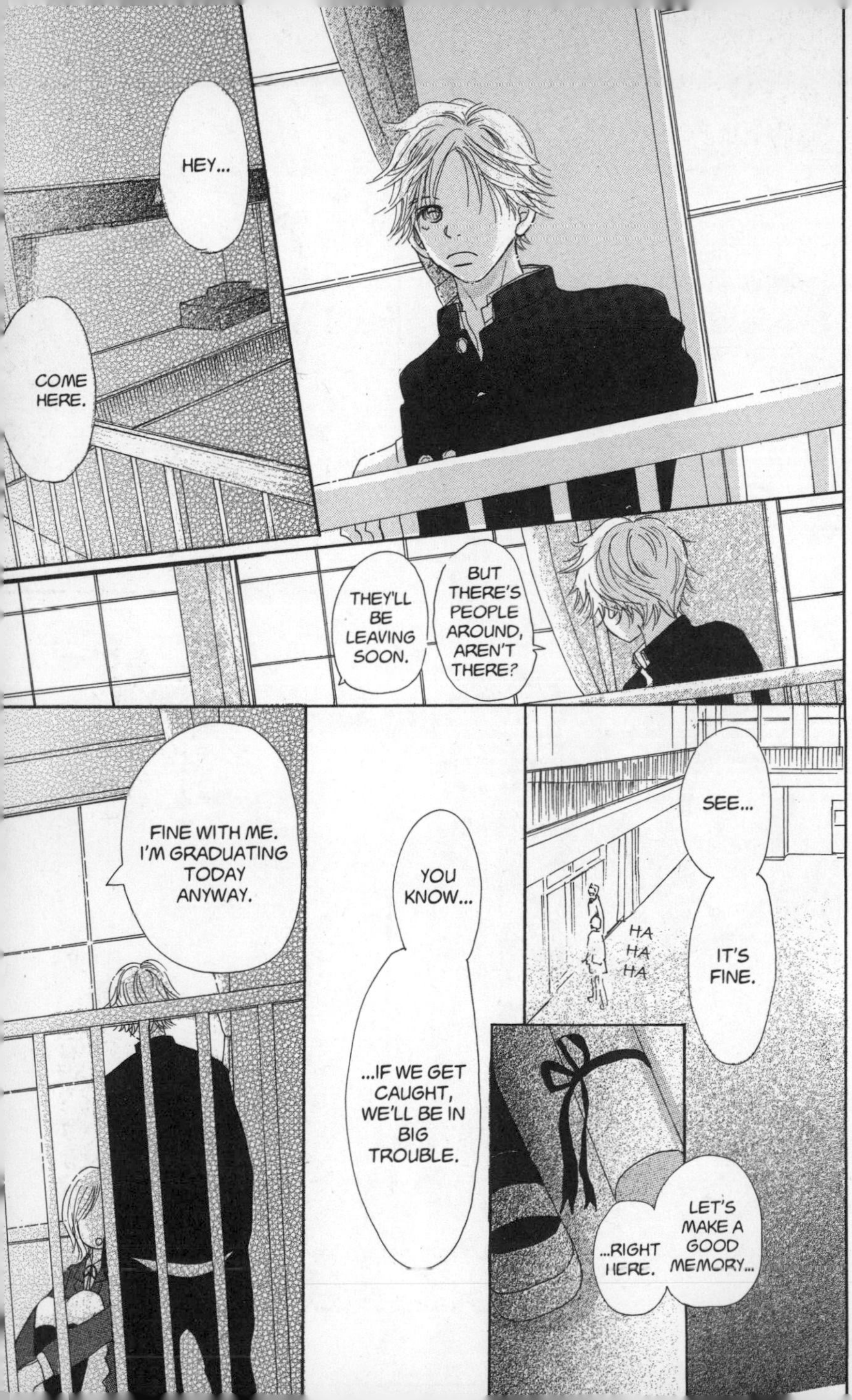
HEY...
COME HERE.
BUT THERE'S PEOPLE AROUND, AREN'T THERE?
THEY'LL BE LEAVING SOON.
SEE...
HA HA HA
IT'S FINE.
LET'S MAKE A GOOD MEMORY...
...RIGHT HERE.
YOU KNOW...
...IF WE GET CAUGHT, WE'LL BE IN BIG TROUBLE.
FINE WITH ME. I'M GRADUATING TODAY ANYWAY.

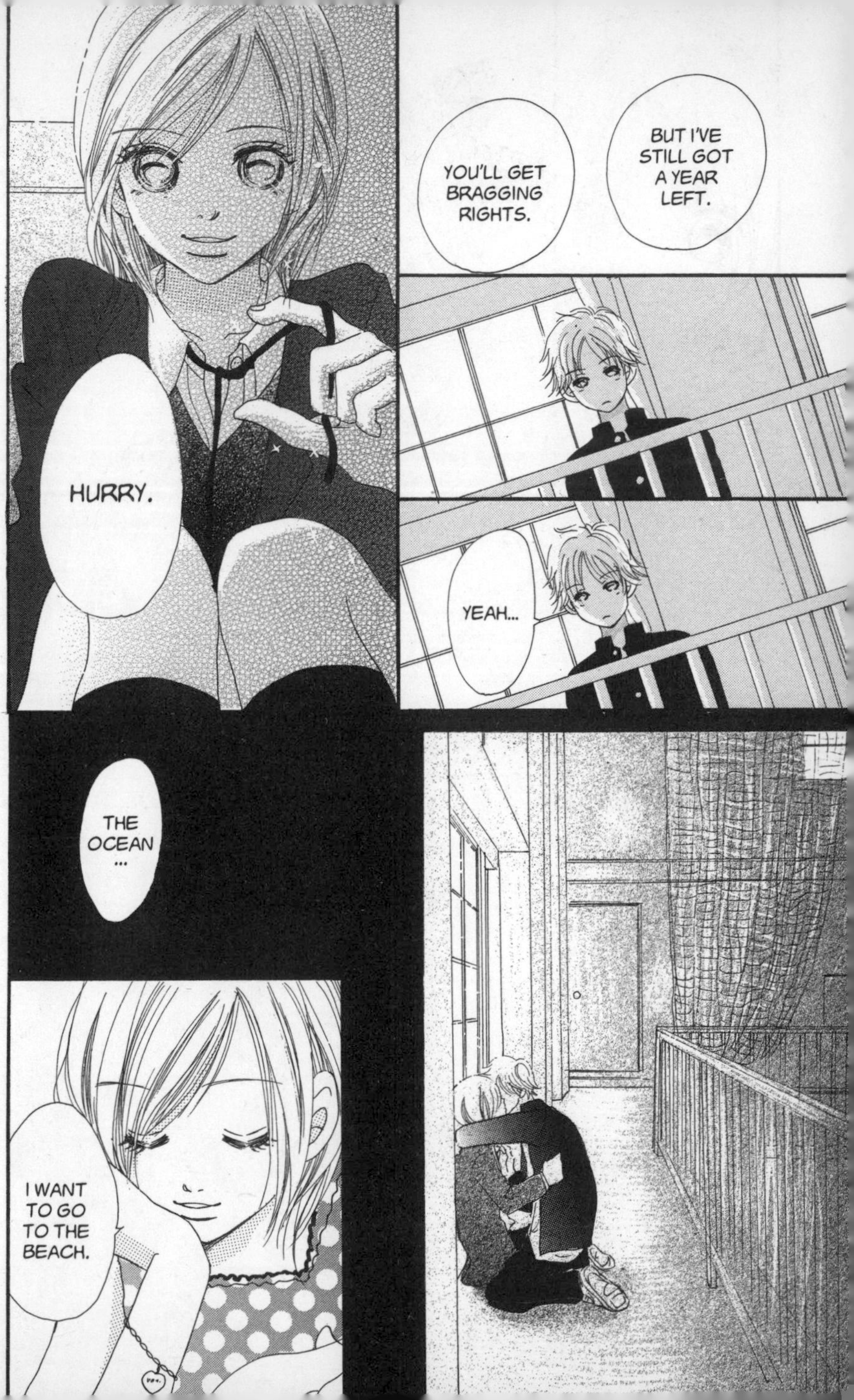
BUT I'VE STILL GOT A YEAR LEFT.
YOU'LL GET BRAGGING RIGHTS.
YEAH...
HURRY.
THE OCEAN ...
I WANT TO GO TO THE BEACH.

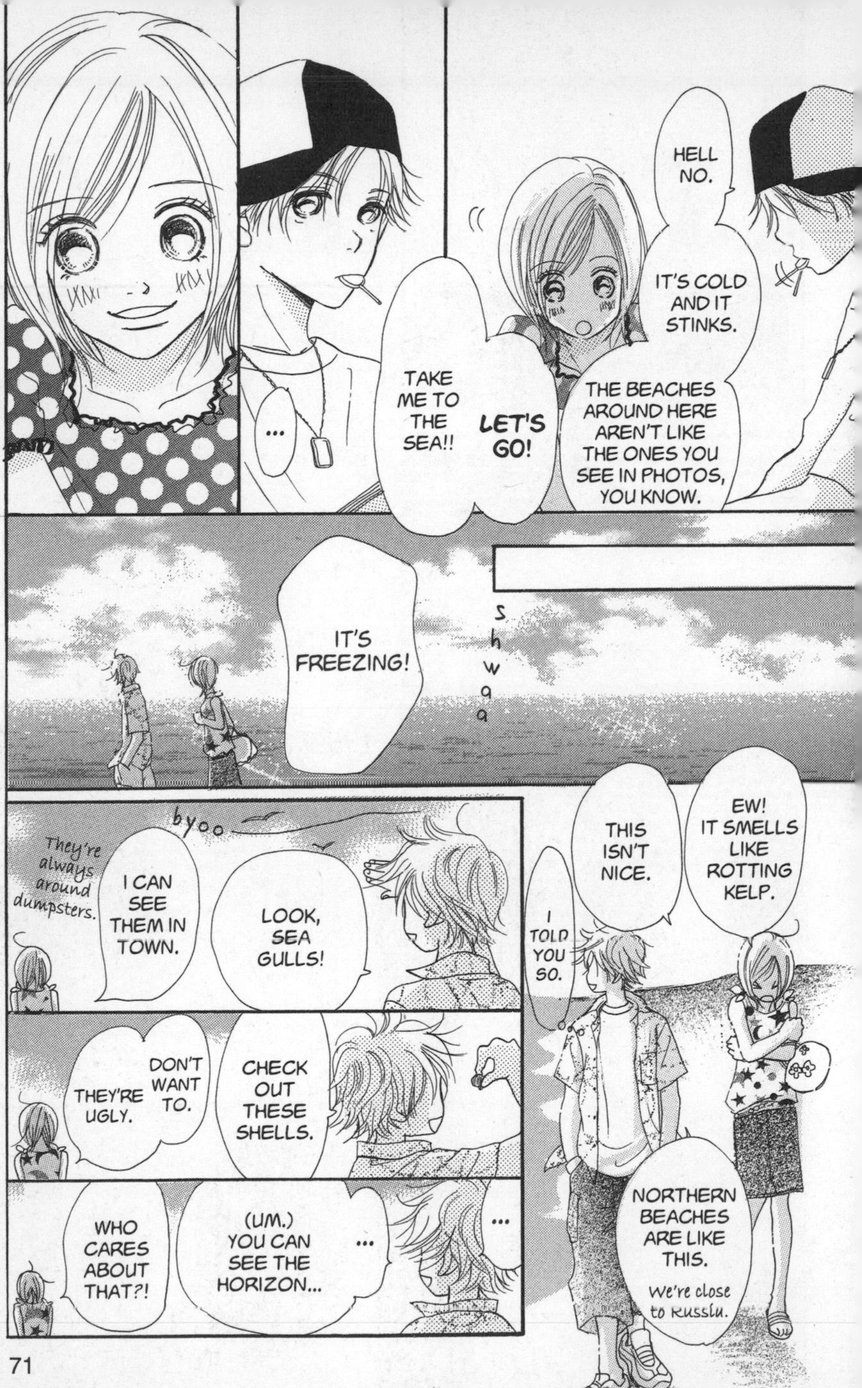
HELL NO.
IT'S COLD AND IT STINKS.
THE BEACHES AROUND HERE AREN'T LIKE THE ONES YOU SEE IN PHOTOS, YOU KNOW.
TAKE ME TO THE SEA!!
LET'S GO!
...
s h w a a
IT'S FREEZING!
EW! IT SMELLS LIKE ROTTING KELP.
THIS ISN'T NICE.
I TOLD YOU SO.
NORTHERN BEACHES ARE LIKE THIS.
We're close to Russia.
byoo
LOOK, SEA GULLS!
I CAN SEE THEM IN TOWN.
They're always around dumpsters.
CHECK OUT THESE SHELLS.
DON'T WANT TO.
THEY'RE UGLY.
...
...
(UM.) YOU CAN SEE THE HORIZON...
WHO CARES ABOUT THAT?!

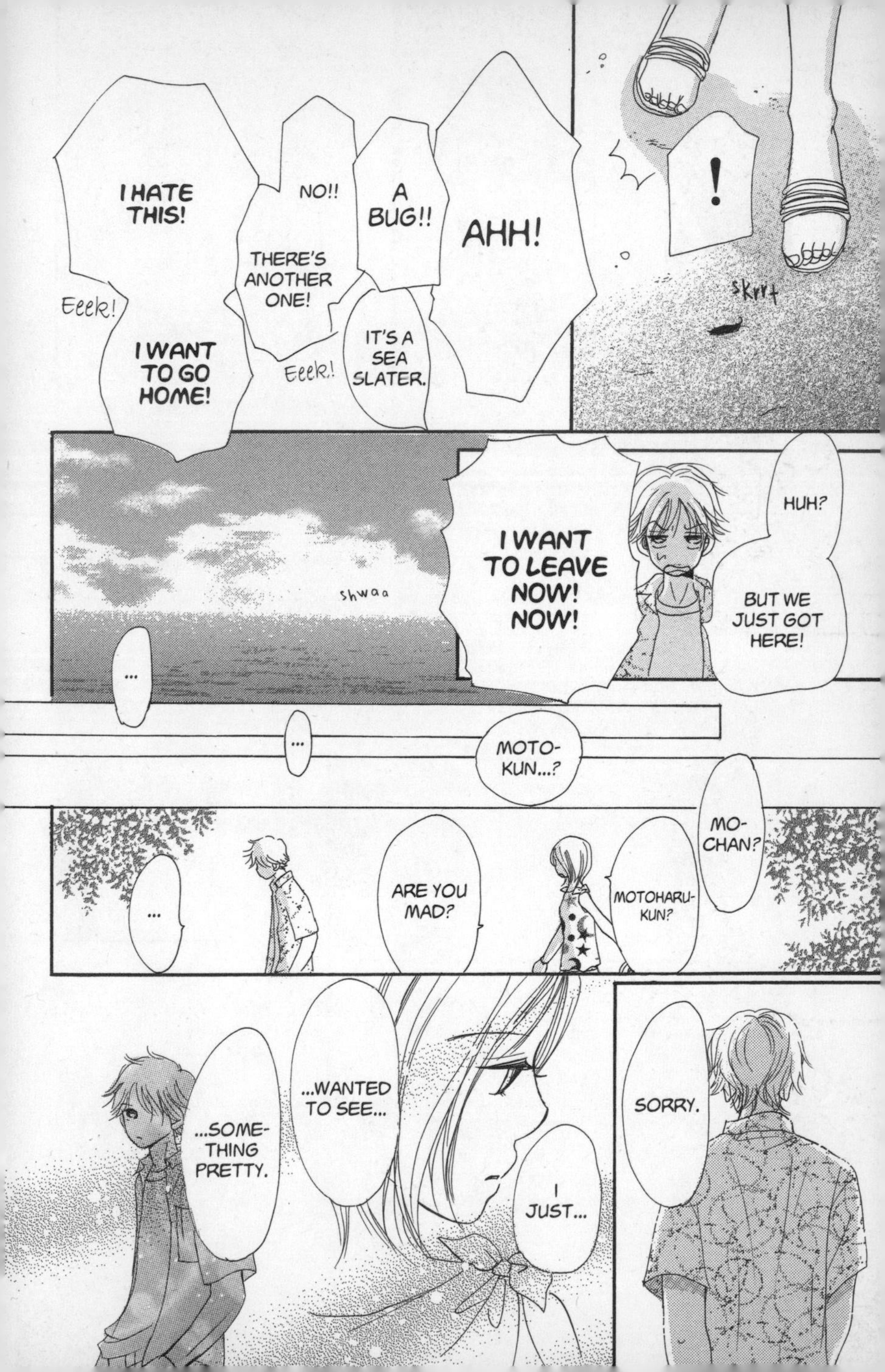
!
skrrt
AHH!
A BUG!!
NO!!
I HATE THIS!
IT'S A SEA SLATER.
THERE'S ANOTHER ONE!
Eeek!
I WANT TO GO HOME!
Eeek!
HUH?
BUT WE JUST GOT HERE!
I WANT TO LEAVE NOW! NOW!
shwaa
...
MOTO-KUN...?
...
MO-CHAN?
MOTOHARU-KUN?
ARE YOU MAD?
...
SORRY.
I JUST...
...WANTED TO SEE...
...SOMETHING PRETTY.

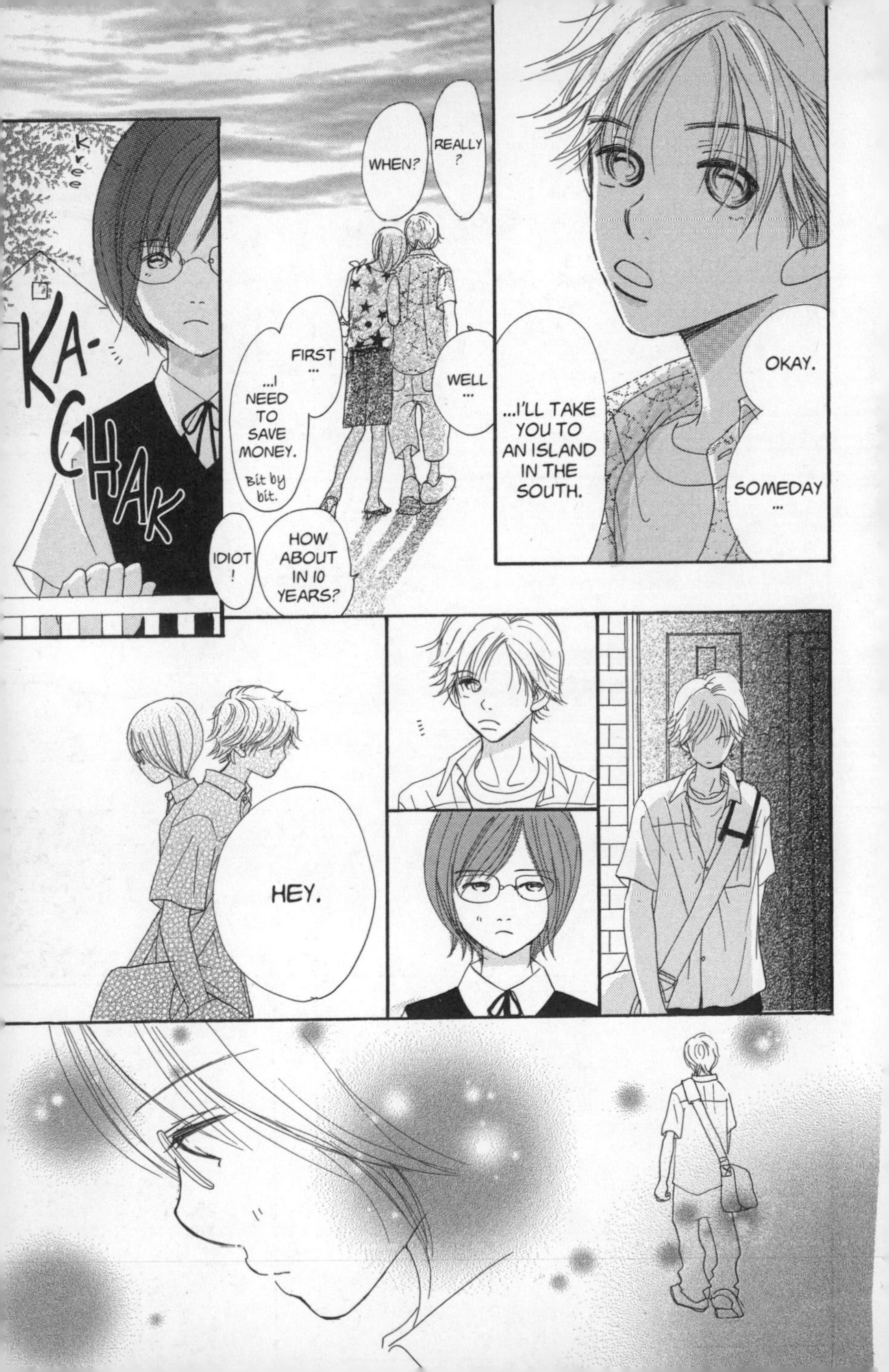
OKAY.
SOMEDAY ...
...I'LL TAKE YOU TO AN ISLAND IN THE SOUTH.
REALLY ?
WHEN?
WELL ...
FIRST ...
...I NEED TO SAVE MONEY.
Bit by bit.
HOW ABOUT IN 10 YEARS?
IDIOT !
Kree
KA-CHAK
HEY.

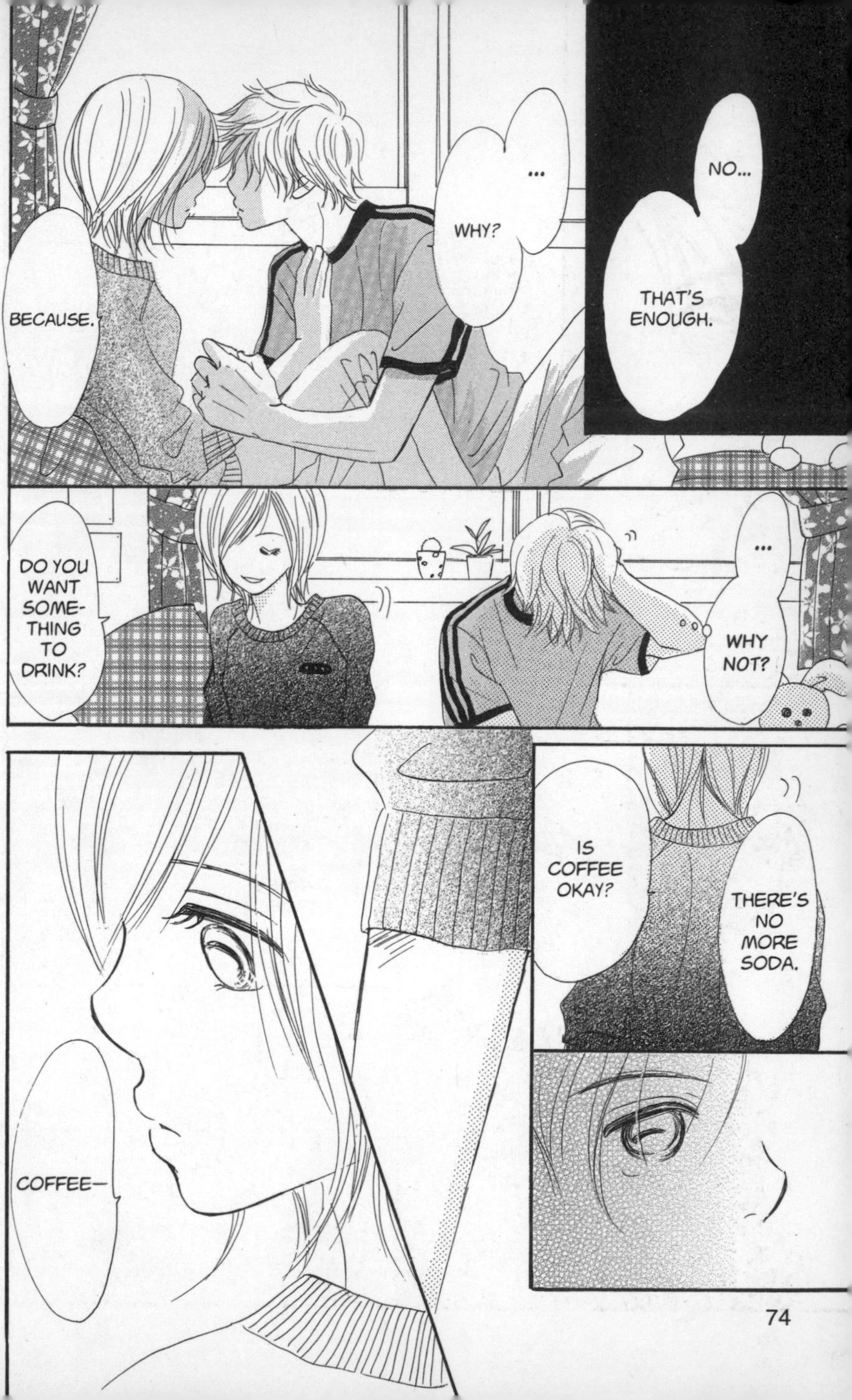
NO...
THAT'S ENOUGH.
...
WHY?
BECAUSE.
...
WHY NOT?
DO YOU WANT SOMETHING TO DRINK?
THERE'S NO MORE SODA.
IS COFFEE OKAY?
COFFEE—

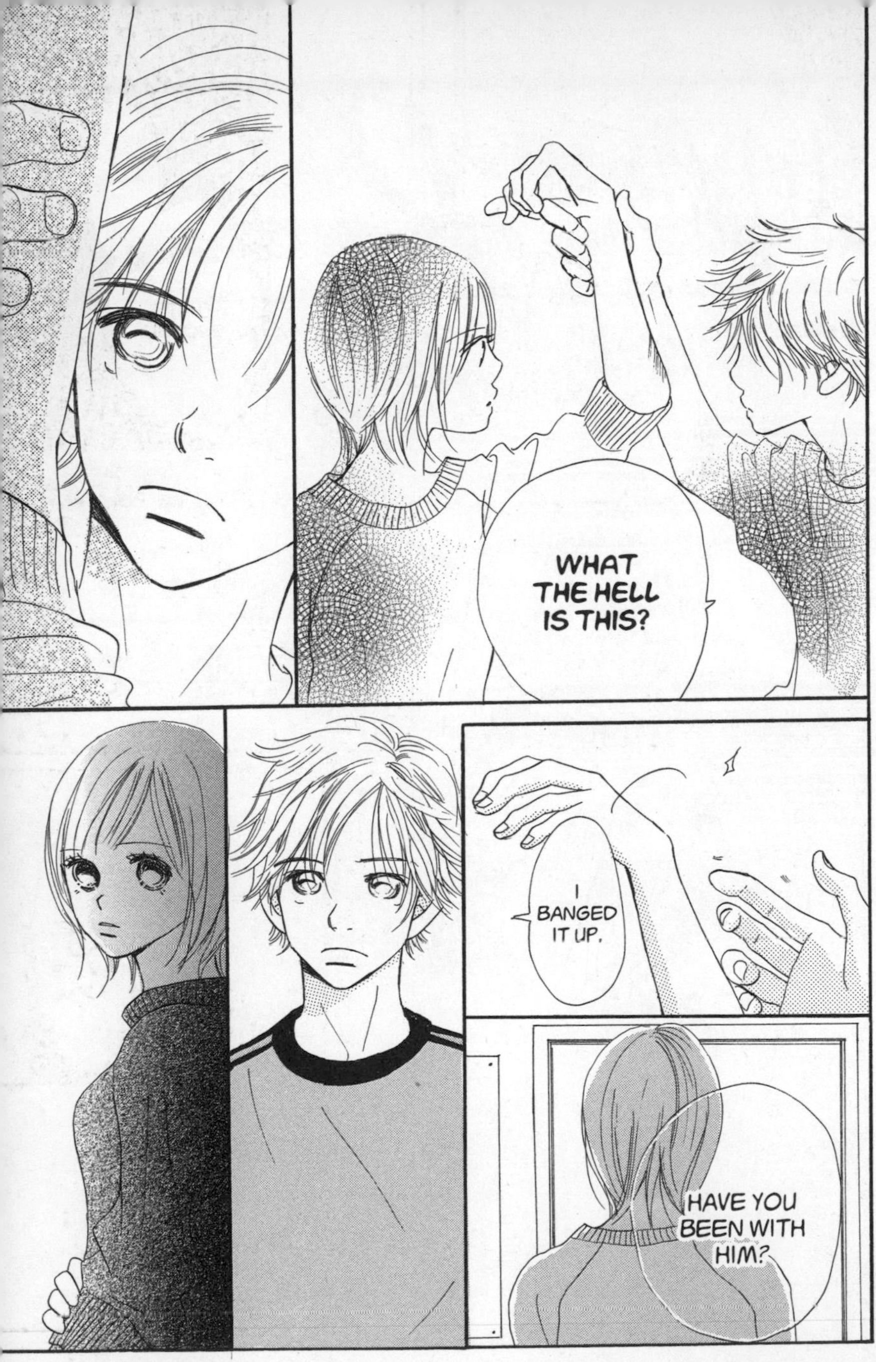
WHAT THE HELL IS THIS?
I BANGED IT UP.
HAVE YOU BEEN WITH HIM?

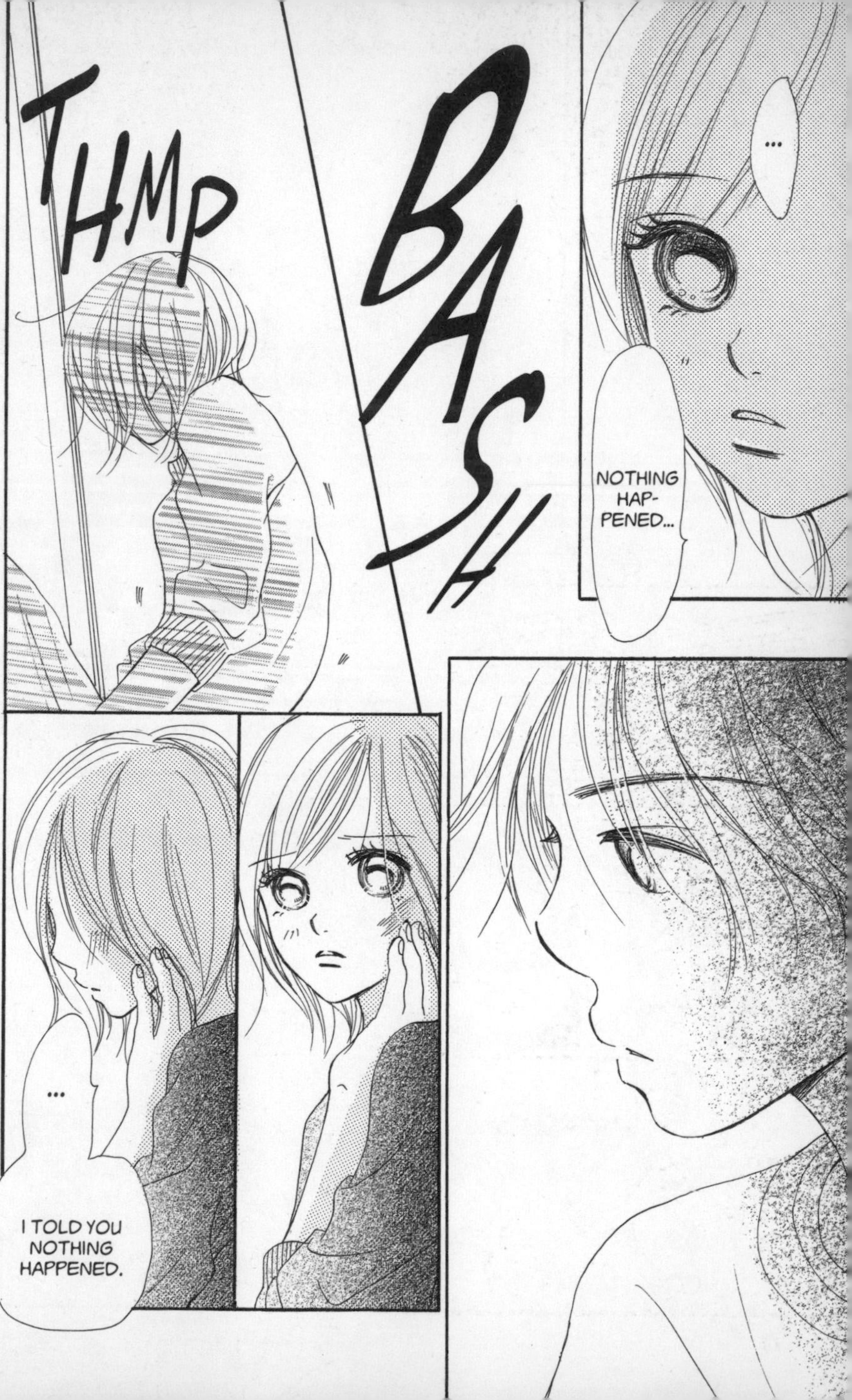
...
NOTHING HAP-PENED...
BASH
THMP
...
I TOLD YOU NOTHING HAPPENED.

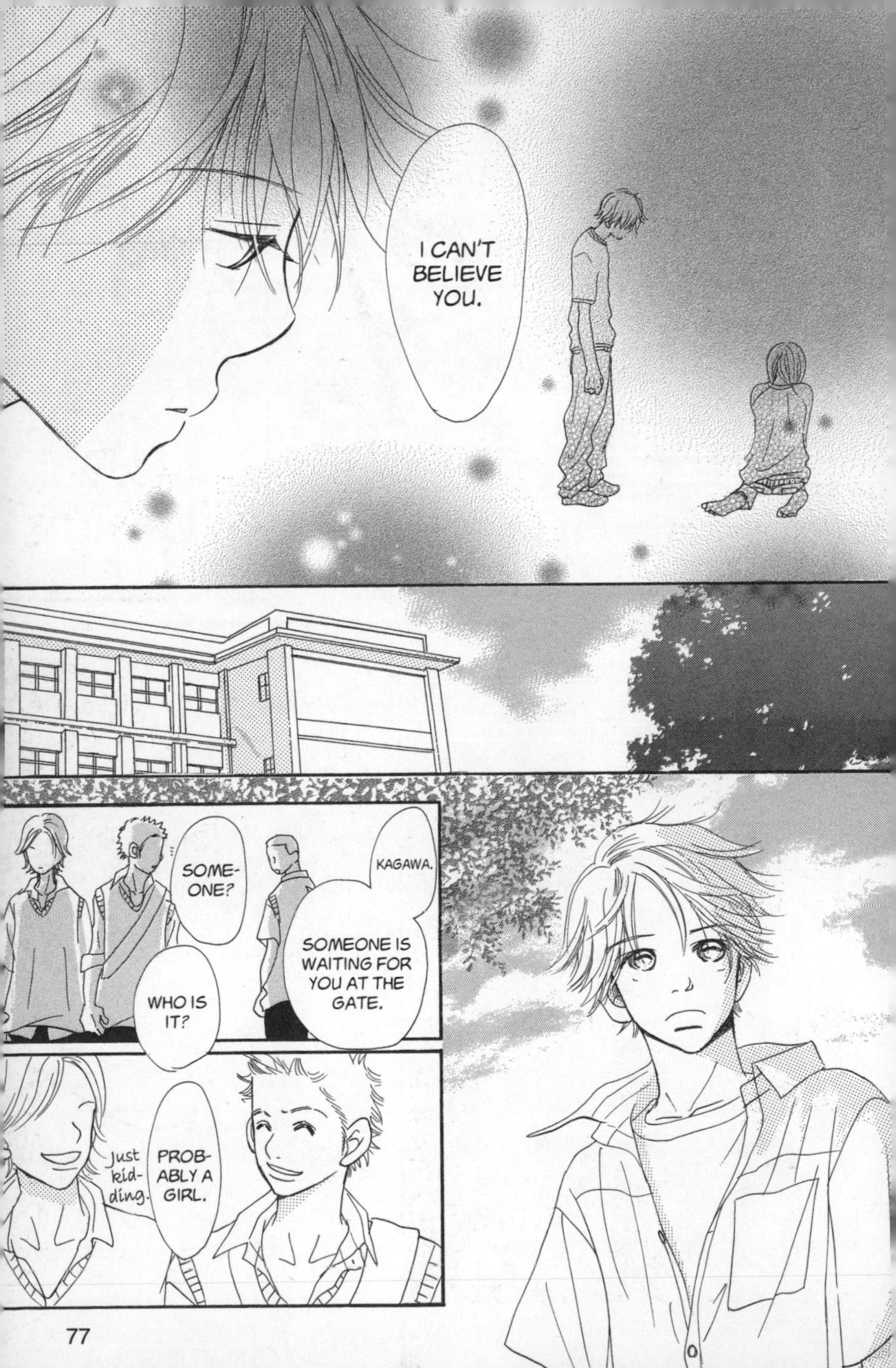
I CAN'T BELIEVE YOU.
KAGAWA.
SOMEONE IS WAITING FOR YOU AT THE GATE.
SOME-ONE?
WHO IS IT?
PROB-ABLY A GIRL.
Just kid-ding.

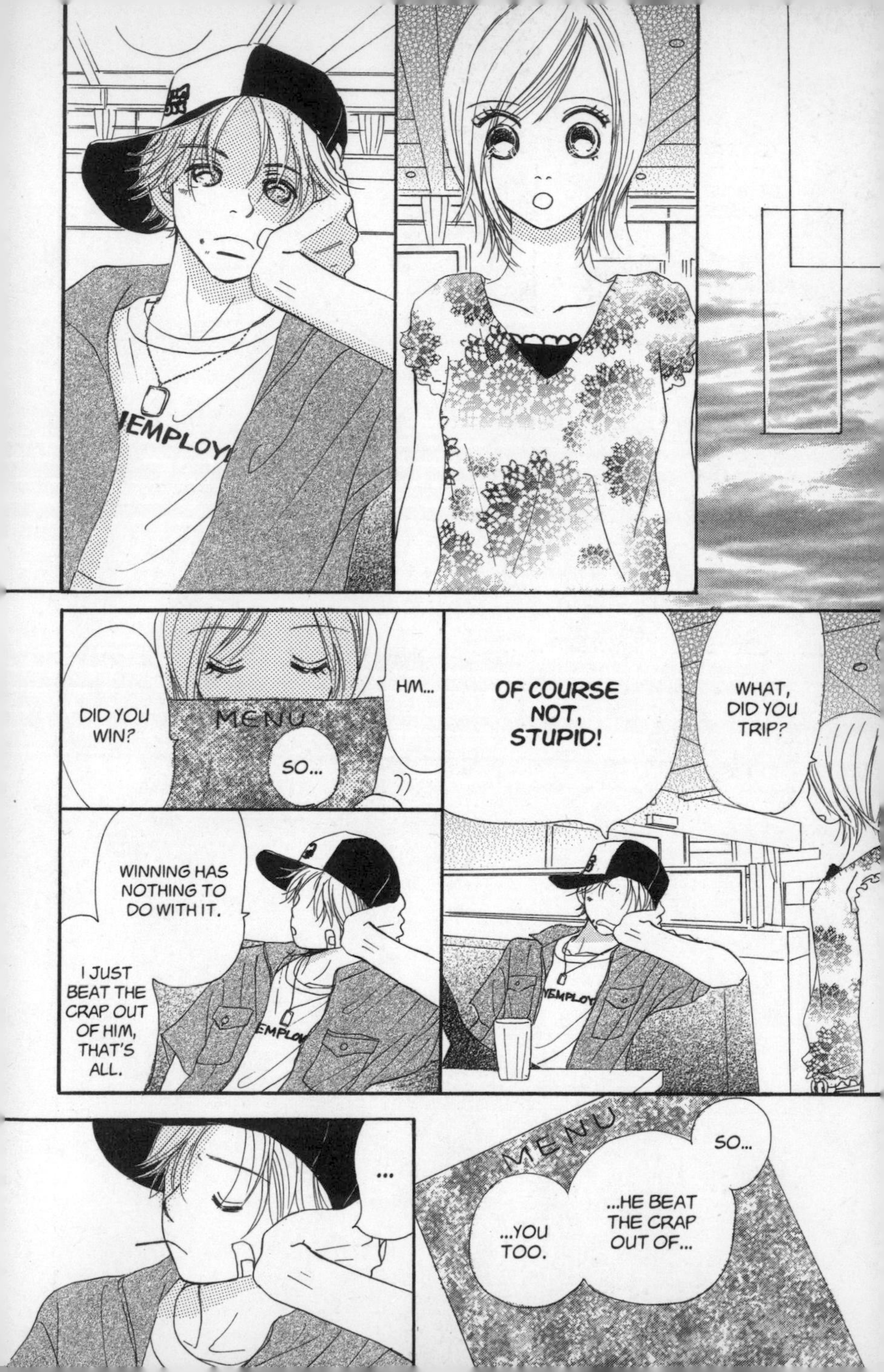
WHAT, DID YOU TRIP?
OF COURSE NOT, STUPID!
HM...
SO...
DID YOU WIN?
WINNING HAS NOTHING TO DO WITH IT.
I JUST BEAT THE CRAP OUT OF HIM, THAT'S ALL.
SO...
...HE BEAT THE CRAP OUT OF...
...YOU TOO.
...

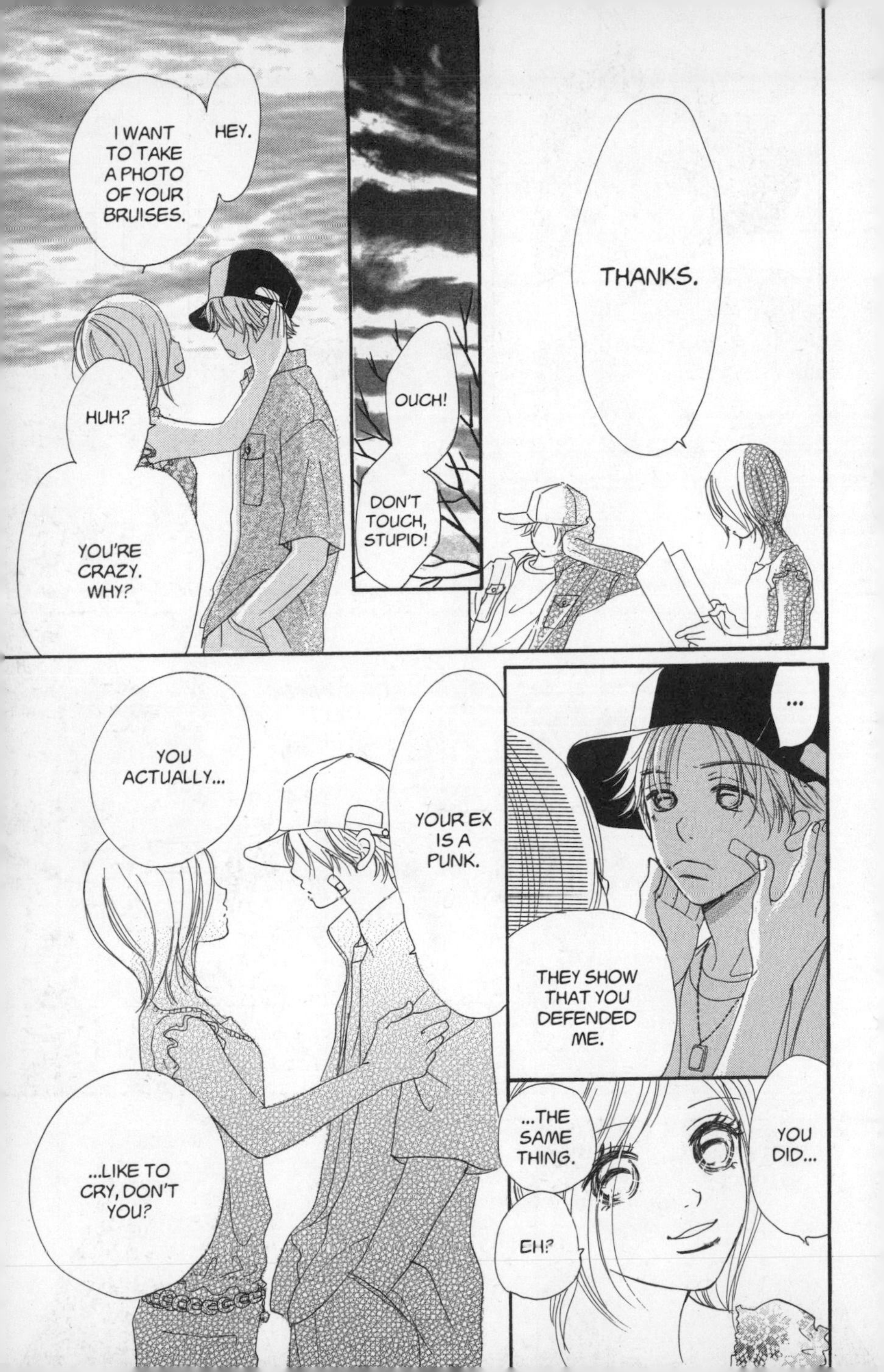
THANKS.
OUCH!
DON'T TOUCH, STUPID!
HEY.
I WANT TO TAKE A PHOTO OF YOUR BRUISES.
HUH?
YOU'RE CRAZY. WHY?
...
THEY SHOW THAT YOU DEFENDED ME.
YOU DID...
...THE SAME THING.
EH?
YOUR EX IS A PUNK.
YOU ACTUALLY...
...LIKE TO CRY, DON'T YOU?

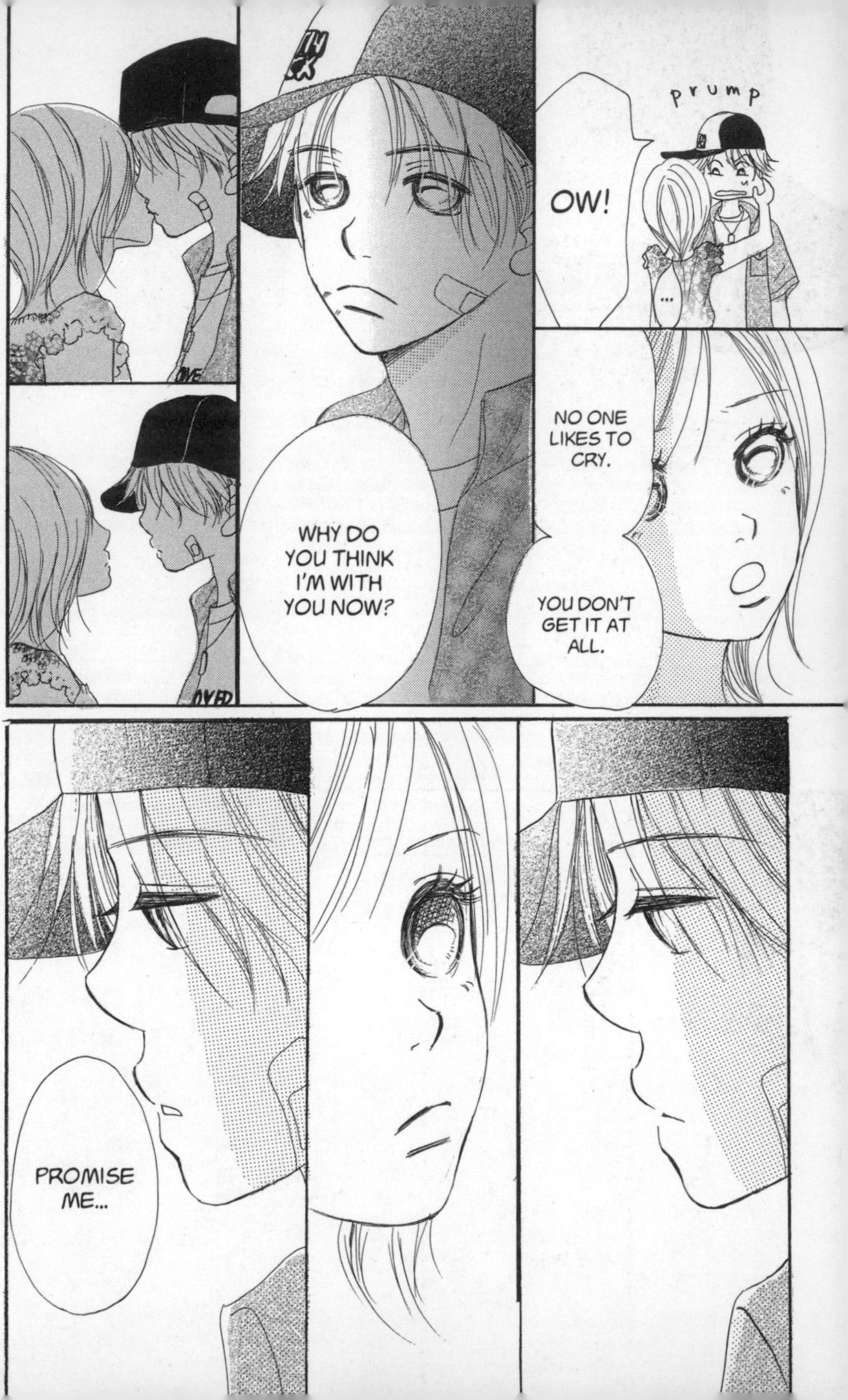
prump
OW!
...
NO ONE LIKES TO CRY.
YOU DON'T GET IT AT ALL.
WHY DO YOU THINK I'M WITH YOU NOW?
PROMISE ME...

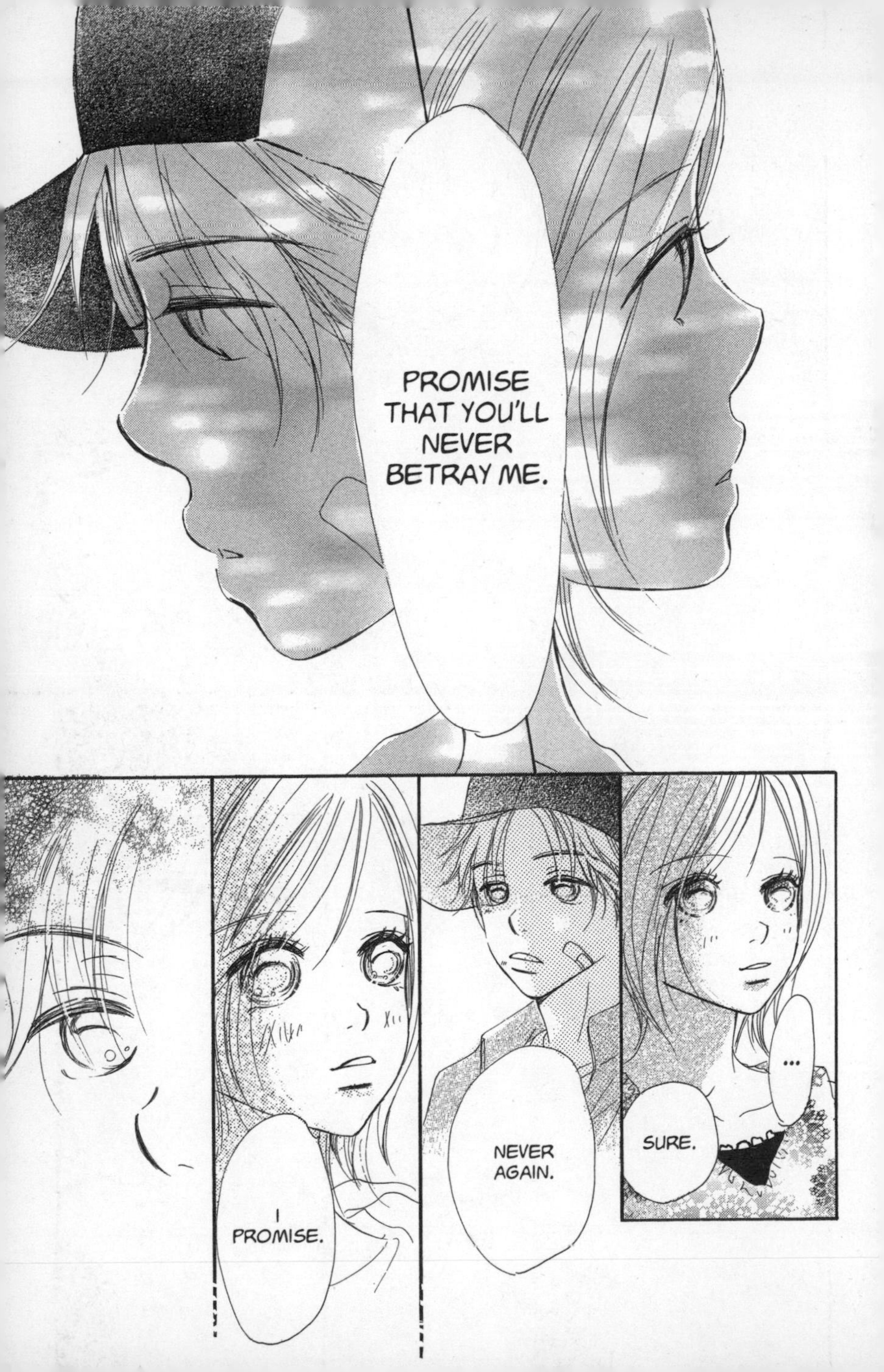
PROMISE THAT YOU'LL NEVER BETRAY ME.
...
SURE.
NEVER AGAIN.
I PROMISE.

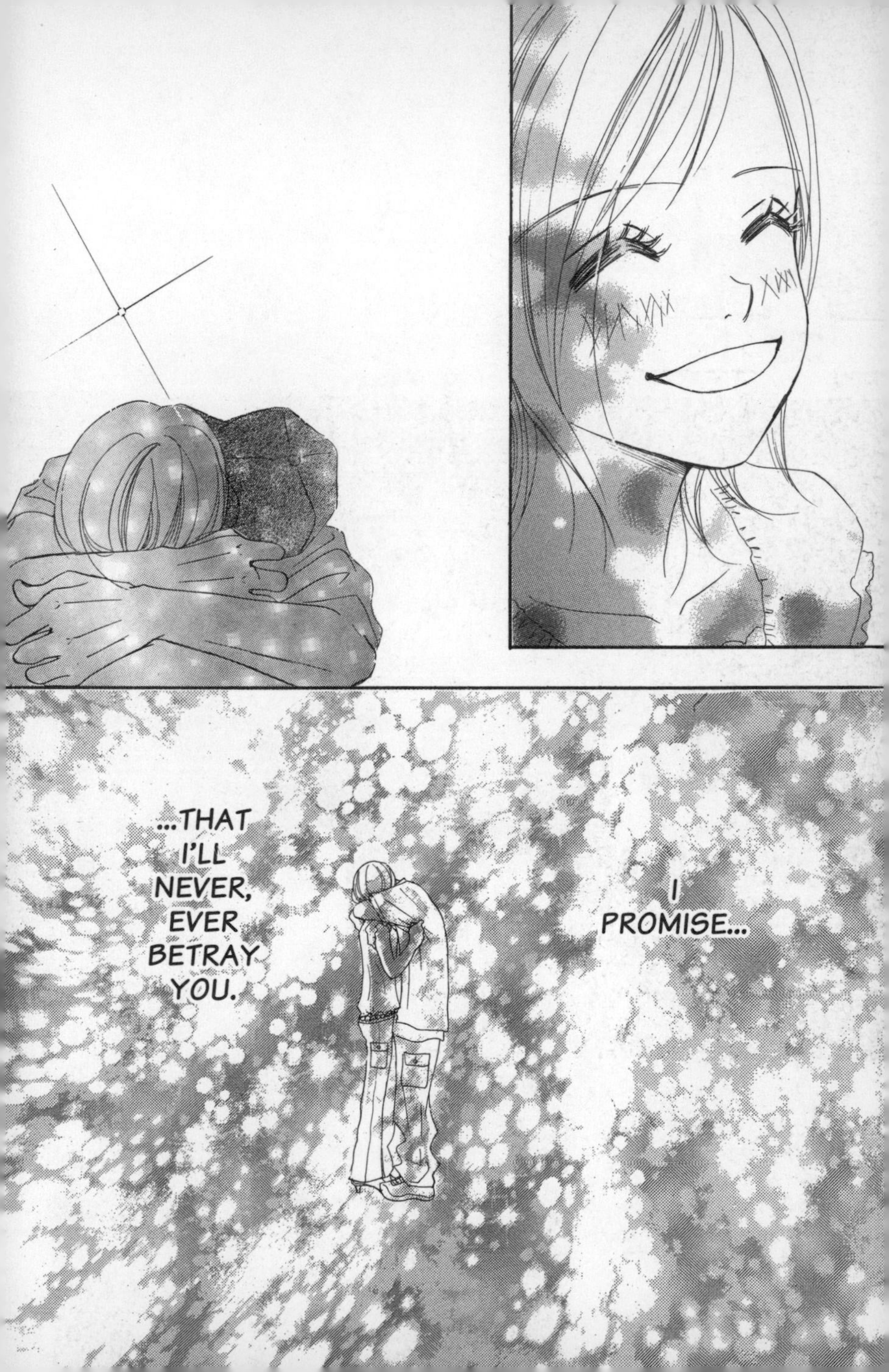
I PROMISE...
...THAT I'LL NEVER, EVER BETRAY YOU.

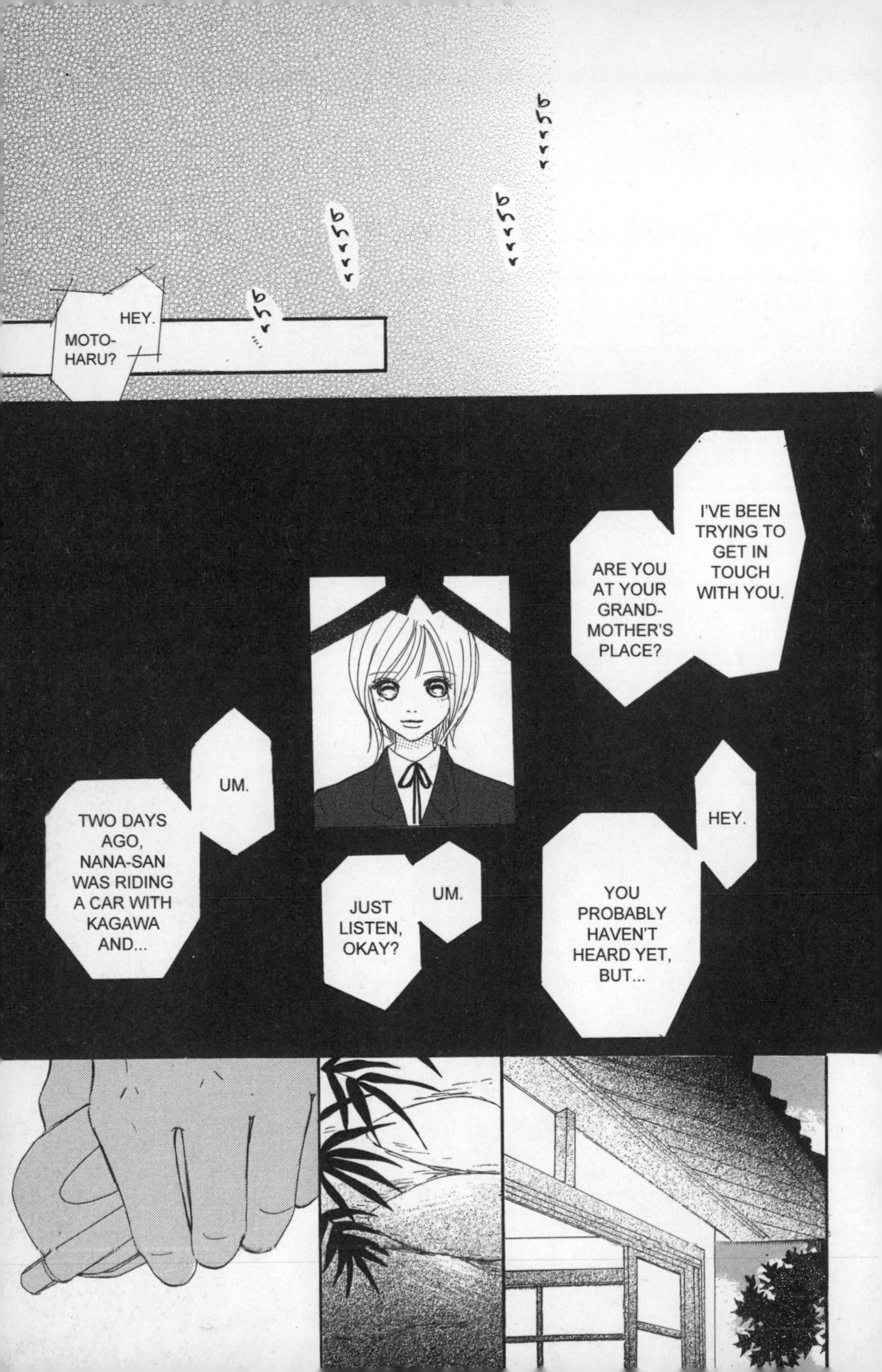
brrrr
brrrr
brrrr
brr...
HEY. MOTO-HARU?
I'VE BEEN TRYING TO GET IN TOUCH WITH YOU.
ARE YOU AT YOUR GRAND-MOTHER'S PLACE?
HEY.
YOU PROBABLY HAVEN'T HEARD YET, BUT...
UM.
JUST LISTEN, OKAY?
UM.
TWO DAYS AGO, NANA-SAN WAS RIDING A CAR WITH KAGAWA AND...

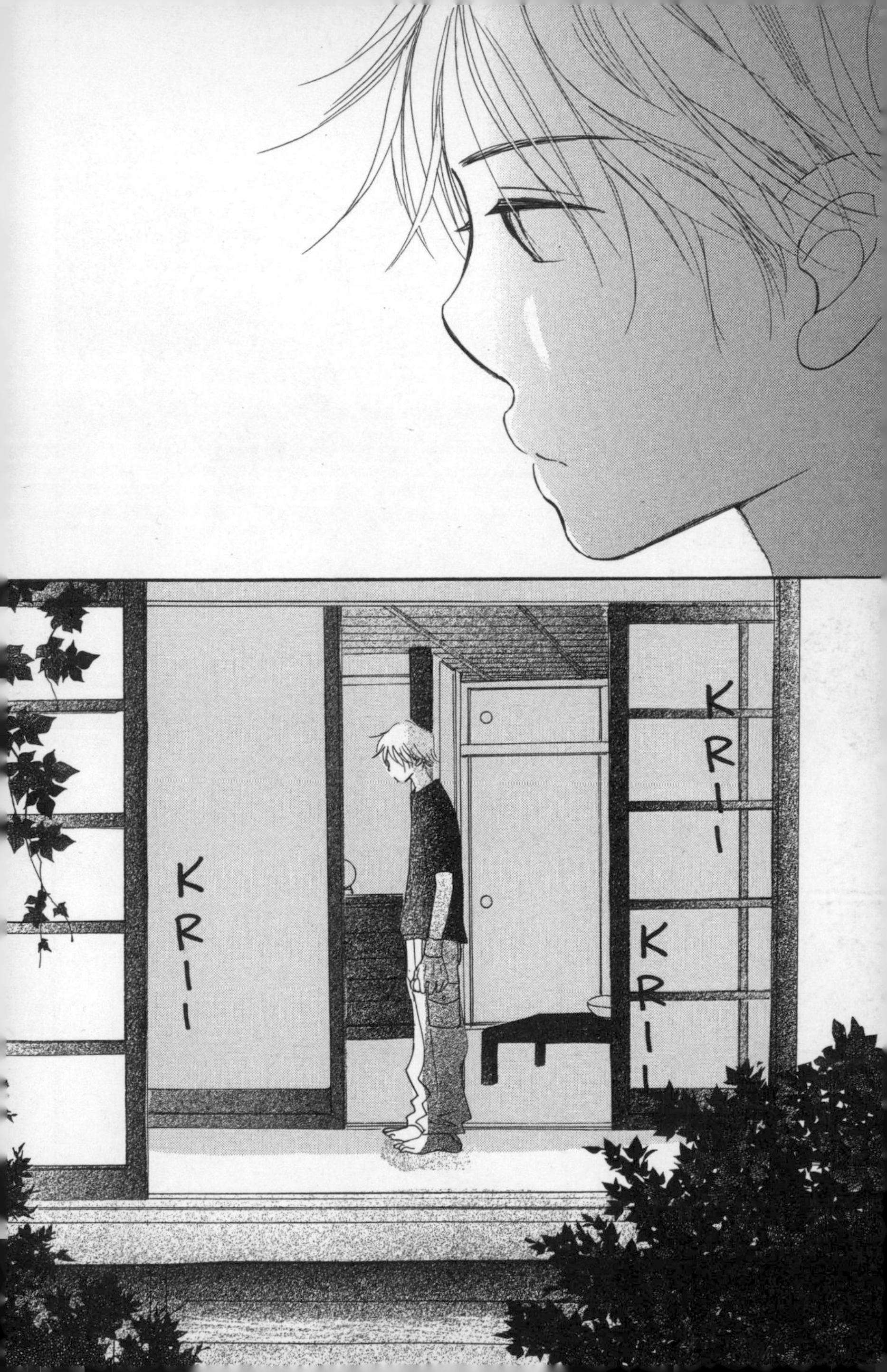
KRII
KRII
KRII

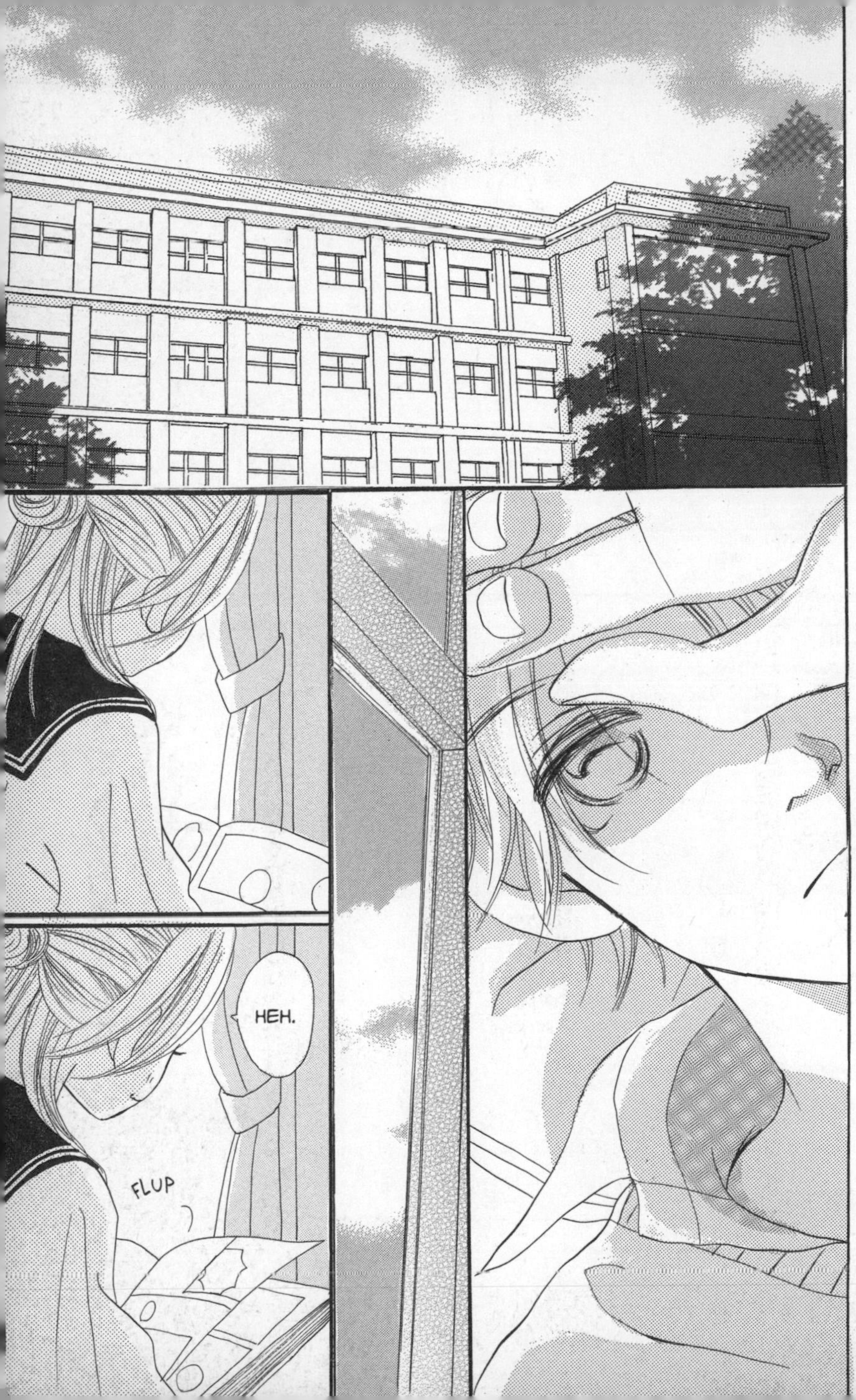
HEH.
FLUP

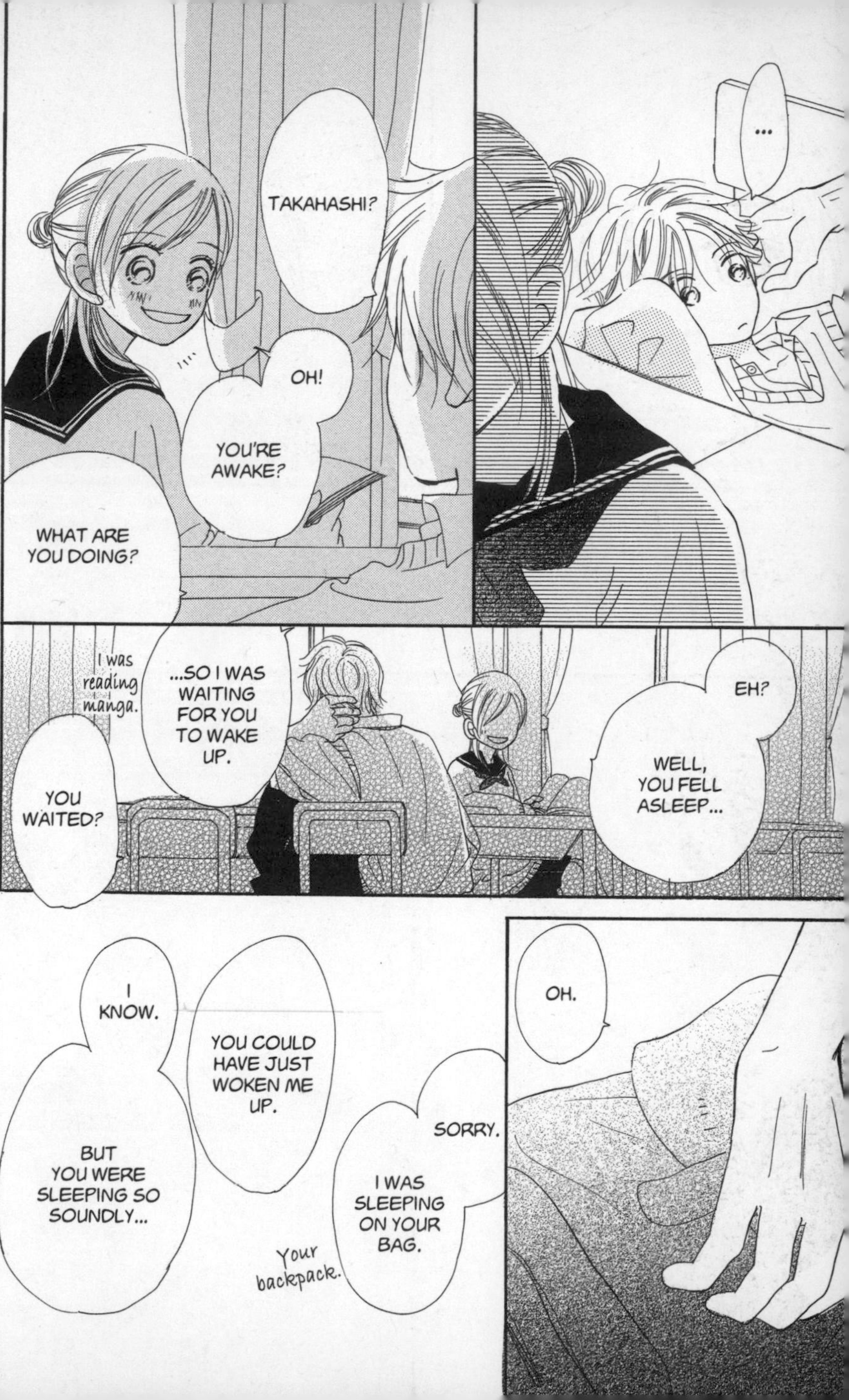
...
TAKAHASHI?
OH!
YOU'RE AWAKE?
WHAT ARE YOU DOING?
EH?
WELL, YOU FELL ASLEEP...
...SO I WAS WAITING FOR YOU TO WAKE UP.
I was reading manga.
YOU WAITED?
OH.
SORRY.
I WAS SLEEPING ON YOUR BAG.
Your backpack.
YOU COULD HAVE JUST WOKEN ME UP.
I KNOW.
BUT YOU WERE SLEEPING SO SOUNDLY...

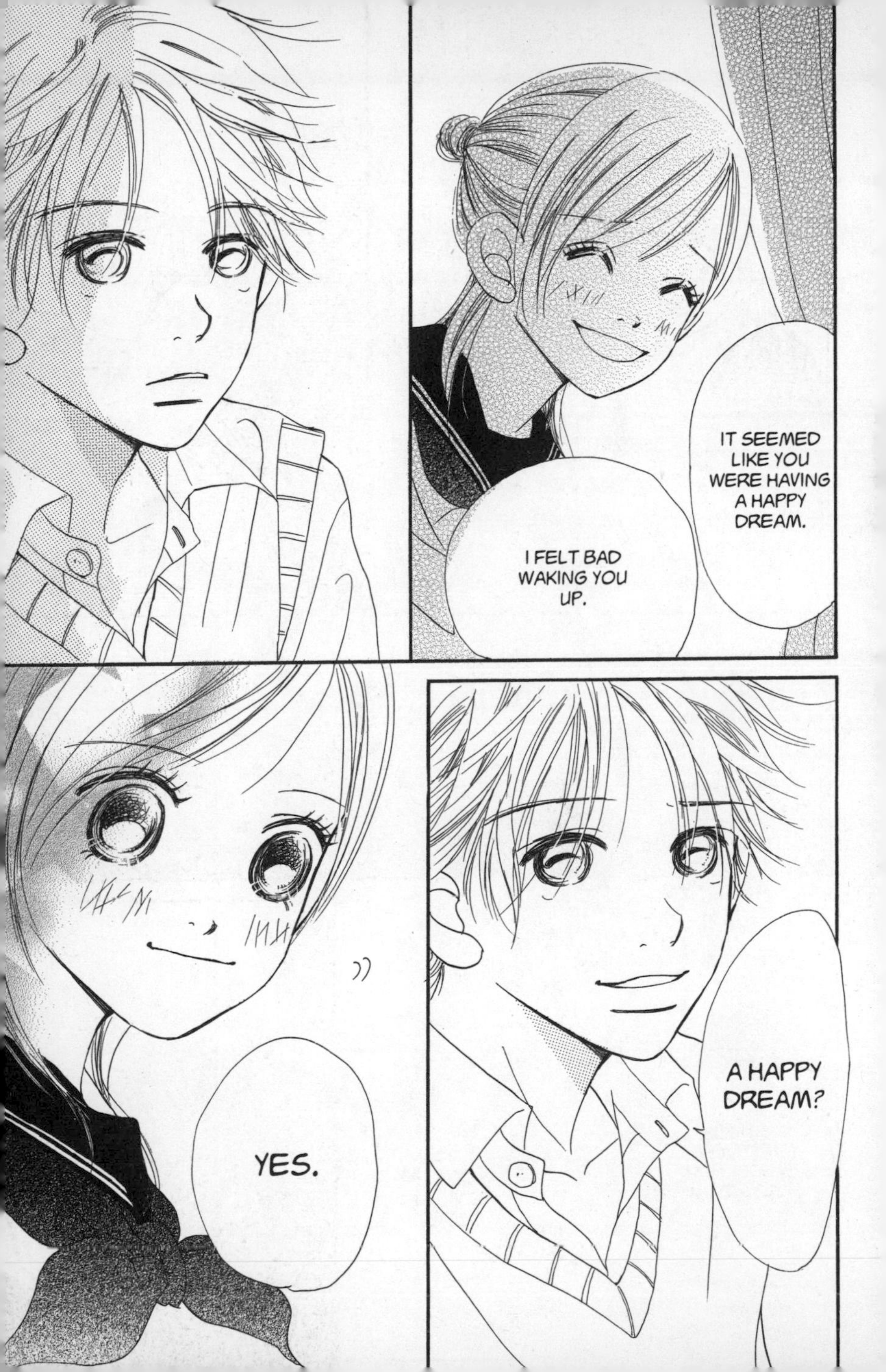
IT SEEMED LIKE YOU WERE HAVING A HAPPY DREAM.
I FELT BAD WAKING YOU UP.
A HAPPY DREAM?
YES.

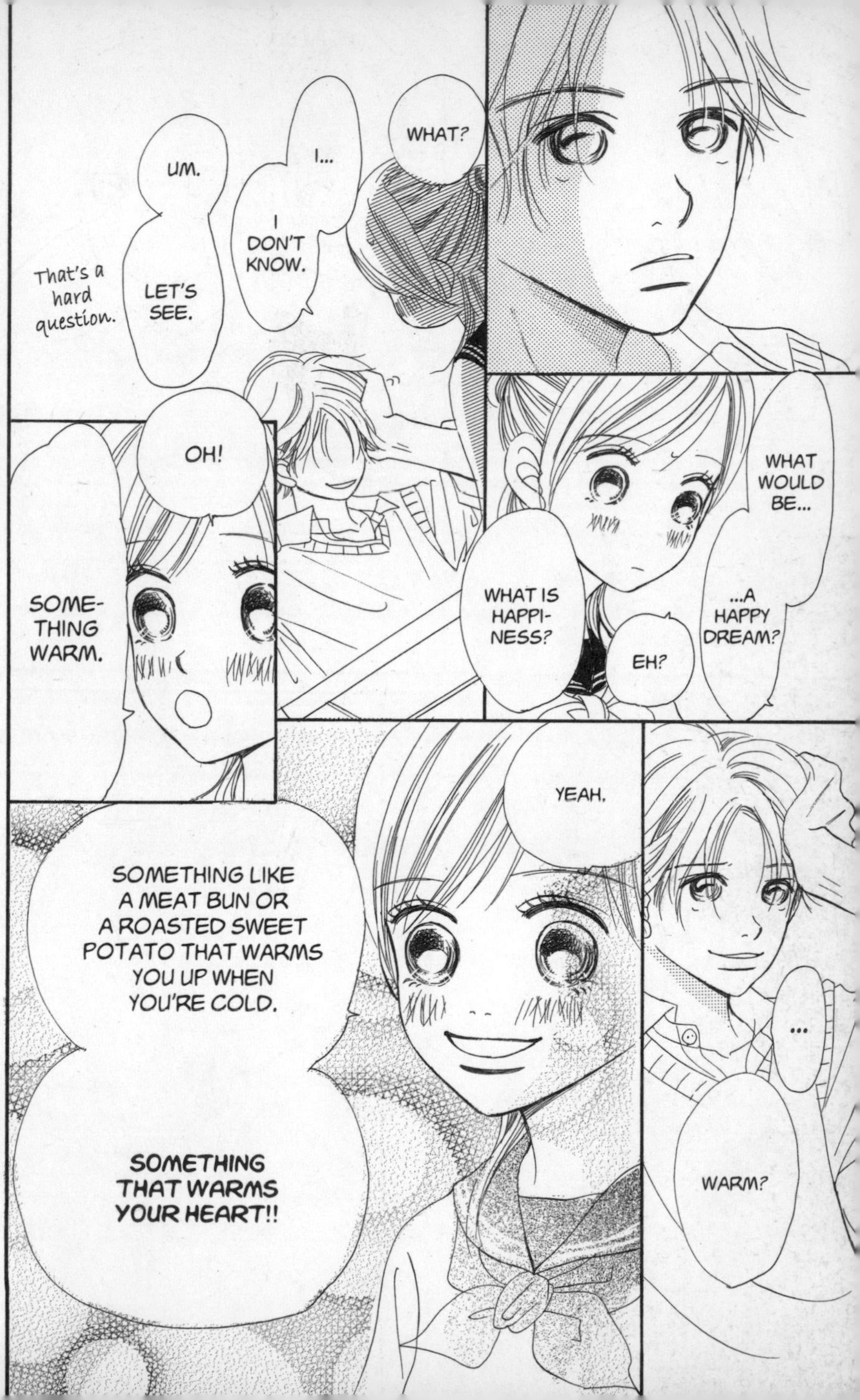
WHAT?
I...
I DON'T KNOW.
UM.
LET'S SEE.
That's a hard question.
WHAT WOULD BE...
...A HAPPY DREAM?
EH?
WHAT IS HAPPINESS?
OH!
SOMETHING WARM.
...
WARM?
YEAH.
SOMETHING LIKE A MEAT BUN OR A ROASTED SWEET POTATO THAT WARMS YOU UP WHEN YOU'RE COLD.
SOMETHING THAT WARMS YOUR HEART!!

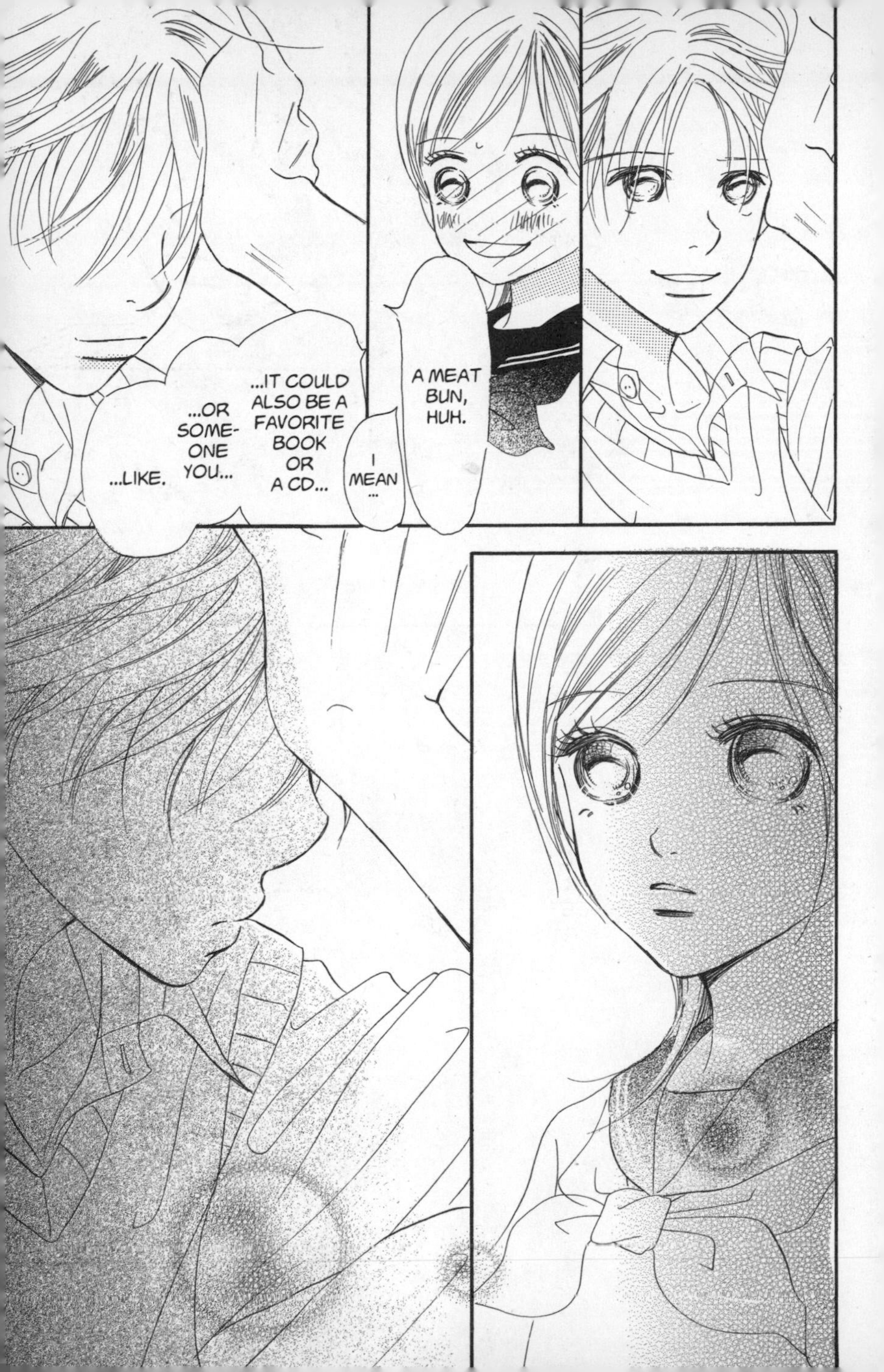
A MEAT BUN, HUH.
I MEAN...
...IT COULD ALSO BE A FAVORITE BOOK OR A CD...
...OR SOMEONE YOU...
...LIKE.

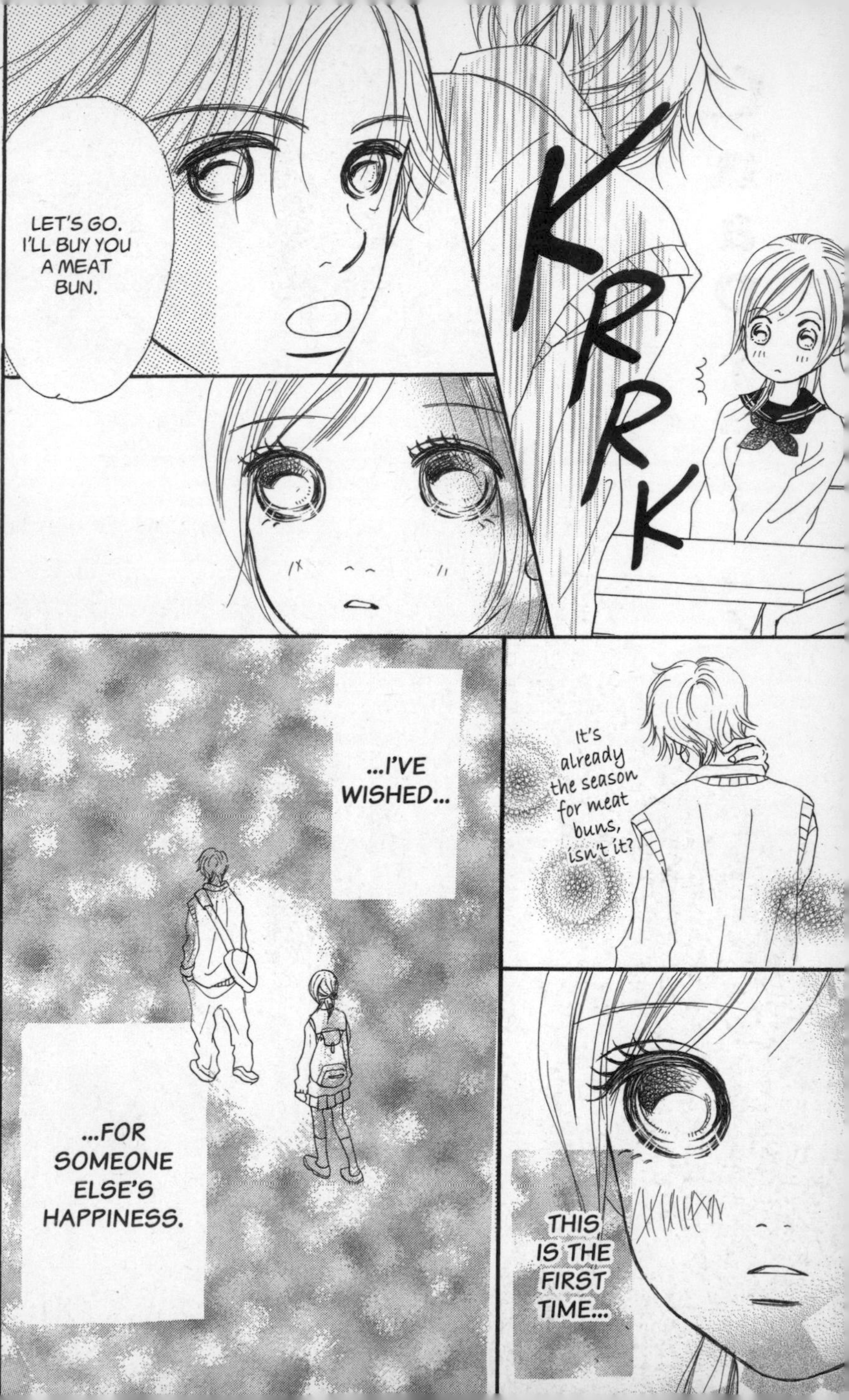
KRRK
LET'S GO. I'LL BUY YOU A MEAT BUN.
It's already the season for meat buns, isn't it?
THIS IS THE FIRST TIME...
...I'VE WISHED...
...FOR SOMEONE ELSE'S HAPPINESS.

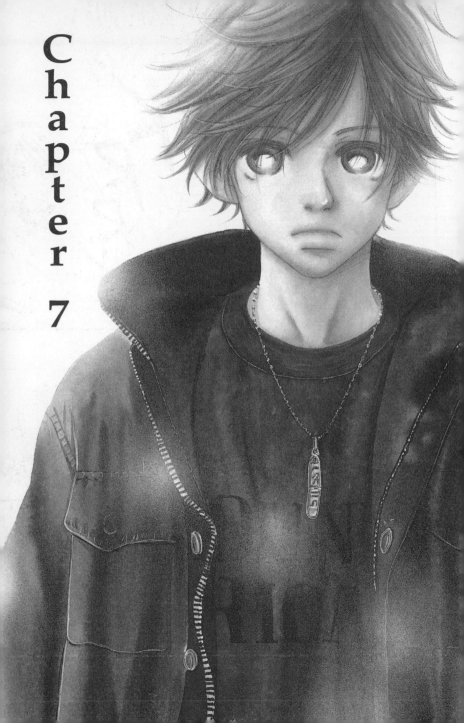

Chapter 7

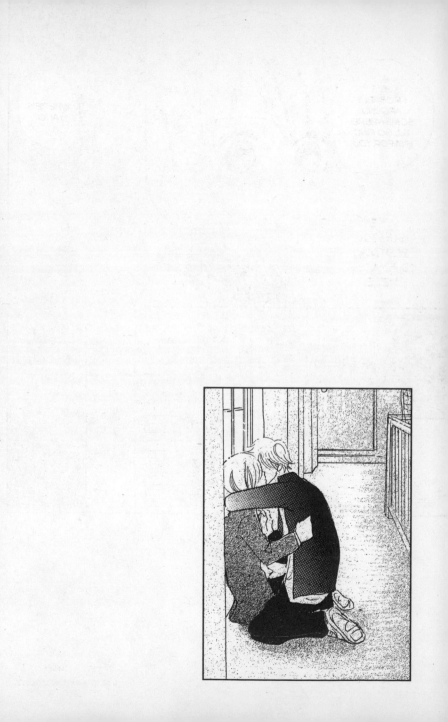

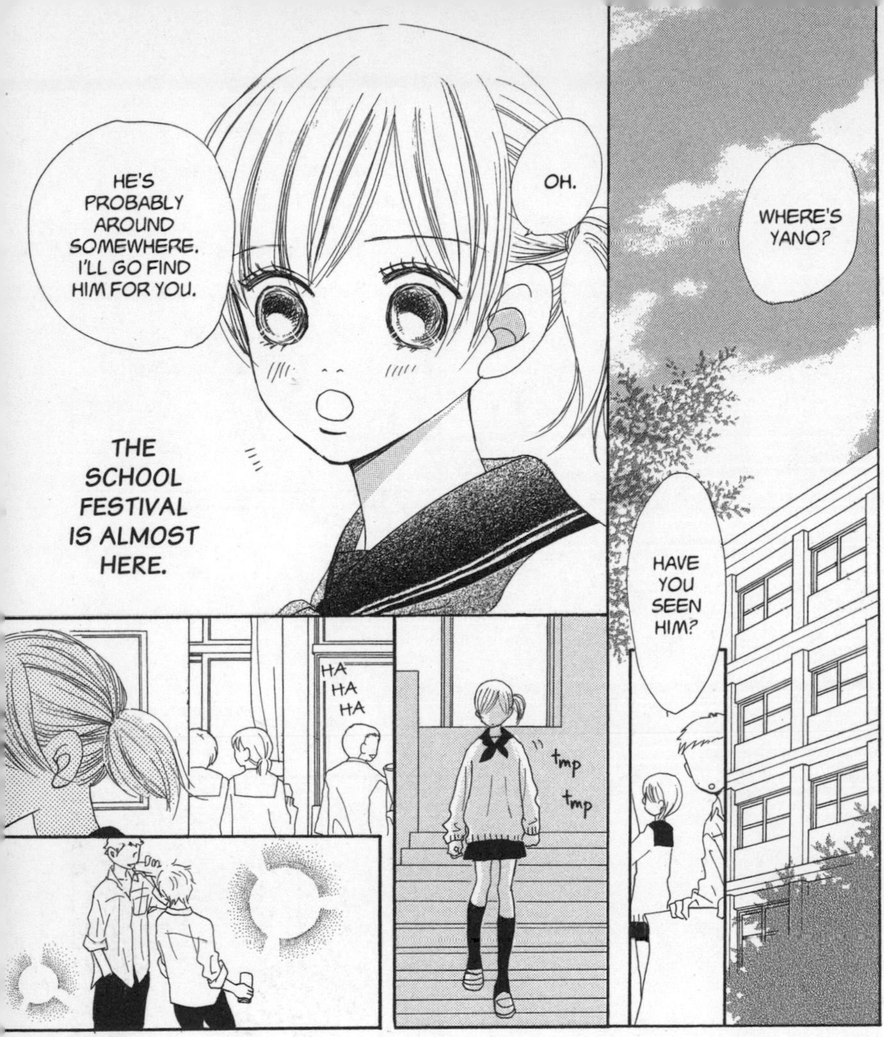
WHERE'S YANO?
HAVE YOU SEEN HIM?
OH.
HE'S PROBABLY AROUND SOMEWHERE. I'LL GO FIND HIM FOR YOU.
THE SCHOOL FESTIVAL IS ALMOST HERE.
tmp
tmp
HA HA HA

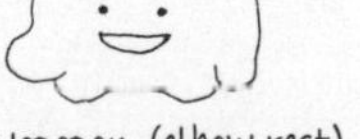
Nopopon (elbow rest)
I can't work without it.

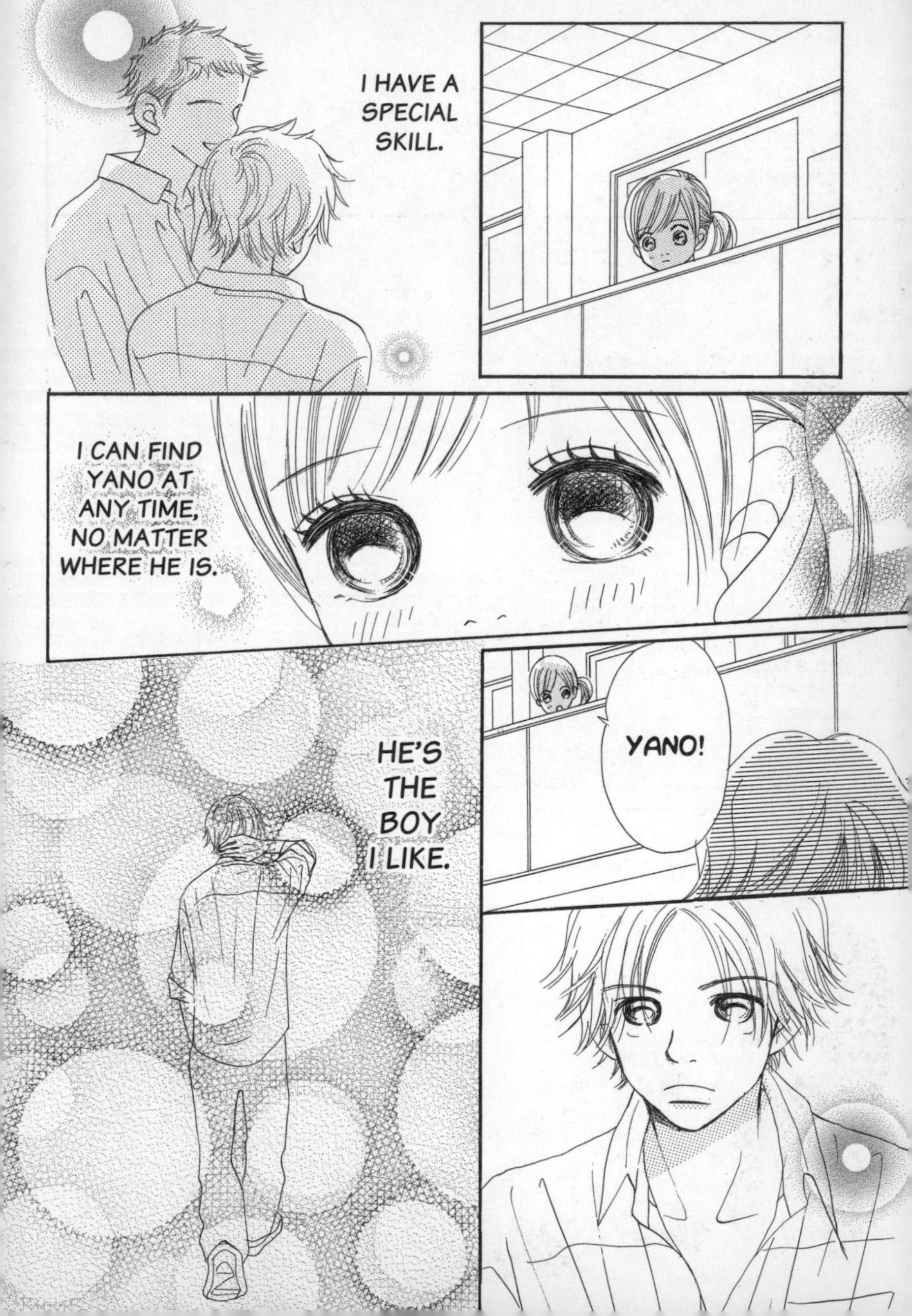
I HAVE A SPECIAL SKILL.
I CAN FIND YANO AT ANY TIME, NO MATTER WHERE HE IS.
YANO!
HE'S THE BOY I LIKE.

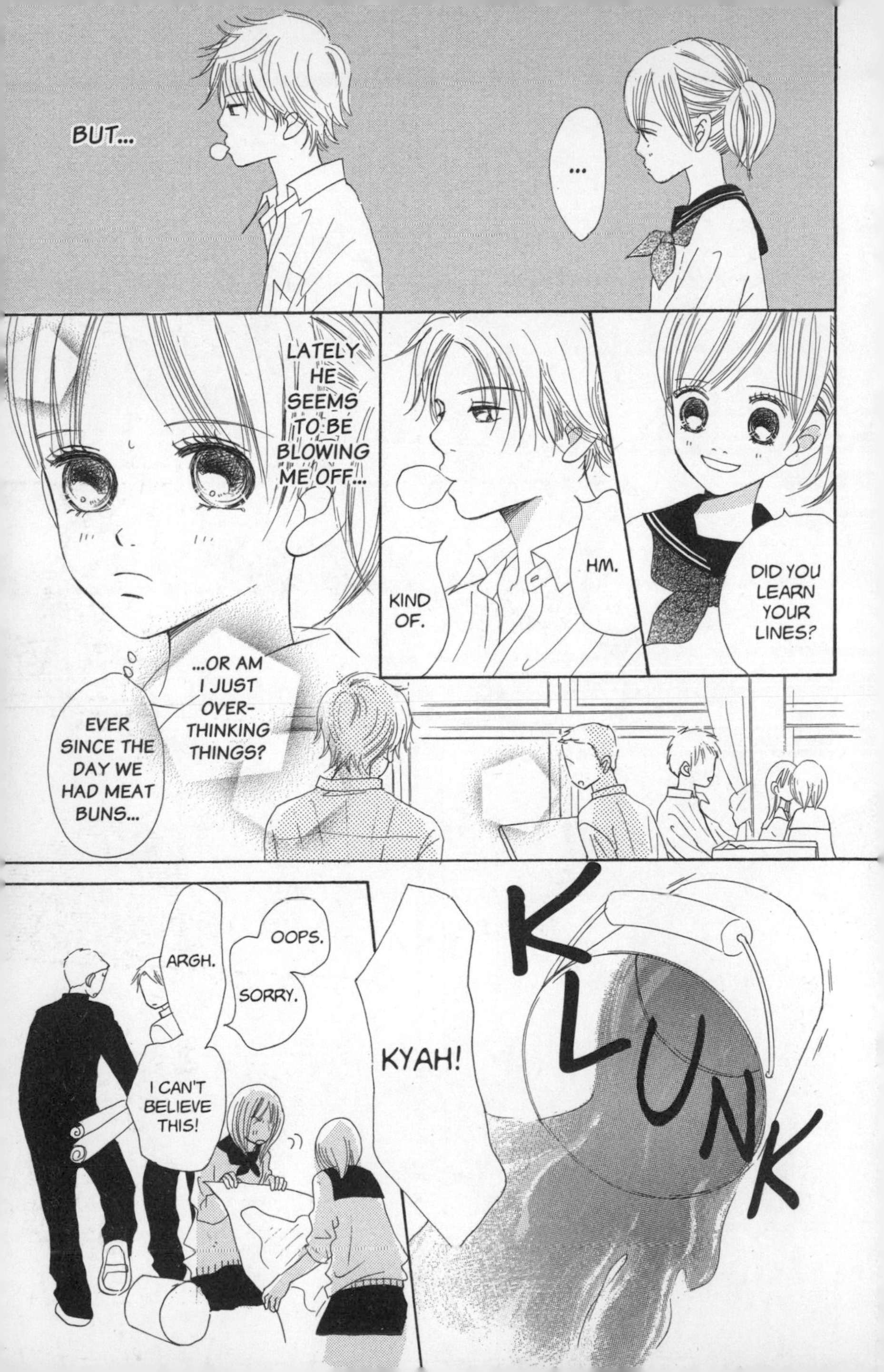
...
BUT...
DID YOU LEARN YOUR LINES?
HM.
KIND OF.
LATELY HE SEEMS TO BE BLOWING ME OFF...
EVER SINCE THE DAY WE HAD MEAT BUNS...
...OR AM I JUST OVER-THINKING THINGS?
KLUNK
KYAH!
OOPS.
SORRY.
ARGH.
I CAN'T BELIEVE THIS!

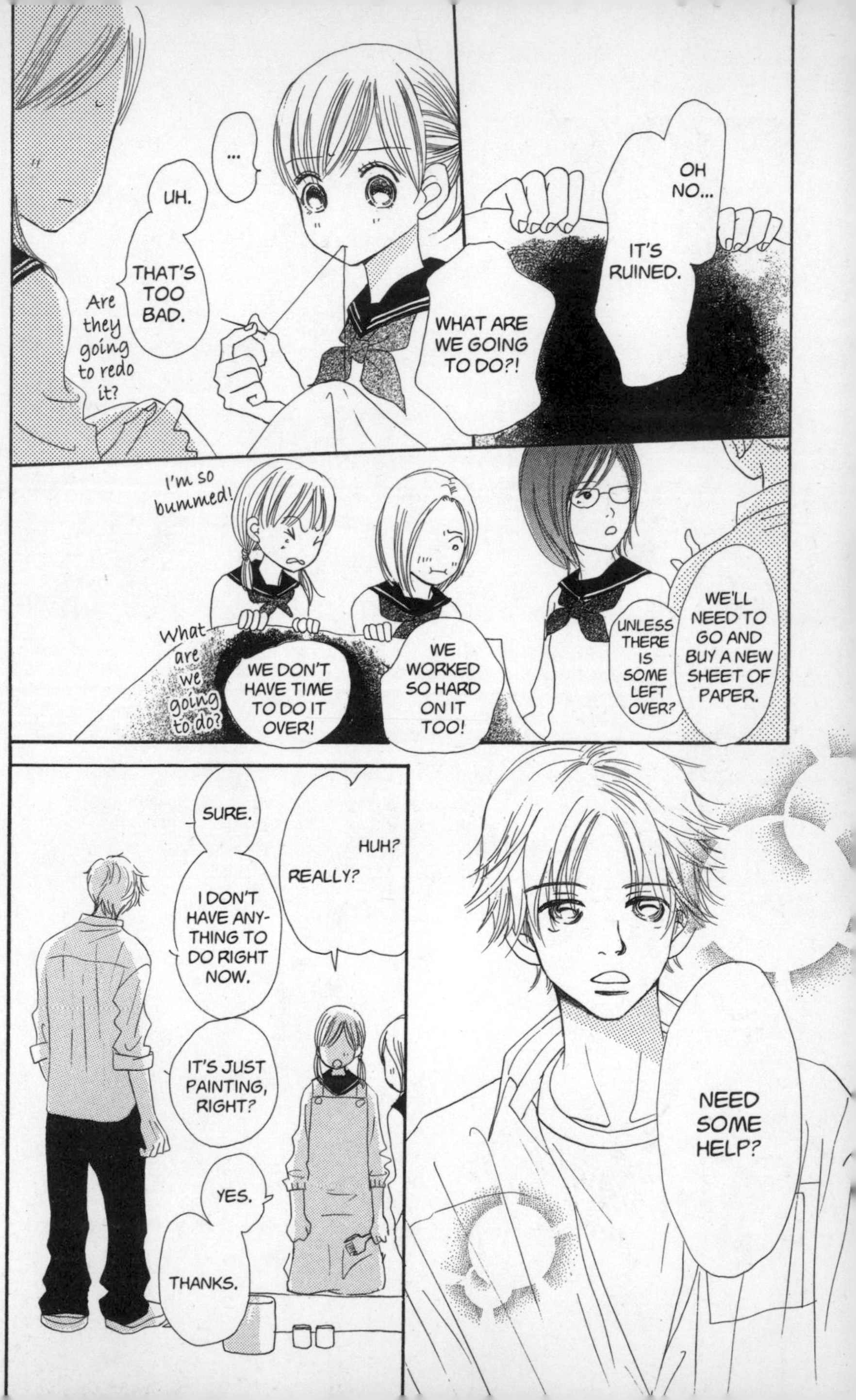
OH NO...
IT'S RUINED.
WHAT ARE WE GOING TO DO?!
...
UH.
THAT'S TOO BAD.
Are they going to redo it?
WE'LL NEED TO GO AND BUY A NEW SHEET OF PAPER.
UNLESS THERE IS SOME LEFT OVER?
WE WORKED SO HARD ON IT TOO!
I'm so bummed!
WE DON'T HAVE TIME TO DO IT OVER!
What are we going to do?
NEED SOME HELP?
HUH?
REALLY?
SURE.
I DON'T HAVE ANY-THING TO DO RIGHT NOW.
IT'S JUST PAINTING, RIGHT?
YES.
THANKS.

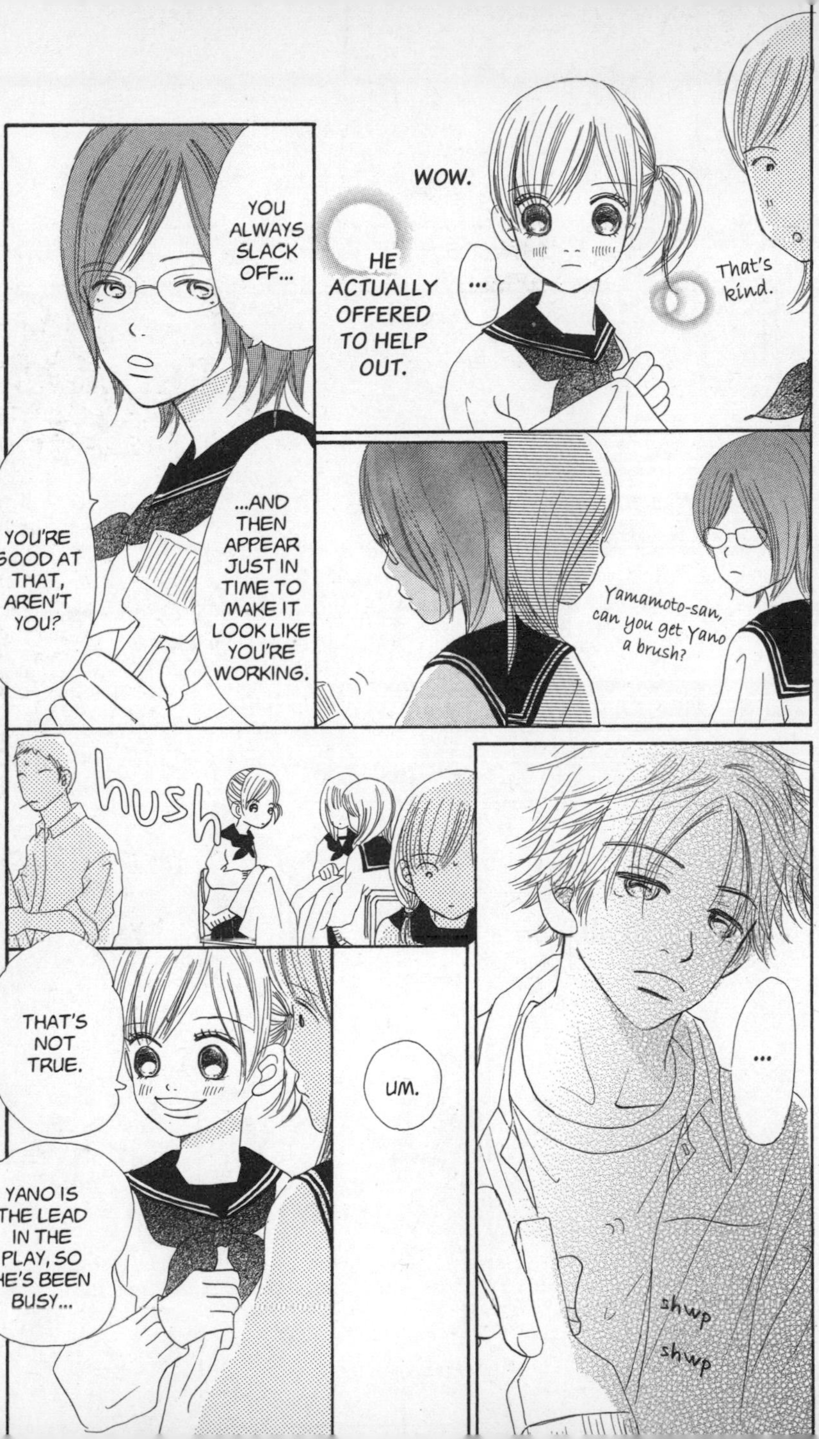
WOW.
HE ACTUALLY OFFERED TO HELP OUT.
...
That's kind.
Yamamoto-san, can you get Yano a brush?
YOU ALWAYS SLACK OFF...
...AND THEN APPEAR JUST IN TIME TO MAKE IT LOOK LIKE YOU'RE WORKING.
YOU'RE GOOD AT THAT, AREN'T YOU?
...
shwp
shwp
hush
UM.
THAT'S NOT TRUE.
YANO IS THE LEAD IN THE PLAY, SO HE'S BEEN BUSY...

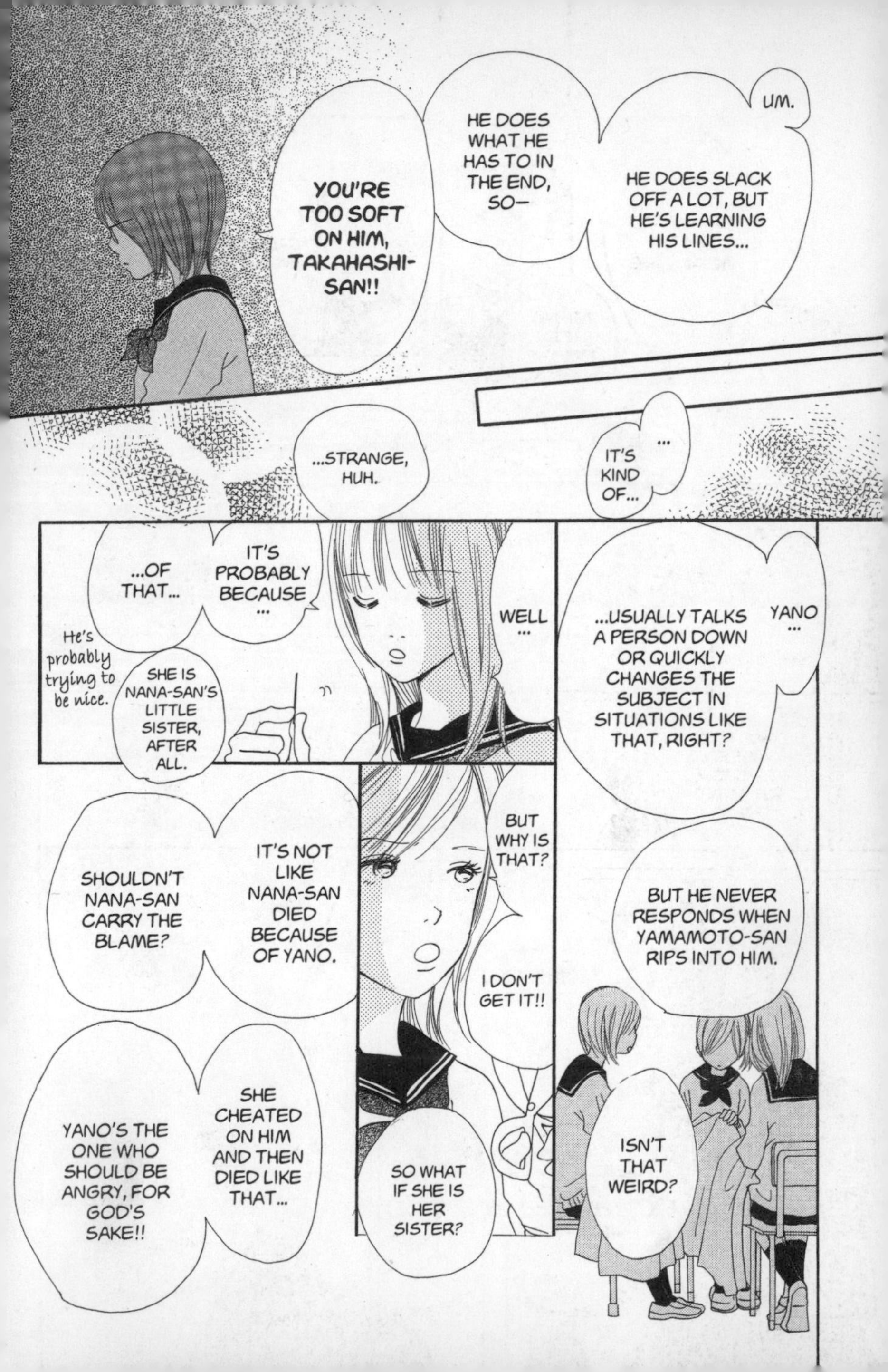
UM.
HE DOES SLACK OFF A LOT, BUT HE'S LEARNING HIS LINES...
HE DOES WHAT HE HAS TO IN THE END, SO—
YOU'RE TOO SOFT ON HIM, TAKAHASHI-SAN!!
...
IT'S KIND OF...
...STRANGE, HUH.
YANO...
...USUALLY TALKS A PERSON DOWN OR QUICKLY CHANGES THE SUBJECT IN SITUATIONS LIKE THAT, RIGHT?
BUT HE NEVER RESPONDS WHEN YAMAMOTO-SAN RIPS INTO HIM.
ISN'T THAT WEIRD?
WELL...
IT'S PROBABLY BECAUSE...
...OF THAT...
SHE IS NANA-SAN'S LITTLE SISTER, AFTER ALL.
He's probably trying to be nice.
BUT WHY IS THAT?
I DON'T GET IT!!
SO WHAT IF SHE IS HER SISTER?
IT'S NOT LIKE NANA-SAN DIED BECAUSE OF YANO.
SHOULDN'T NANA-SAN CARRY THE BLAME?
SHE CHEATED ON HIM AND THEN DIED LIKE THAT...
YANO'S THE ONE WHO SHOULD BE ANGRY, FOR GOD'S SAKE!!

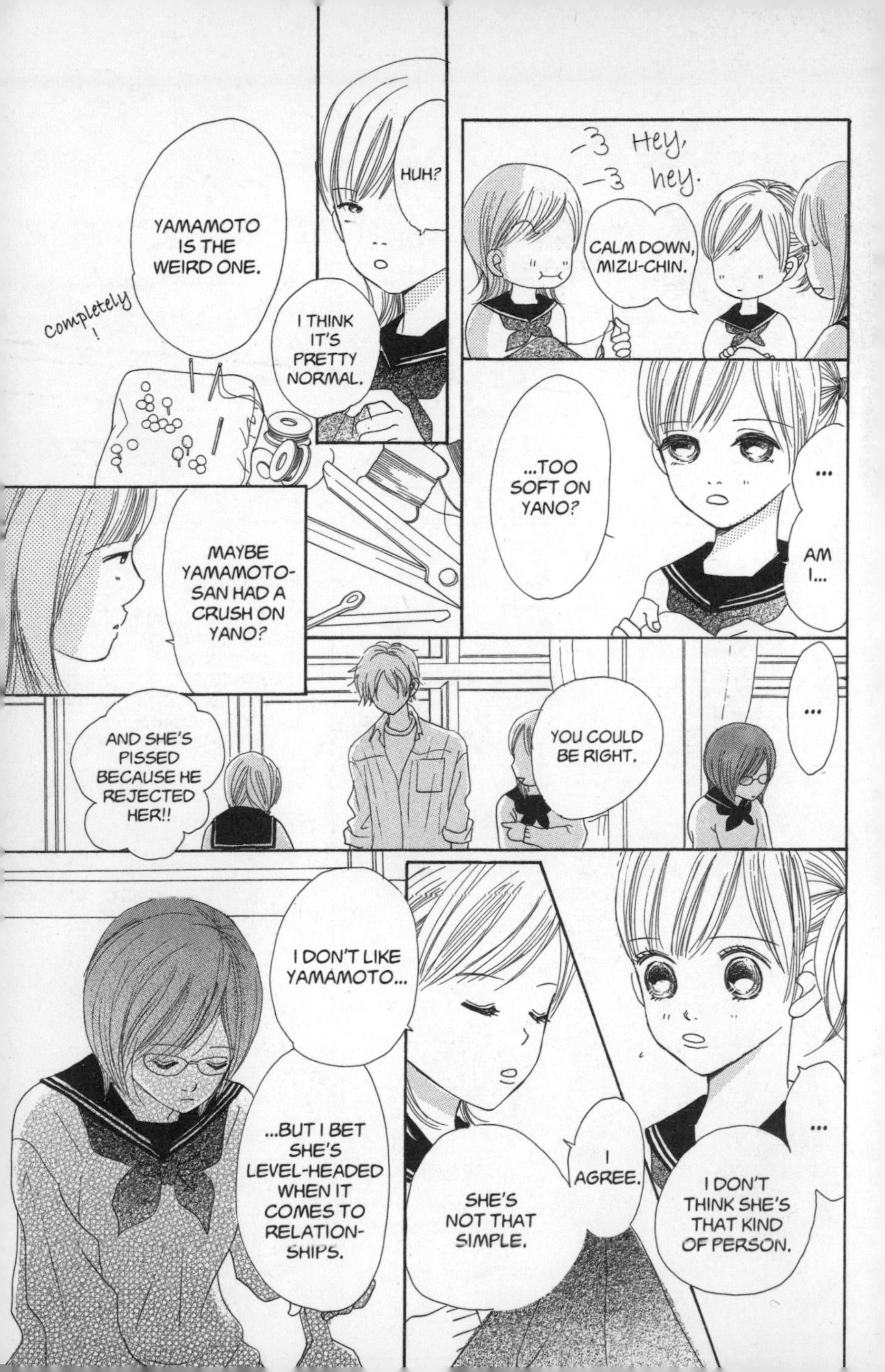
HUH?
I THINK IT'S PRETTY NORMAL.
YAMAMOTO IS THE WEIRD ONE.
Completely!
Hey, hey.
CALM DOWN, MIZU-CHIN.
...
AM I...
...TOO SOFT ON YANO?
MAYBE YAMAMOTO-SAN HAD A CRUSH ON YANO?
...
YOU COULD BE RIGHT.
AND SHE'S PISSED BECAUSE HE REJECTED HER!!
...
I DON'T THINK SHE'S THAT KIND OF PERSON.
I AGREE.
SHE'S NOT THAT SIMPLE.
I DON'T LIKE YAMAMOTO...
...BUT I BET SHE'S LEVEL-HEADED WHEN IT COMES TO RELATION-SHIPS.

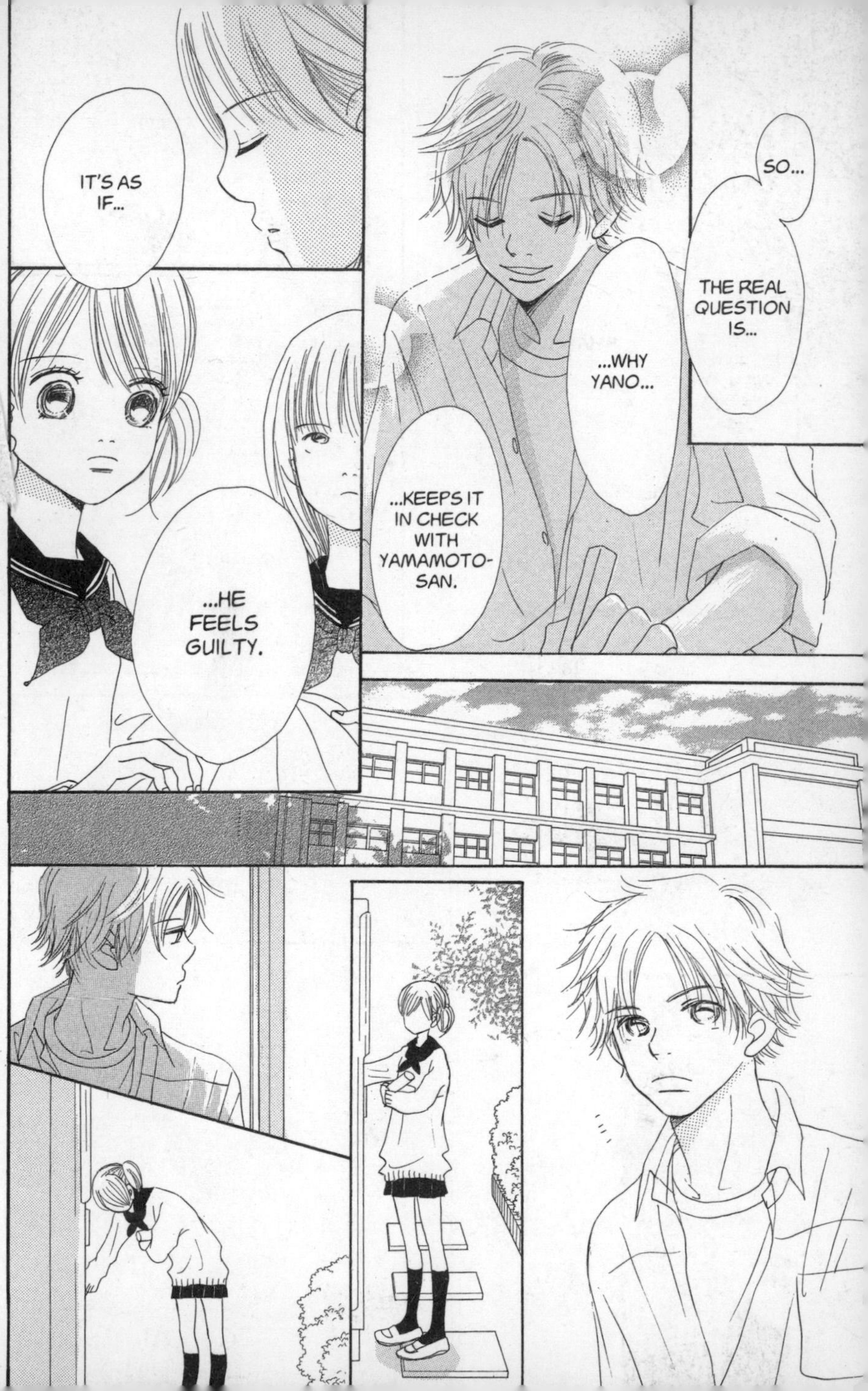
SO...
THE REAL QUESTION IS...
...WHY YANO...
...KEEPS IT IN CHECK WITH YAMAMOTO-SAN.
IT'S AS IF...
...HE FEELS GUILTY.
...

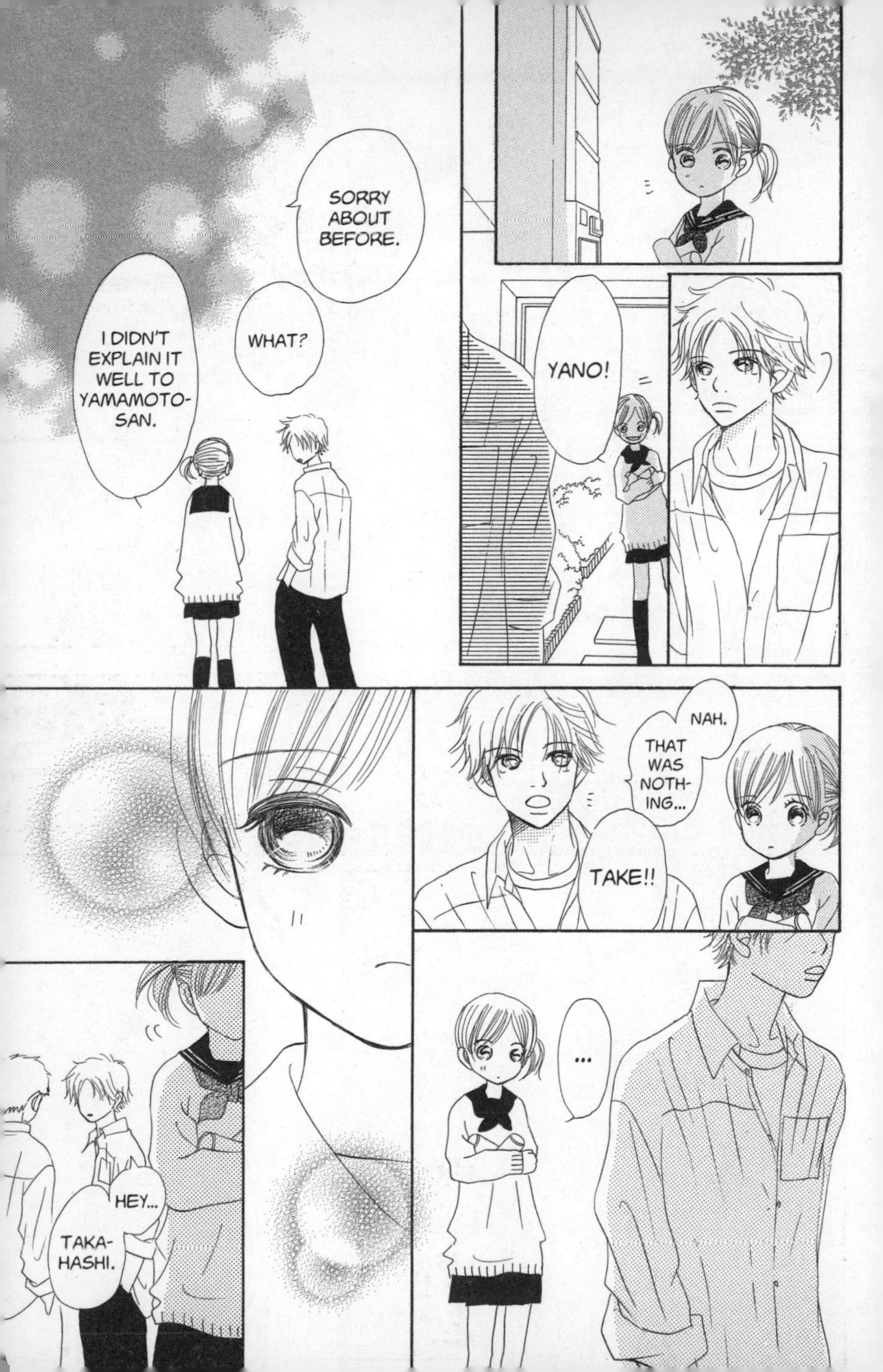
YANO!
SORRY ABOUT BEFORE.
WHAT?
I DIDN'T EXPLAIN IT WELL TO YAMAMOTO-SAN.
NAH. THAT WAS NOTHING...
TAKE!!
...
HEY... TAKAHASHI.

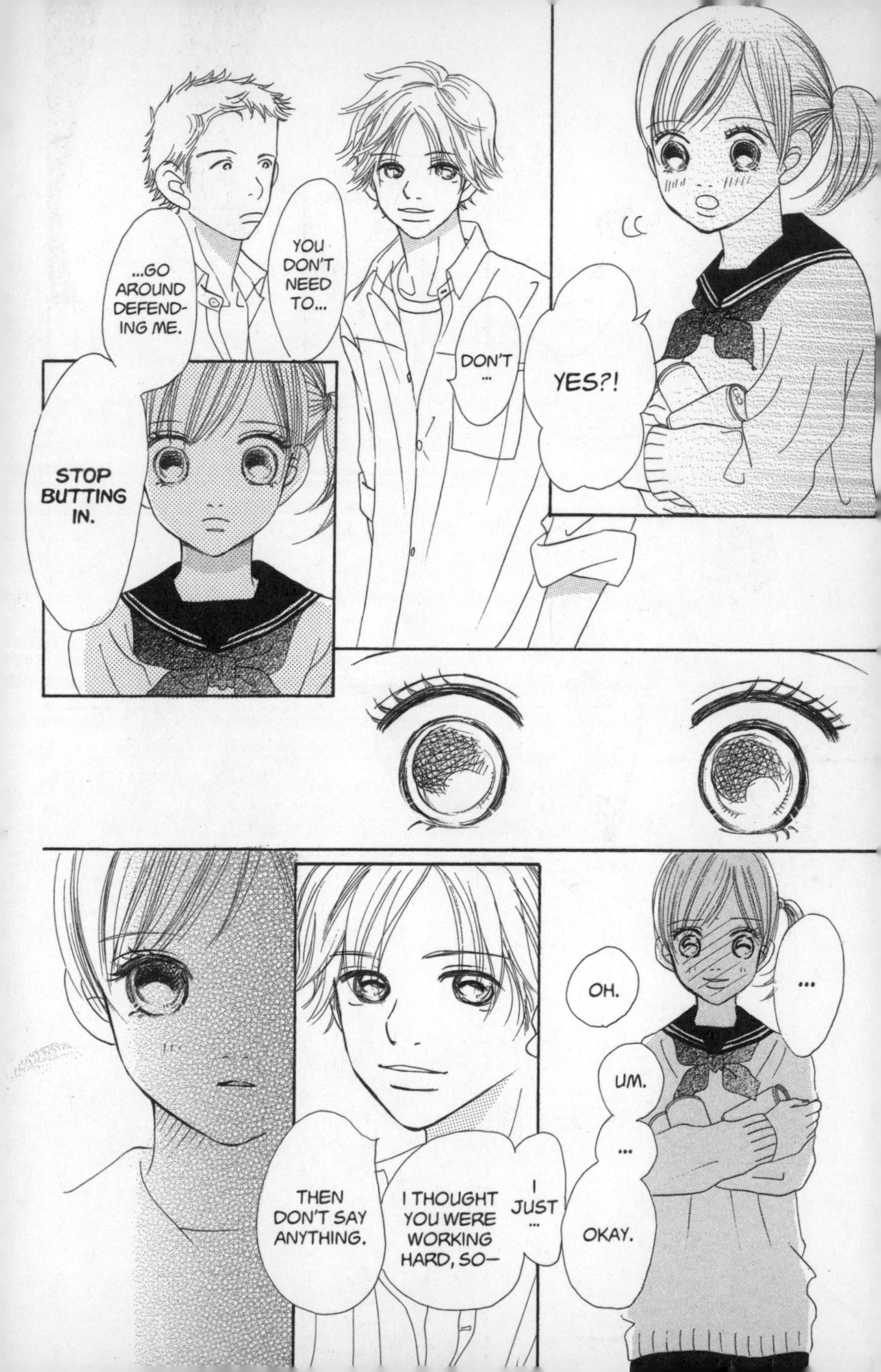
YES?!
DON'T ...
YOU DON'T NEED TO...
...GO AROUND DEFEND-ING ME.
STOP BUTTING IN.
...
OH.
UM.
...
OKAY.
I JUST ...
I THOUGHT YOU WERE WORKING HARD, SO—
THEN DON'T SAY ANYTHING.

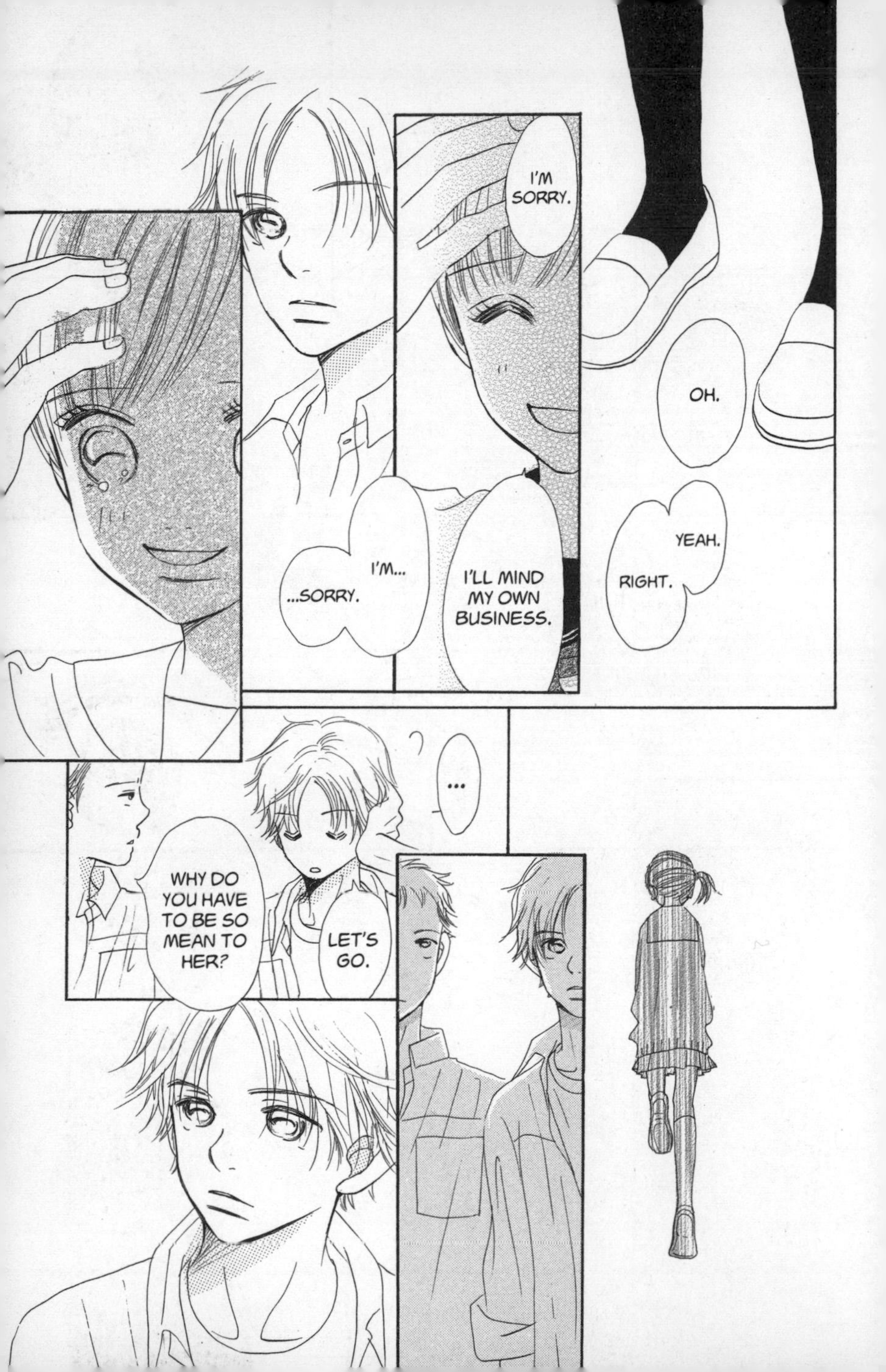
OH.
YEAH. RIGHT.
I'M SORRY.
I'LL MIND MY OWN BUSINESS.
I'M... ...SORRY.
...
LET'S GO.
WHY DO YOU HAVE TO BE SO MEAN TO HER?

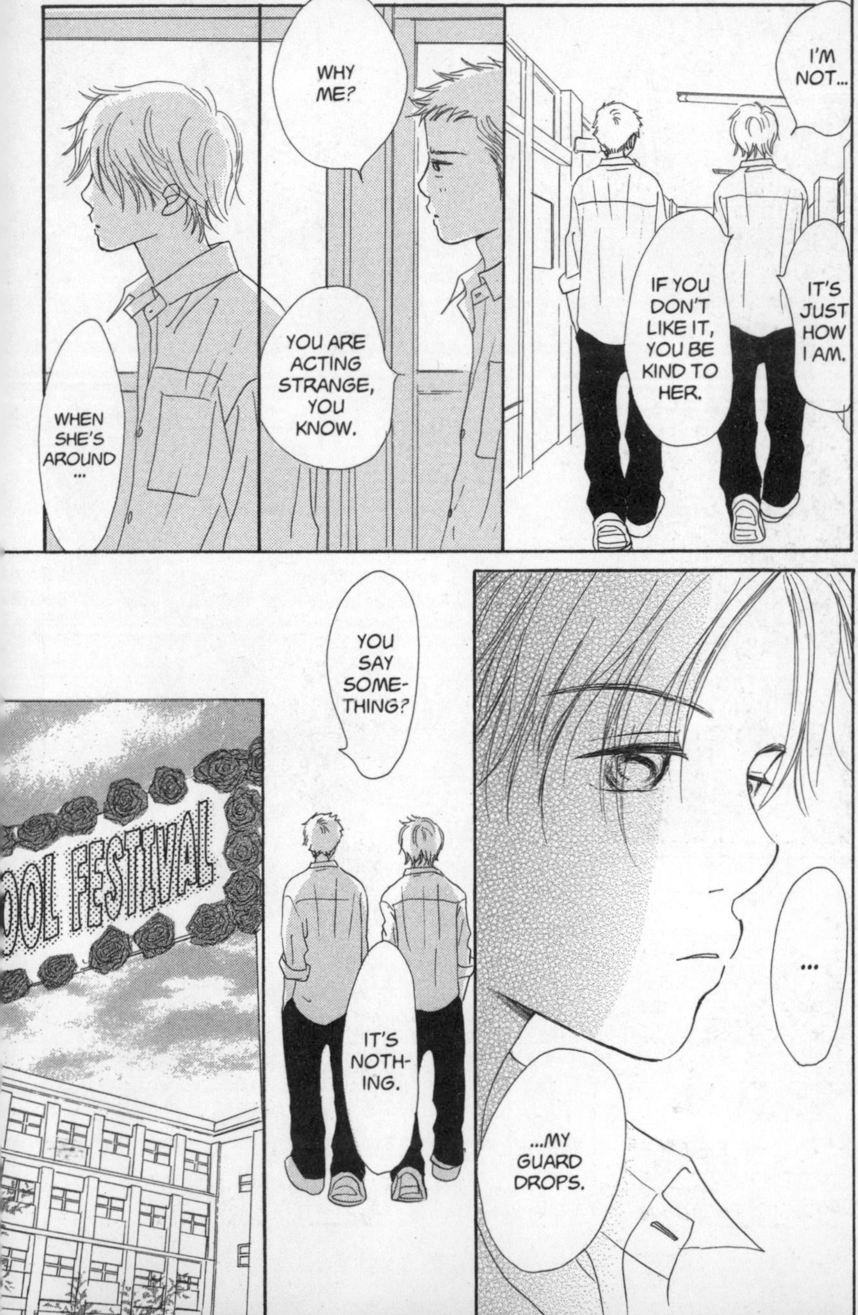
I'M NOT...
IT'S JUST HOW I AM.
IF YOU DON'T LIKE IT, YOU BE KIND TO HER.
WHY ME?
YOU ARE ACTING STRANGE, YOU KNOW.
WHEN SHE'S AROUND ...
...
...MY GUARD DROPS.
YOU SAY SOME-THING?
IT'S NOTH-ING.
OOL FESTIVAL

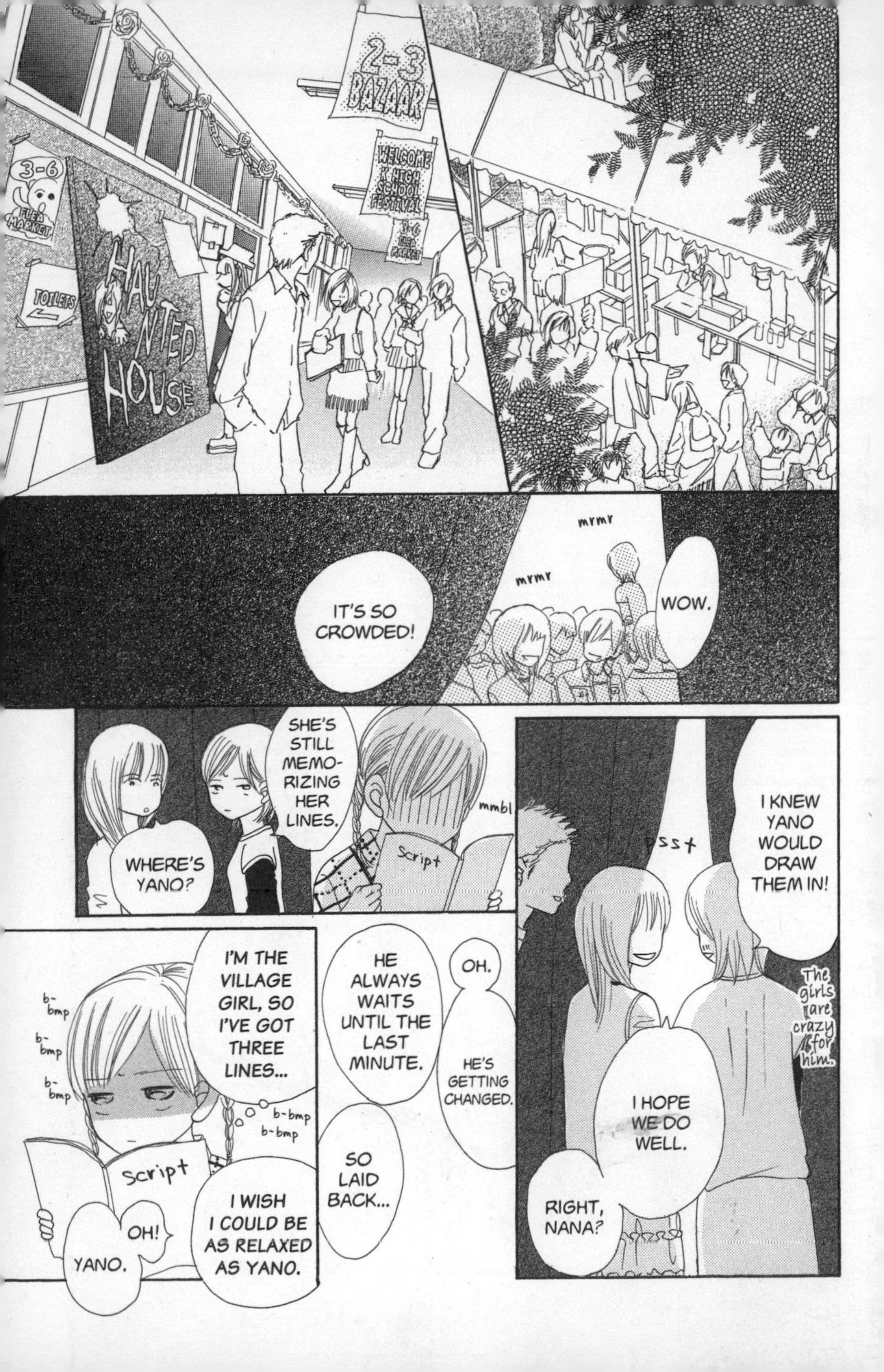
2-3 BAZAAR
WELCOME K HIGH SCHOOL FESTIVAL
3-6 FLEA MARKET
3-6 FLEA MARKET
HAUNTED HOUSE
TOILETS
mrmr
mrmr
WOW.
IT'S SO CROWDED!
I KNEW YANO WOULD DRAW THEM IN!
psst
The girls are crazy for him.
I HOPE WE DO WELL.
RIGHT, NANA?
SHE'S STILL MEMORIZING HER LINES.
mmbl
Script
WHERE'S YANO?
OH.
HE'S GETTING CHANGED.
HE ALWAYS WAITS UNTIL THE LAST MINUTE.
SO LAID BACK...
I'M THE VILLAGE GIRL, SO I'VE GOT THREE LINES...
b-bmp b-bmp b-bmp
b-bmp b-bmp
Script
I WISH I COULD BE AS RELAXED AS YANO.
OH!
YANO.

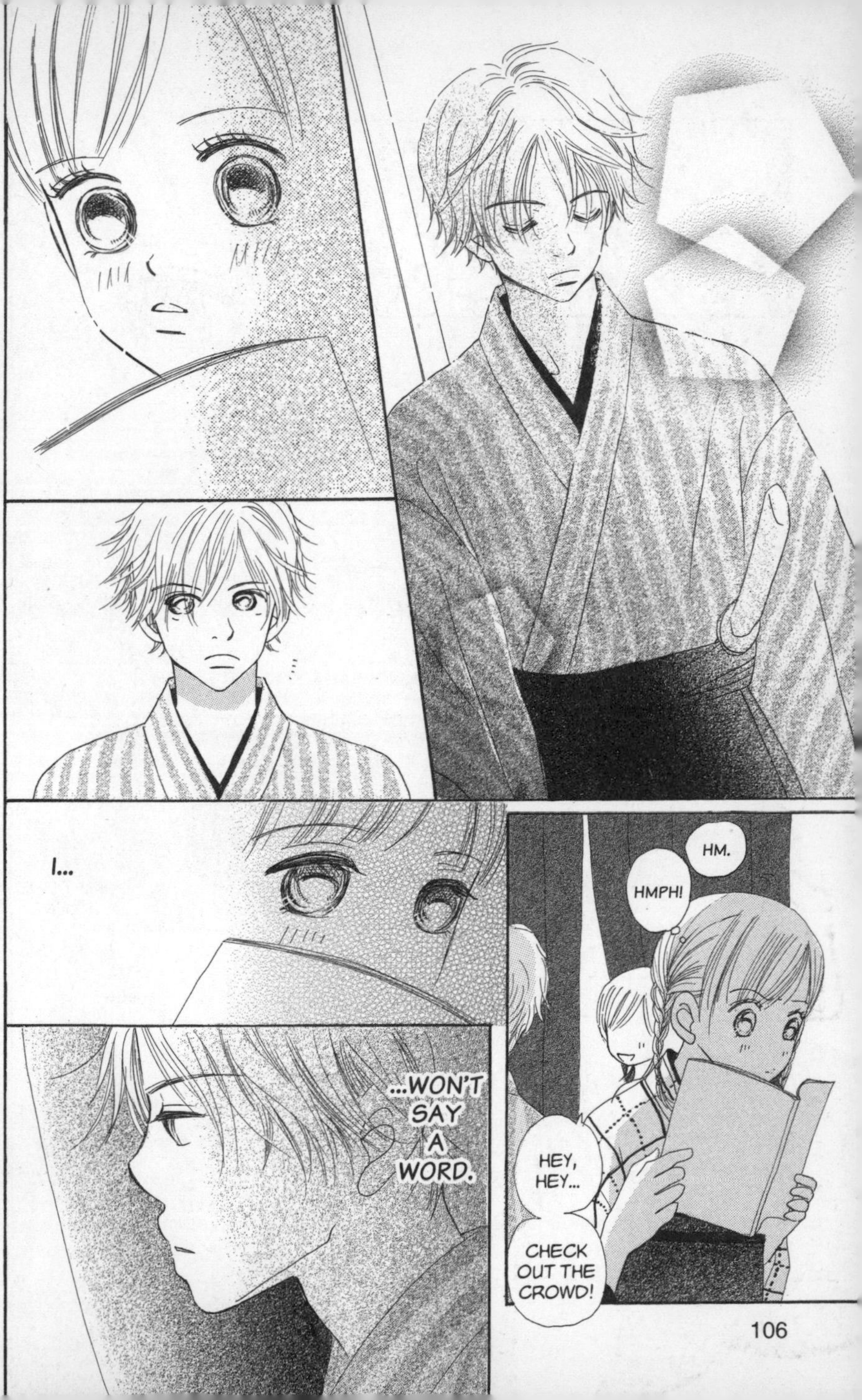
HM.
HMPH!
HEY, HEY...
CHECK OUT THE CROWD!
I...
...WON'T SAY A WORD.

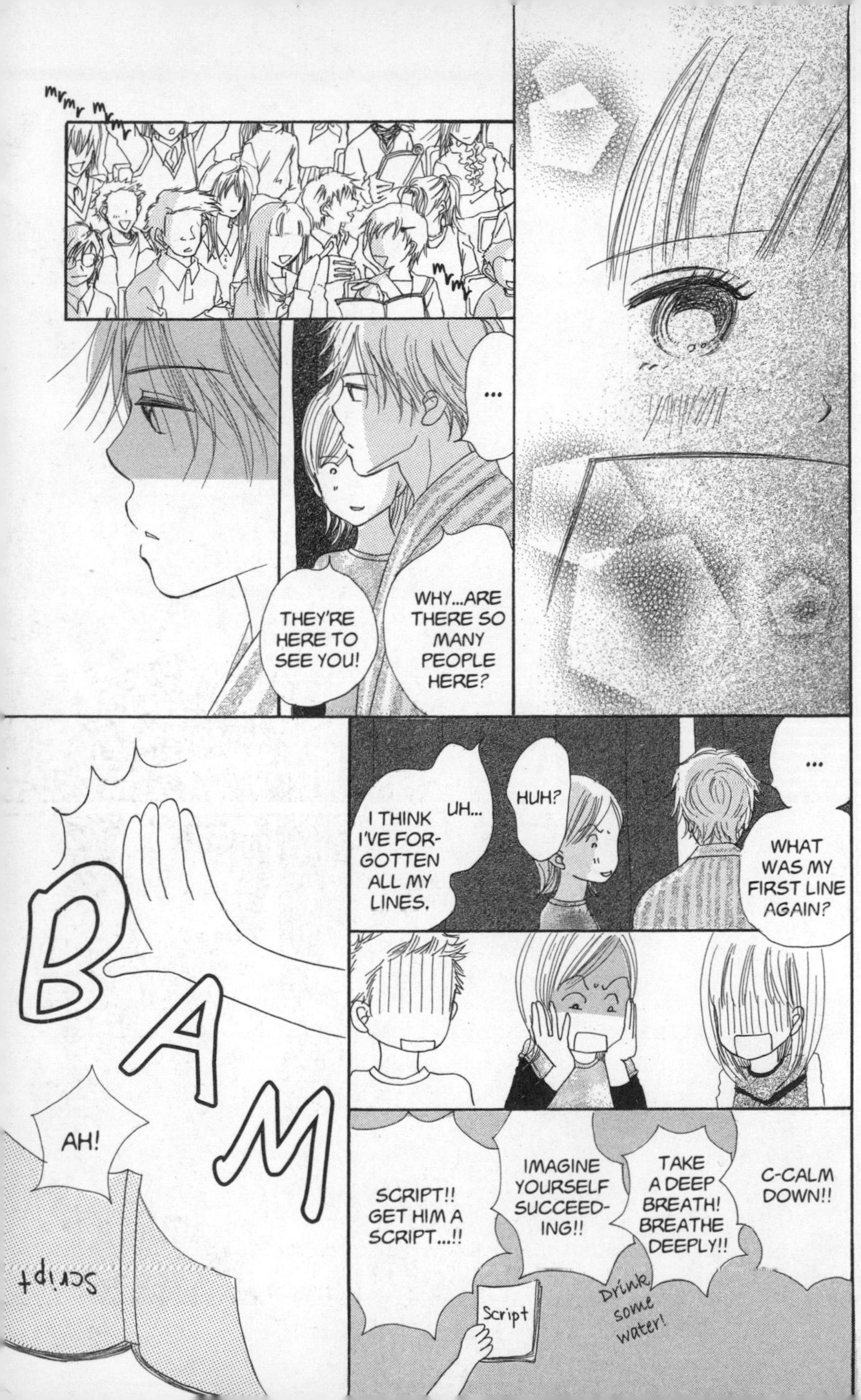
mrmr mrmr
mrmr
...
WHY...ARE THERE SO MANY PEOPLE HERE?
THEY'RE HERE TO SEE YOU!
...
WHAT WAS MY FIRST LINE AGAIN?
HUH?
UH...
I THINK I'VE FORGOTTEN ALL MY LINES.
C-CALM DOWN!!
TAKE A DEEP BREATH! BREATHE DEEPLY!!
IMAGINE YOURSELF SUCCEEDING!!
SCRIPT!! GET HIM A SCRIPT...!!
Drink some water!
Script
BAM
AH!

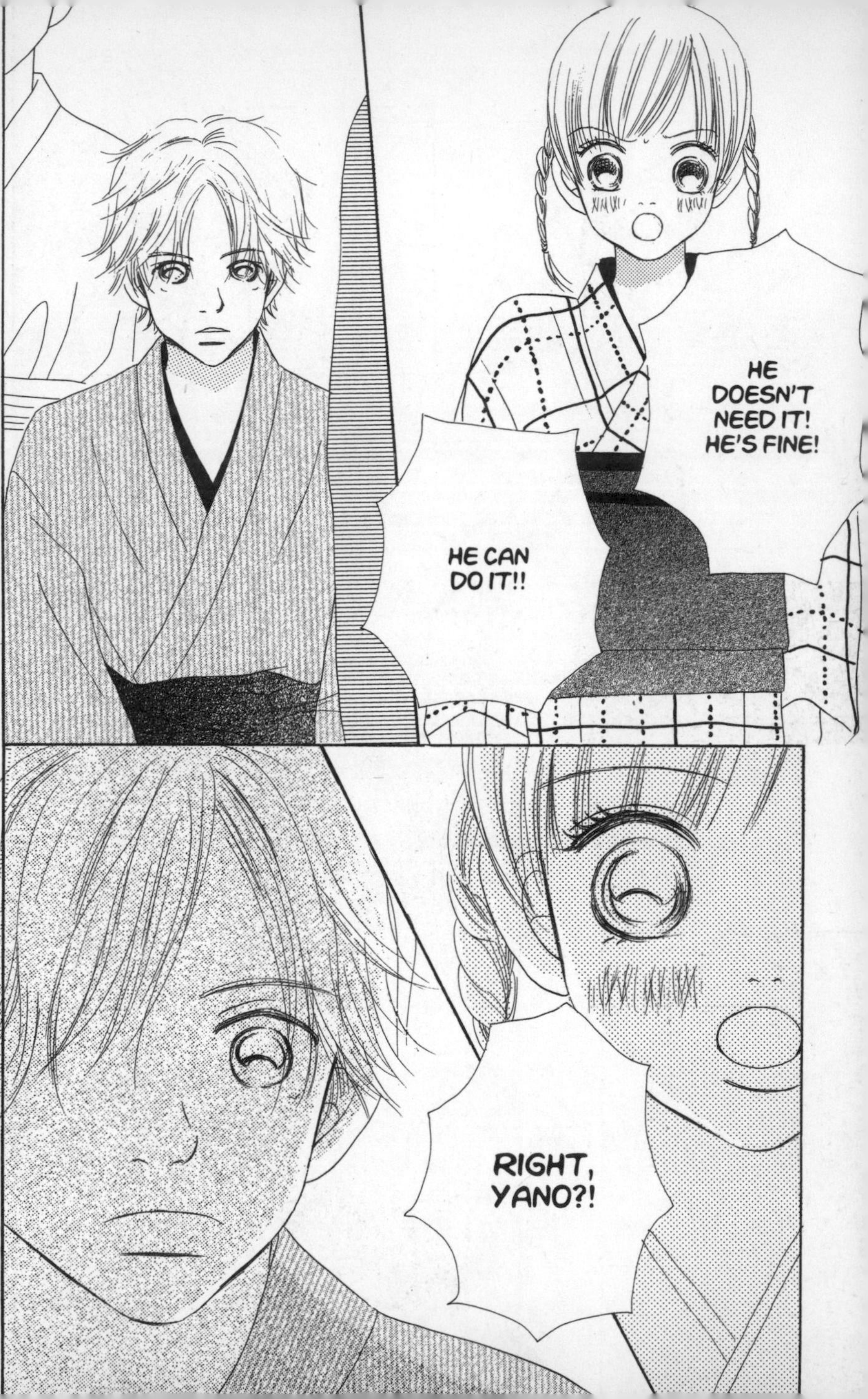
HE DOESN'T NEED IT! HE'S FINE!
HE CAN DO IT!!
RIGHT, YANO?!

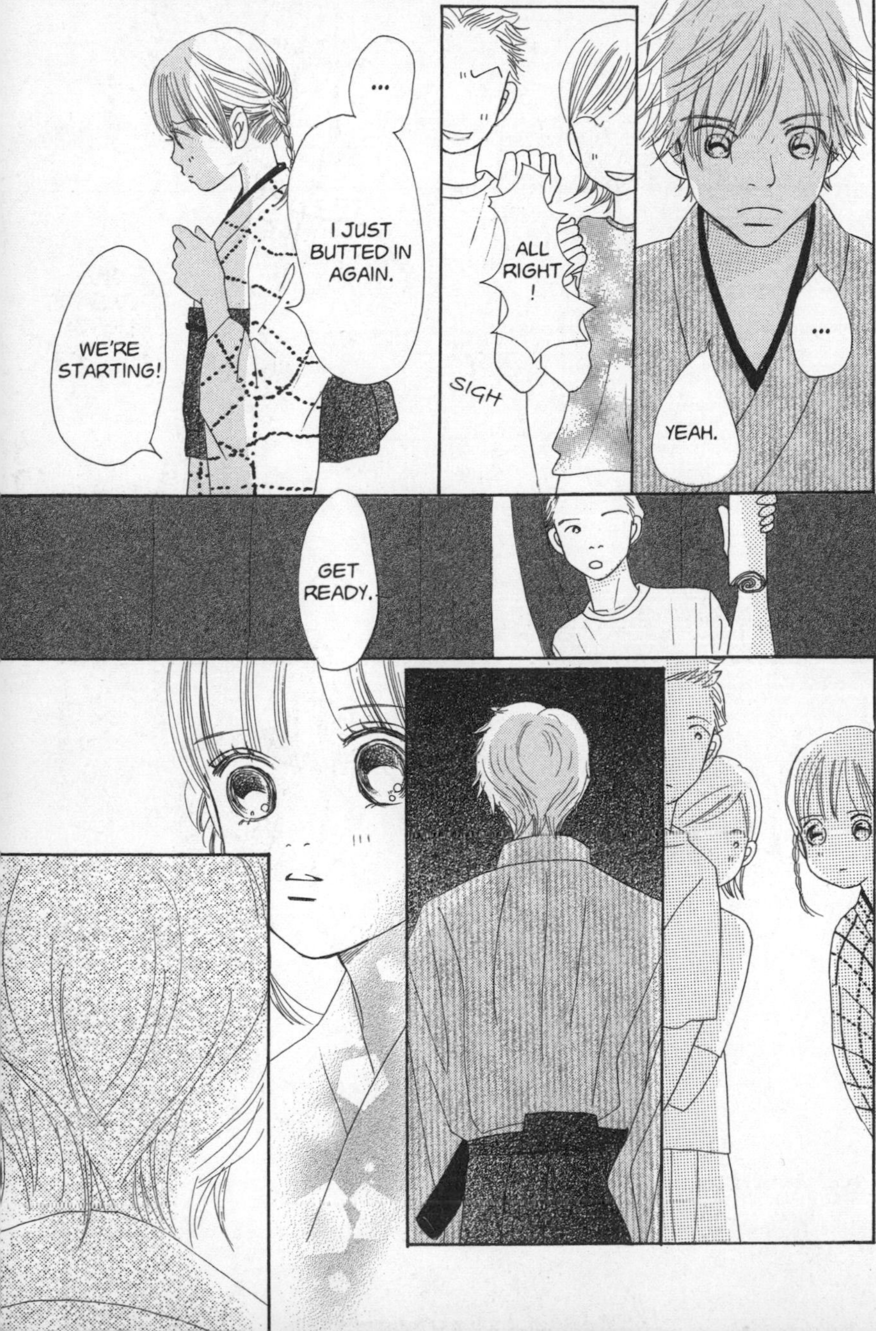
...
YEAH.
ALL RIGHT!
SIGH
...
I JUST BUTTED IN AGAIN.
WE'RE STARTING!
GET READY.

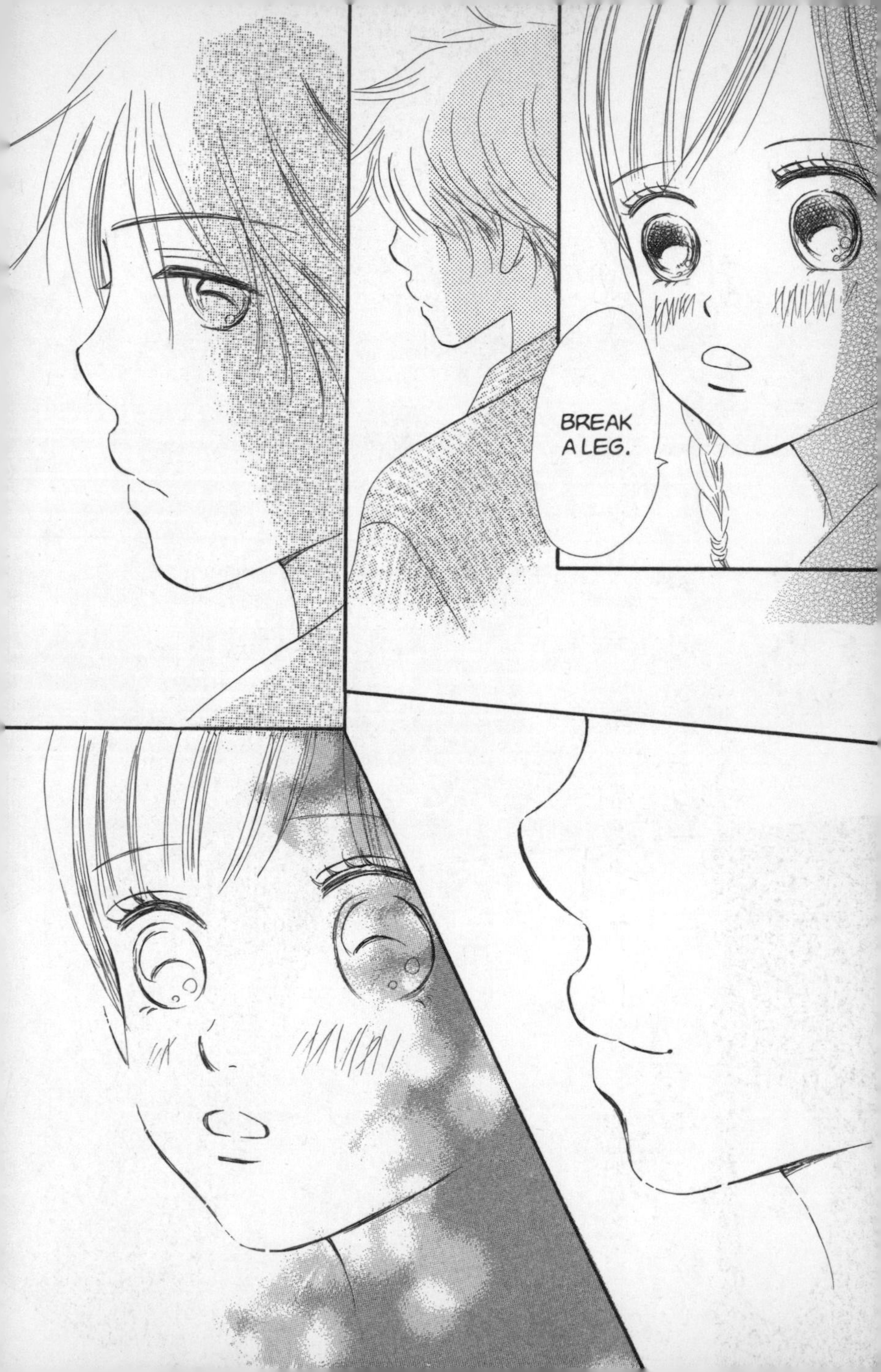
BREAK A LEG.

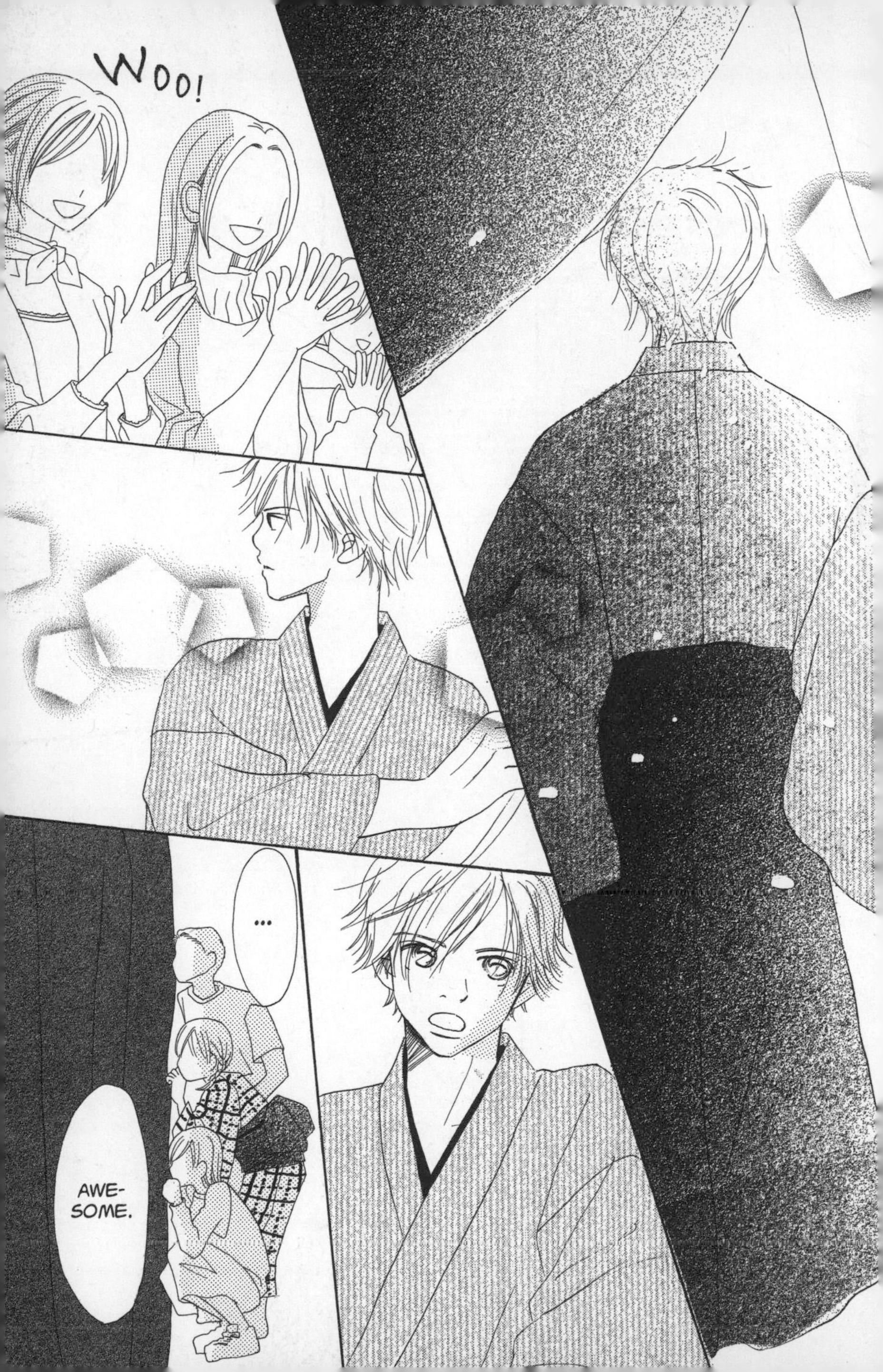
WOO!
...
AWE-SOME.

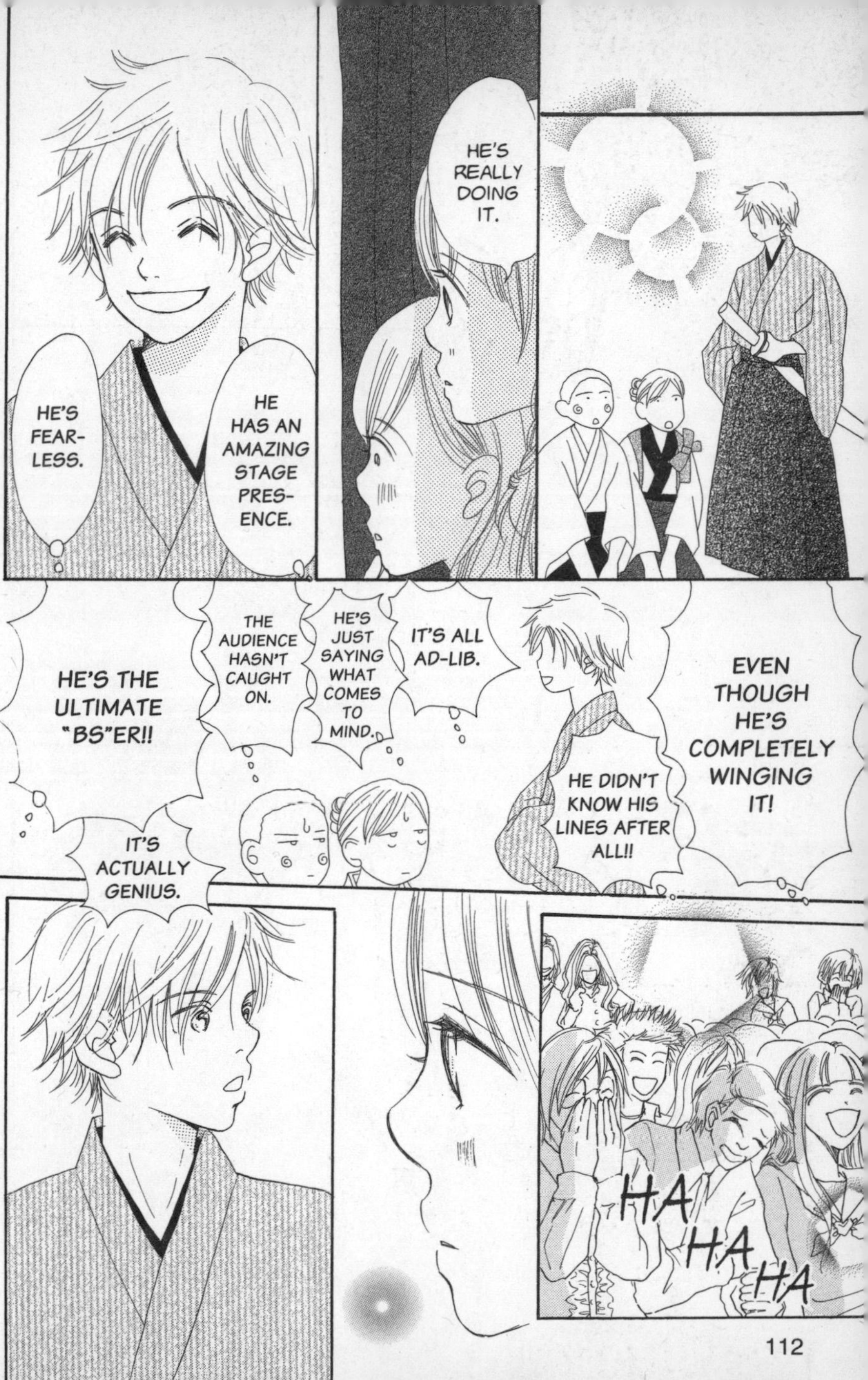
HE'S REALLY DOING IT.
HE HAS AN AMAZING STAGE PRESENCE.
HE'S FEARLESS.
EVEN THOUGH HE'S COMPLETELY WINGING IT!
HE DIDN'T KNOW HIS LINES AFTER ALL!!
IT'S ALL AD-LIB.
HE'S JUST SAYING WHAT COMES TO MIND.
THE AUDIENCE HASN'T CAUGHT ON.
HE'S THE ULTIMATE "BS"ER!!
IT'S ACTUALLY GENIUS.
HA HA HA

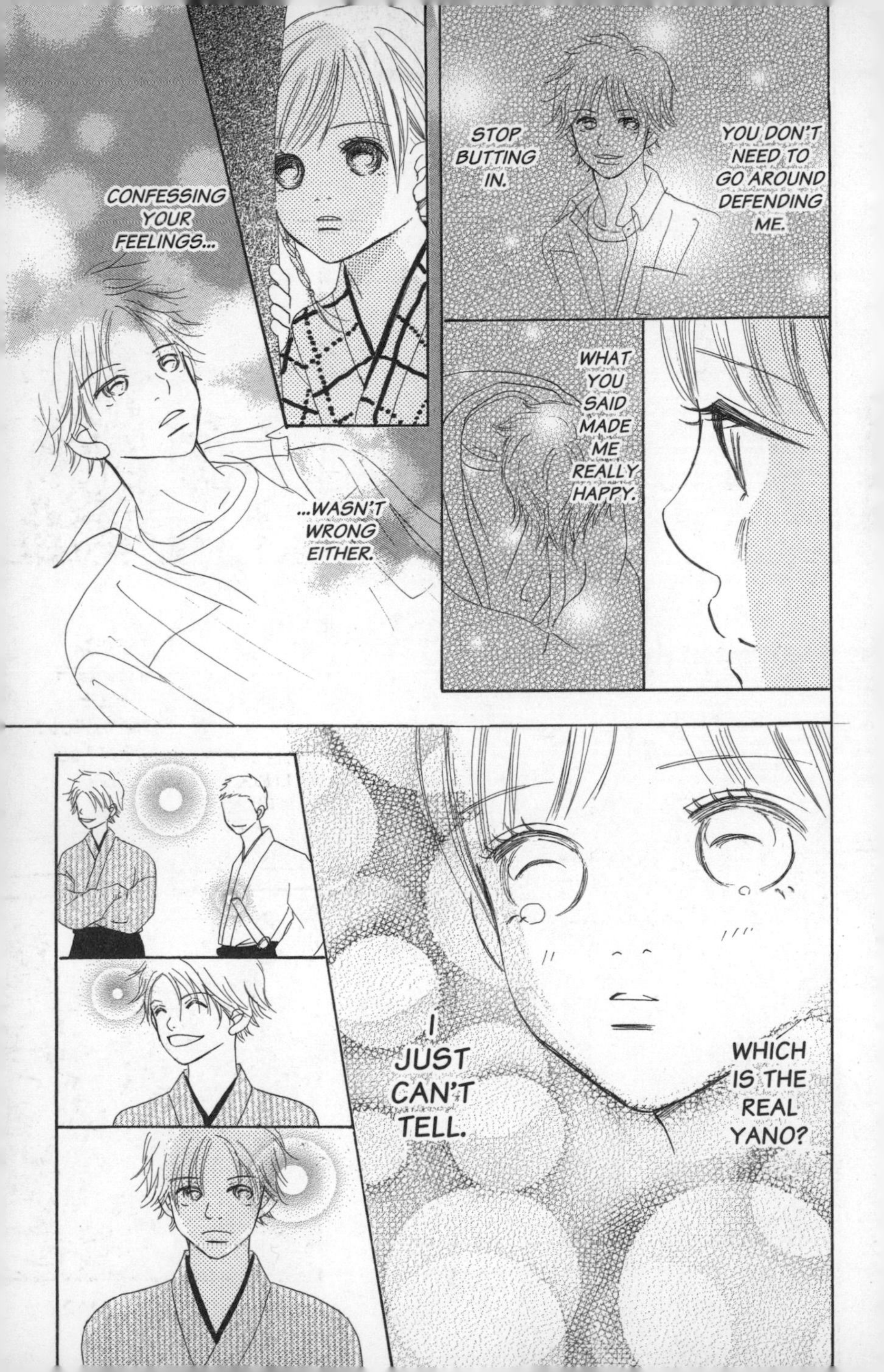
YOU DON'T NEED TO GO AROUND DEFENDING ME.
STOP BUTTING IN.
WHAT YOU SAID MADE ME REALLY HAPPY.
CONFESSING YOUR FEELINGS...
...WASN'T WRONG EITHER.
WHICH IS THE REAL YANO?
I JUST CAN'T TELL.

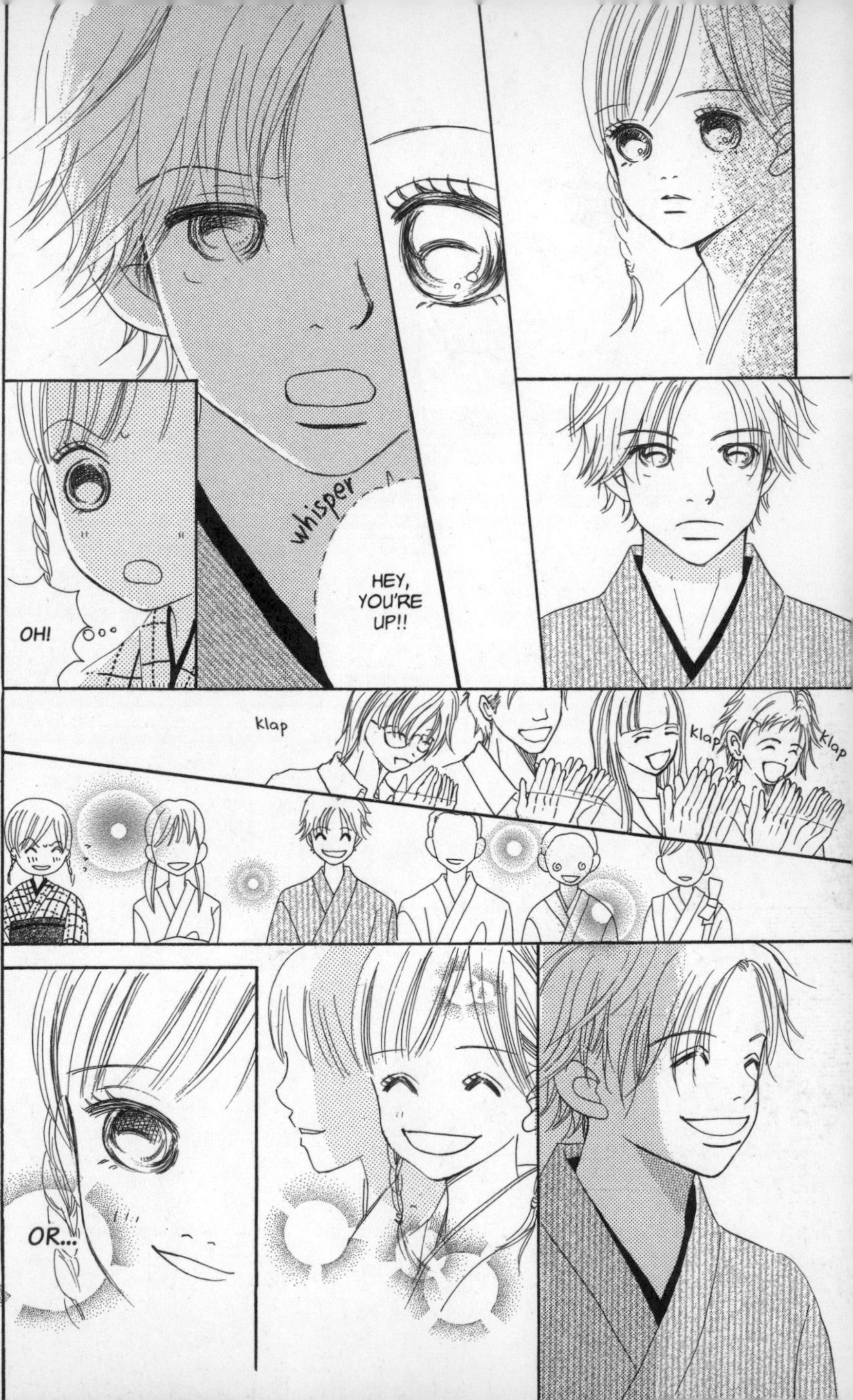

whisper
HEY, YOU'RE UP!!
OH!
Klap
Klap
Klap
OR...

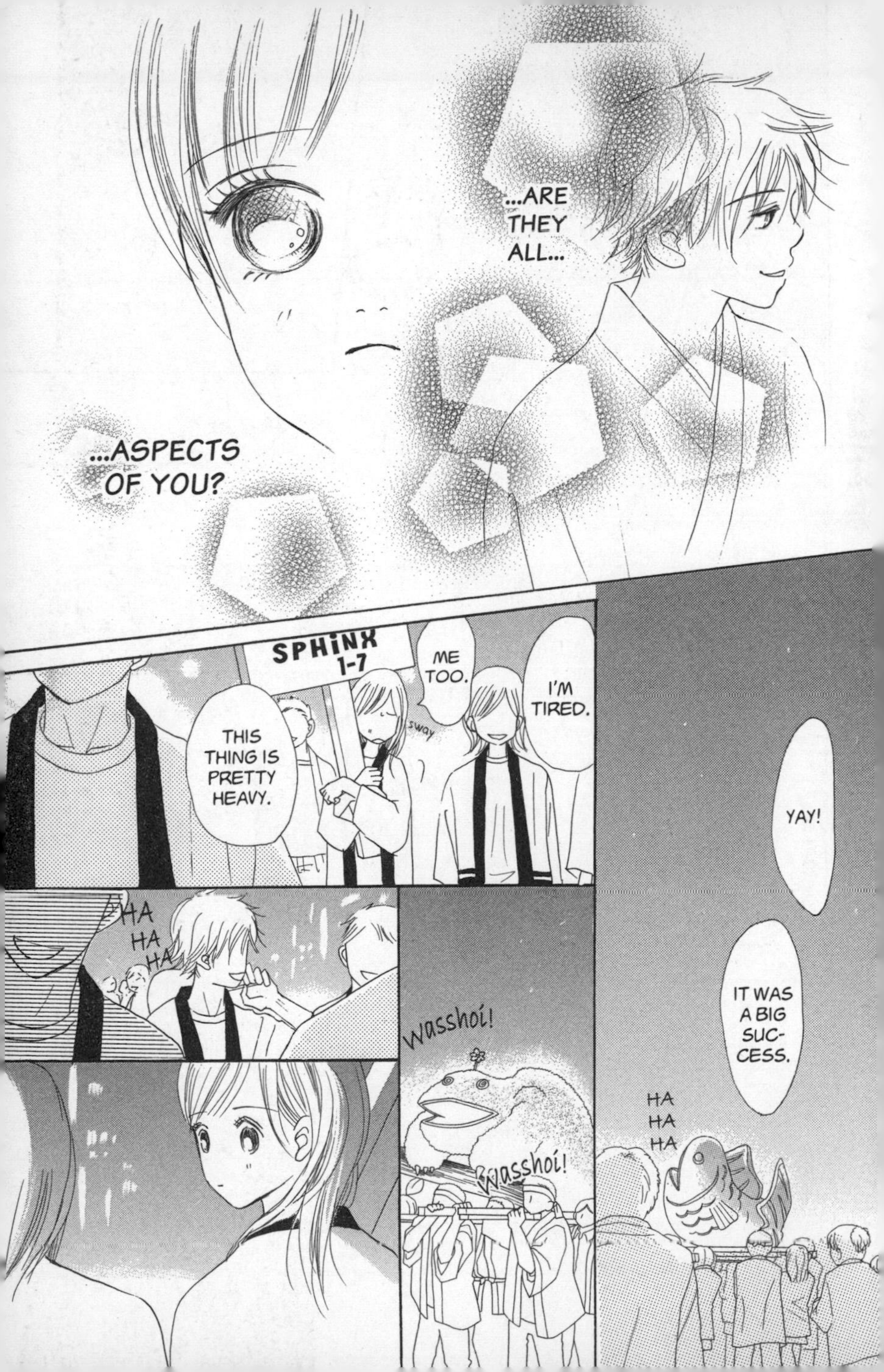
...ARE THEY ALL...
...ASPECTS OF YOU?
YAY!
IT WAS A BIG SUC-CESS.
HA HA HA
SPHINX 1-7
I'M TIRED.
ME TOO.
sway
THIS THING IS PRETTY HEAVY.
Wasshoi!
Wasshoi!
HA HA HA

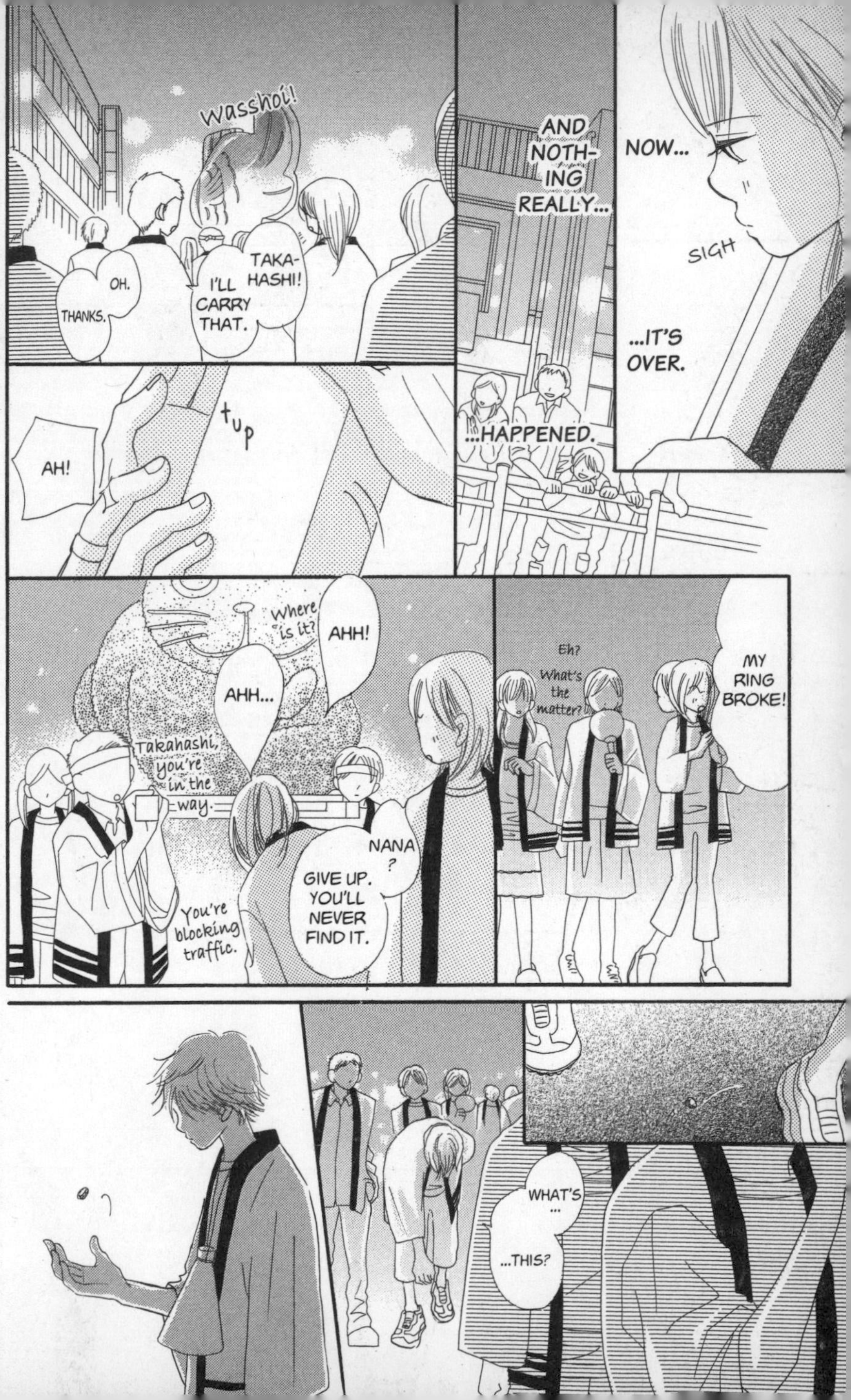
NOW...
SIGH
...IT'S OVER.
AND NOTHING REALLY...
...HAPPENED.
Wasshoi!
TAKAHASHI!
I'LL CARRY THAT.
OH. THANKS.
tup
AH!
MY RING BROKE!
Eh? What's the matter?
AHH!
Where is it?
AHH...
Takahashi, you're in the way.
NANA?
GIVE UP. YOU'LL NEVER FIND IT.
You're blocking traffic.
WHAT'S...
...THIS?

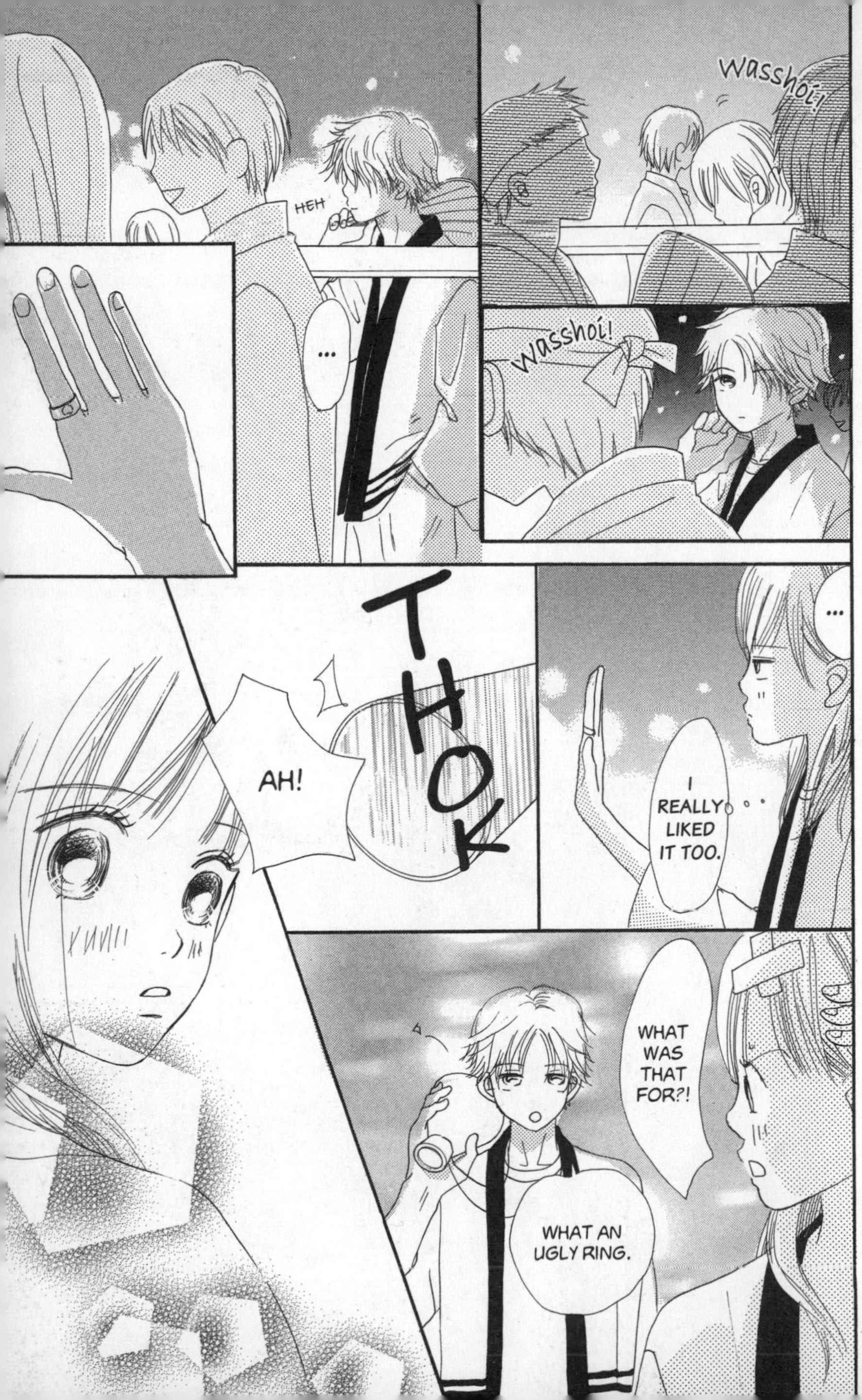
Wasshoi!
Wasshoi!
HEH
...
...
I REALLY LIKED IT TOO.
THOK
AH!
WHAT WAS THAT FOR?!
WHAT AN UGLY RING.

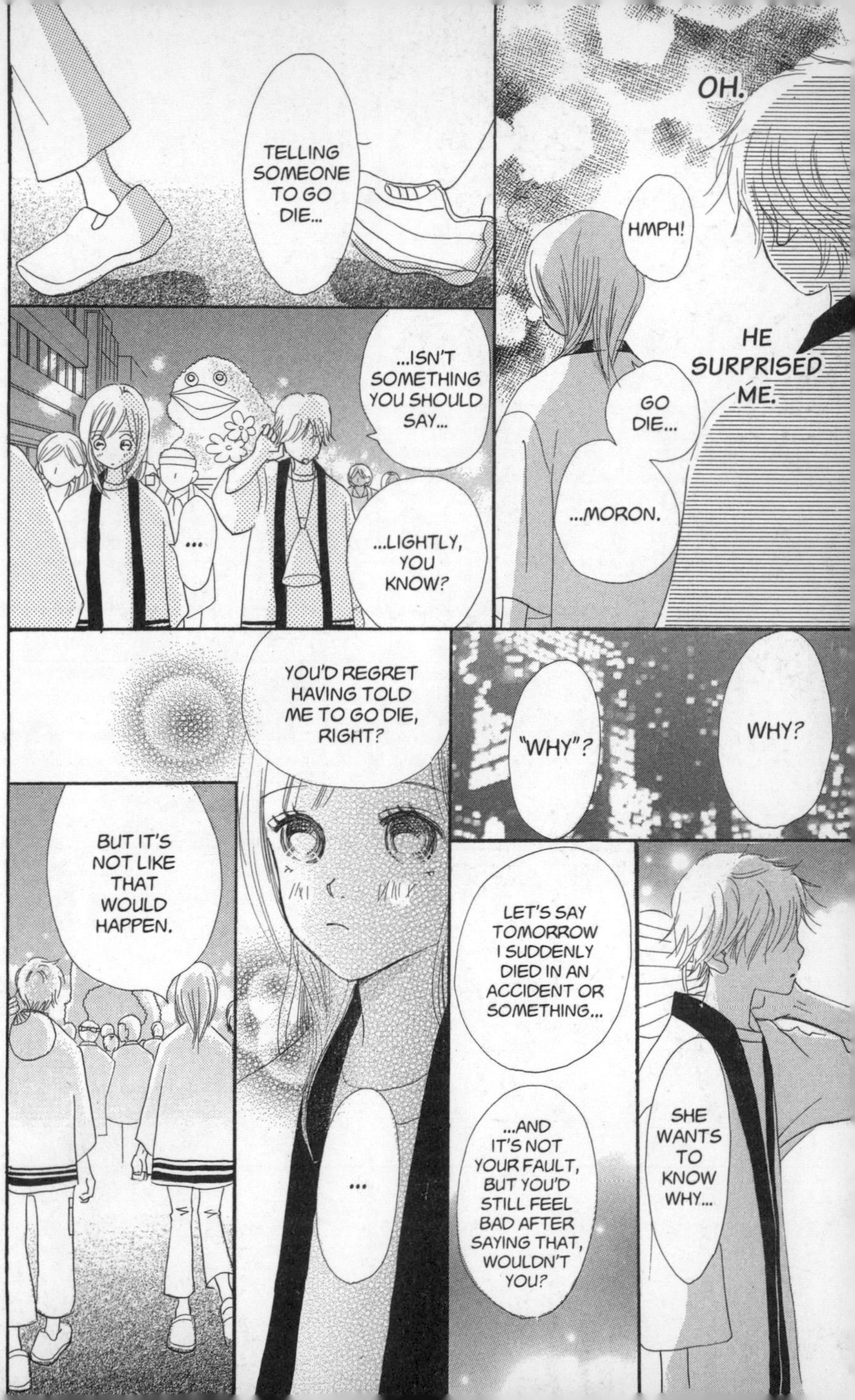
OH.
HMPH!
HE SURPRISED ME.
GO DIE...
...MORON.
TELLING SOMEONE TO GO DIE...
...ISN'T SOMETHING YOU SHOULD SAY...
...
...LIGHTLY, YOU KNOW?
WHY?
"WHY"?
SHE WANTS TO KNOW WHY...
LET'S SAY TOMORROW I SUDDENLY DIED IN AN ACCIDENT OR SOMETHING...
...AND IT'S NOT YOUR FAULT, BUT YOU'D STILL FEEL BAD AFTER SAYING THAT, WOULDN'T YOU?
YOU'D REGRET HAVING TOLD ME TO GO DIE, RIGHT?
...
BUT IT'S NOT LIKE THAT WOULD HAPPEN.

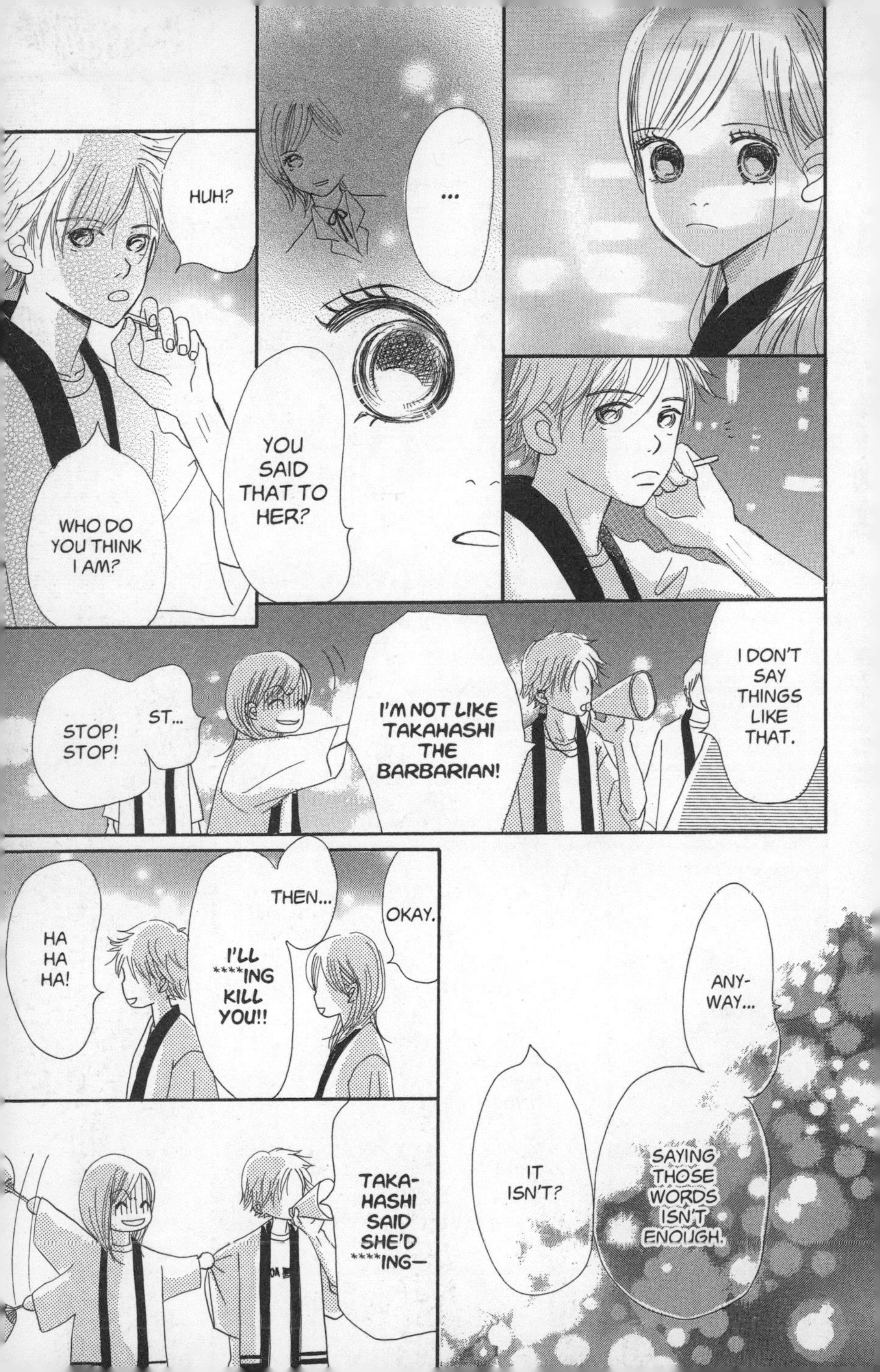
...
YOU SAID THAT TO HER?
HUH?
WHO DO YOU THINK I AM?
I DON'T SAY THINGS LIKE THAT.
I'M NOT LIKE TAKAHASHI THE BARBARIAN!
ST...
STOP! STOP!
ANY-WAY...
SAYING THOSE WORDS ISN'T ENOUGH.
IT ISN'T?
OKAY.
THEN...
I'LL ****ING KILL YOU!!
HA HA HA!
TAKA-HASHI SAID SHE'D ****ING—

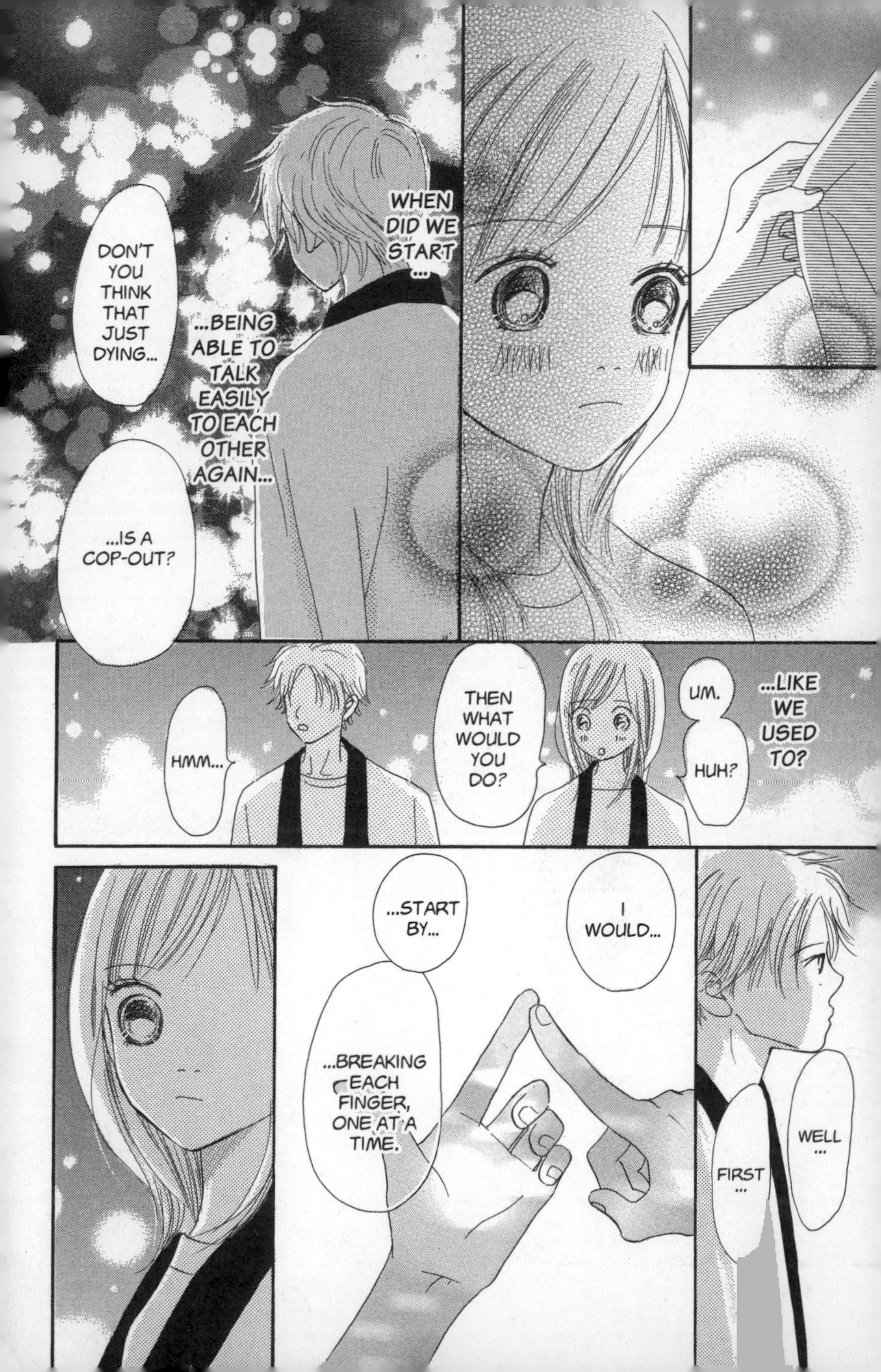
WHEN DID WE START...
...BEING ABLE TO TALK EASILY TO EACH OTHER AGAIN...
DON'T YOU THINK THAT JUST DYING...
...IS A COP-OUT?
...LIKE WE USED TO?
UM.
HUH?
THEN WHAT WOULD YOU DO?
HMM...
WELL...
FIRST...
I WOULD...
...START BY...
...BREAKING EACH FINGER, ONE AT A TIME.

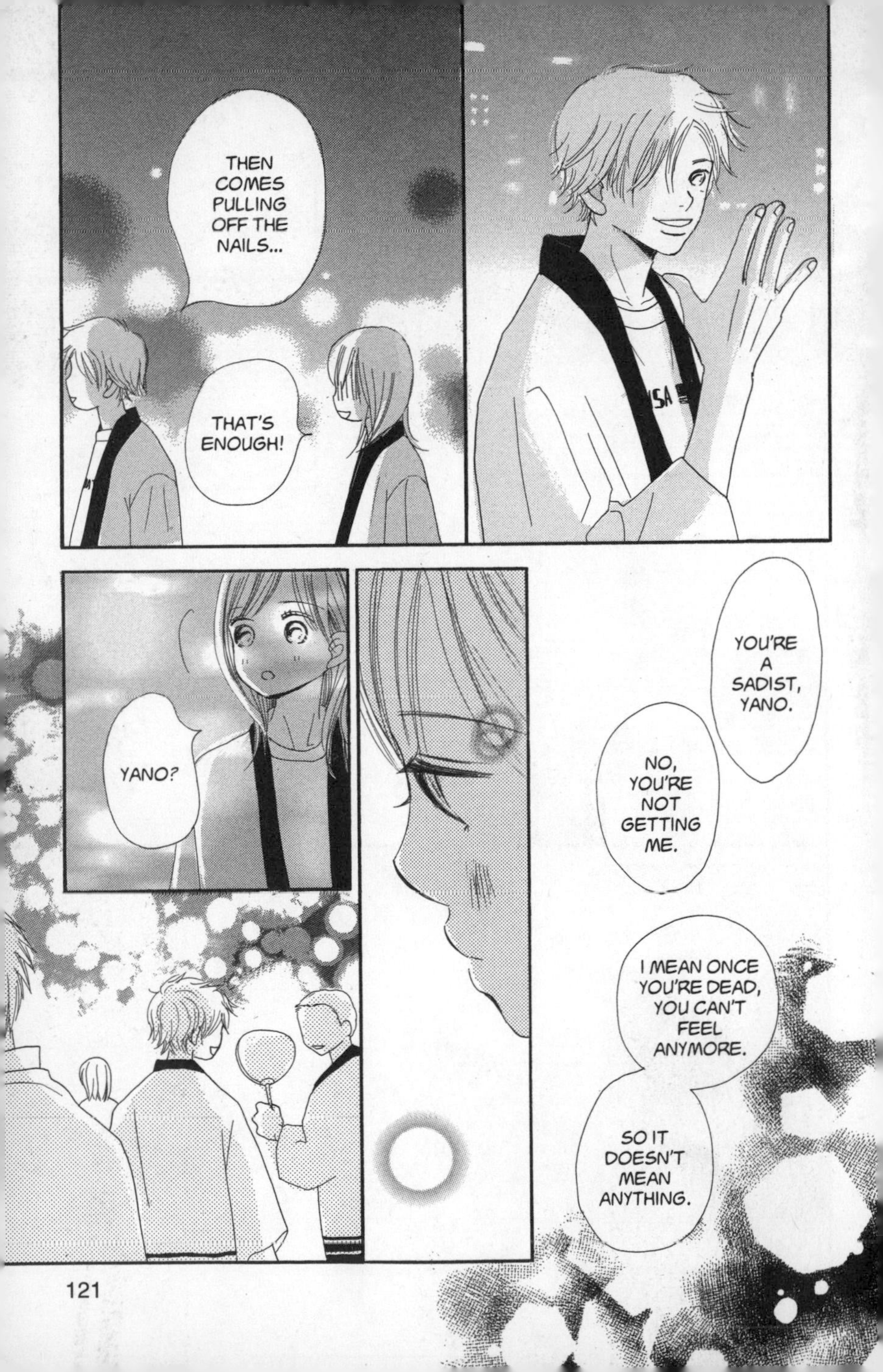
THEN COMES PULLING OFF THE NAILS...
THAT'S ENOUGH!
YOU'RE A SADIST, YANO.
NO, YOU'RE NOT GETTING ME.
I MEAN ONCE YOU'RE DEAD, YOU CAN'T FEEL ANYMORE.
SO IT DOESN'T MEAN ANYTHING.
YANO?

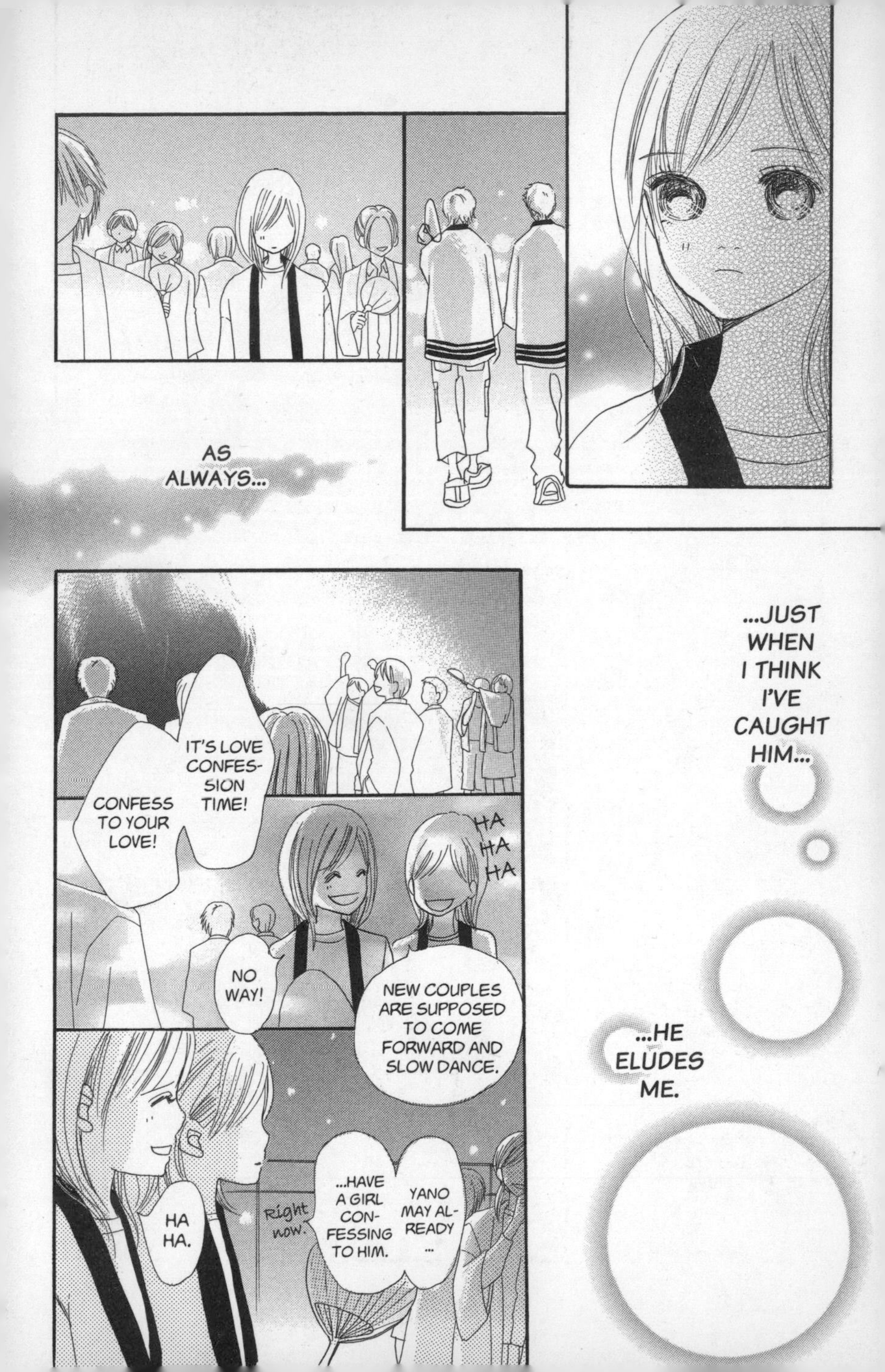
AS ALWAYS...
...JUST WHEN I THINK I'VE CAUGHT HIM...
...HE ELUDES ME.
IT'S LOVE CONFES-SION TIME!
CONFESS TO YOUR LOVE!
HA HA HA
NEW COUPLES ARE SUPPOSED TO COME FORWARD AND SLOW DANCE.
NO WAY!
YANO MAY AL-READY ...
...HAVE A GIRL CON-FESSING TO HIM.
Right now.
HA HA.

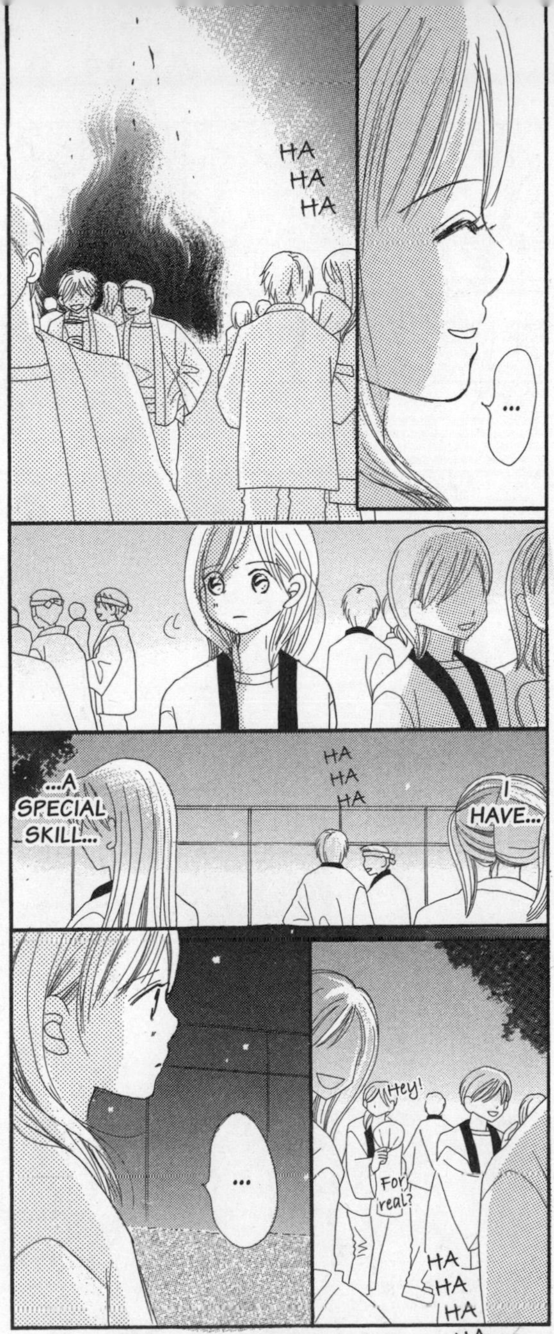
...
HA
HA
HA
I HAVE...
HA
HA
HA
...A SPECIAL SKILL...
Hey!
For real?
HA
HA
HA
HA
...

Juri (little sister)
She hasn't dropped by my place to help me lately.

Hagi (my editor)
She's always smiling.

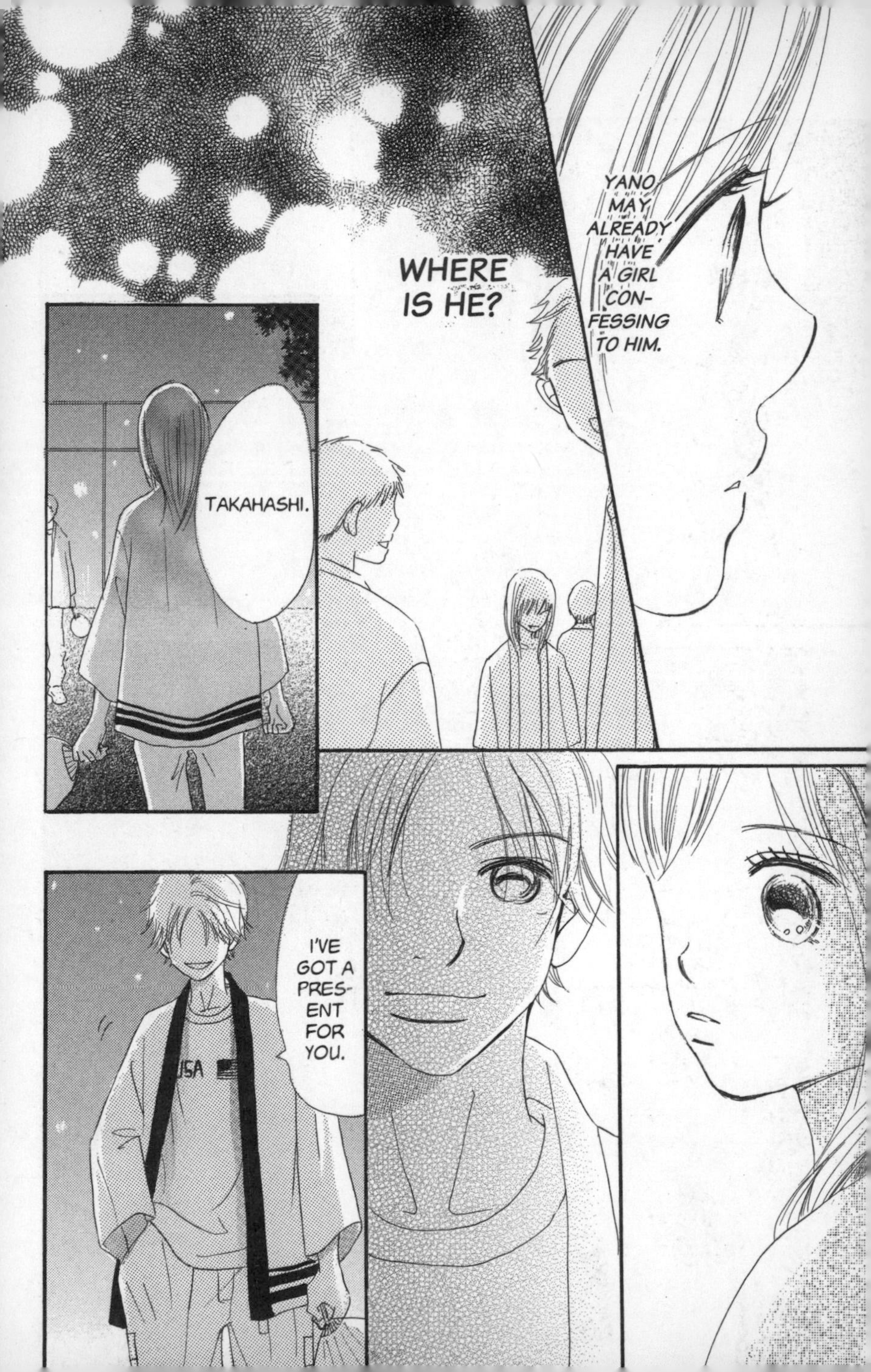
YANO MAY ALREADY HAVE A GIRL CON-FESSING TO HIM.
WHERE IS HE?
TAKAHASHI.
I'VE GOT A PRES-ENT FOR YOU.

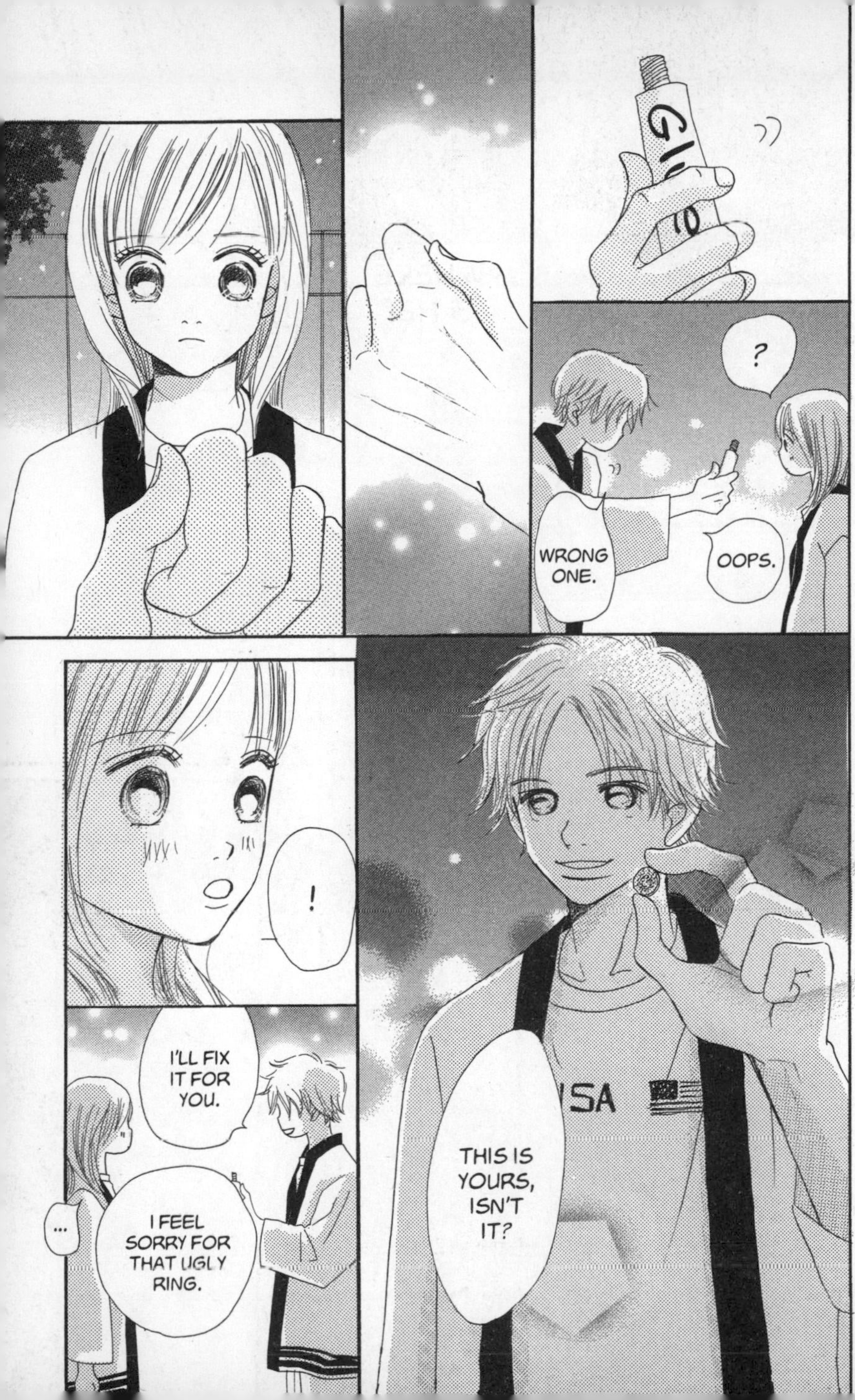
?
OOPS.
WRONG ONE.
THIS IS YOURS, ISN'T IT?
!
I'LL FIX IT FOR YOU.
I FEEL SORRY FOR THAT UGLY RING.
...

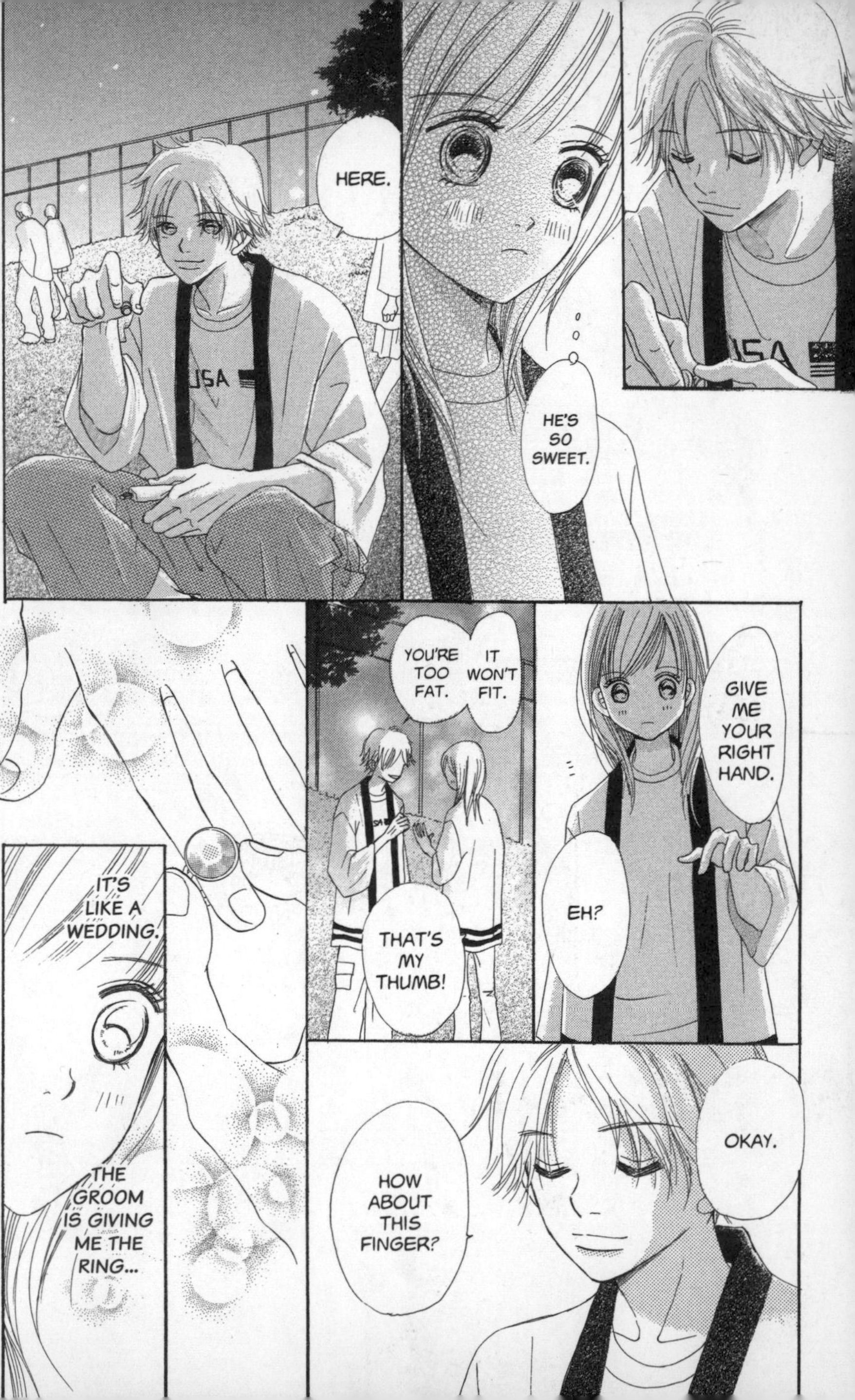
HE'S SO SWEET.
HERE.
GIVE ME YOUR RIGHT HAND.
EH?
IT WON'T FIT.
YOU'RE TOO FAT.
THAT'S MY THUMB!
OKAY.
HOW ABOUT THIS FINGER?
IT'S LIKE A WEDDING.
THE GROOM IS GIVING ME THE RING...

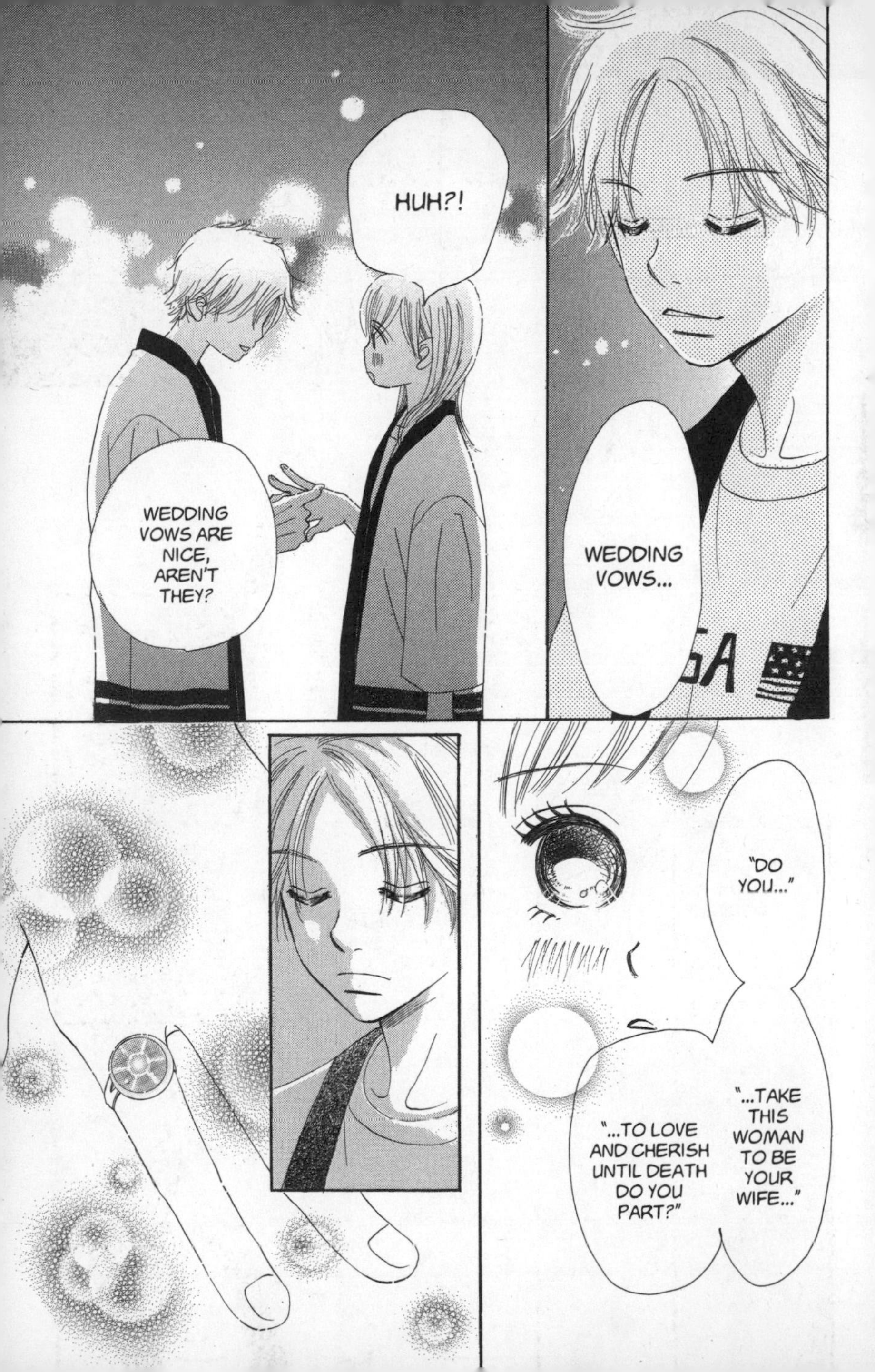
WEDDING VOWS...
HUH?!
WEDDING VOWS ARE NICE, AREN'T THEY?
"DO YOU..."
"...TAKE THIS WOMAN TO BE YOUR WIFE..."
"...TO LOVE AND CHERISH UNTIL DEATH DO YOU PART?"

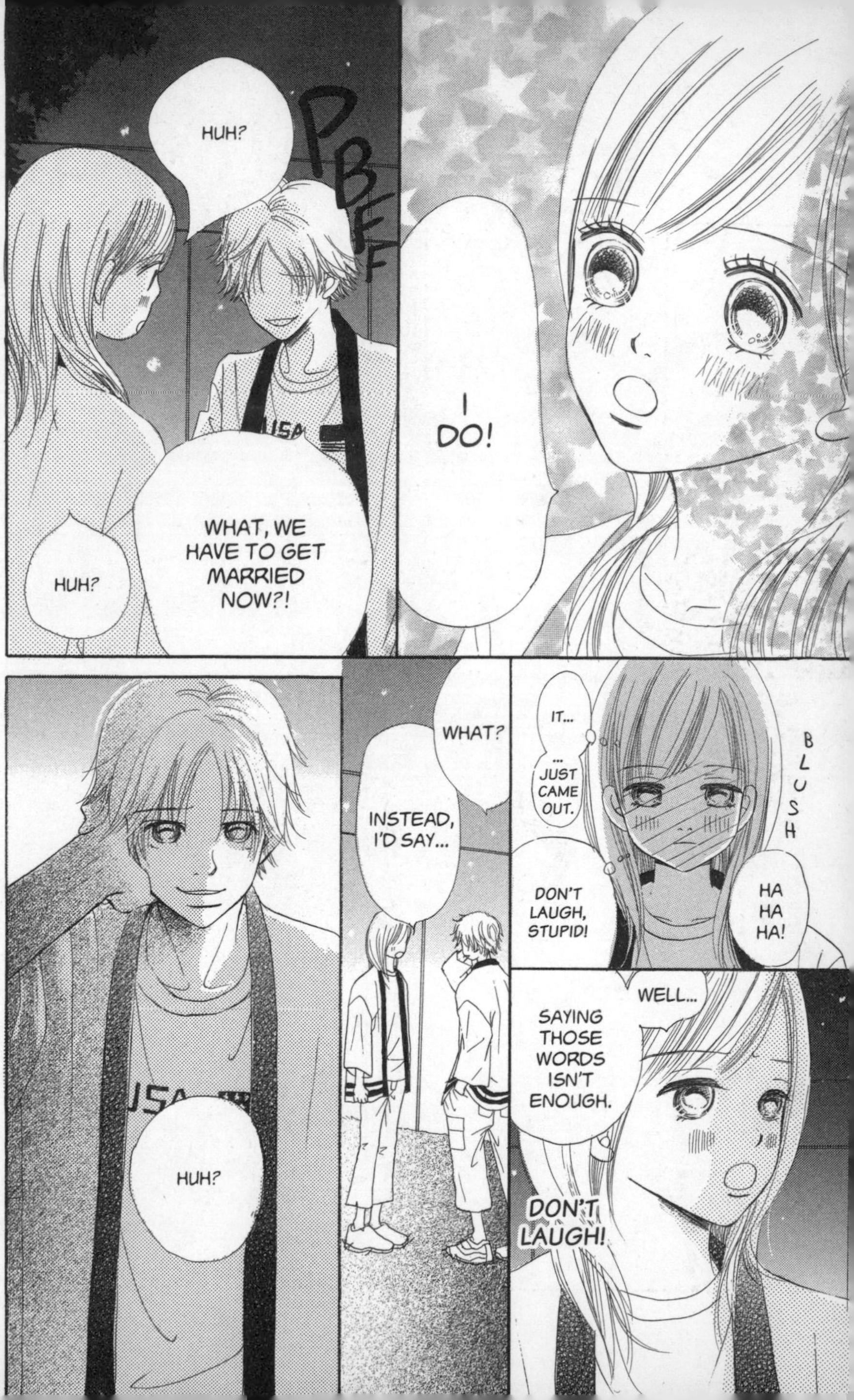
I DO!
PBFF
HUH?
WHAT, WE HAVE TO GET MARRIED NOW?!
HUH?
BLUSH
IT...
... JUST CAME OUT.
HA HA HA!
DON'T LAUGH, STUPID!
WELL...
SAYING THOSE WORDS ISN'T ENOUGH.
DON'T LAUGH!
WHAT?
INSTEAD, I'D SAY...
HUH?

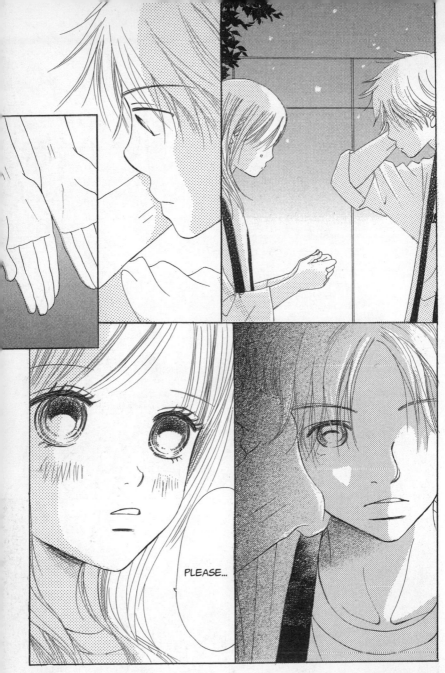

PLEASE...

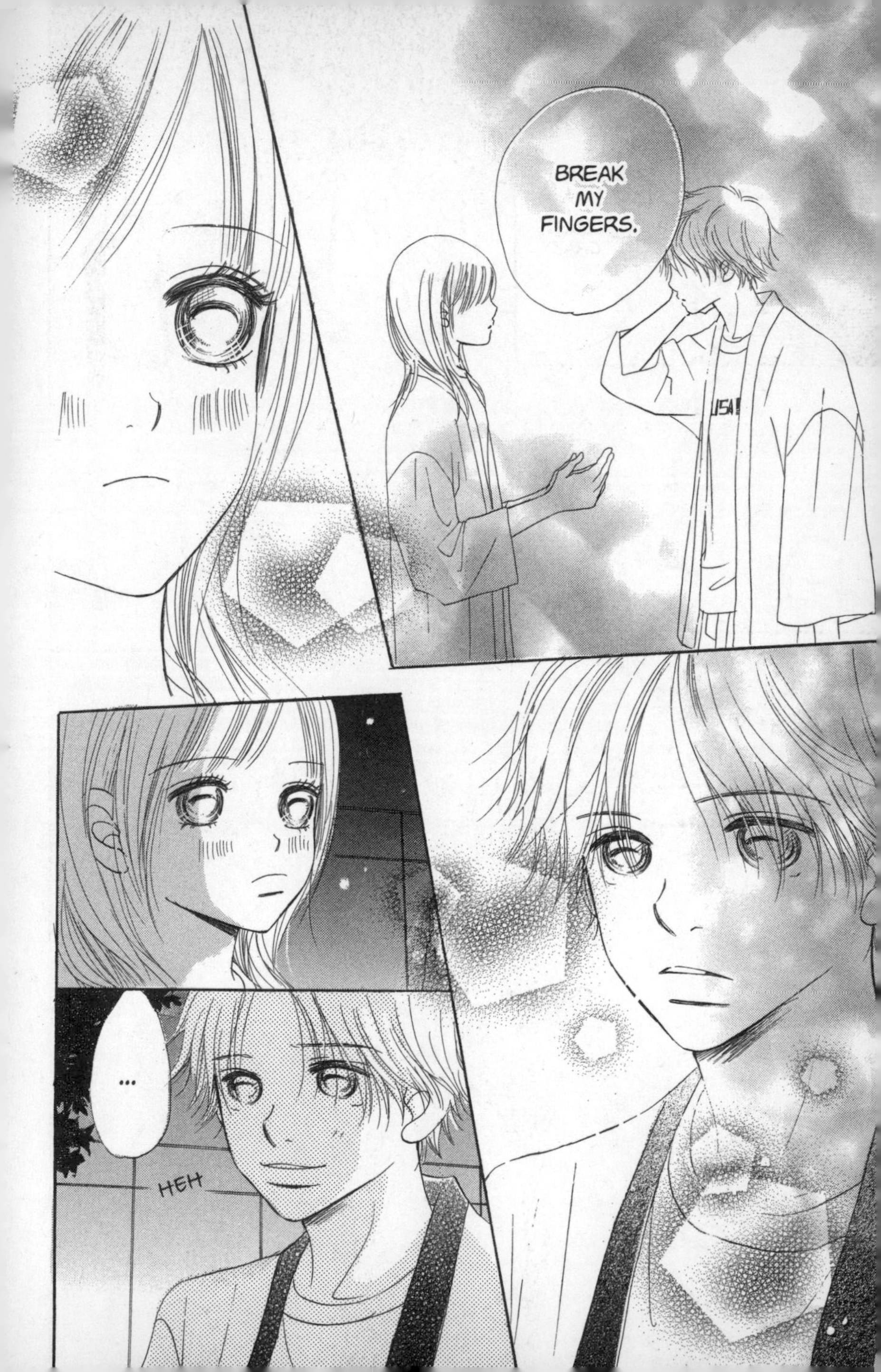
BREAK MY FINGERS.
...
HEH

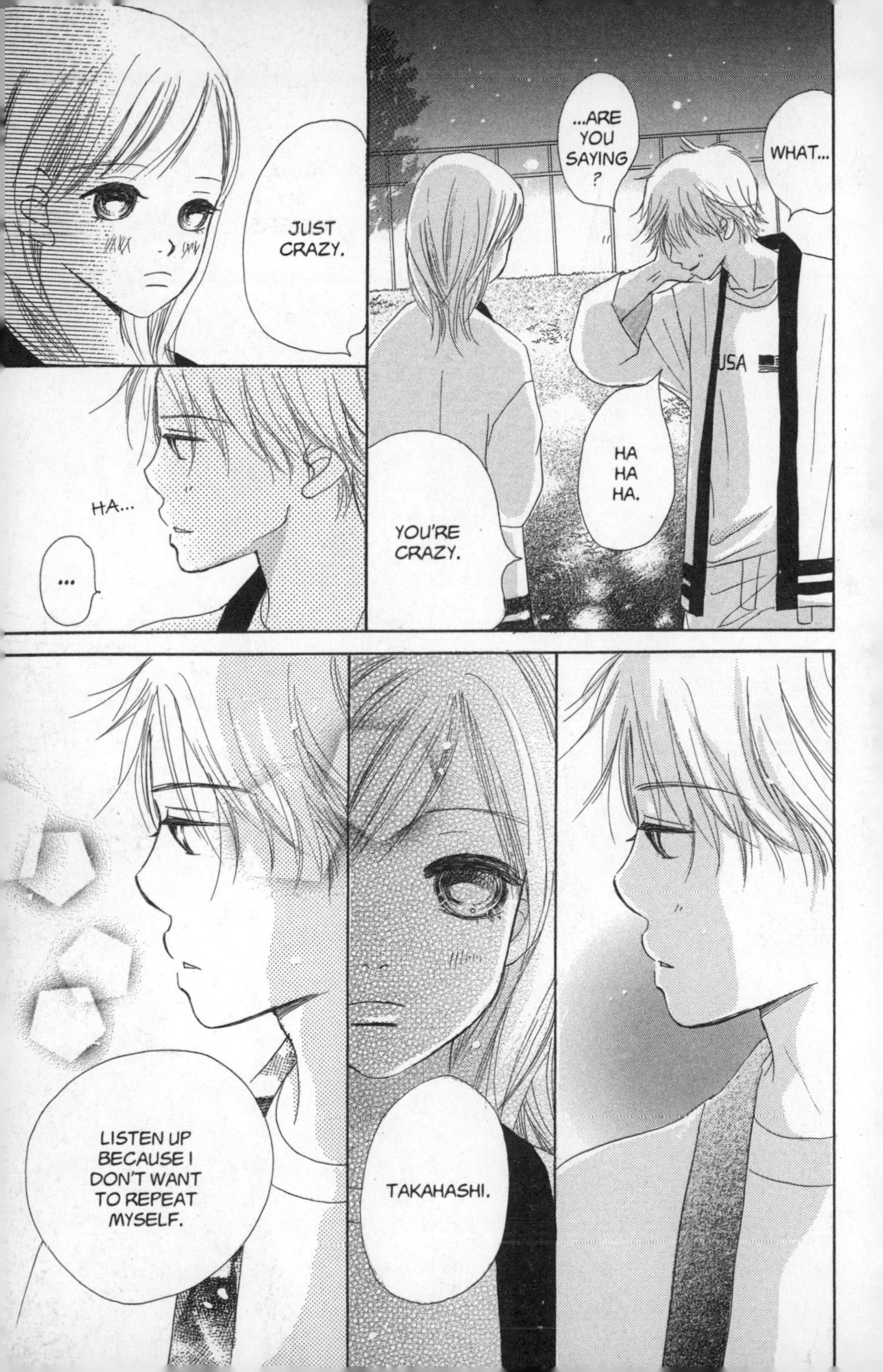
WHAT...
...ARE YOU SAYING?
HA HA HA.
YOU'RE CRAZY.
JUST CRAZY.
HA...
...
TAKAHASHI.
LISTEN UP BECAUSE I DON'T WANT TO REPEAT MYSELF.

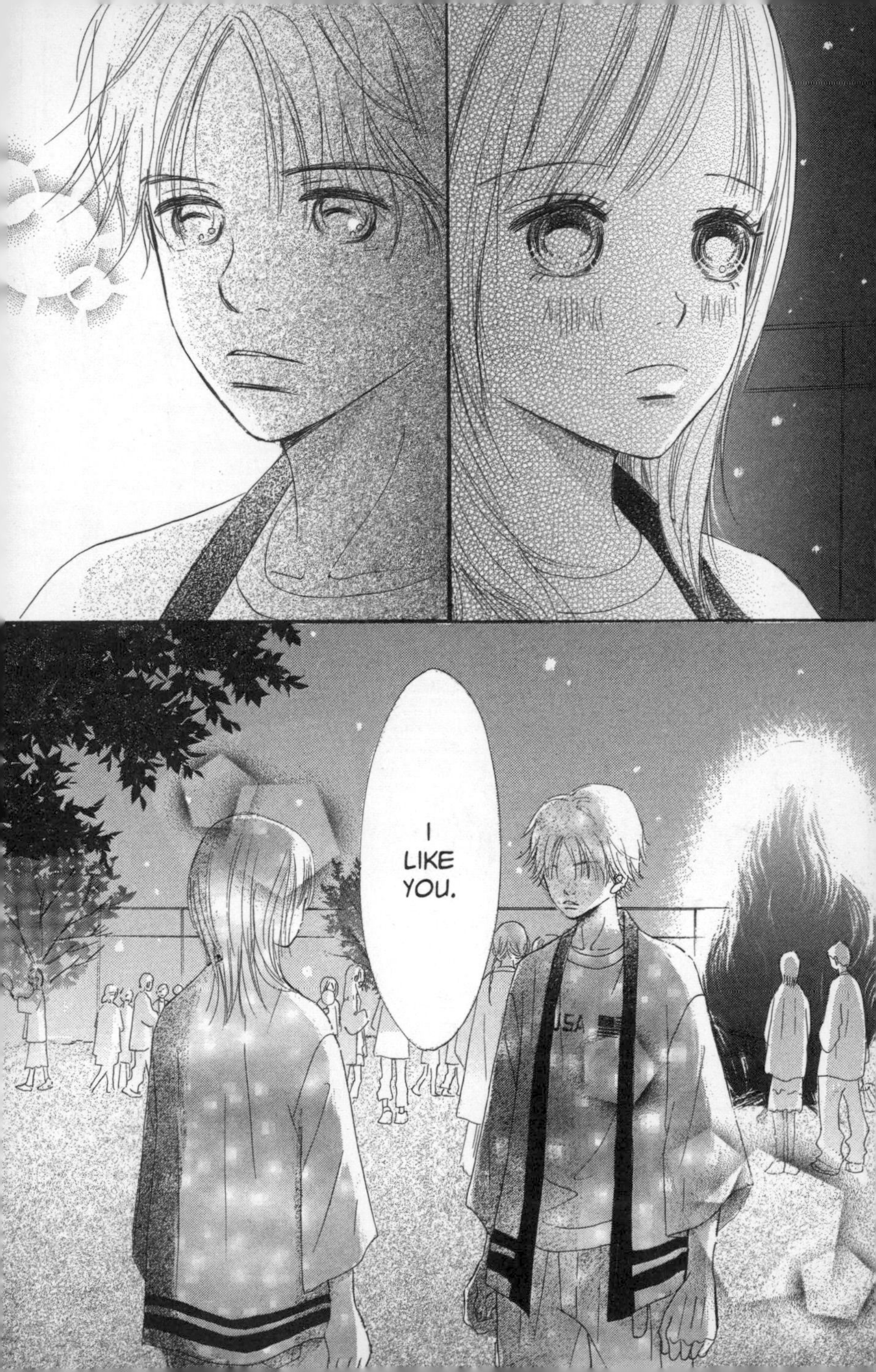
I LIKE YOU.

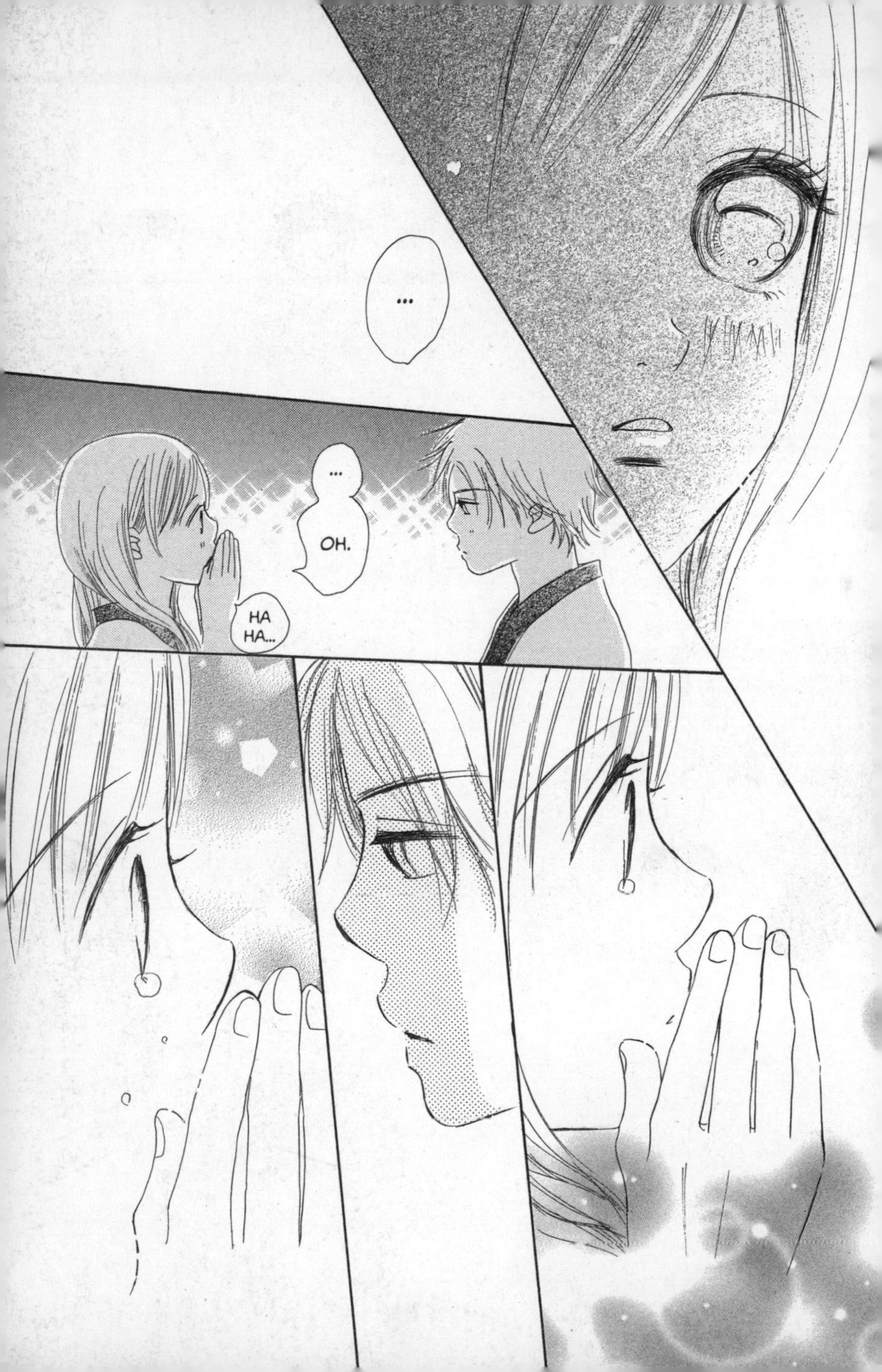
...
...
OH.
HA HA...

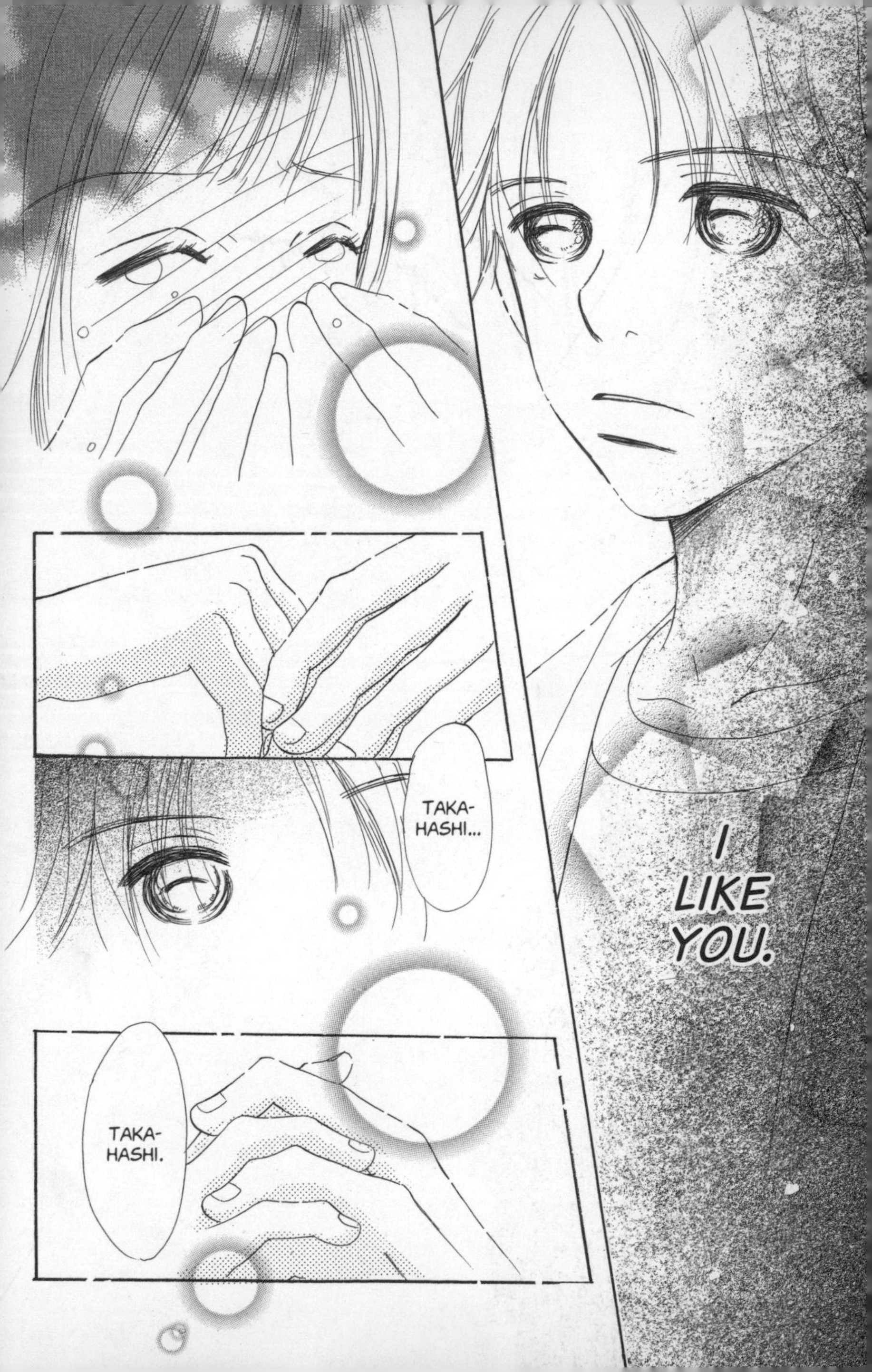
I LIKE YOU.
TAKA-HASHI...
TAKA-HASHI.

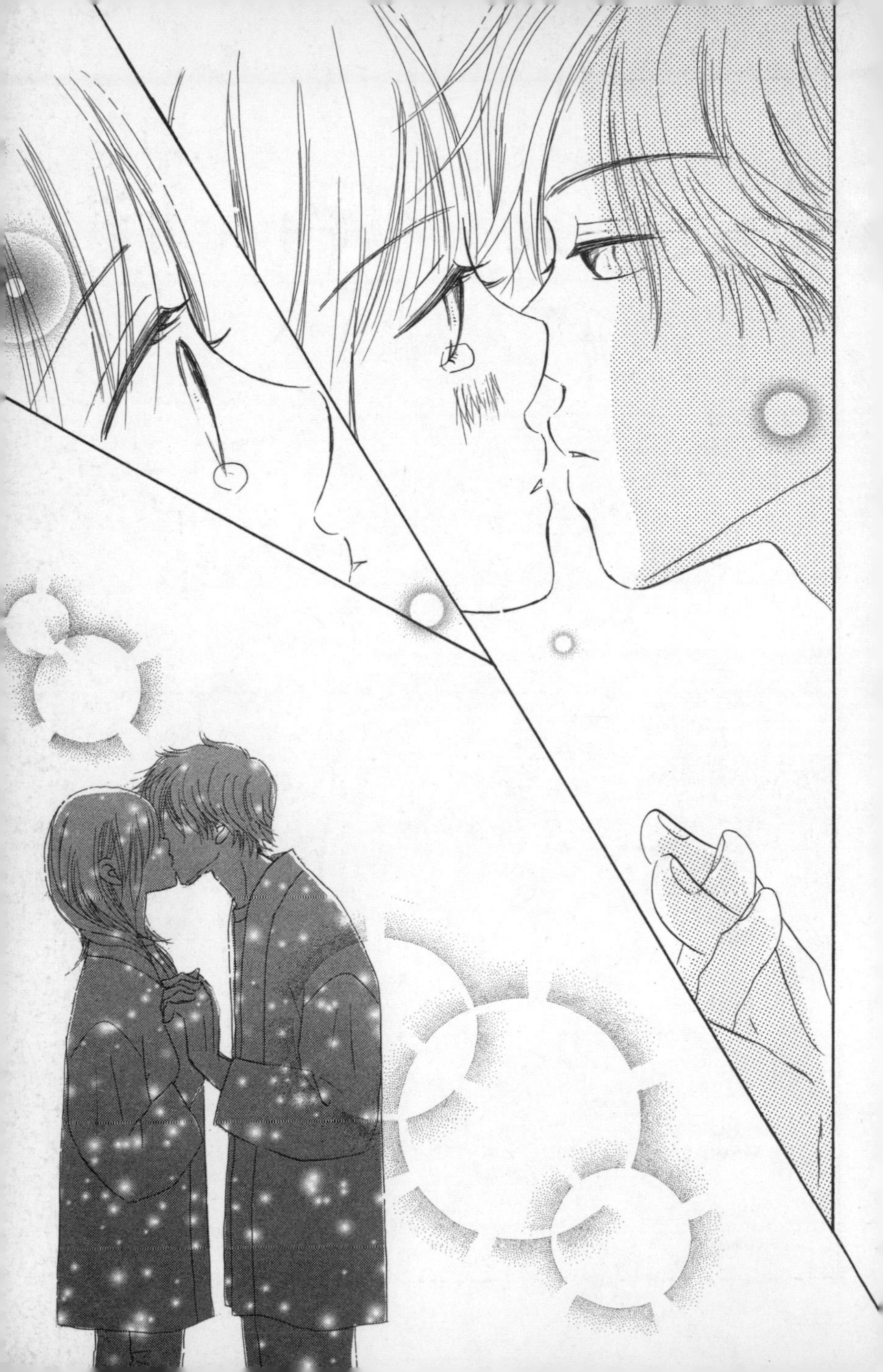

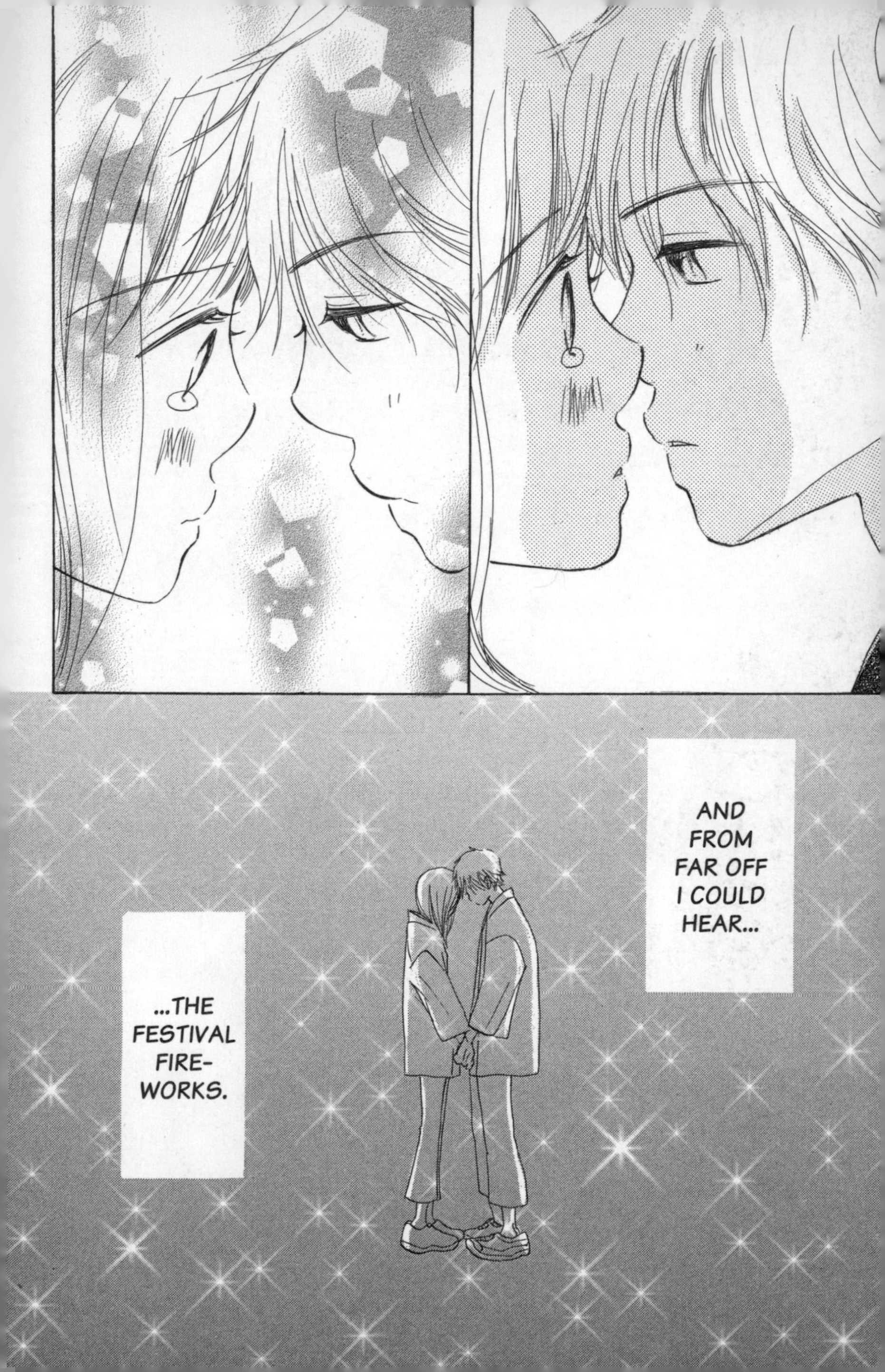
AND FROM FAR OFF I COULD HEAR...
...THE FESTIVAL FIRE-WORKS.

Chapter 8

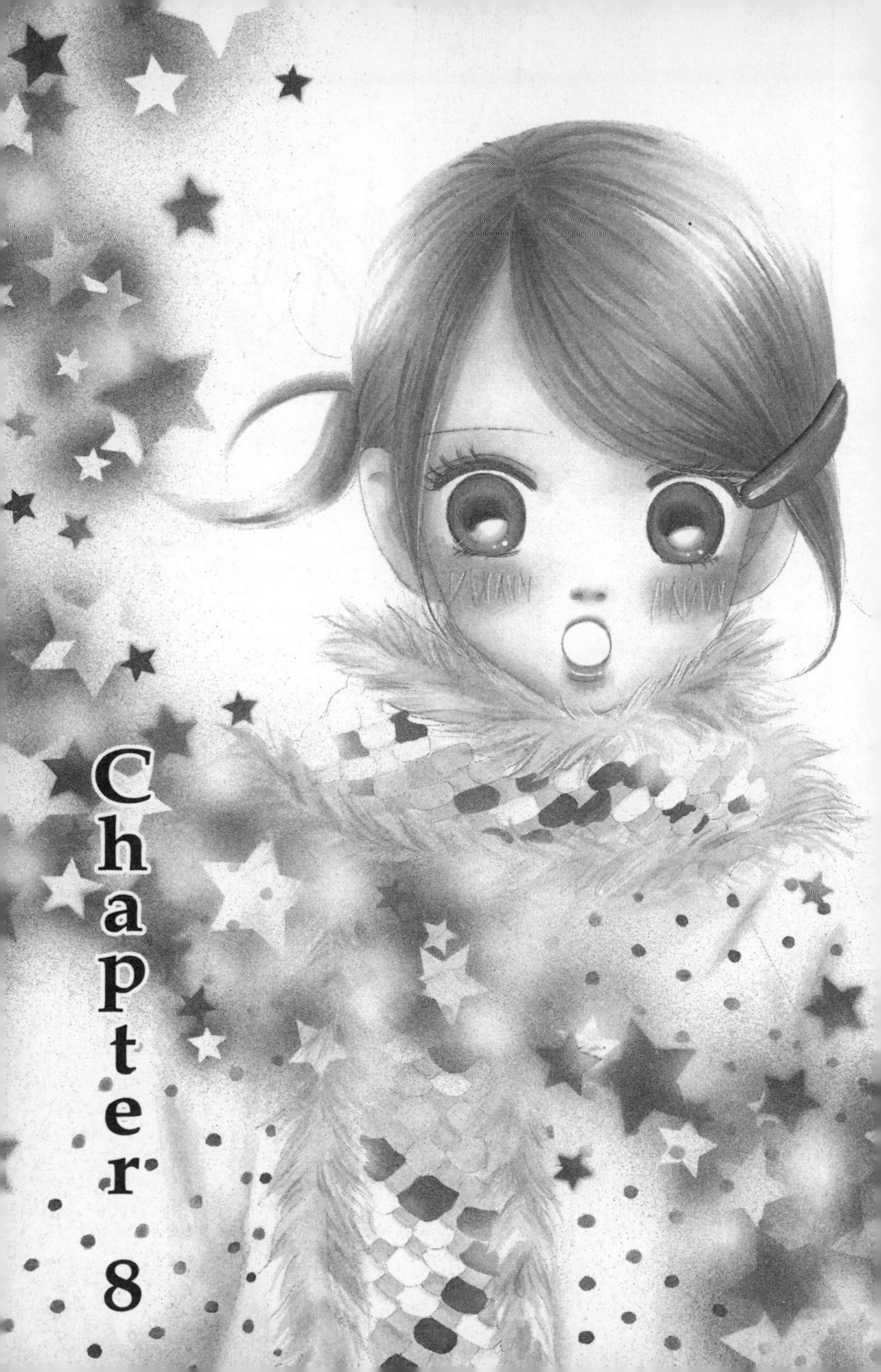

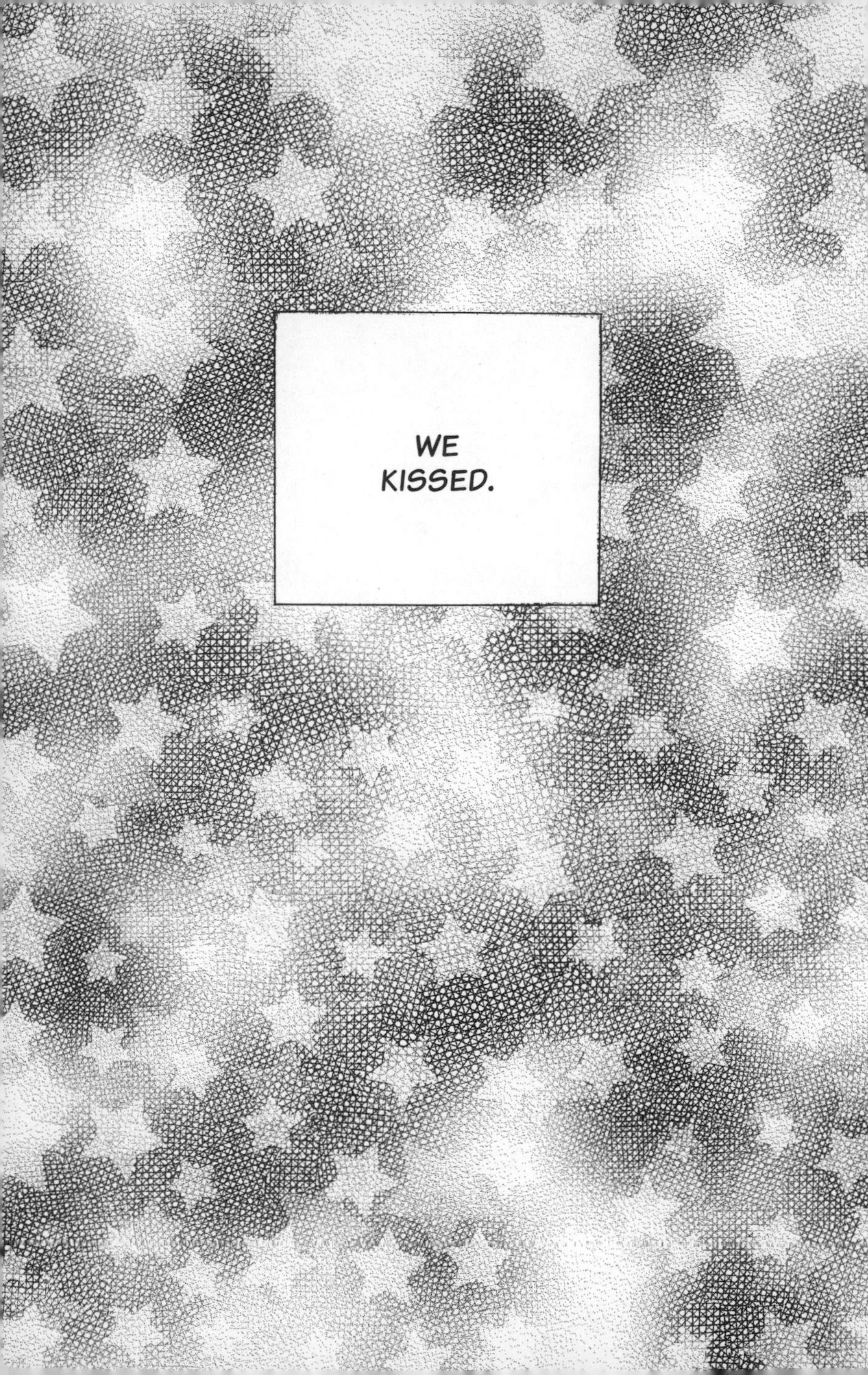
WE KISSED.

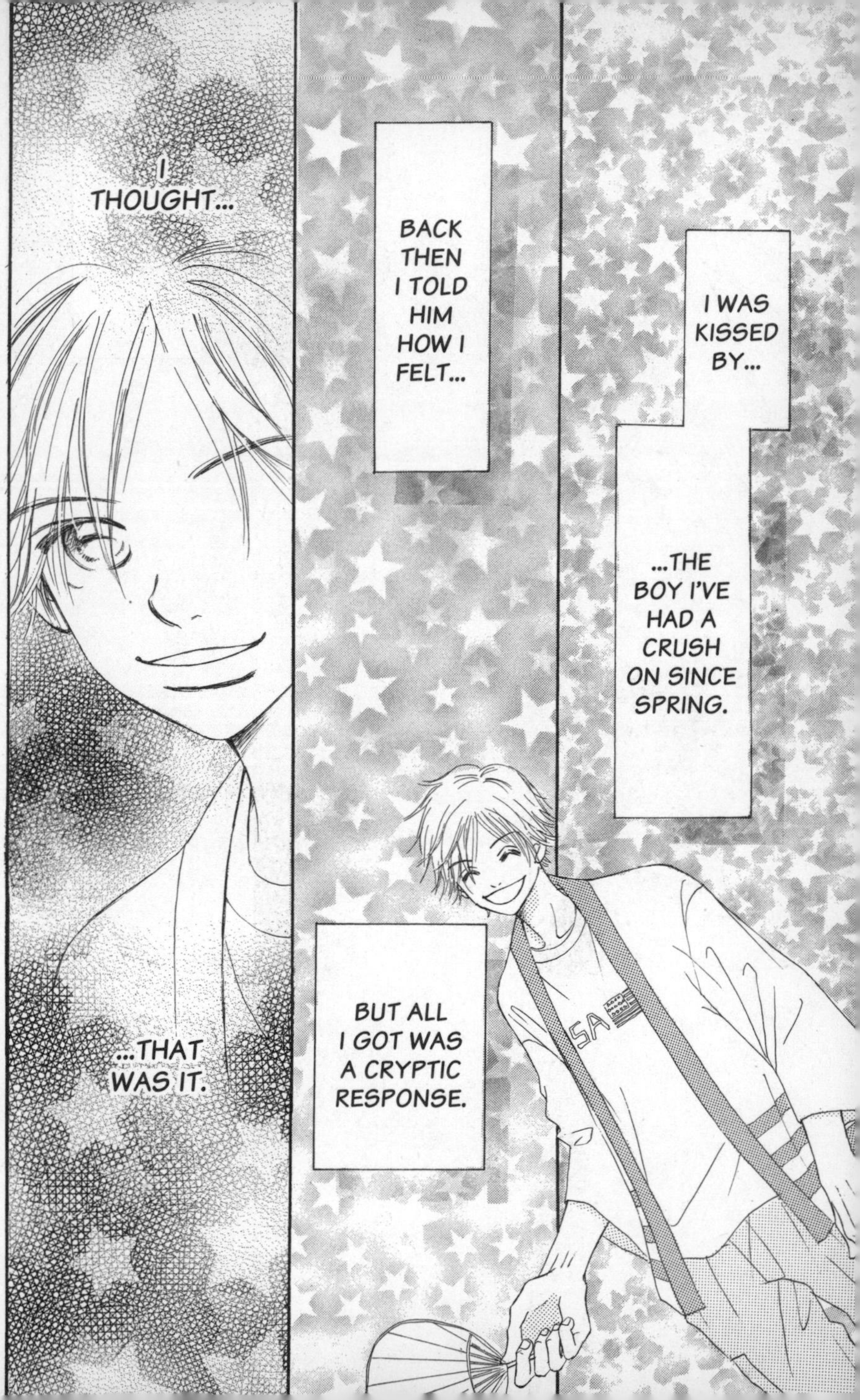
I WAS KISSED BY...
...THE BOY I'VE HAD A CRUSH ON SINCE SPRING.
BACK THEN I TOLD HIM HOW I FELT...
BUT ALL I GOT WAS A CRYPTIC RESPONSE.
I THOUGHT...
...THAT WAS IT.

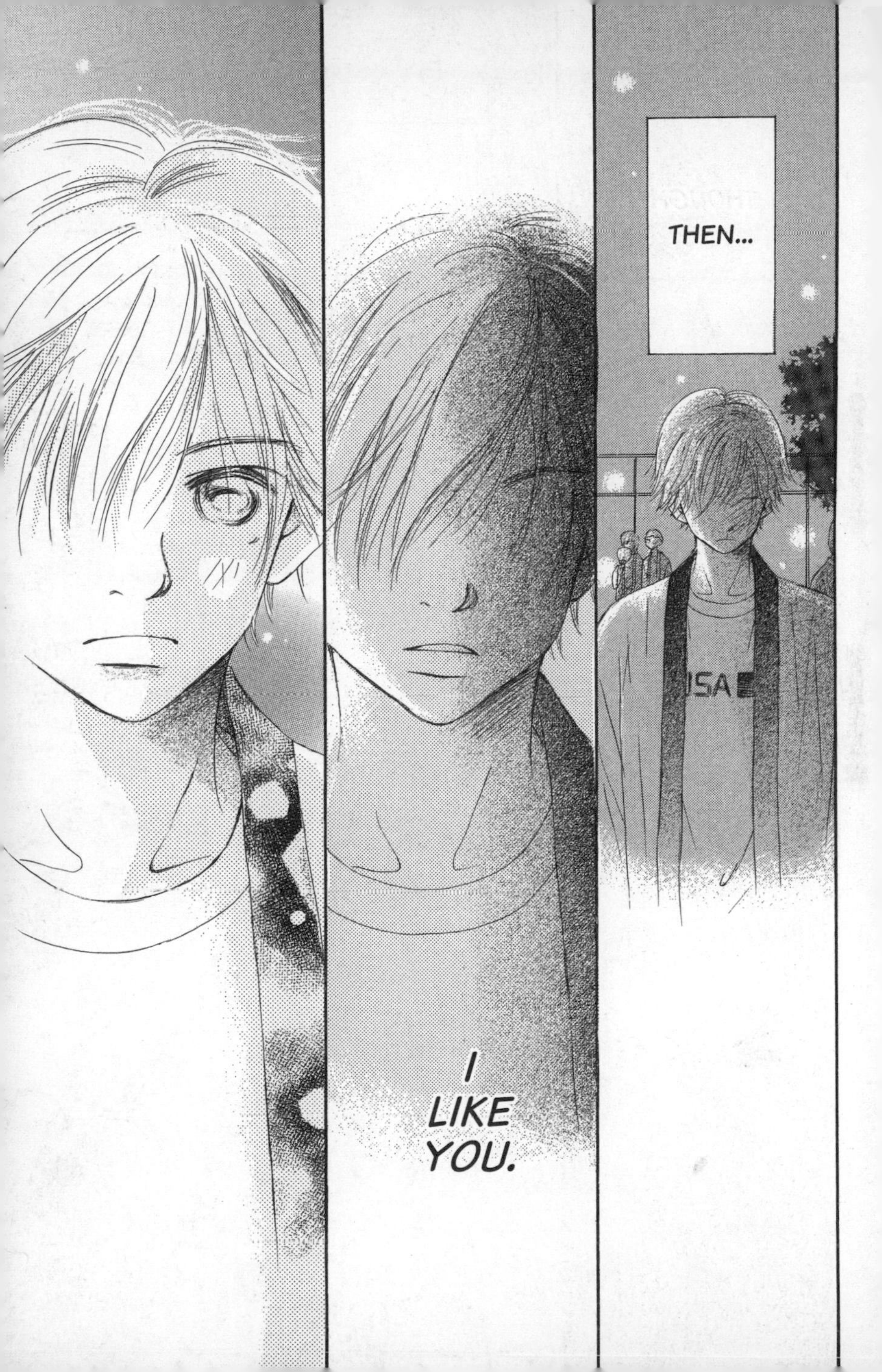
THEN...
I LIKE YOU.

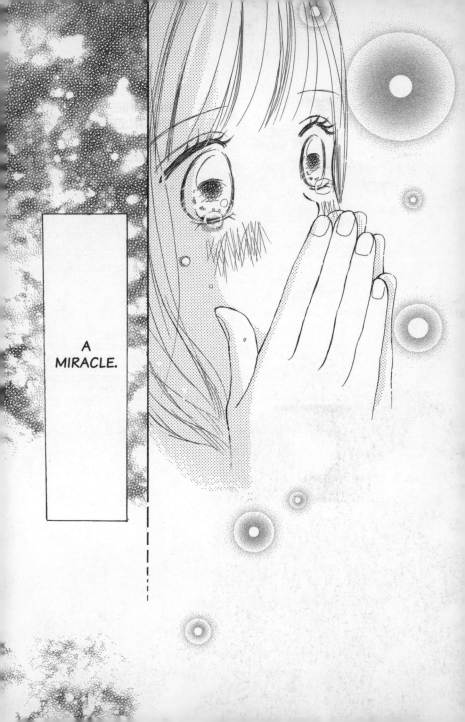

A
MIRACLE.

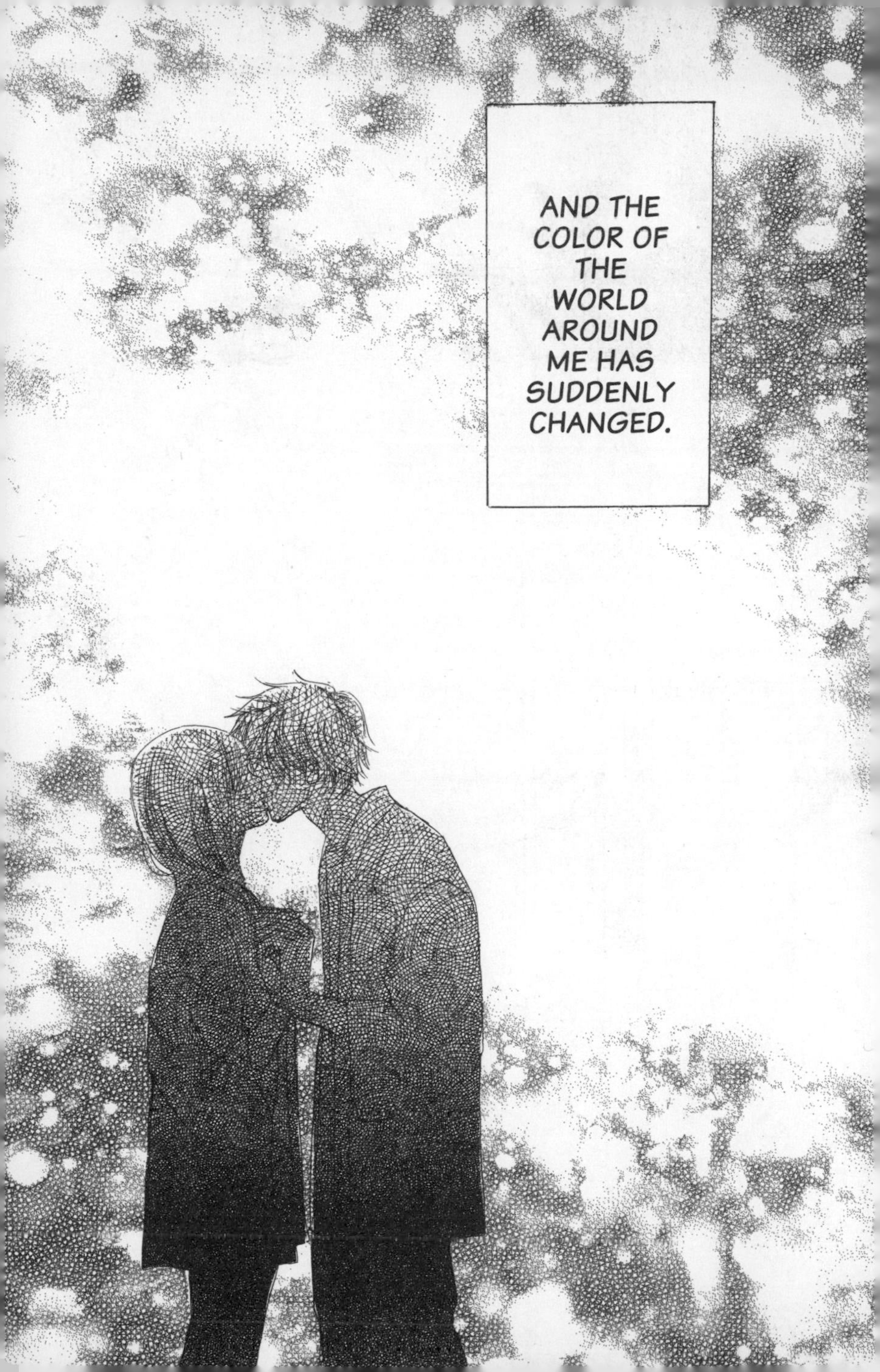
AND THE COLOR OF THE WORLD AROUND ME HAS SUDDENLY CHANGED.

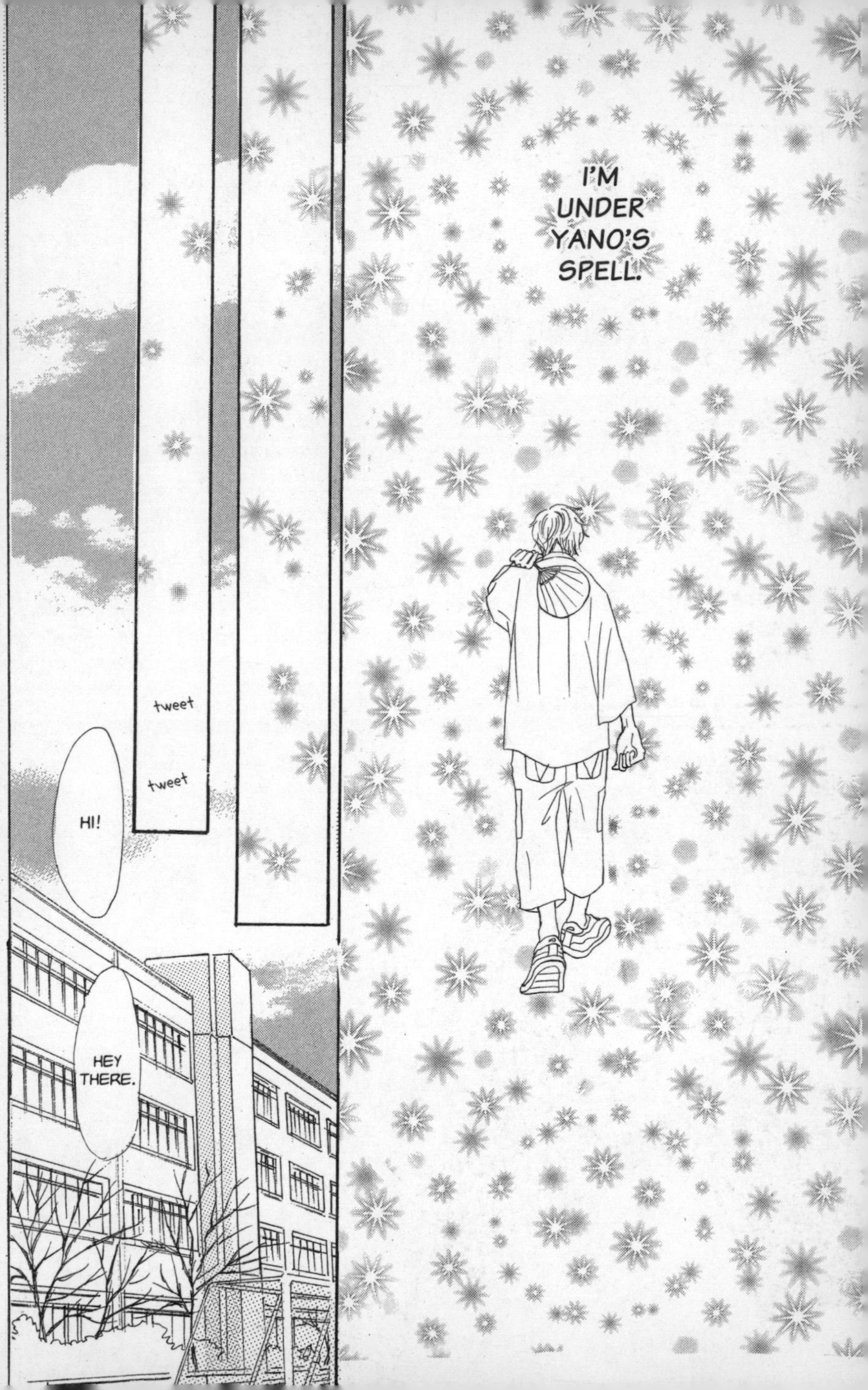
I'M UNDER YANO'S SPELL.
tweet
tweet
HI!
HEY THERE.

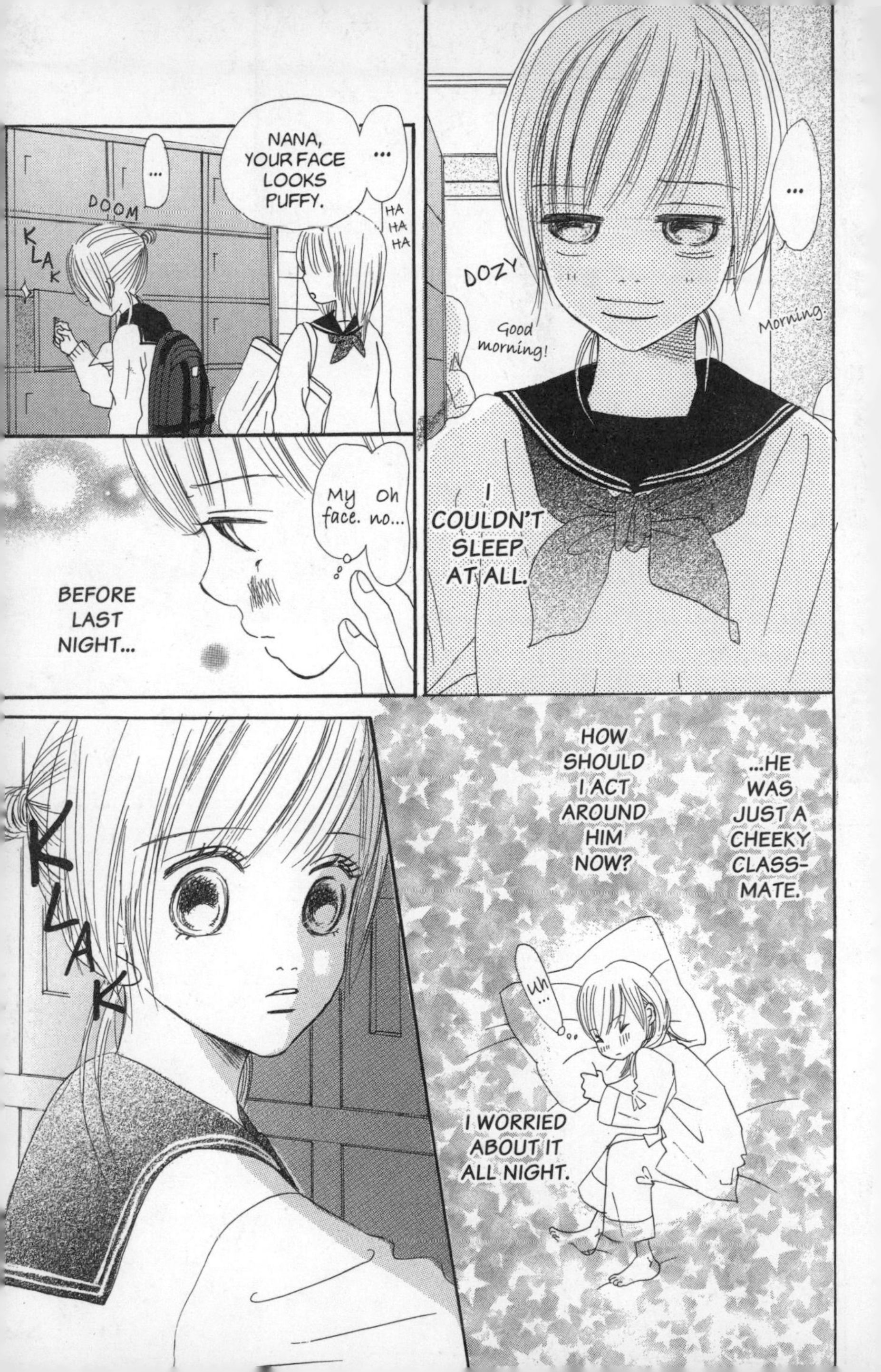
...
Morning.
DOZY
Good morning!
I COULDN'T SLEEP AT ALL.
...
HA HA HA
NANA, YOUR FACE LOOKS PUFFY.
...
DOOM
KLAK
My face. Oh no...
BEFORE LAST NIGHT...
...HE WAS JUST A CHEEKY CLASS-MATE.
HOW SHOULD I ACT AROUND HIM NOW?
uh...
I WORRIED ABOUT IT ALL NIGHT.
KLAK

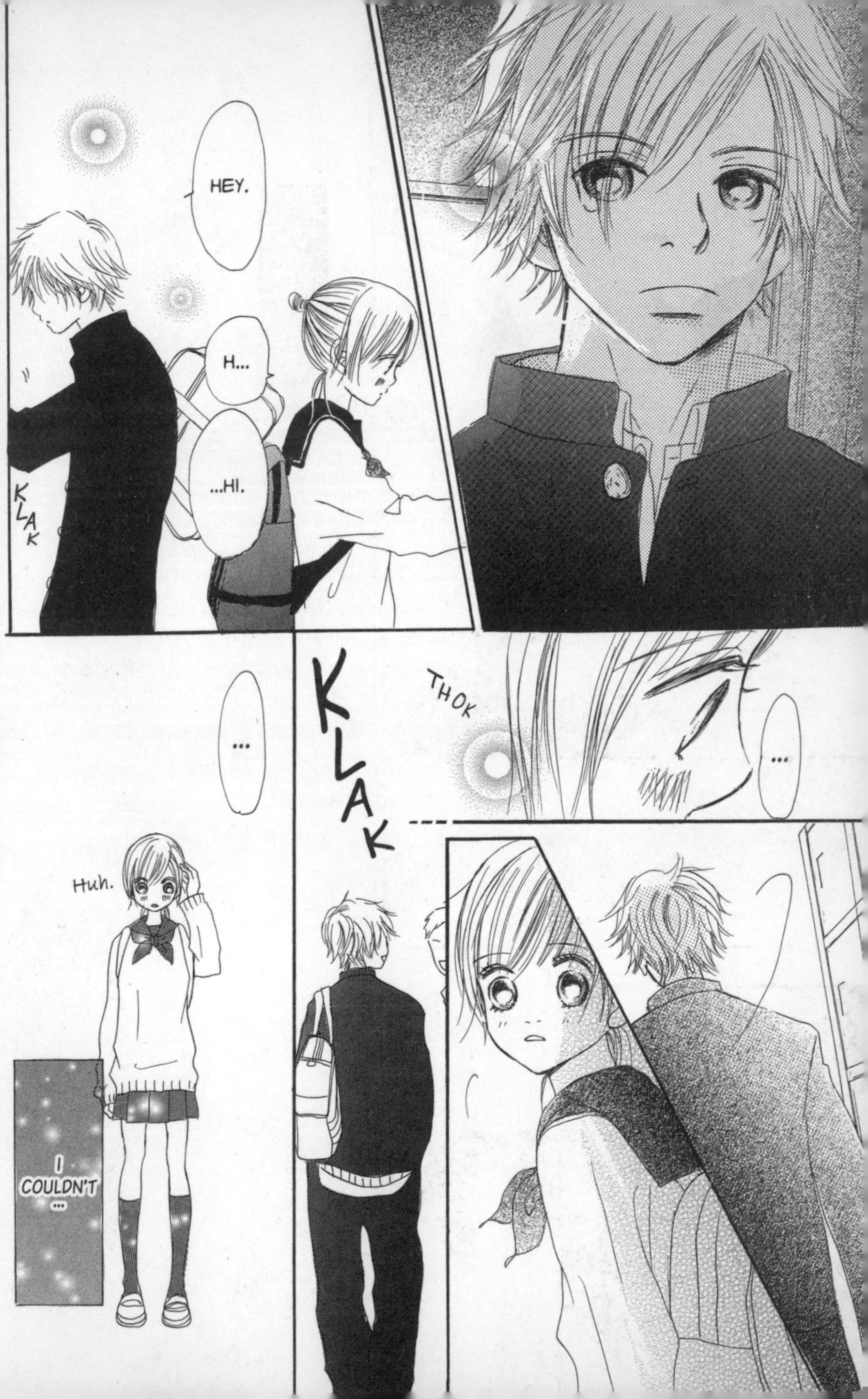
HEY.
H...
...HI.
KLAK
...
THOK
KLAK
...
Huh.
I COULDN'T ...

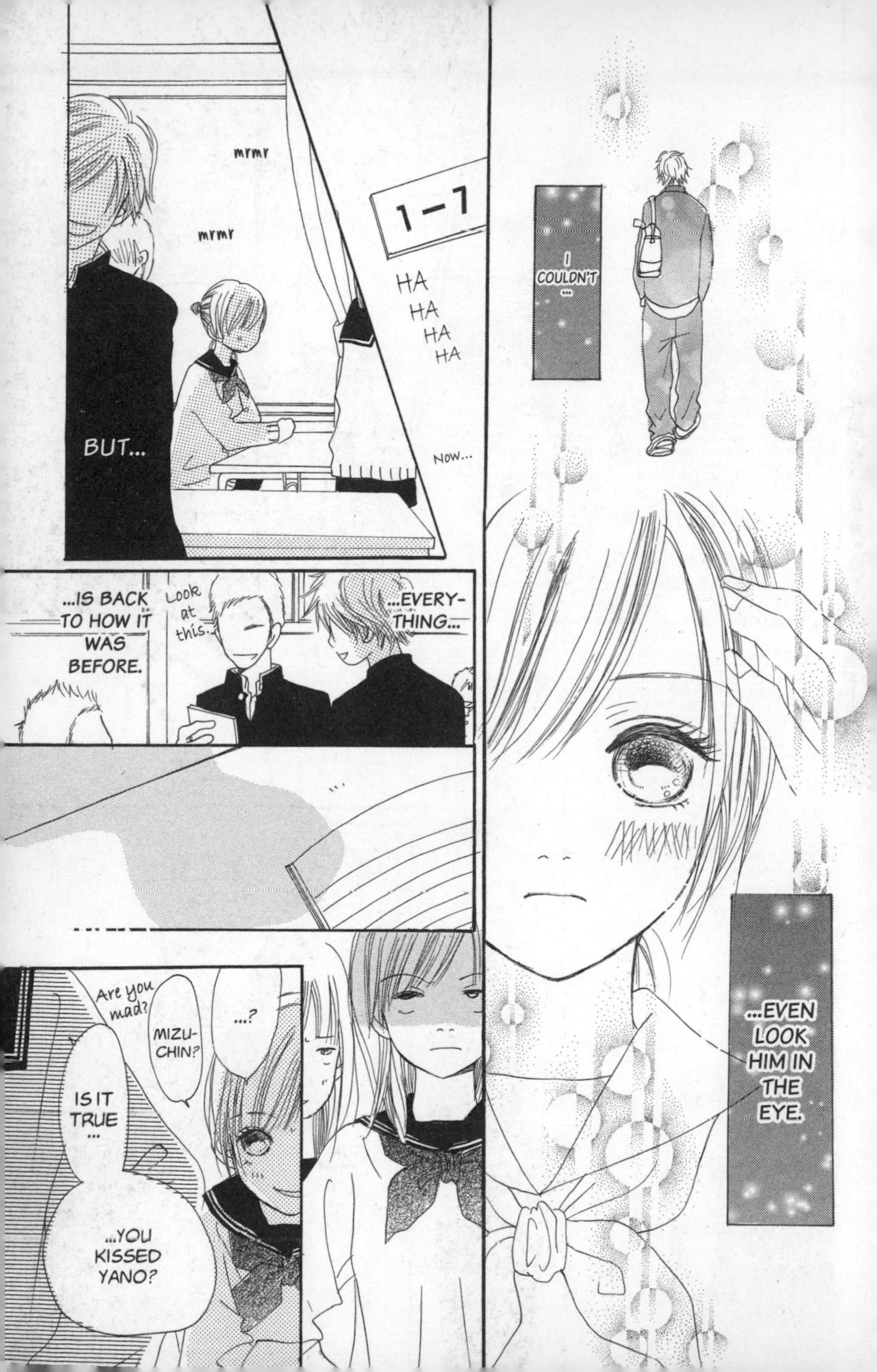
I COULDN'T ...
...EVEN LOOK HIM IN THE EYE.
1-7
HA HA HA HA
mrmr
mrmr
Now...
BUT...
...EVERY-THING...
Look at this.
...IS BACK TO HOW IT WAS BEFORE.
...?
MIZU-CHIN?
Are you mad?
IS IT TRUE ...
...YOU KISSED YANO?

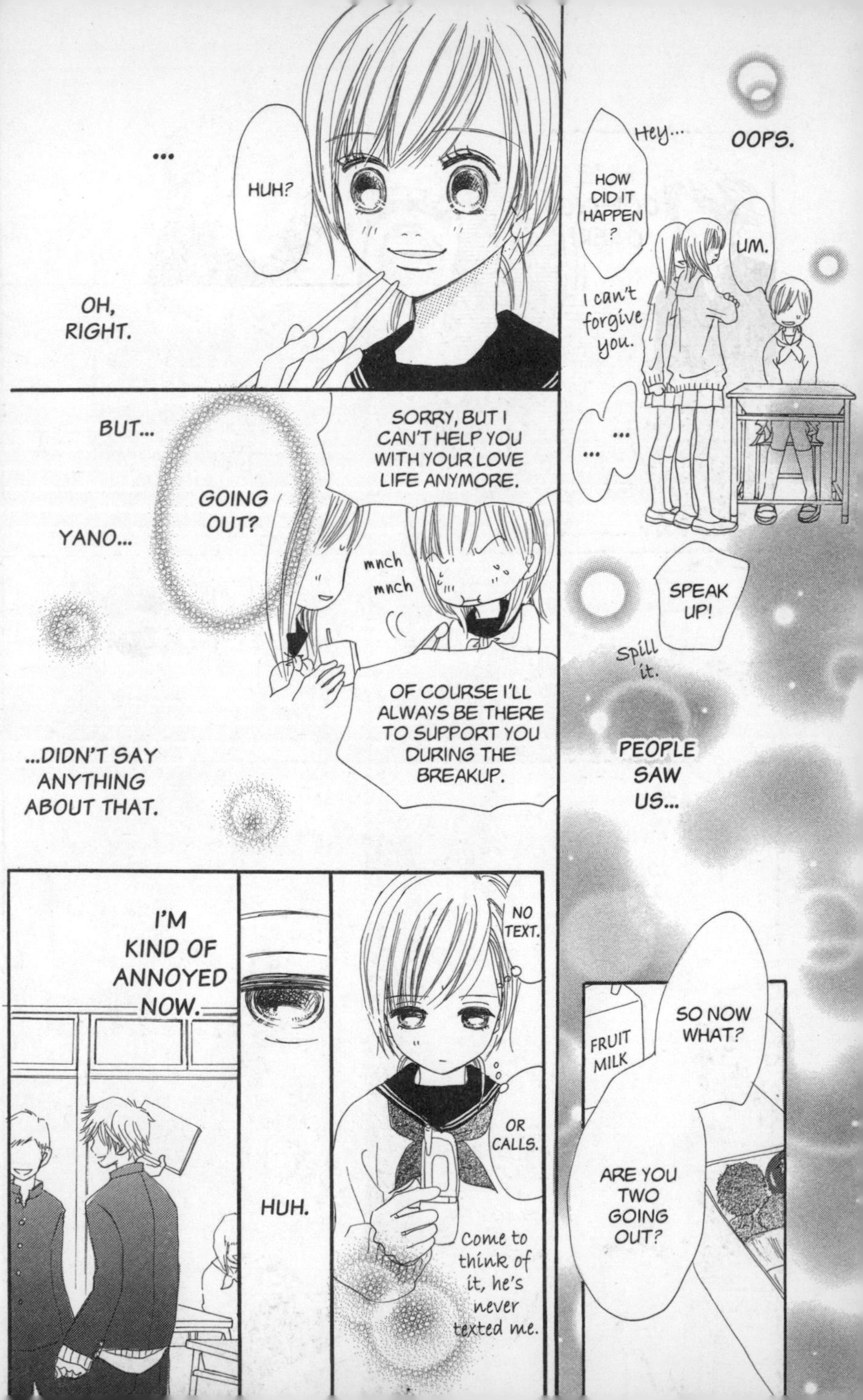
OOPS.
Hey...
HOW DID IT HAPPEN?
UM.
I can't forgive you.
... ...
SPEAK UP!
Spill it.
PEOPLE SAW US...
SO NOW WHAT?
FRUIT MILK
ARE YOU TWO GOING OUT?
HUH?
...
OH, RIGHT.
SORRY, BUT I CAN'T HELP YOU WITH YOUR LOVE LIFE ANYMORE.
GOING OUT?
BUT...
YANO...
mnch mnch
OF COURSE I'LL ALWAYS BE THERE TO SUPPORT YOU DURING THE BREAKUP.
...DIDN'T SAY ANYTHING ABOUT THAT.
NO TEXT.
OR CALLS.
Come to think of it, he's never texted me.
HUH.
I'M KIND OF ANNOYED NOW.

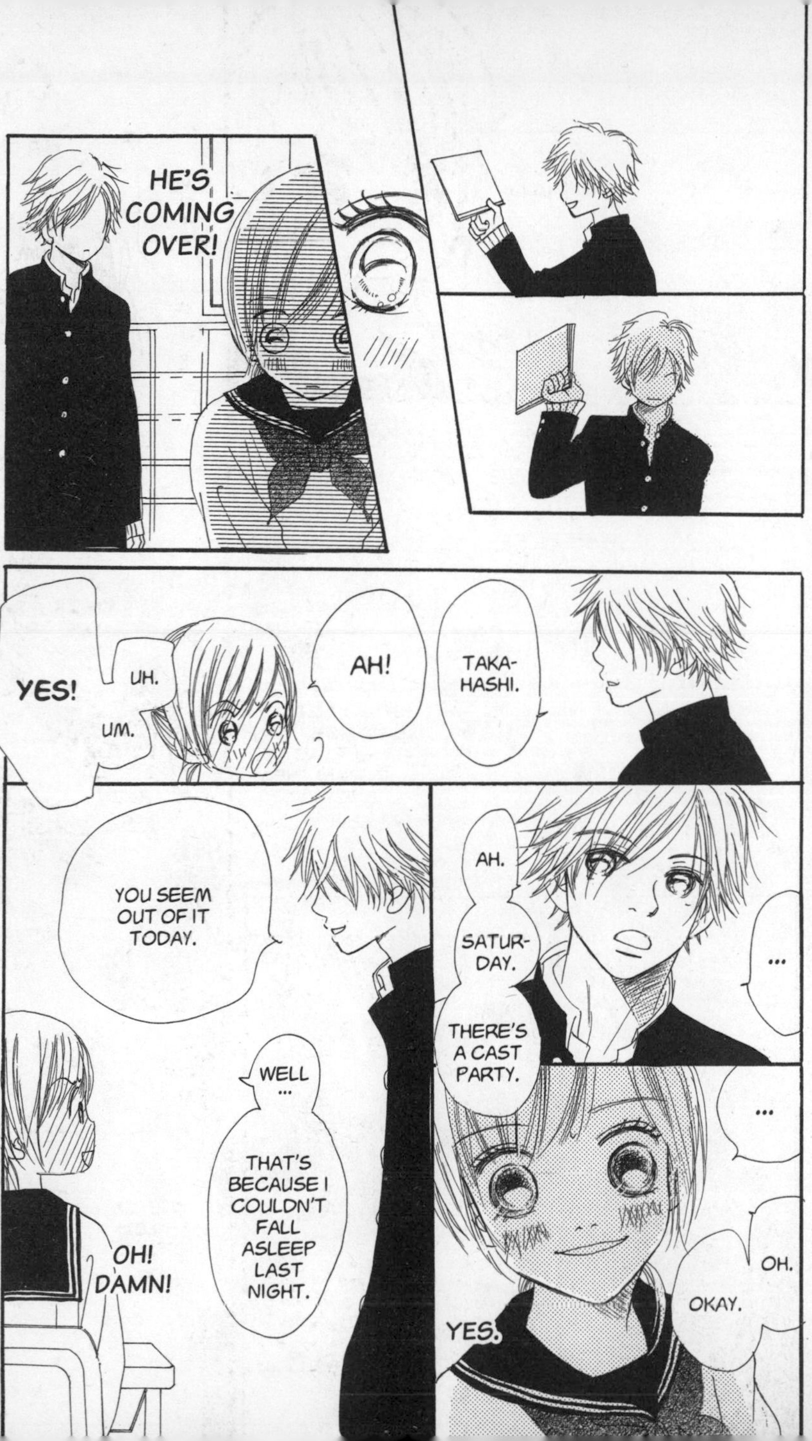
HE'S COMING OVER!
TAKA-HASHI.
AH!
UH.
UM.
YES!
AH.
SATURDAY.
THERE'S A CAST PARTY.
...
...
OH.
OKAY.
YES.
YOU SEEM OUT OF IT TODAY.
WELL...
THAT'S BECAUSE I COULDN'T FALL ASLEEP LAST NIGHT.
OH! DAMN!

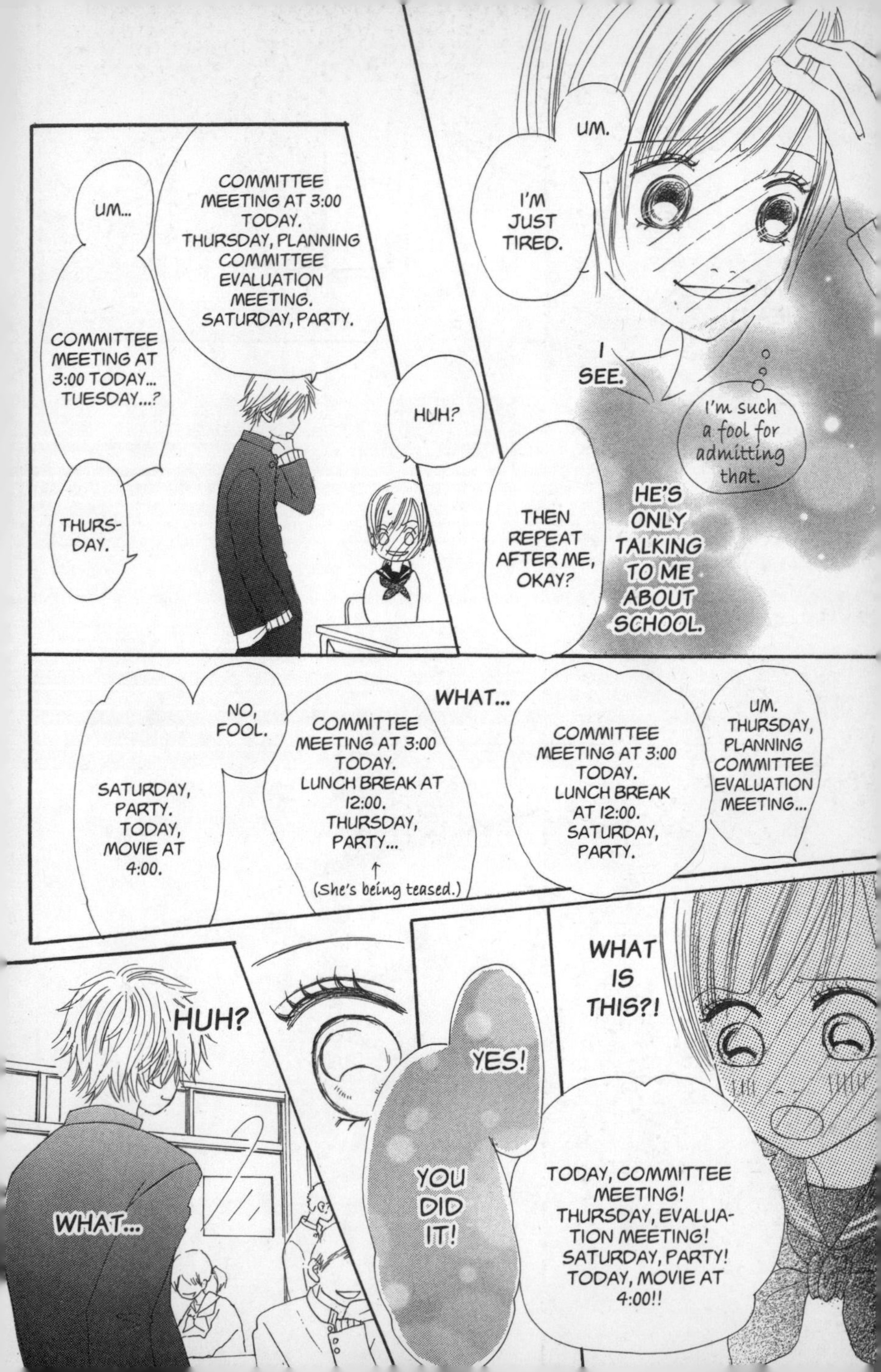
UM.
I'M JUST TIRED.
I SEE.
I'm such a fool for admitting that.
HE'S ONLY TALKING TO ME ABOUT SCHOOL.
THEN REPEAT AFTER ME, OKAY?
HUH?
COMMITTEE MEETING AT 3:00 TODAY. THURSDAY, PLANNING COMMITTEE EVALUATION MEETING. SATURDAY, PARTY.
UM...
COMMITTEE MEETING AT 3:00 TODAY... TUESDAY...?
THURS-DAY.
UM. THURSDAY, PLANNING COMMITTEE EVALUATION MEETING...
COMMITTEE MEETING AT 3:00 TODAY. LUNCH BREAK AT 12:00. SATURDAY, PARTY.
WHAT...
COMMITTEE MEETING AT 3:00 TODAY. LUNCH BREAK AT 12:00. THURSDAY, PARTY...
↑ (She's being teased.)
NO, FOOL.
SATURDAY, PARTY. TODAY, MOVIE AT 4:00.
WHAT IS THIS?!
TODAY, COMMITTEE MEETING! THURSDAY, EVALUA-TION MEETING! SATURDAY, PARTY! TODAY, MOVIE AT 4:00!!
YES!
YOU DID IT!
HUH?
WHAT...

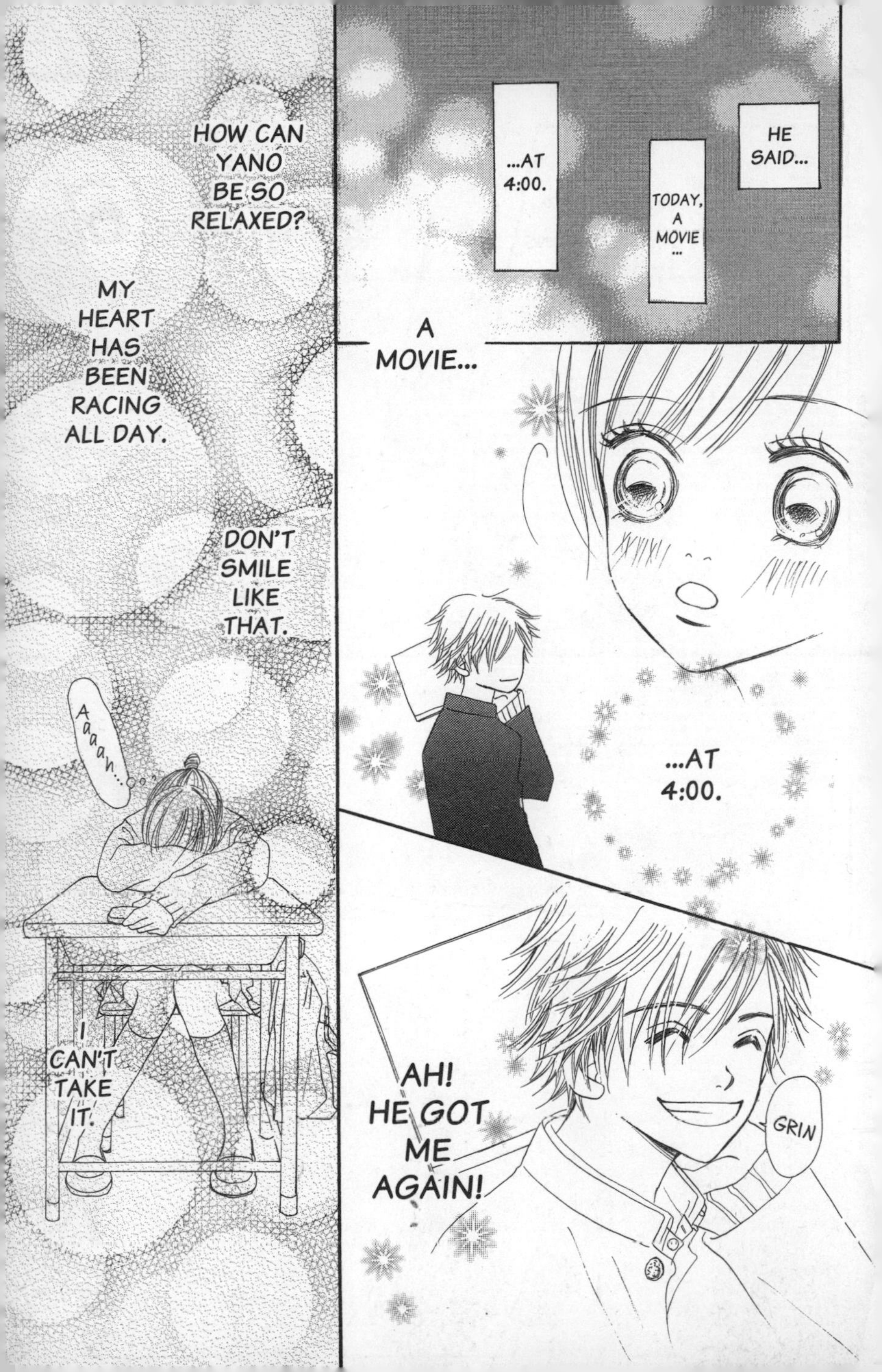
HE SAID...
TODAY, A MOVIE...
...AT 4:00.
A MOVIE...
...AT 4:00.
GRIN
AH! HE GOT ME AGAIN!
HOW CAN YANO BE SO RELAXED?
MY HEART HAS BEEN RACING ALL DAY.
DON'T SMILE LIKE THAT.
Aaaan...
I CAN'T TAKE IT.

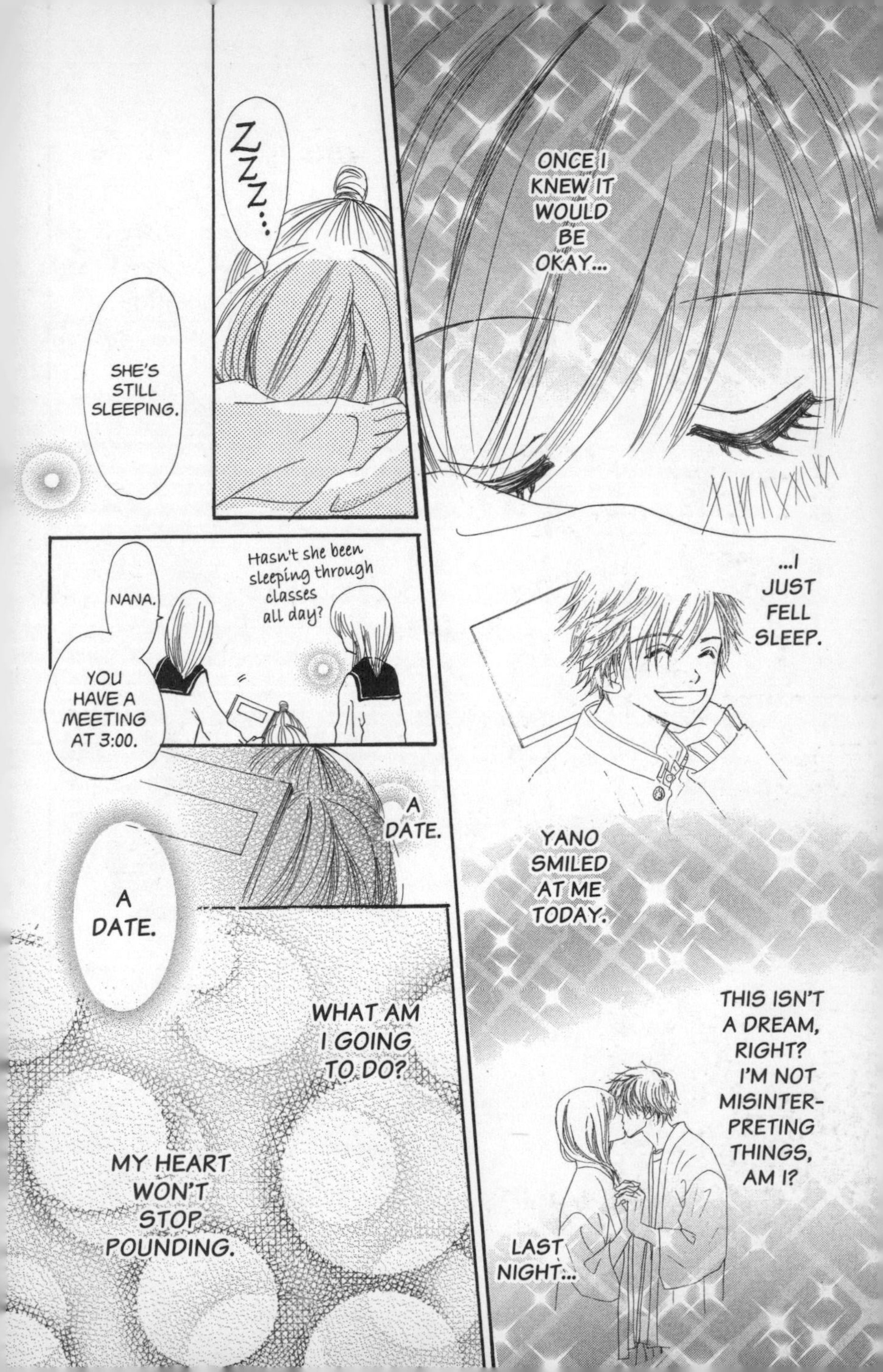

ONCE I KNEW IT WOULD BE OKAY...
...I JUST FELL SLEEP.
YANO SMILED AT ME TODAY.
THIS ISN'T A DREAM, RIGHT? I'M NOT MISINTERPRETING THINGS, AM I?
LAST NIGHT...
ZZZ...
SHE'S STILL SLEEPING.
Hasn't she been sleeping through classes all day?
NANA.
YOU HAVE A MEETING AT 3:00.
A DATE.
A DATE.
WHAT AM I GOING TO DO?
MY HEART WON'T STOP POUNDING.

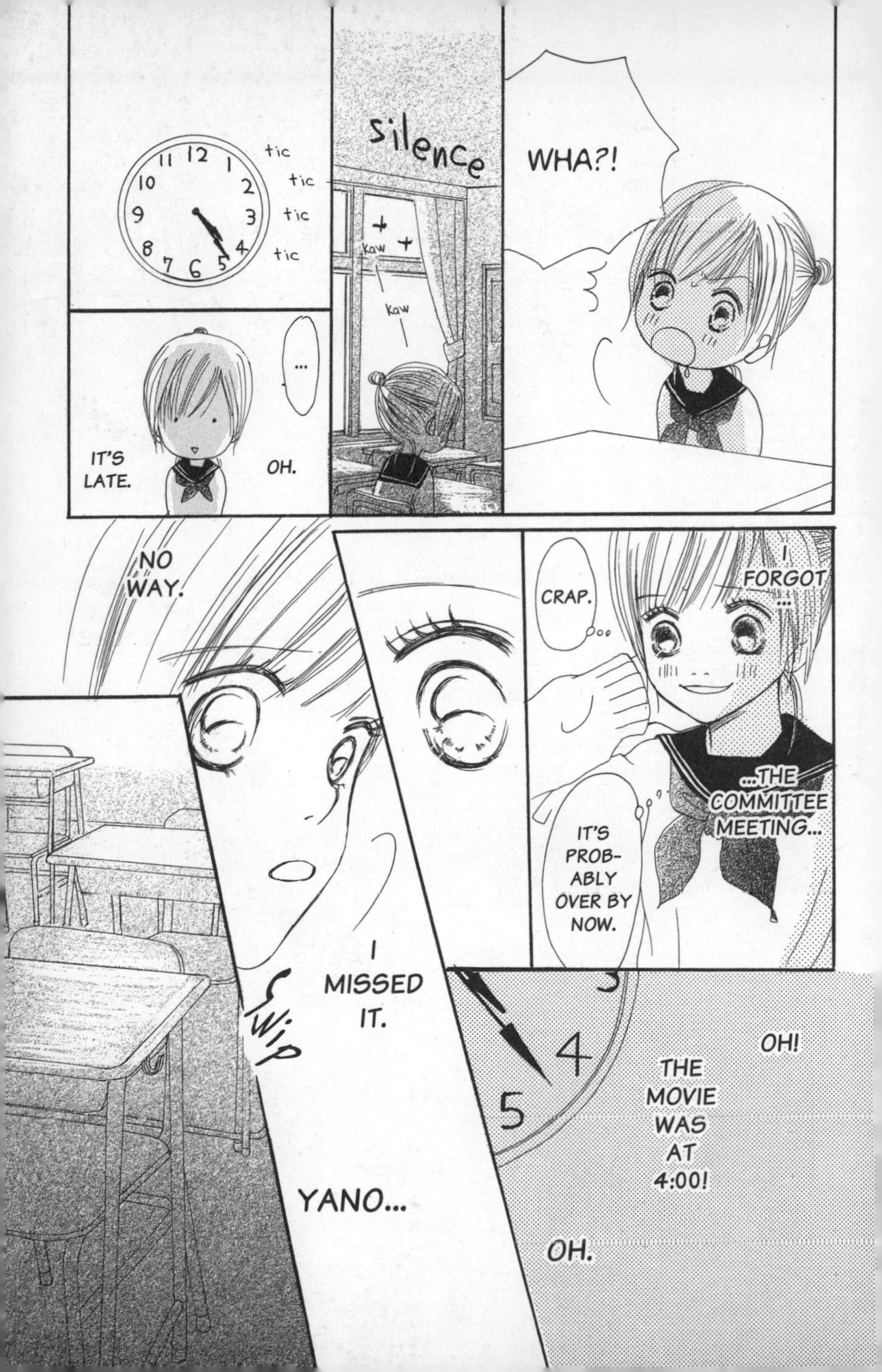
WHA?!
Silence
kaw
kaw
tic
tic
tic
tic
...
OH.
IT'S LATE.
I FORGOT...
CRAP.
...THE COMMITTEE MEETING...
IT'S PROBABLY OVER BY NOW.
NO WAY.
OH!
THE MOVIE WAS AT 4:00!
OH.
I MISSED IT.
SWIP
YANO...

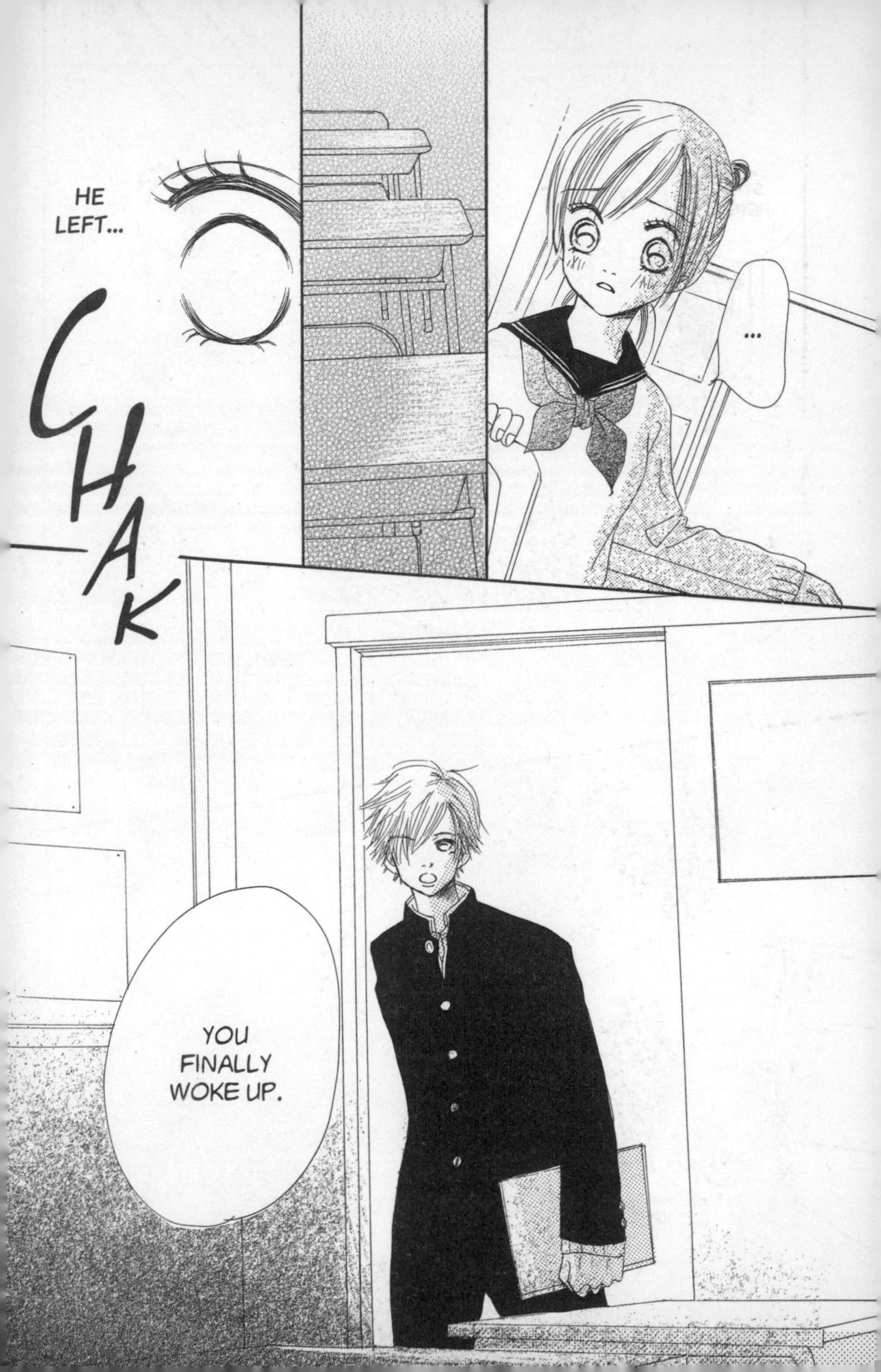
...
HE LEFT...
CHAK
YOU FINALLY WOKE UP.

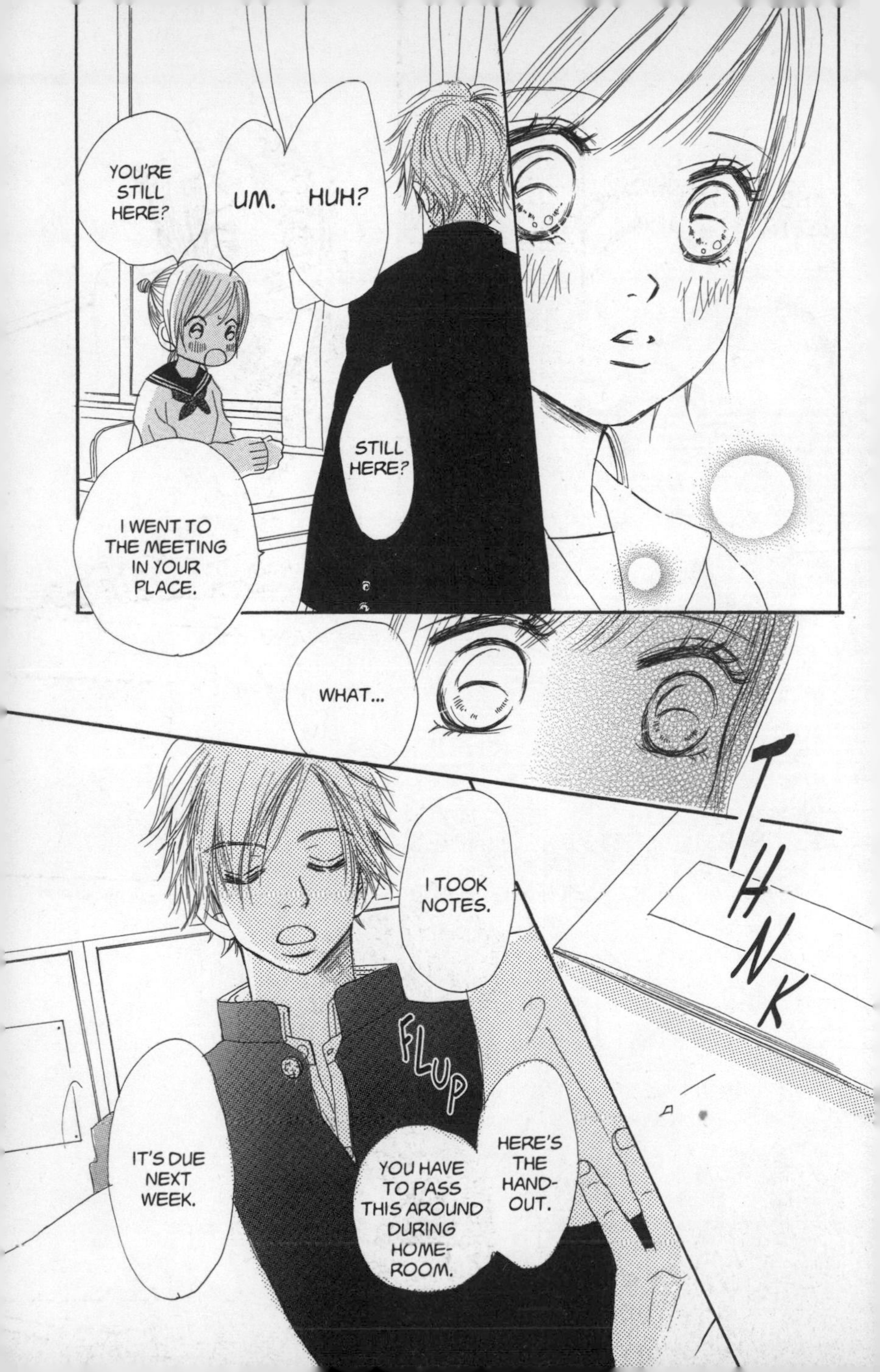

YOU'RE STILL HERE?
UM. HUH?
STILL HERE?
I WENT TO THE MEETING IN YOUR PLACE.
WHAT...
THNK
I TOOK NOTES.
HERE'S THE HAND-OUT.
YOU HAVE TO PASS THIS AROUND DURING HOME-ROOM.
FLUP
IT'S DUE NEXT WEEK.

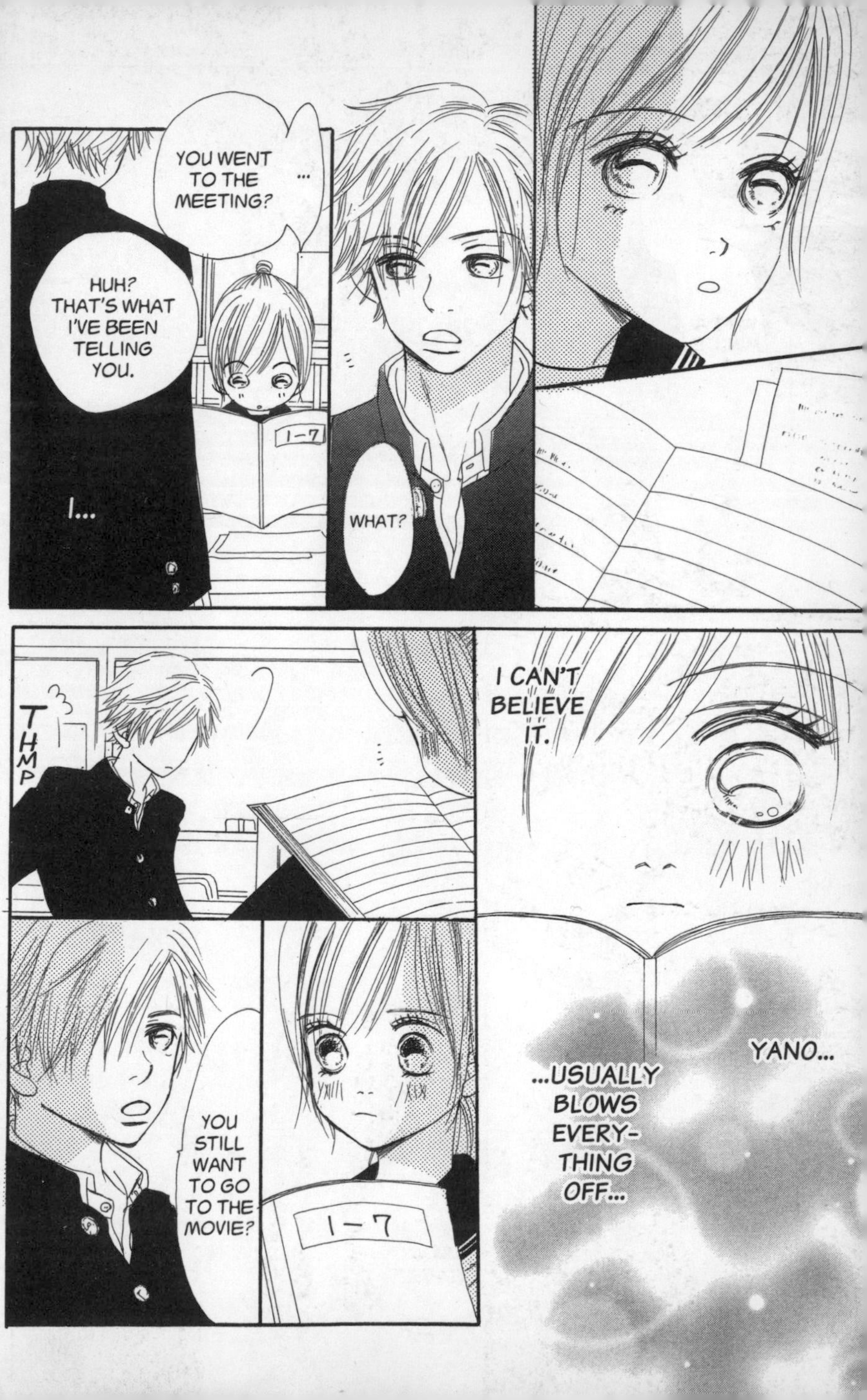
WHAT?
...
YOU WENT TO THE MEETING?
HUH? THAT'S WHAT I'VE BEEN TELLING YOU.
I...
I CAN'T BELIEVE IT.
YANO...
...USUALLY BLOWS EVERY-THING OFF...
THMP
YOU STILL WANT TO GO TO THE MOVIE?

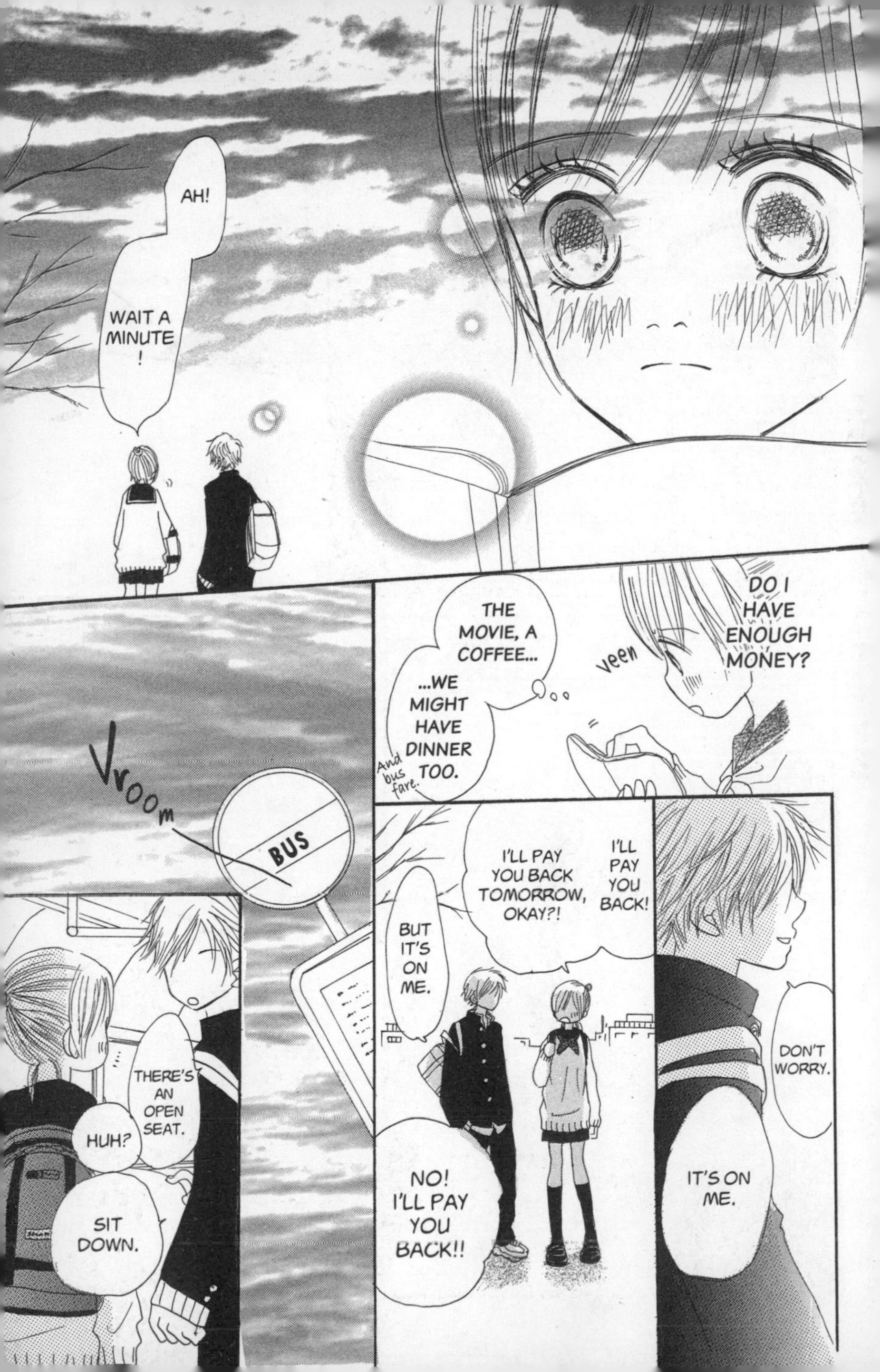
AH!
WAIT A MINUTE!
DO I HAVE ENOUGH MONEY?
veen
THE MOVIE, A COFFEE...
...WE MIGHT HAVE DINNER TOO.
And bus fare.
DON'T WORRY.
IT'S ON ME.
I'LL PAY YOU BACK!
I'LL PAY YOU BACK TOMORROW, OKAY?!
BUT IT'S ON ME.
NO! I'LL PAY YOU BACK!!
Vroom
BUS
THERE'S AN OPEN SEAT.
HUH?
SIT DOWN.

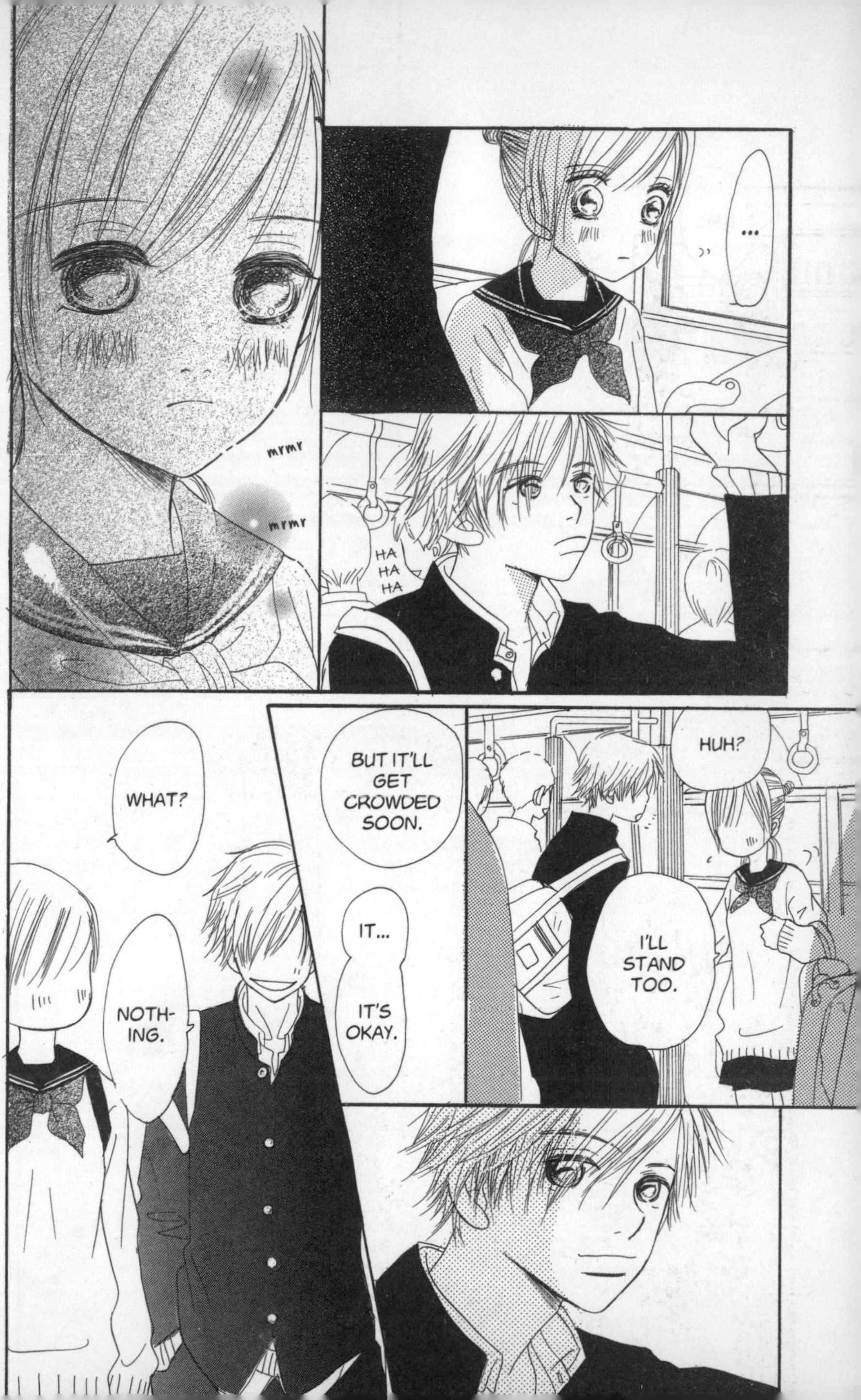
...
HA HA HA
mrmr
mrmr
HUH?
I'LL STAND TOO.
BUT IT'LL GET CROWDED SOON.
IT...
IT'S OKAY.
WHAT?
NOTHING.

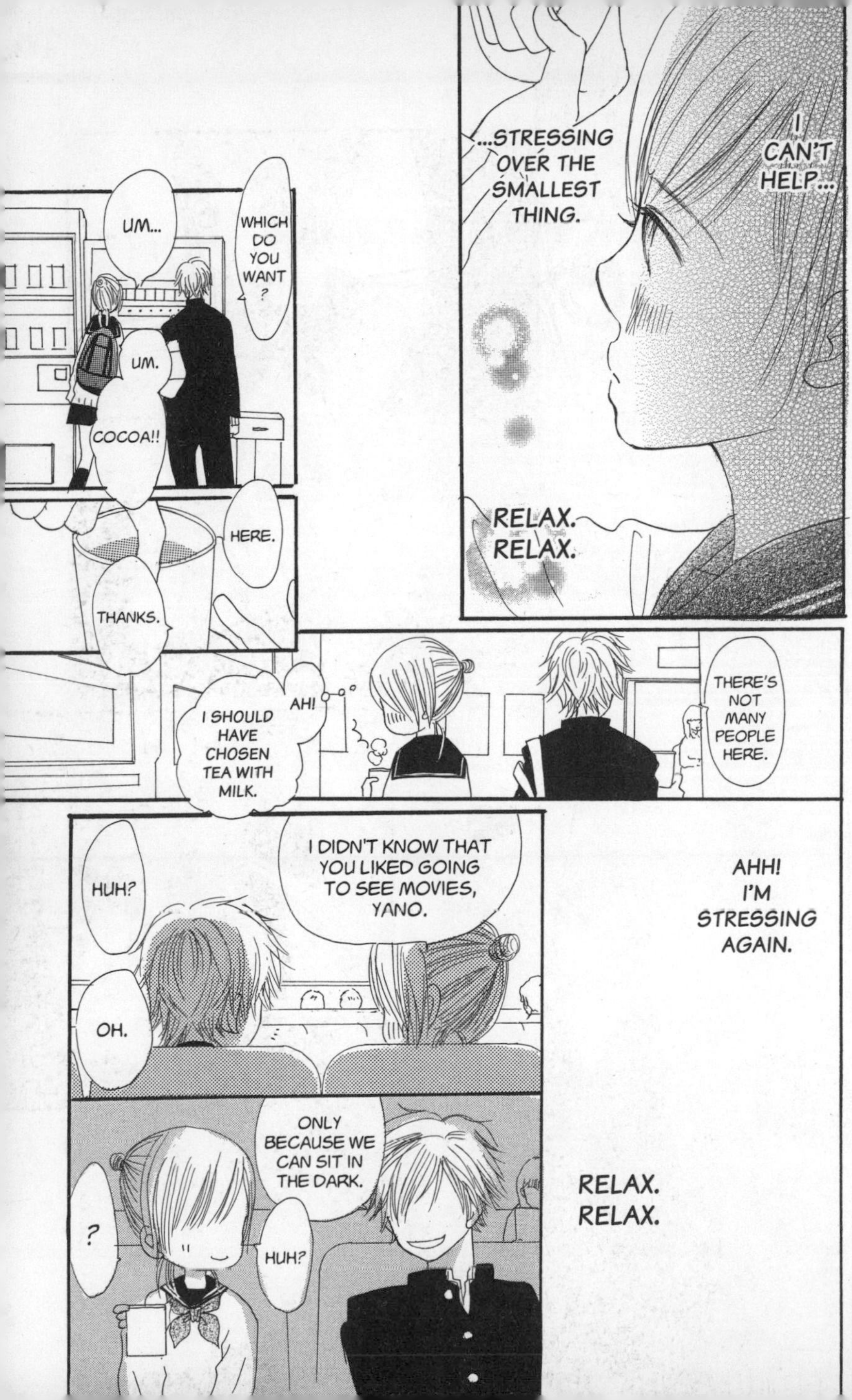
I CAN'T HELP...
...STRESSING OVER THE SMALLEST THING.
RELAX. RELAX.
WHICH DO YOU WANT ?
UM...
UM.
COCOA!!
HERE.
THANKS.
THERE'S NOT MANY PEOPLE HERE.
AH!
I SHOULD HAVE CHOSEN TEA WITH MILK.
AHH! I'M STRESSING AGAIN.
RELAX. RELAX.
I DIDN'T KNOW THAT YOU LIKED GOING TO SEE MOVIES, YANO.
HUH?
OH.
ONLY BECAUSE WE CAN SIT IN THE DARK.
HUH?
?

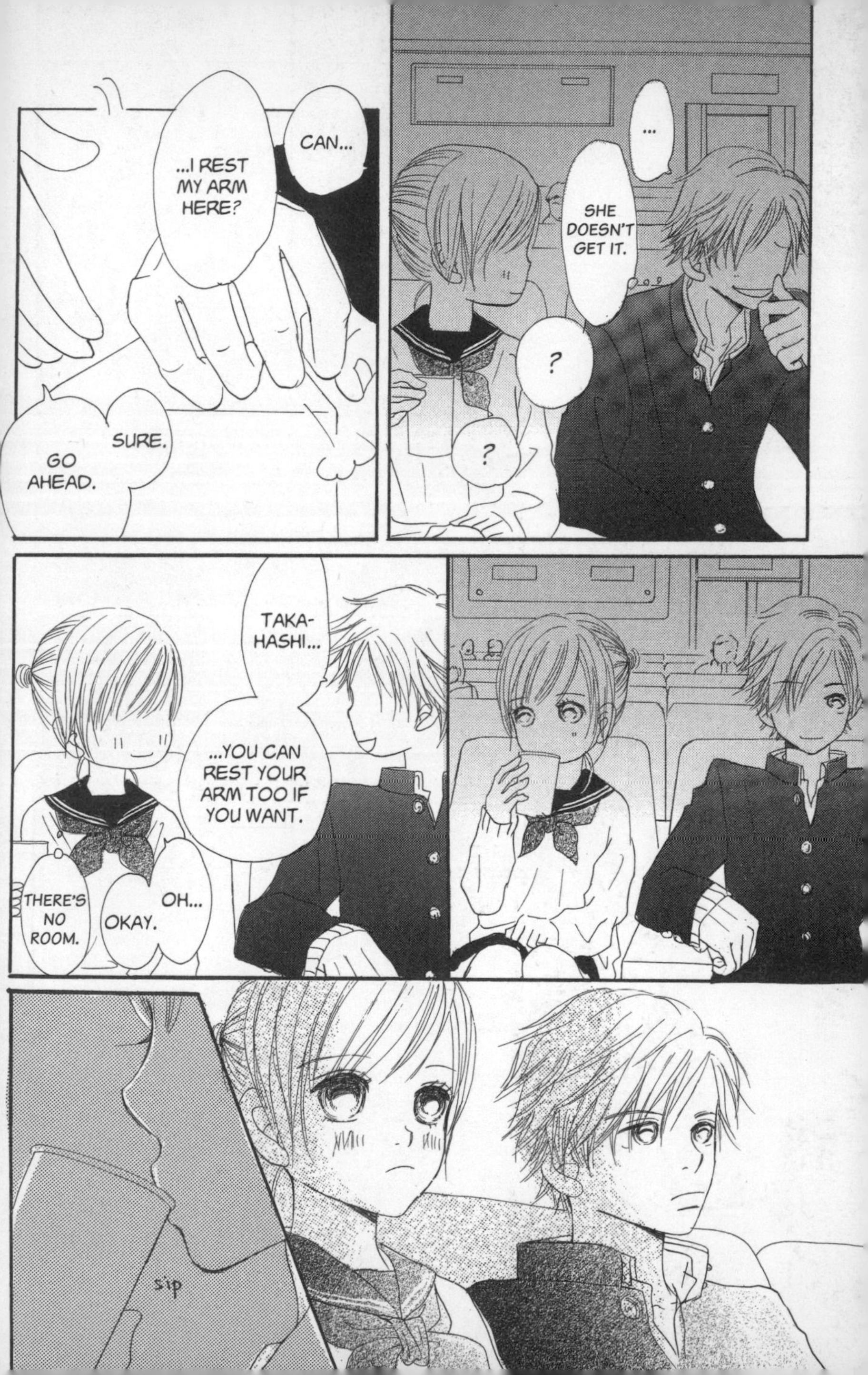
...
SHE DOESN'T GET IT.
?
?
CAN...
...I REST MY ARM HERE?
SURE. GO AHEAD.
TAKA-HASHI...
...YOU CAN REST YOUR ARM TOO IF YOU WANT.
OH... OKAY.
THERE'S NO ROOM.
sip

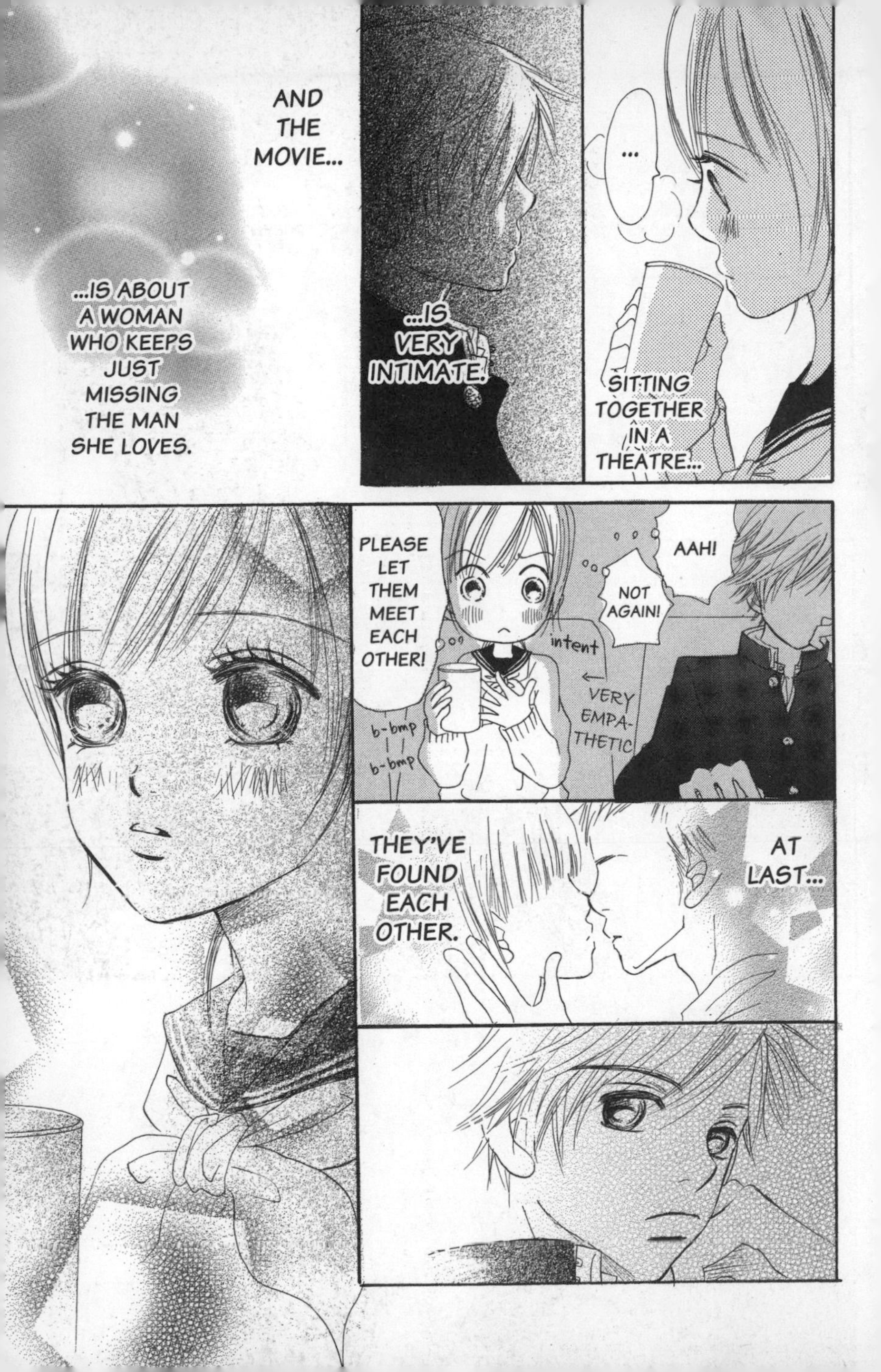
...
SITTING TOGETHER IN A THEATRE...
...IS VERY INTIMATE.
AND THE MOVIE...
...IS ABOUT A WOMAN WHO KEEPS JUST MISSING THE MAN SHE LOVES.
AAH!
NOT AGAIN!
PLEASE LET THEM MEET EACH OTHER!
intent
VERY EMPATHETIC
b-bmp
b-bmp
AT LAST...
THEY'VE FOUND EACH OTHER.

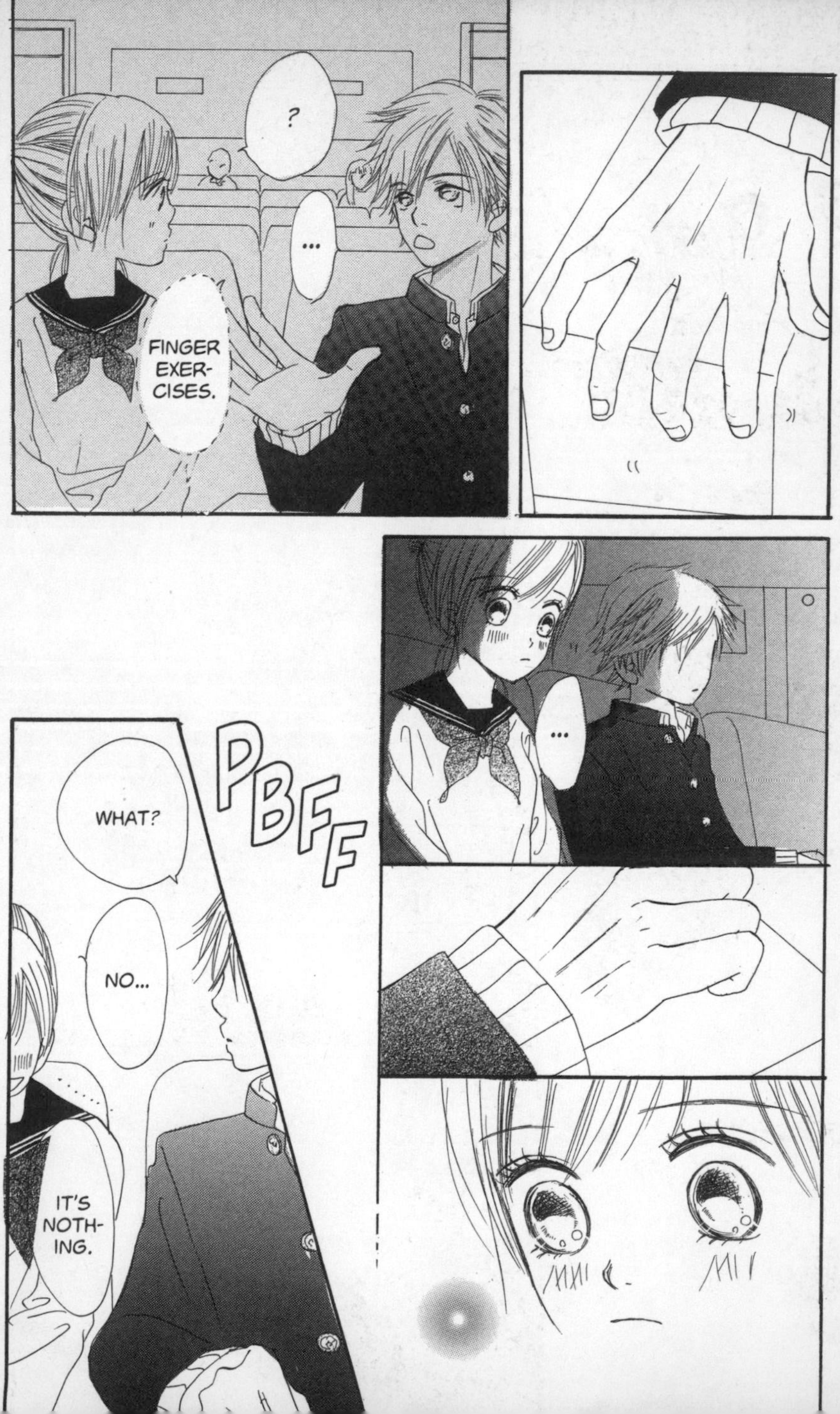
?
...
FINGER EXER-CISES.
...
PBFFF
WHAT?
NO...
IT'S NOTH-ING.

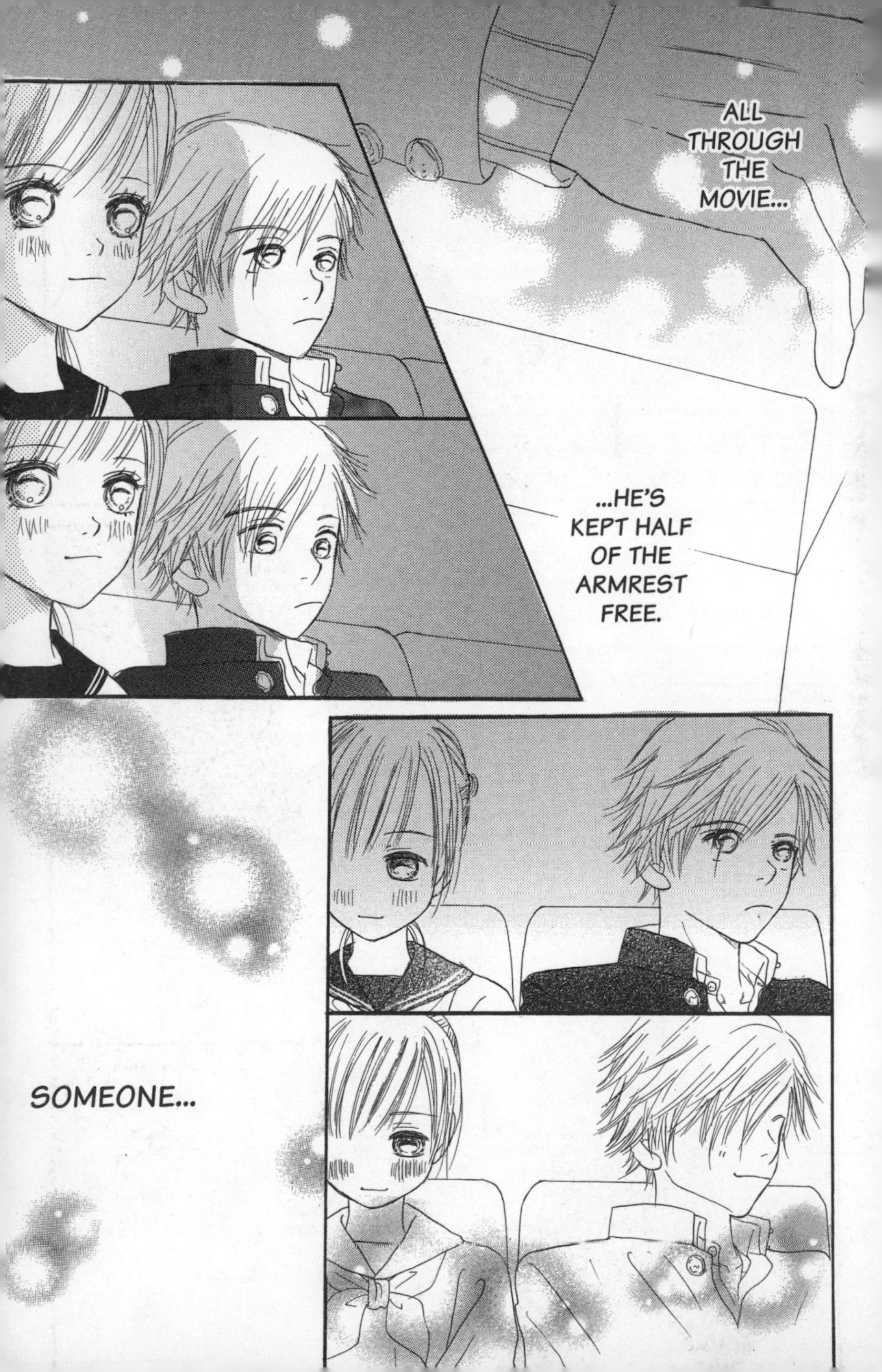
ALL THROUGH THE MOVIE...
...HE'S KEPT HALF OF THE ARMREST FREE.
SOMEONE...

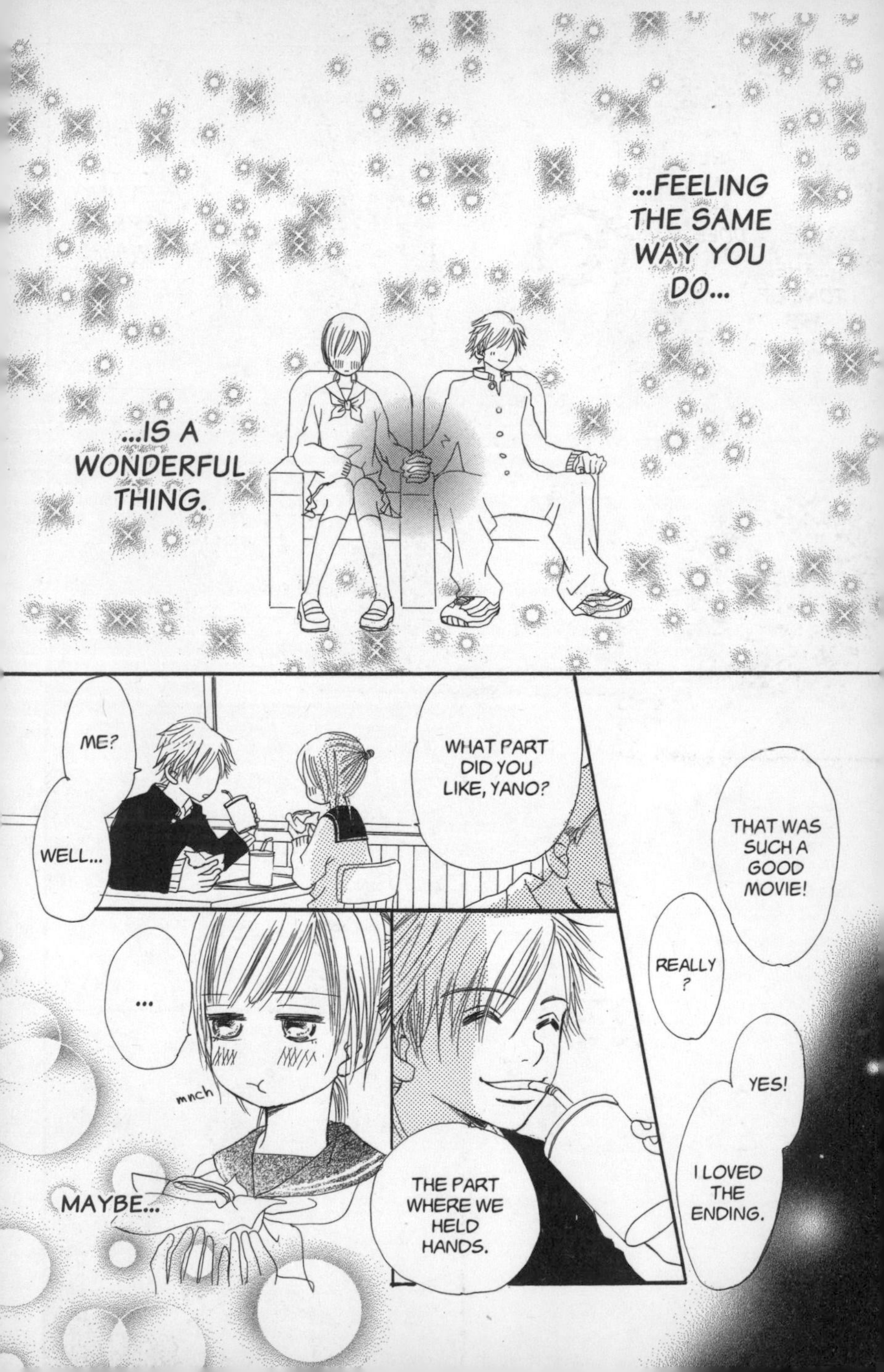
...FEELING THE SAME WAY YOU DO...
...IS A WONDERFUL THING.
THAT WAS SUCH A GOOD MOVIE!
REALLY?
YES!
I LOVED THE ENDING.
WHAT PART DID YOU LIKE, YANO?
ME?
WELL...
THE PART WHERE WE HELD HANDS.
...
mnch
MAYBE...

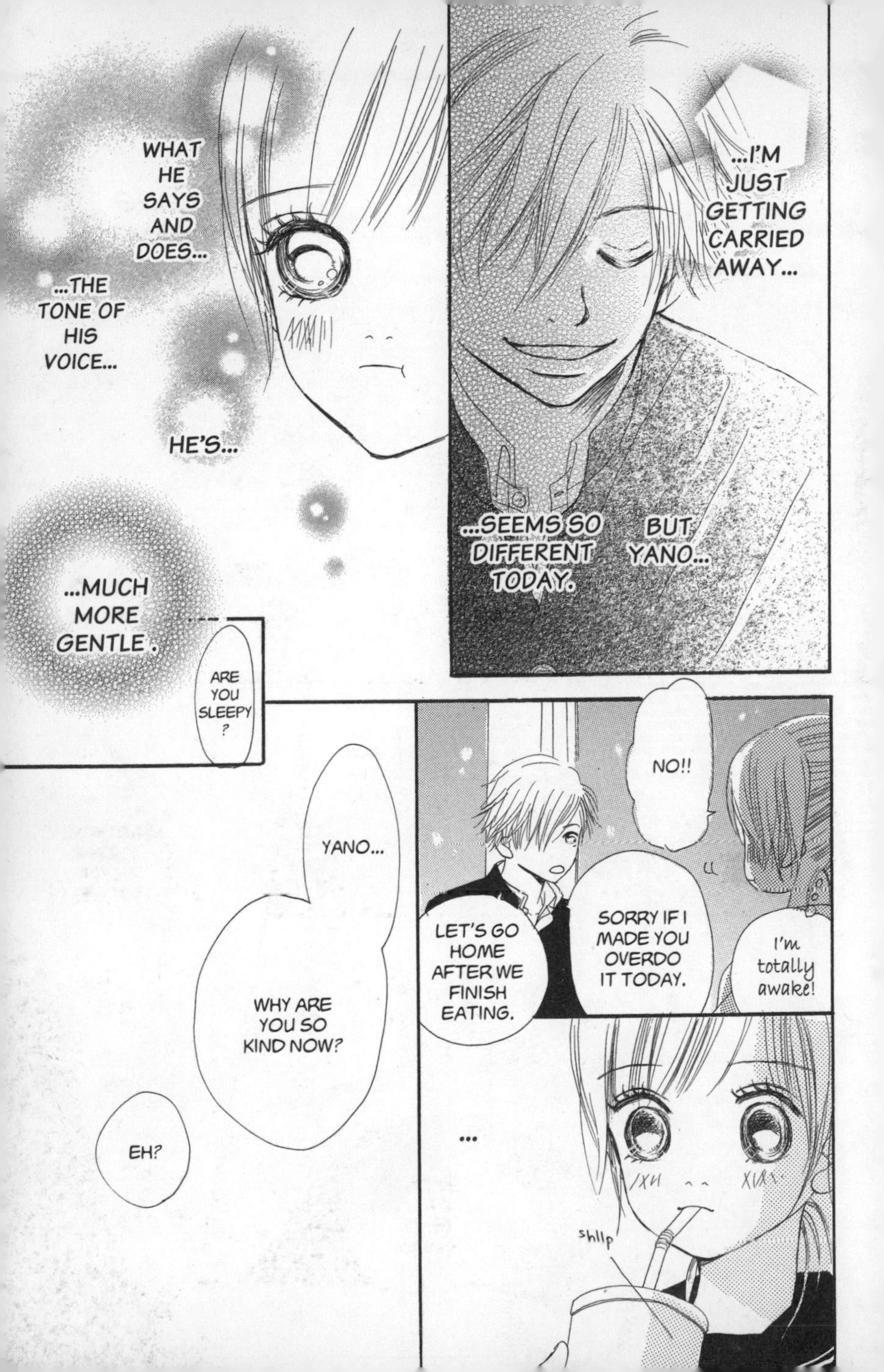
...I'M JUST GETTING CARRIED AWAY...
BUT YANO...
...SEEMS SO DIFFERENT TODAY.
WHAT HE SAYS AND DOES...
...THE TONE OF HIS VOICE...
HE'S...
...MUCH MORE GENTLE.
ARE YOU SLEEPY?
NO!!
I'm totally awake!
SORRY IF I MADE YOU OVERDO IT TODAY.
LET'S GO HOME AFTER WE FINISH EATING.
...
shllp
YANO...
WHY ARE YOU SO KIND NOW?
EH?

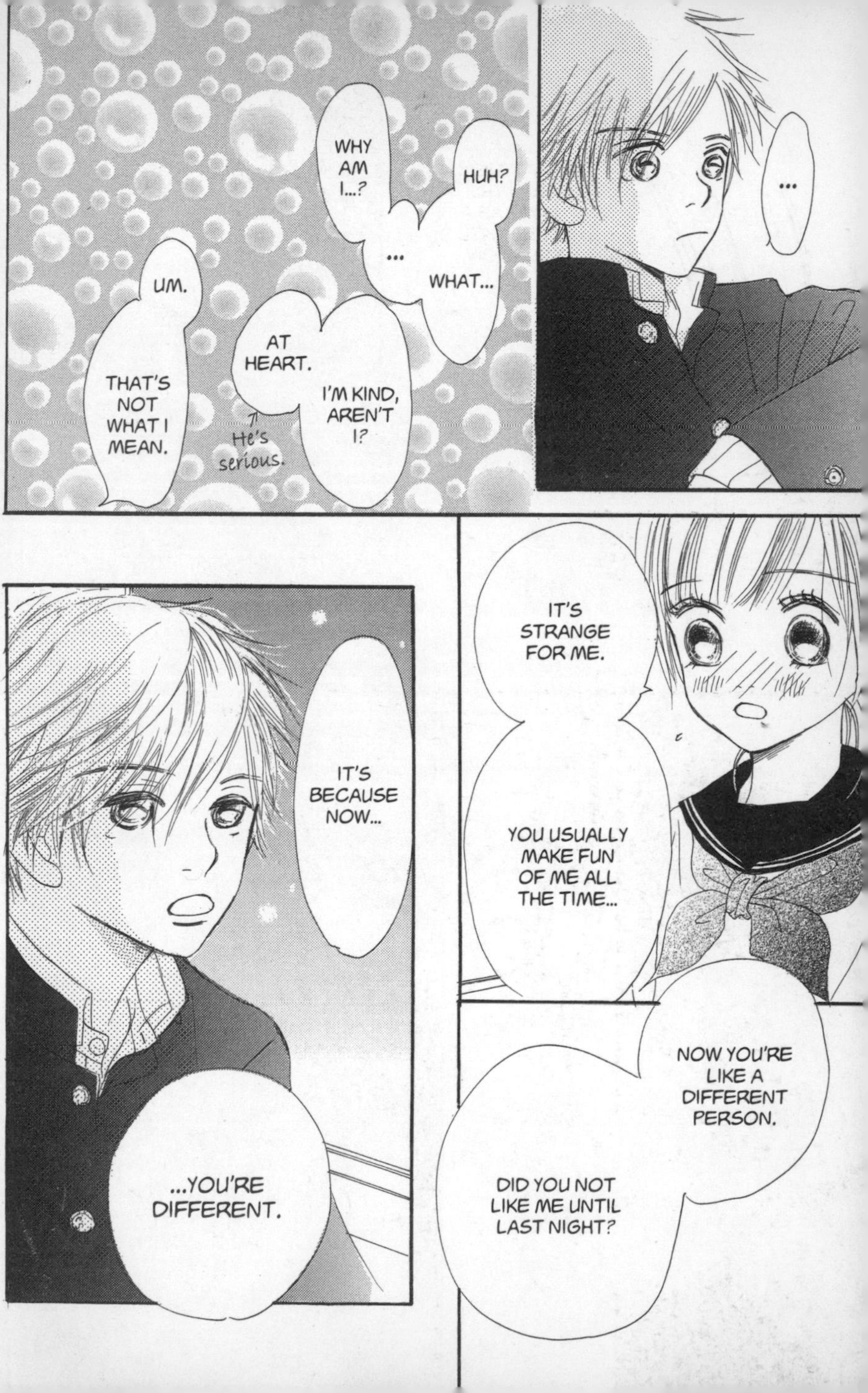
...
HUH?
WHY AM I...?
...
WHAT...
I'M KIND, AREN'T I?
AT HEART.
He's serious.
UM.
THAT'S NOT WHAT I MEAN.
IT'S STRANGE FOR ME.
YOU USUALLY MAKE FUN OF ME ALL THE TIME...
NOW YOU'RE LIKE A DIFFERENT PERSON.
DID YOU NOT LIKE ME UNTIL LAST NIGHT?
IT'S BECAUSE NOW...
...YOU'RE DIFFERENT.

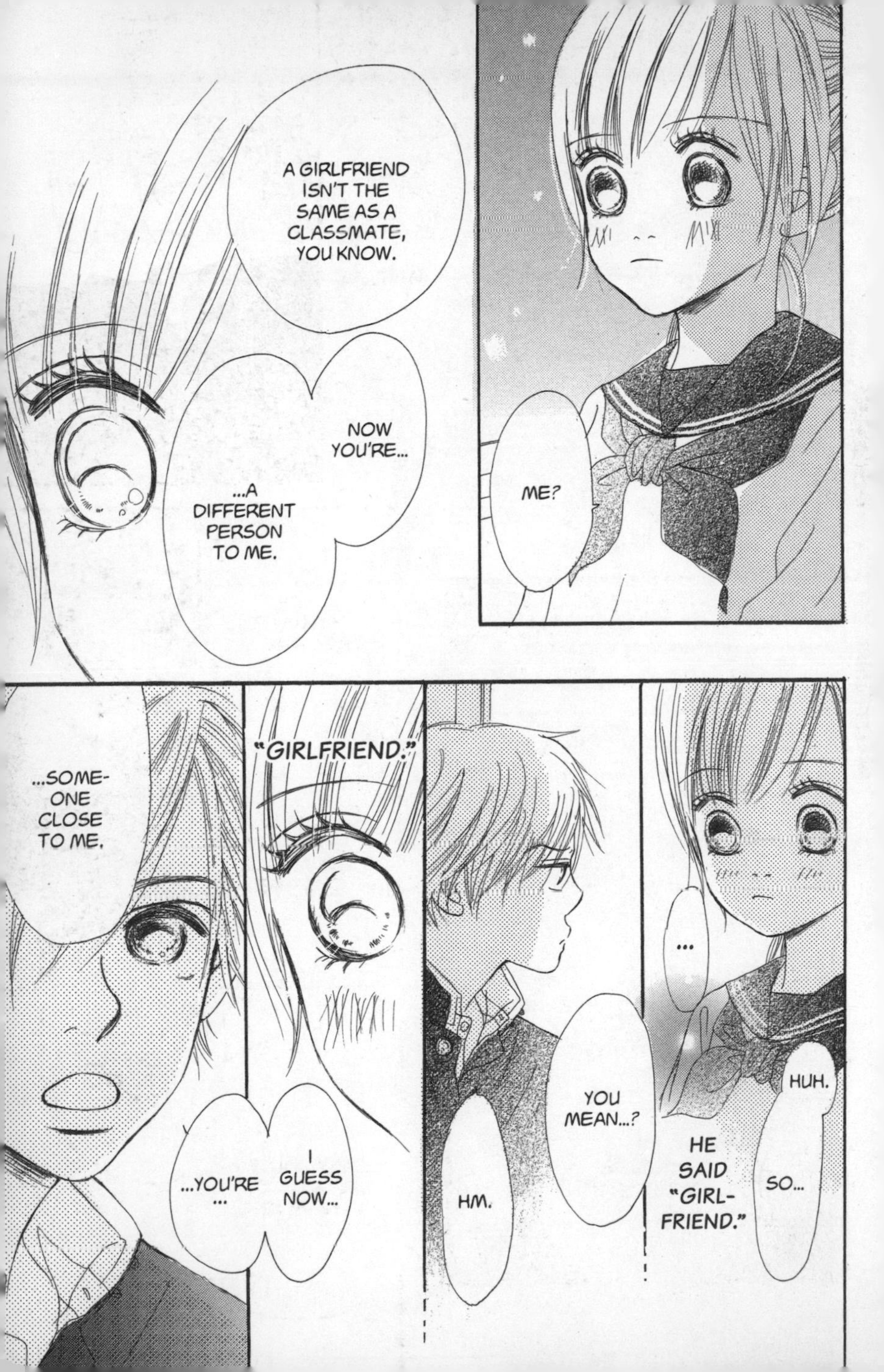
ME?
A GIRLFRIEND ISN'T THE SAME AS A CLASSMATE, YOU KNOW.
NOW YOU'RE...
...A DIFFERENT PERSON TO ME.
...
HUH.
SO...
HE SAID "GIRL-FRIEND."
YOU MEAN...?
HM.
"GIRLFRIEND."
I GUESS NOW...
...YOU'RE ...
...SOME-ONE CLOSE TO ME.

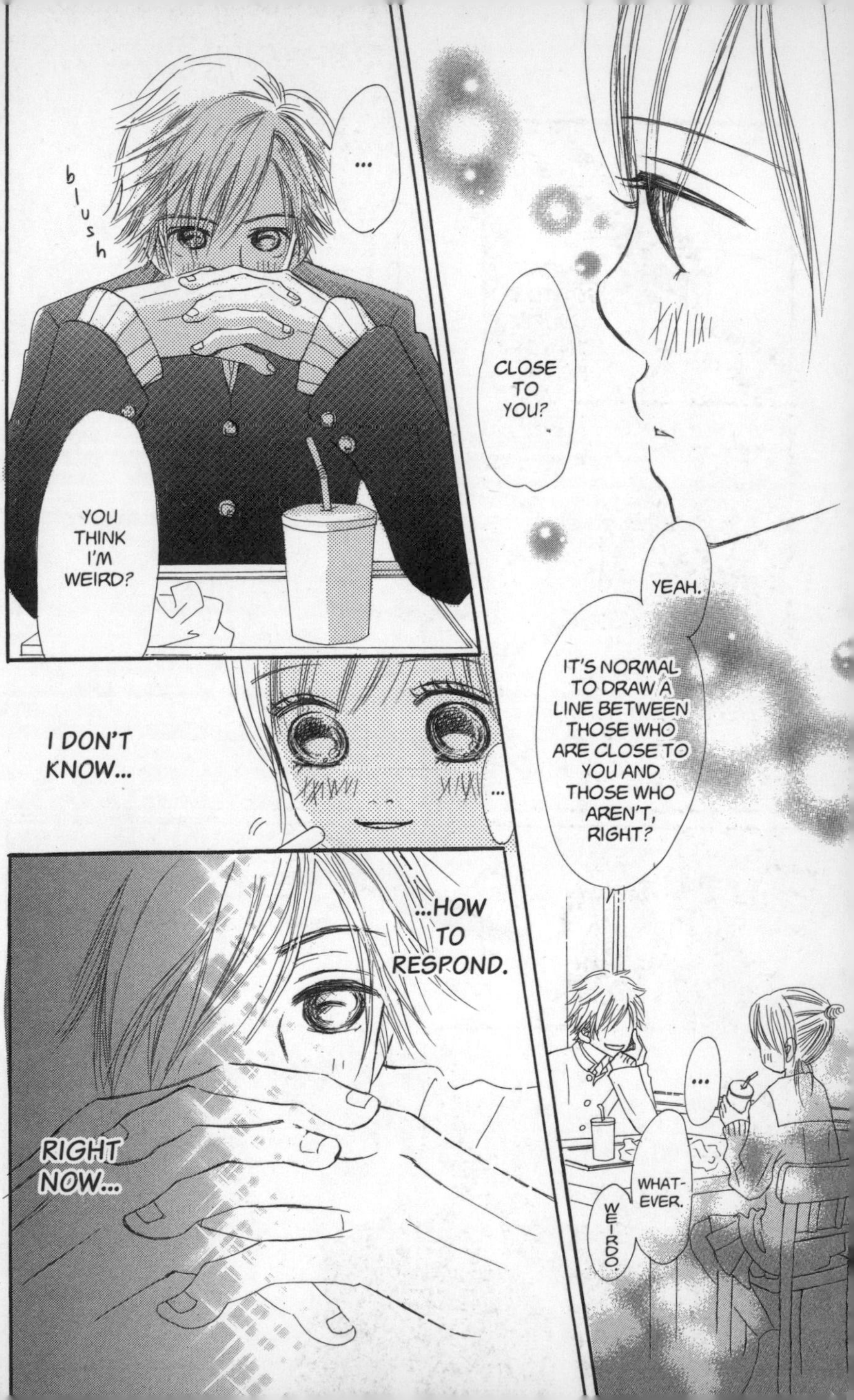
CLOSE TO YOU?
YEAH.
IT'S NORMAL TO DRAW A LINE BETWEEN THOSE WHO ARE CLOSE TO YOU AND THOSE WHO AREN'T, RIGHT?
...
WHAT-EVER.
WEIRDO.
...
blush
YOU THINK I'M WEIRD?
...
I DON'T KNOW...
...HOW TO RESPOND.
RIGHT NOW...

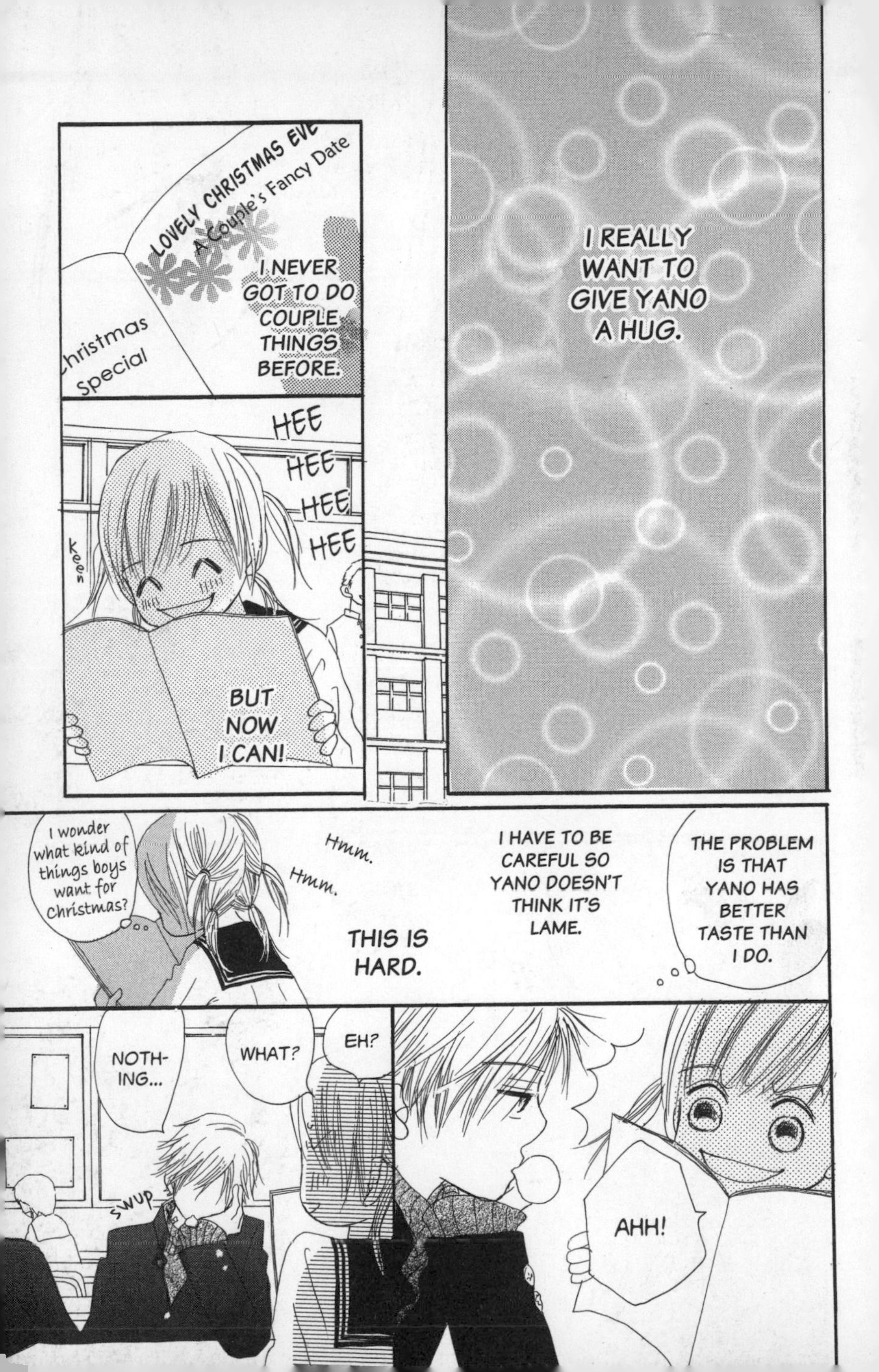
I REALLY WANT TO GIVE YANO A HUG.
LOVELY CHRISTMAS EVE
A Couple's Fancy Date
Christmas Special
I NEVER GOT TO DO COUPLE THINGS BEFORE.
HEE HEE HEE HEE
keen
BUT NOW I CAN!
THE PROBLEM IS THAT YANO HAS BETTER TASTE THAN I DO.
I HAVE TO BE CAREFUL SO YANO DOESN'T THINK IT'S LAME.
THIS IS HARD.
Hmm.
Hmm.
I wonder what kind of things boys want for Christmas?
AHH!
EH?
WHAT?
NOTH-ING...
swup

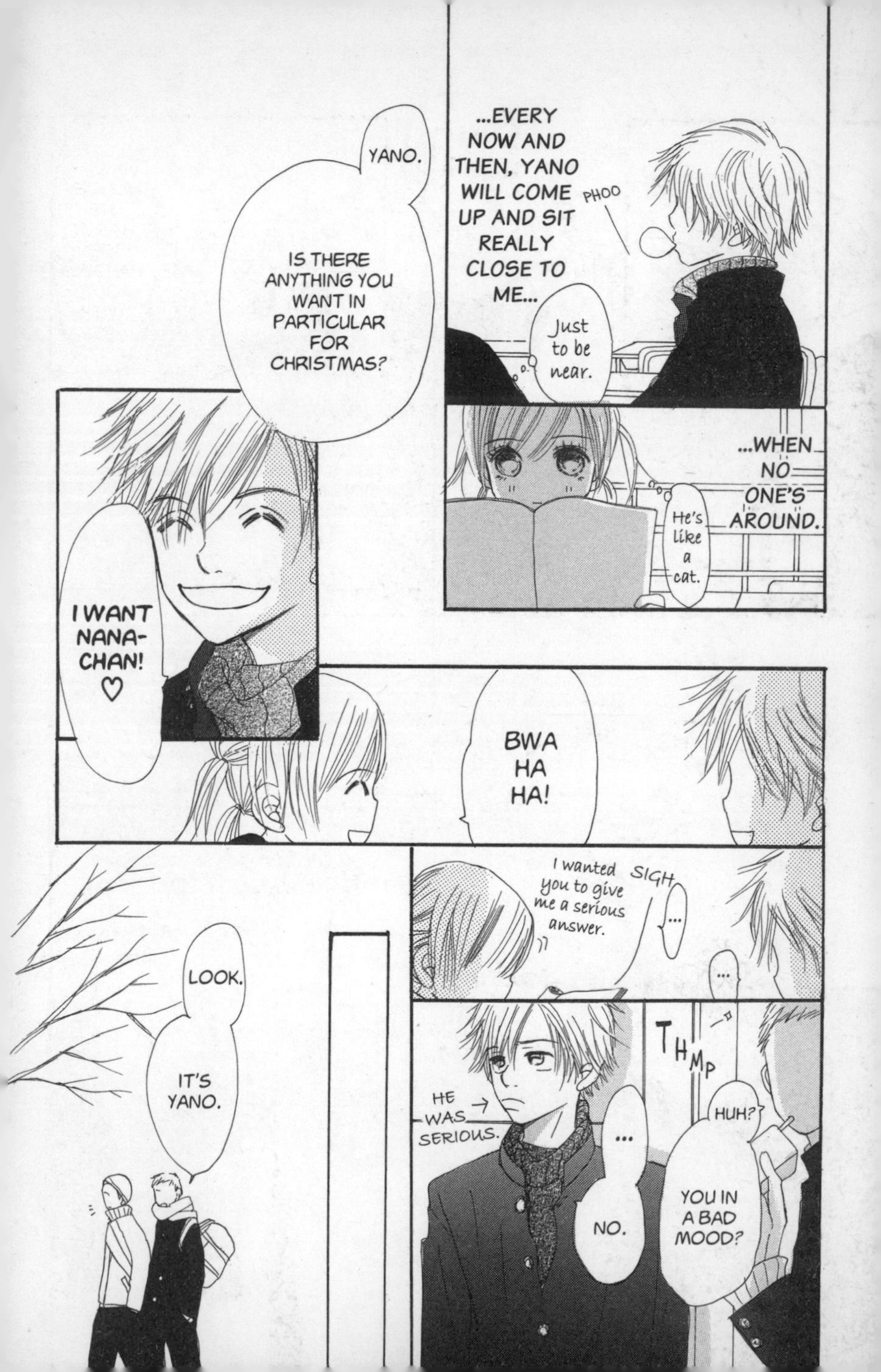
...EVERY NOW AND THEN, YANO WILL COME UP AND SIT REALLY CLOSE TO ME...
PHOO
Just to be near.
...WHEN NO ONE'S AROUND.
He's like a cat.
YANO.
IS THERE ANYTHING YOU WANT IN PARTICULAR FOR CHRISTMAS?
I WANT NANA-CHAN! ♡
BWA HA HA!
SIGH
...
I wanted you to give me a serious answer.
...
THMP
HUH?
YOU IN A BAD MOOD?
...
NO.
HE WAS SERIOUS.
LOOK.
IT'S YANO.

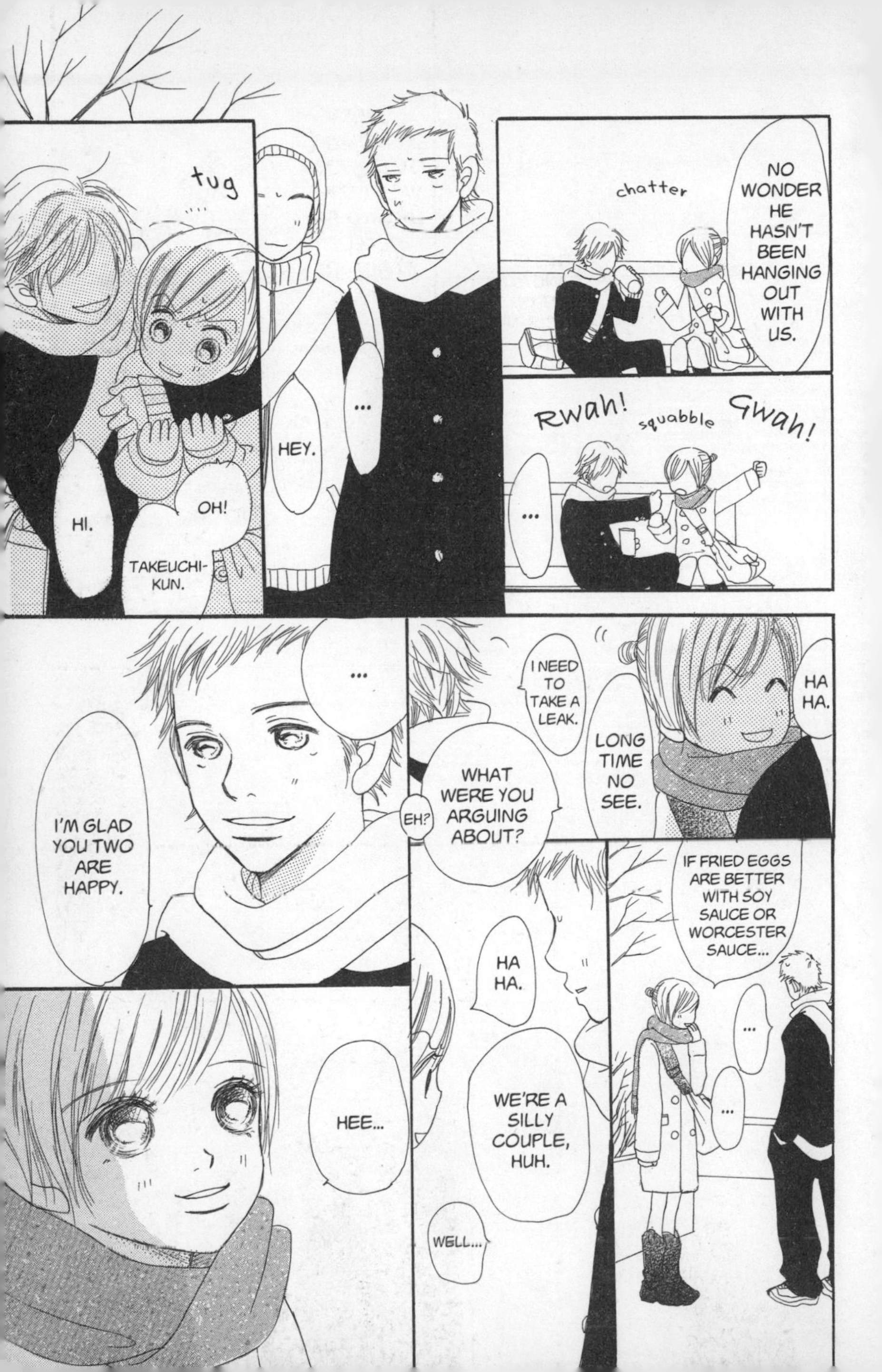
NO WONDER HE HASN'T BEEN HANGING OUT WITH US.
chatter
Gwah!
squabble
Rwah!
...
...
HEY.
tug
OH!
TAKEUCHI-KUN.
HI.
HA HA.
LONG TIME NO SEE.
I NEED TO TAKE A LEAK.
WHAT WERE YOU ARGUING ABOUT?
EH?
...
I'M GLAD YOU TWO ARE HAPPY.
IF FRIED EGGS ARE BETTER WITH SOY SAUCE OR WORCESTER SAUCE...
...
...
HA HA.
WE'RE A SILLY COUPLE, HUH.
WELL...
HEE...

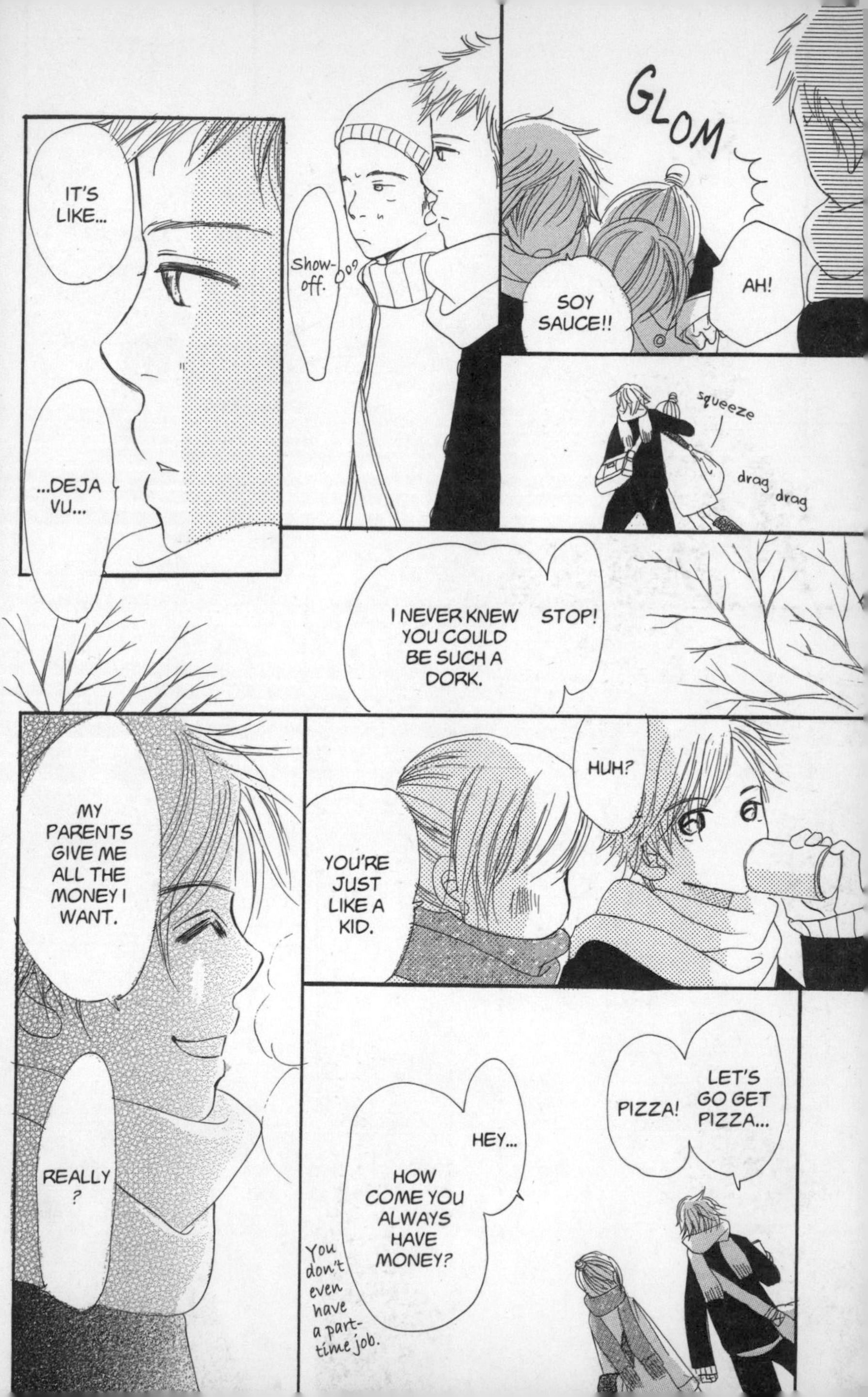

GLOM
AH!
SOY SAUCE!!
squeeze
drag drag
Show-off.
IT'S LIKE...
...DEJA VU...
STOP!
I NEVER KNEW YOU COULD BE SUCH A DORK.
HUH?
YOU'RE JUST LIKE A KID.
LET'S GO GET PIZZA...
PIZZA!
HEY...
HOW COME YOU ALWAYS HAVE MONEY?
You don't even have a part-time job.
MY PARENTS GIVE ME ALL THE MONEY I WANT.
REALLY?

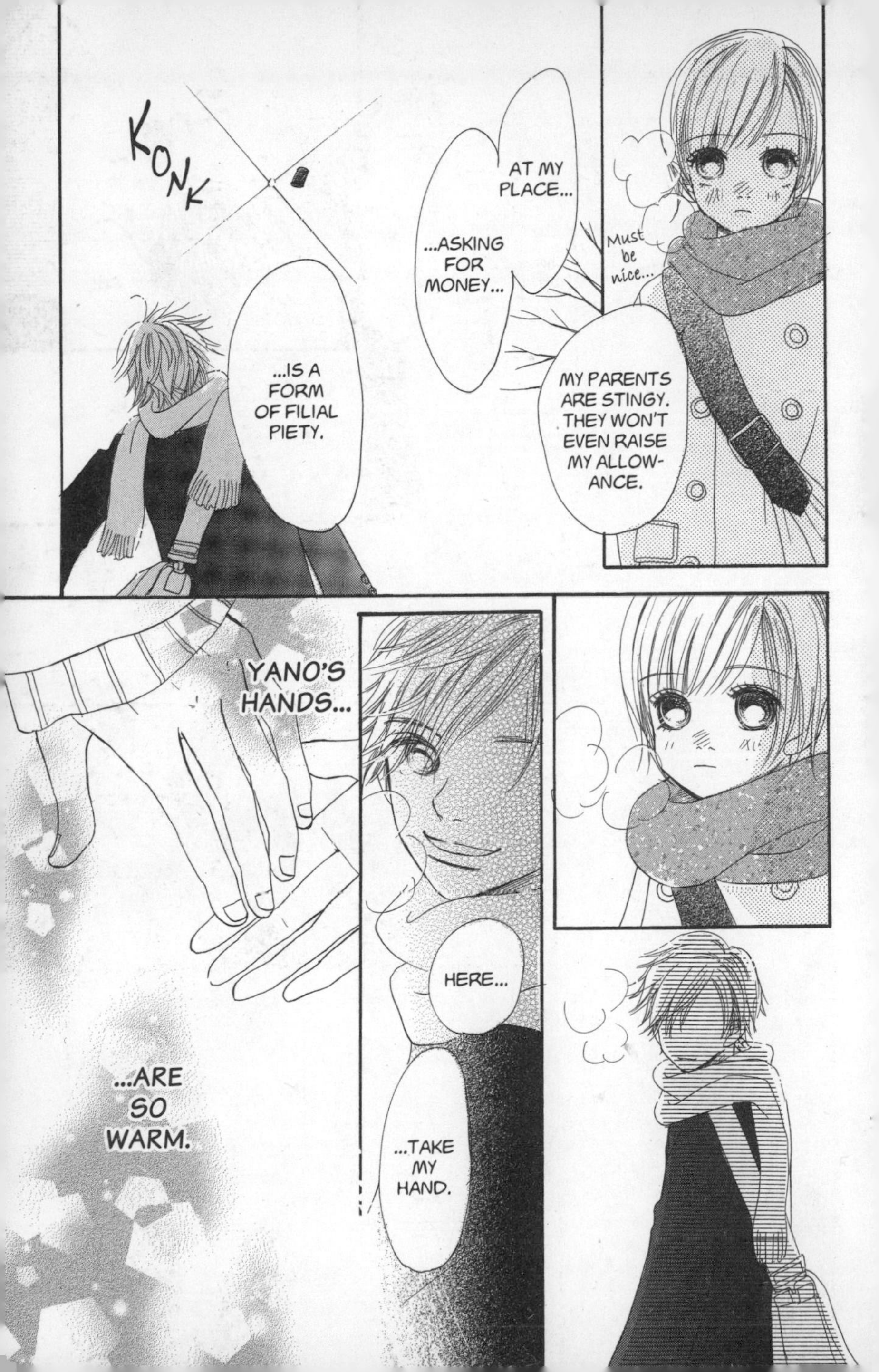
Must be nice...
MY PARENTS ARE STINGY. THEY WON'T EVEN RAISE MY ALLOW-ANCE.
AT MY PLACE...
...ASKING FOR MONEY...
...IS A FORM OF FILIAL PIETY.
KONK
HERE...
...TAKE MY HAND.
YANO'S HANDS...
...ARE SO WARM.

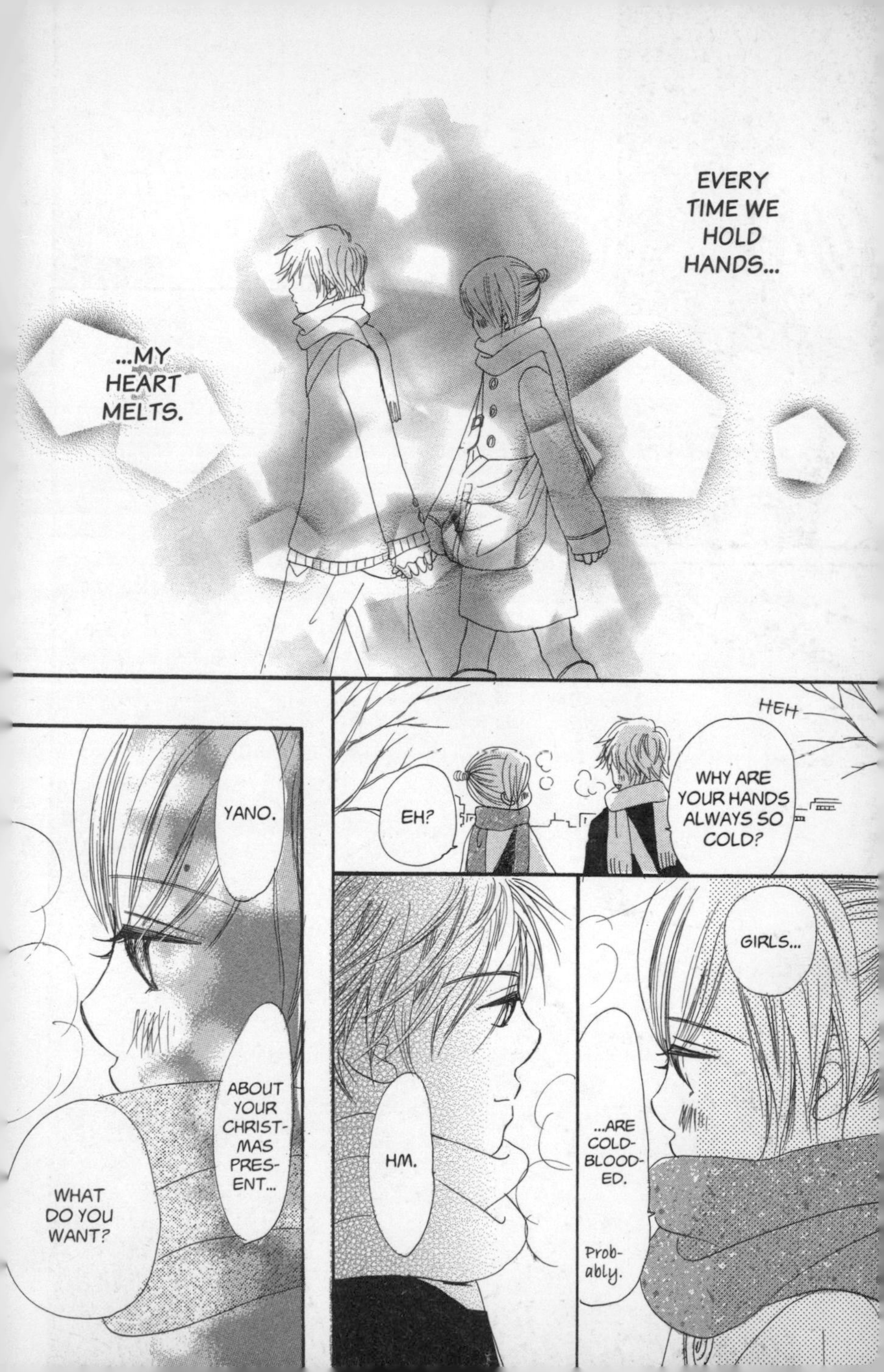
EVERY TIME WE HOLD HANDS...
...MY HEART MELTS.
HEH
WHY ARE YOUR HANDS ALWAYS SO COLD?
EH?
GIRLS...
...ARE COLD-BLOODED.
Probably.
HM.
YANO.
ABOUT YOUR CHRISTMAS PRESENT...
WHAT DO YOU WANT?

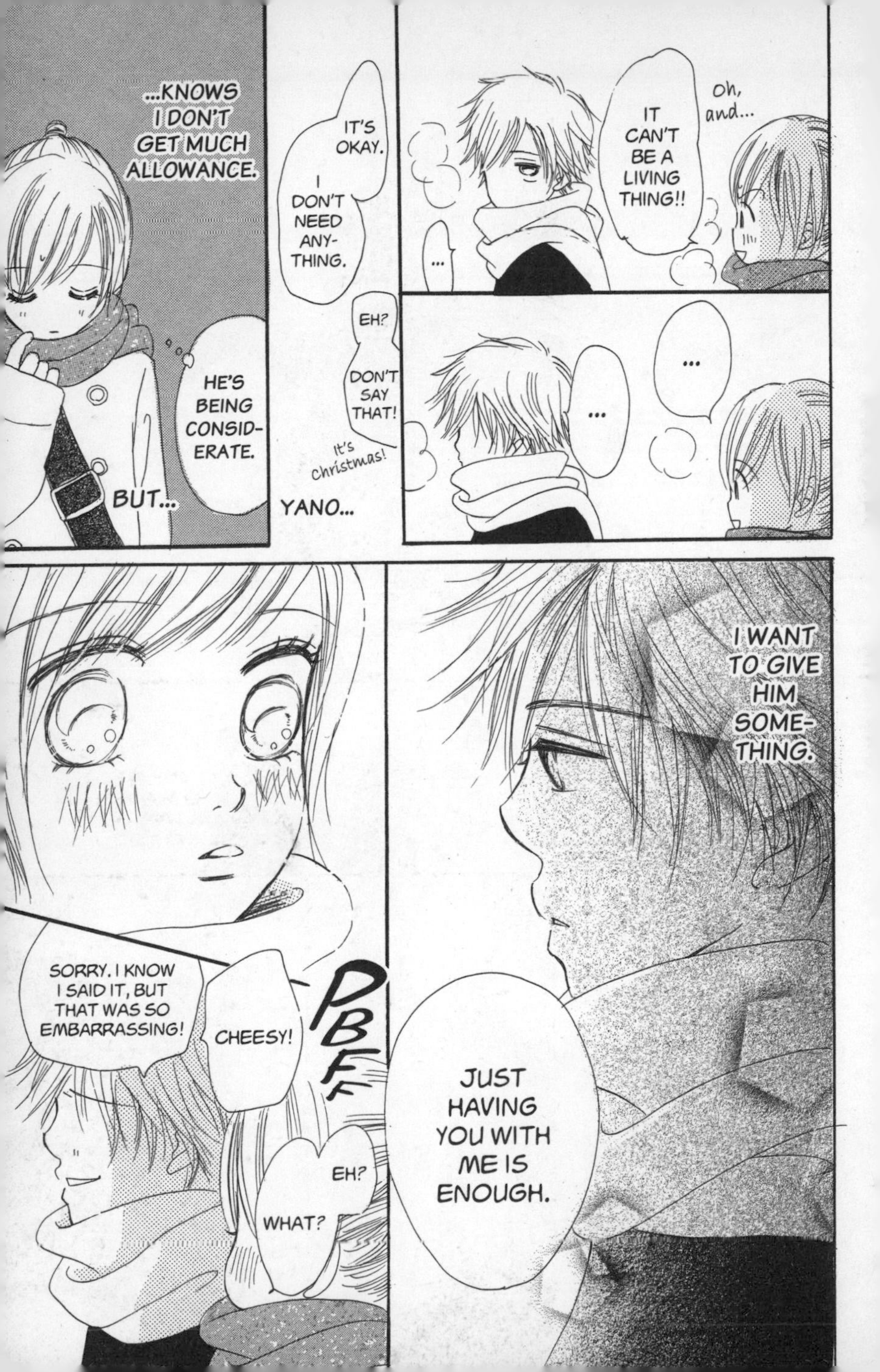
Oh, and...
IT CAN'T BE A LIVING THING!!
...
...
...
IT'S OKAY. I DON'T NEED ANYTHING.
EH? DON'T SAY THAT!
It's Christmas!
YANO...
...KNOWS I DON'T GET MUCH ALLOWANCE.
HE'S BEING CONSIDERATE.
BUT...
I WANT TO GIVE HIM SOMETHING.
JUST HAVING YOU WITH ME IS ENOUGH.
EH? WHAT?
PBFF
CHEESY!
SORRY. I KNOW I SAID IT, BUT THAT WAS SO EMBARRASSING!

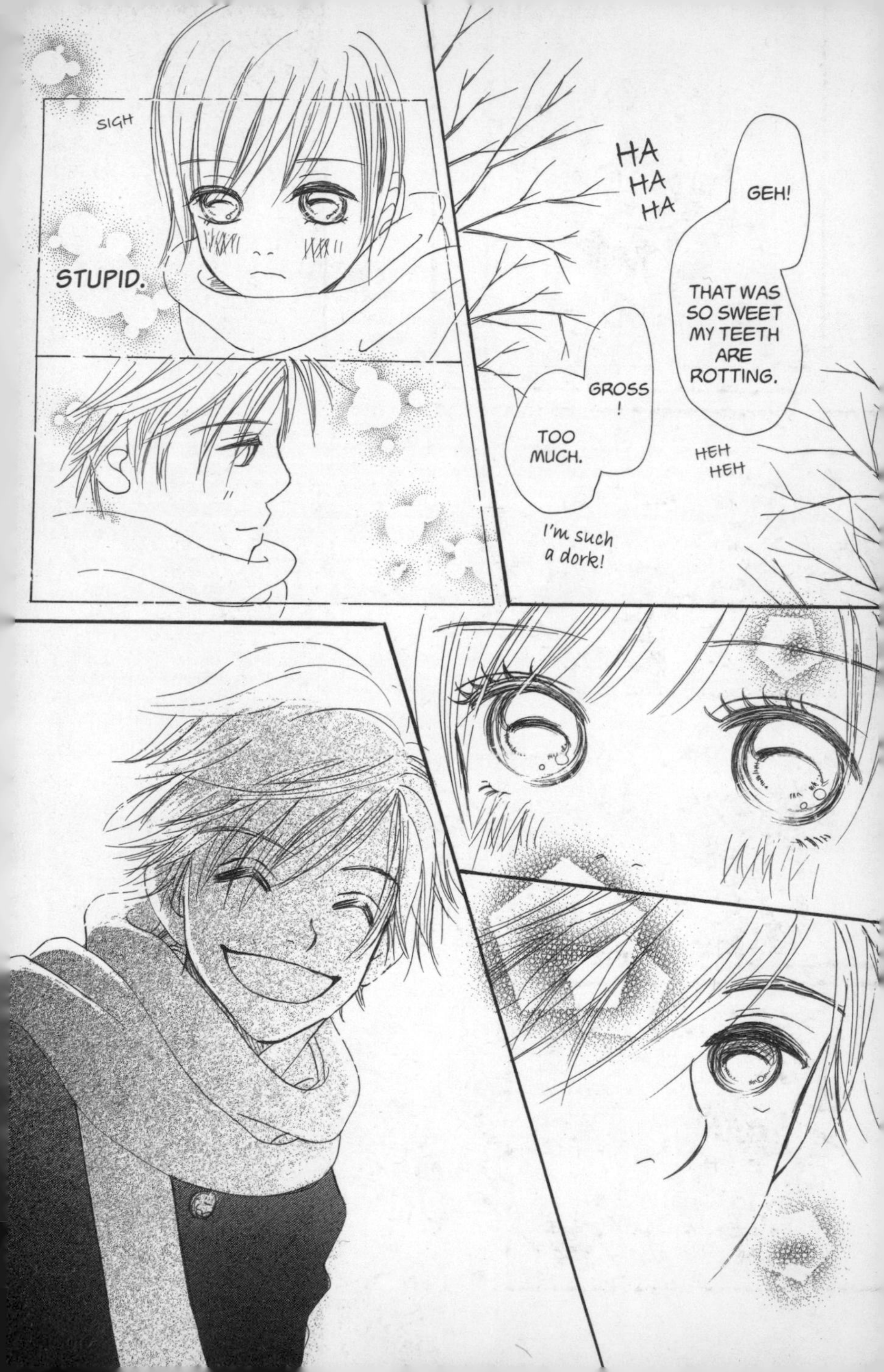
GEH!
THAT WAS SO SWEET MY TEETH ARE ROTTING.
HA HA HA
HEH HEH
GROSS! TOO MUCH.
I'm such a dork!
SIGH
STUPID.

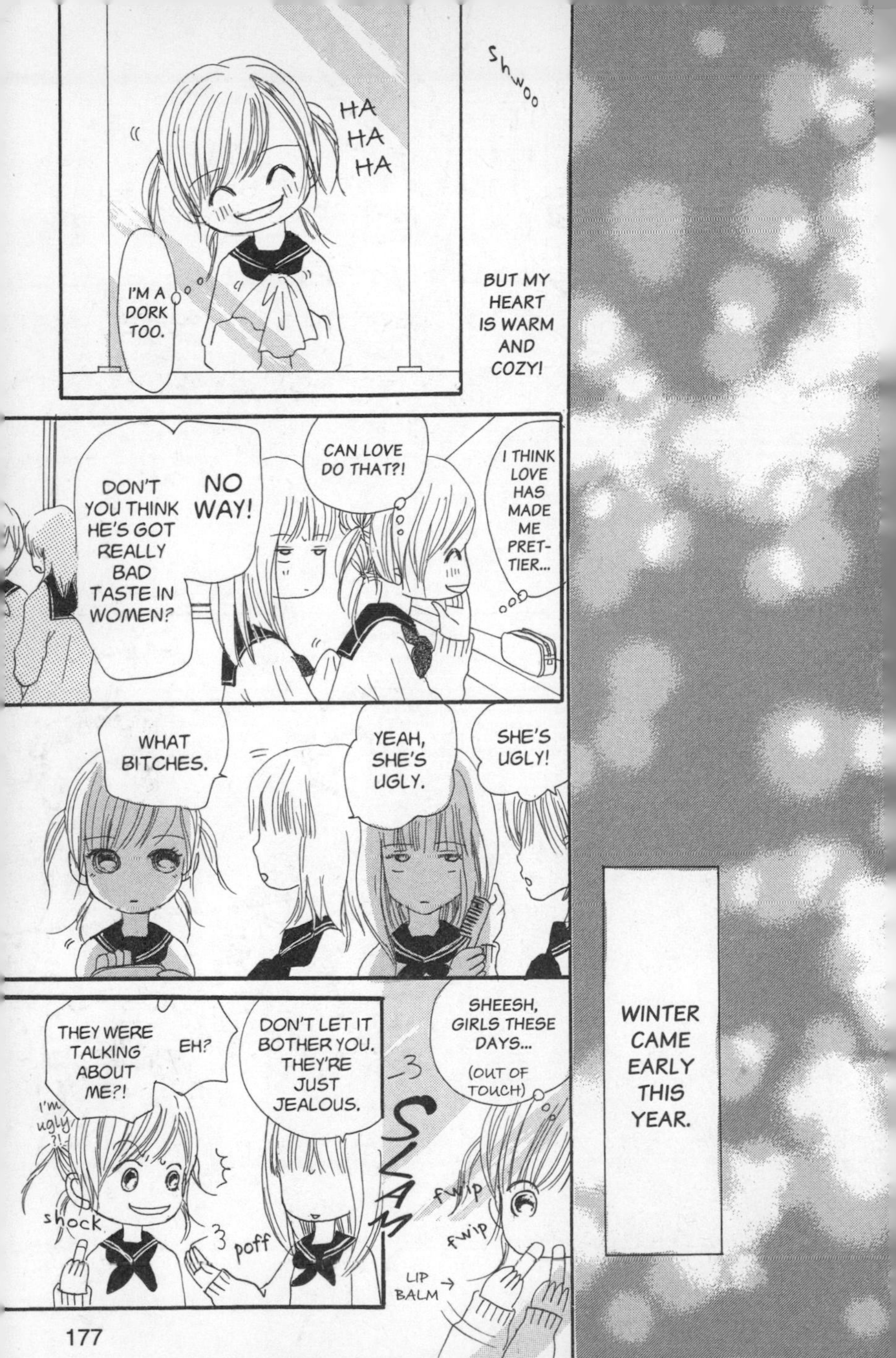
WINTER CAME EARLY THIS YEAR.
Shwoo
BUT MY HEART IS WARM AND COZY!
HA HA HA
I'M A DORK TOO.
I THINK LOVE HAS MADE ME PRETTIER...
CAN LOVE DO THAT?!
NO WAY!
DON'T YOU THINK HE'S GOT REALLY BAD TASTE IN WOMEN?
SHE'S UGLY!
YEAH, SHE'S UGLY.
WHAT BITCHES.
SHEESH, GIRLS THESE DAYS...
(OUT OF TOUCH)
LIP BALM →
fwip
fwip
SLAM
DON'T LET IT BOTHER YOU. THEY'RE JUST JEALOUS.
poff
EH?
THEY WERE TALKING ABOUT ME?!
I'm ugly?!
shock

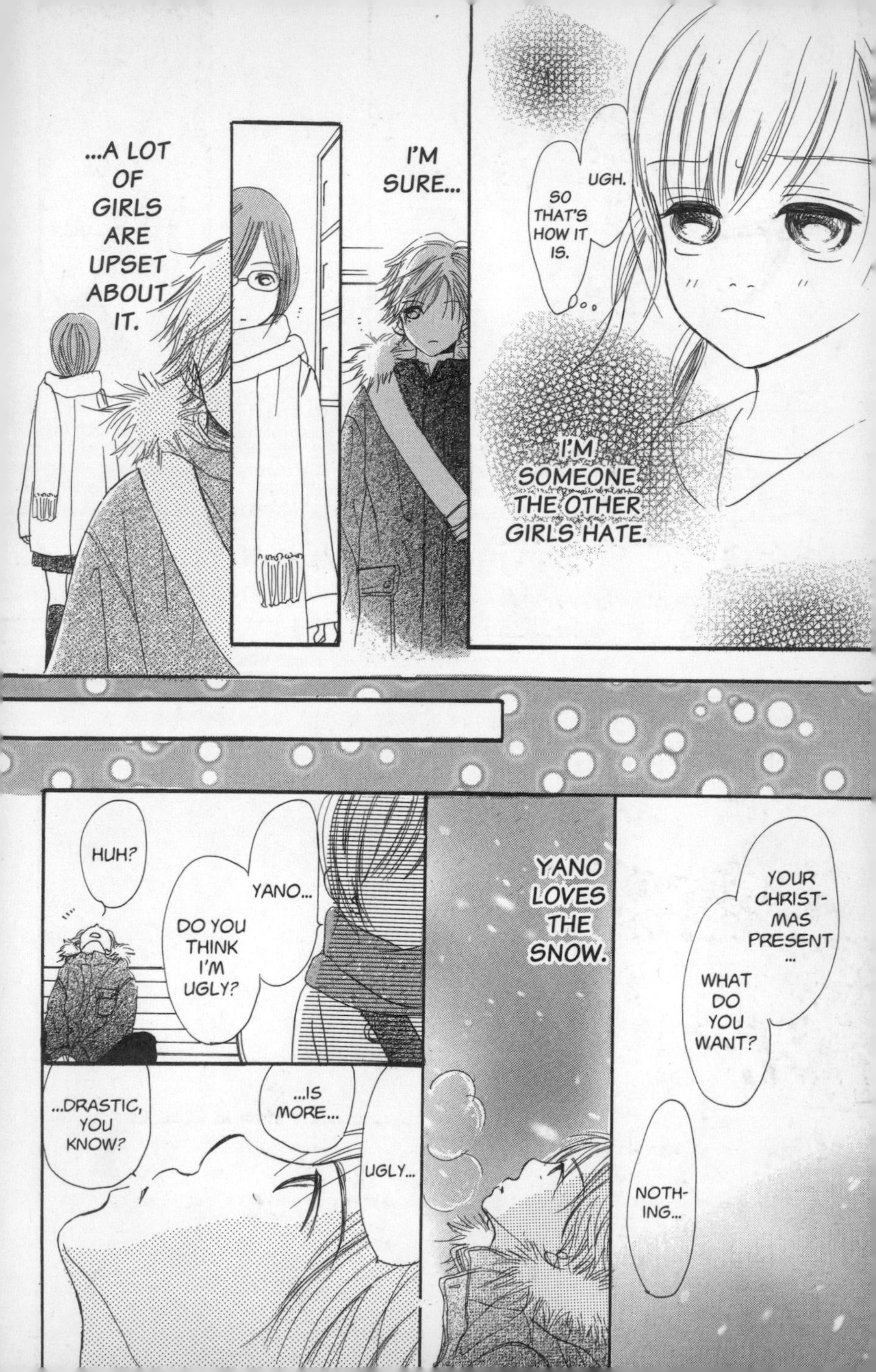
UGH.
SO THAT'S HOW IT IS.
I'M SOMEONE THE OTHER GIRLS HATE.
I'M SURE...
...A LOT OF GIRLS ARE UPSET ABOUT IT.
YOUR CHRIST-MAS PRESENT ...
WHAT DO YOU WANT?
NOTH-ING...
YANO LOVES THE SNOW.
YANO...
DO YOU THINK I'M UGLY?
HUH?
UGLY...
...IS MORE...
...DRASTIC, YOU KNOW?

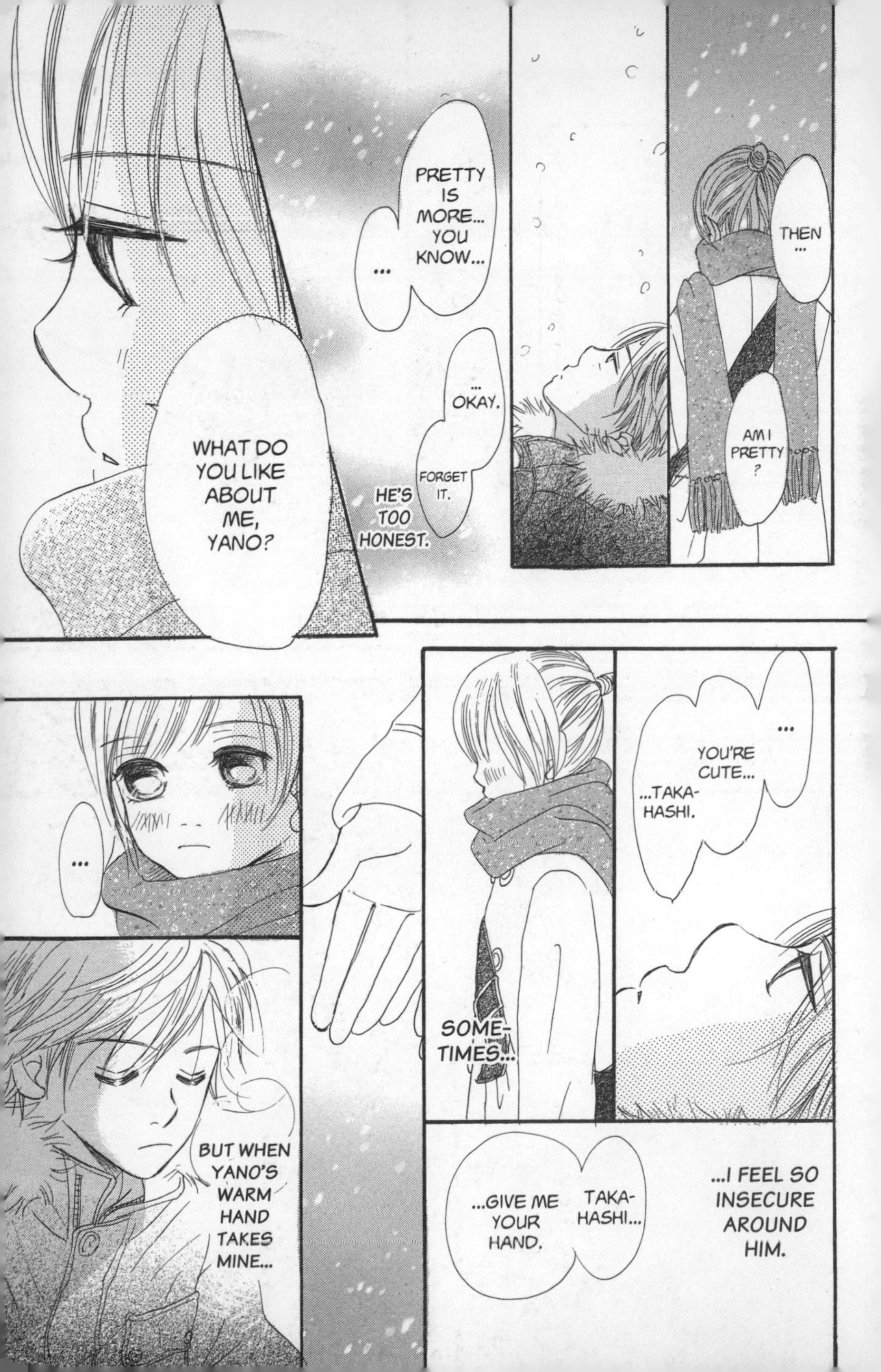

THEN...
AM I PRETTY?
...
PRETTY IS MORE... YOU KNOW...
... OKAY.
FORGET IT.
HE'S TOO HONEST.
WHAT DO YOU LIKE ABOUT ME, YANO?
...
YOU'RE CUTE...
...TAKA-HASHI.
SOME-TIMES...
...I FEEL SO INSECURE AROUND HIM.
TAKA-HASHI...
...GIVE ME YOUR HAND.
...
BUT WHEN YANO'S WARM HAND TAKES MINE...

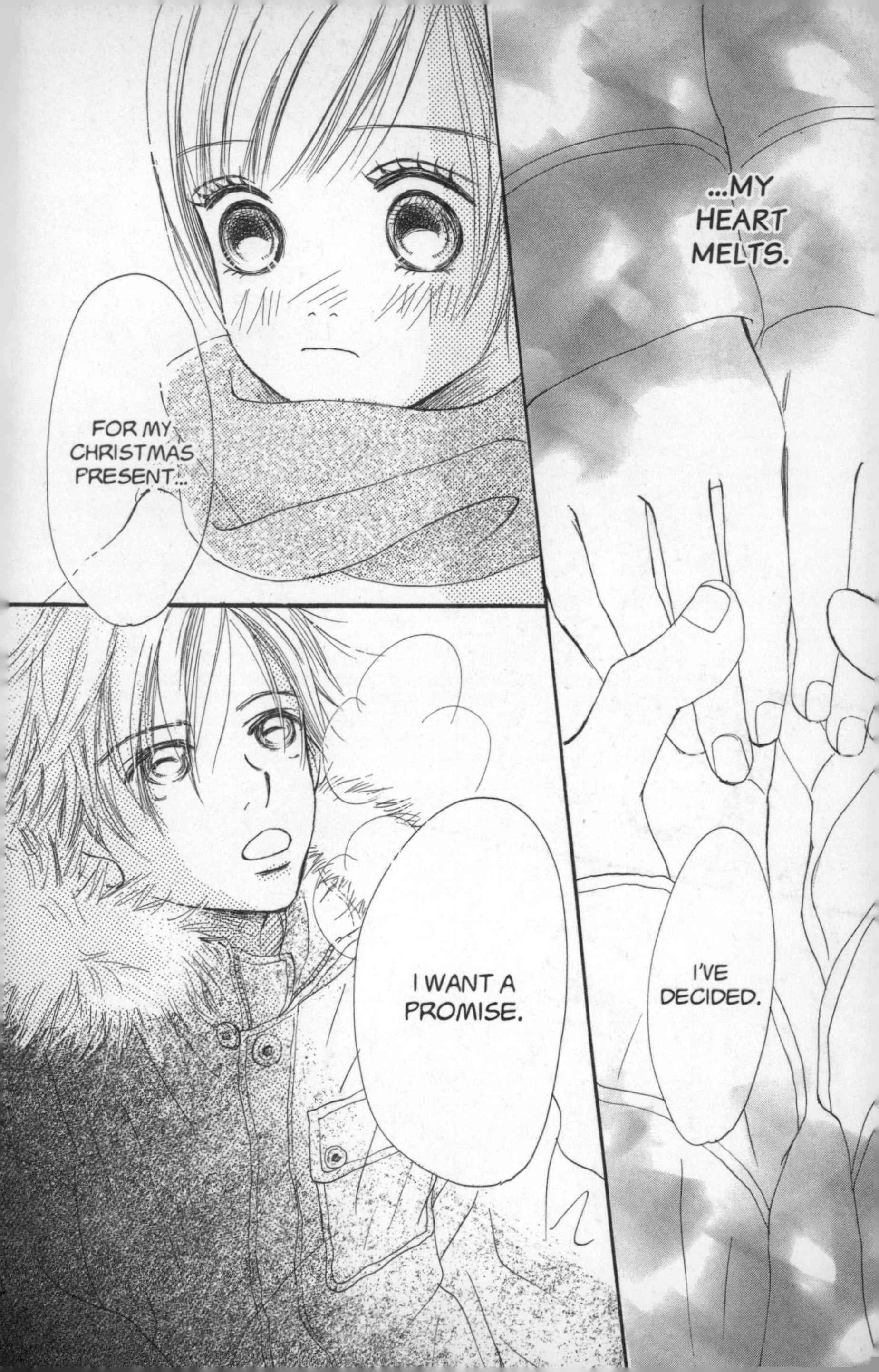
...MY HEART MELTS.
I'VE DECIDED.
FOR MY CHRISTMAS PRESENT...
I WANT A PROMISE.

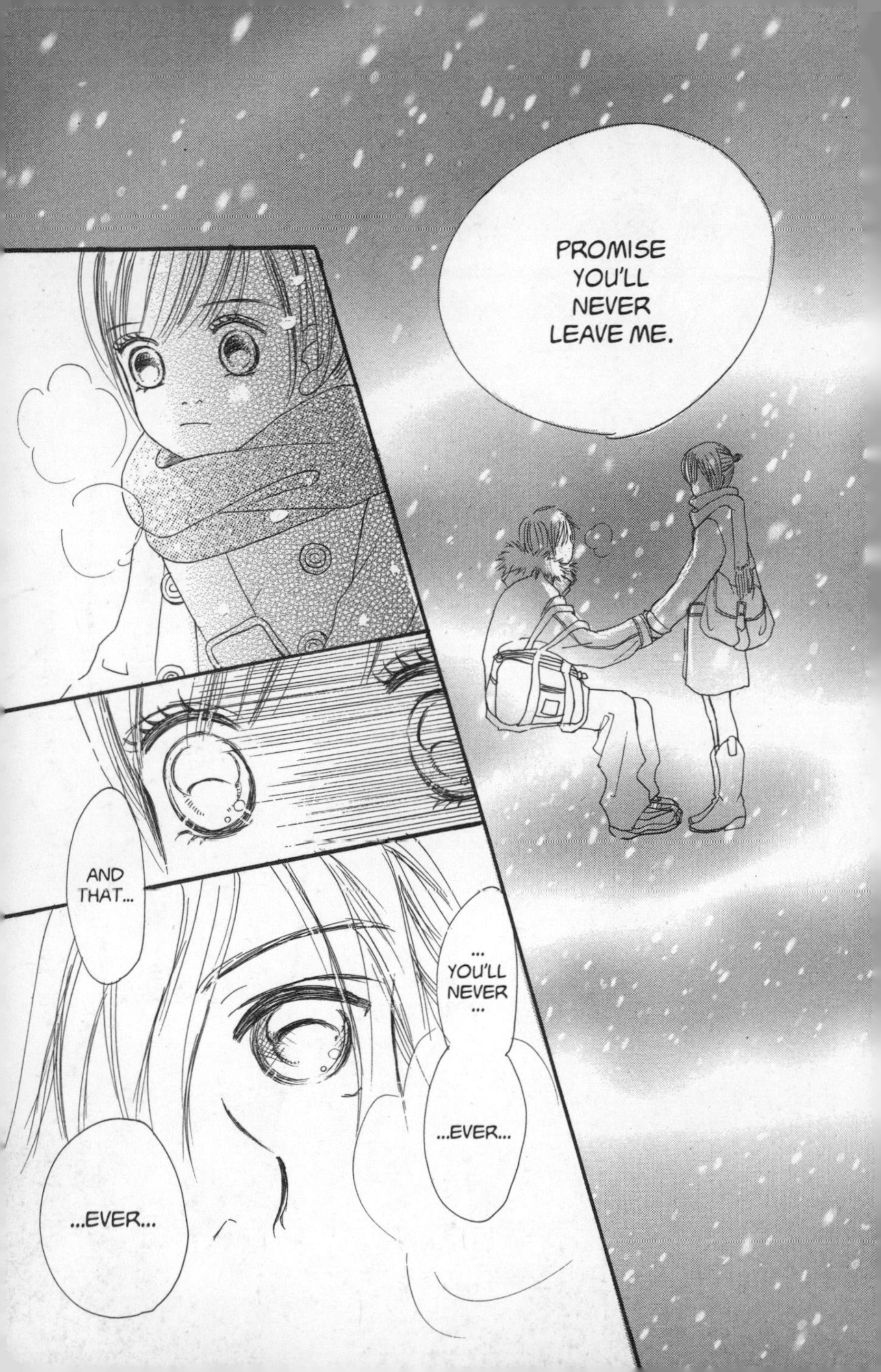
PROMISE YOU'LL NEVER LEAVE ME.
AND THAT...
... YOU'LL NEVER ...
...EVER...
...EVER...

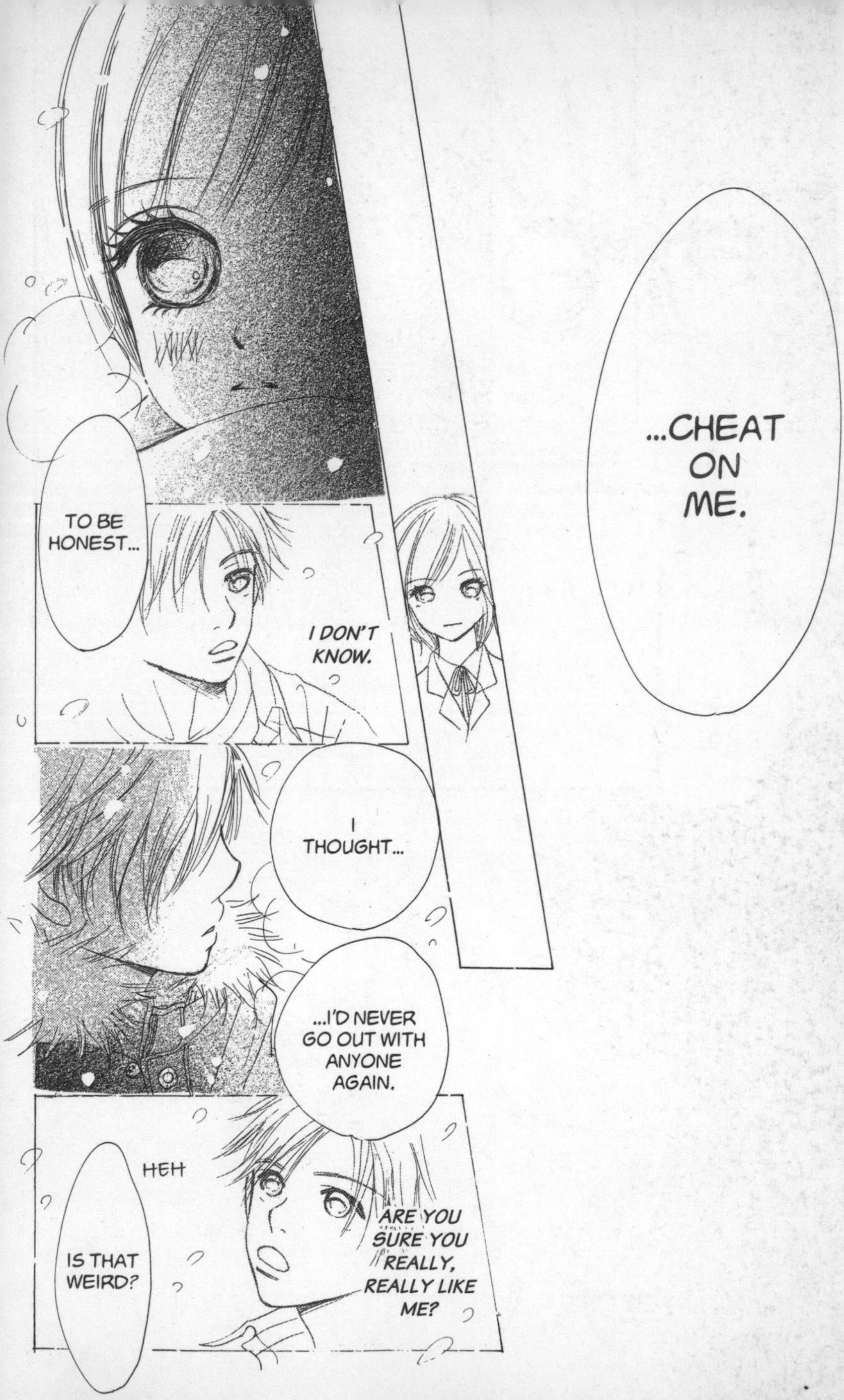
...CHEAT ON ME.
TO BE HONEST...
I DON'T KNOW.
I THOUGHT...
...I'D NEVER GO OUT WITH ANYONE AGAIN.
ARE YOU SURE YOU REALLY, REALLY LIKE ME?
HEH
IS THAT WEIRD?

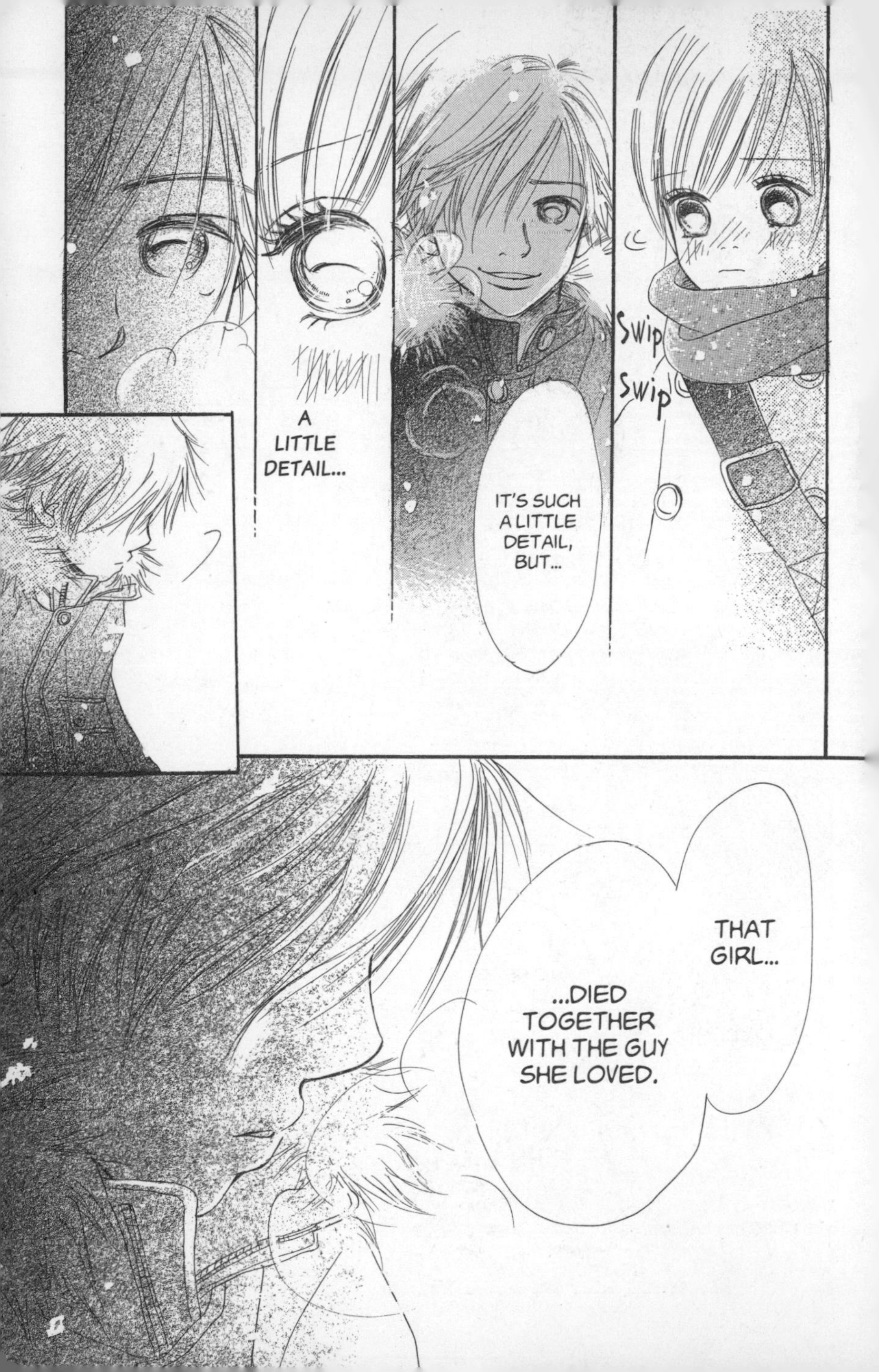
Swip
Swip
IT'S SUCH A LITTLE DETAIL, BUT...
A LITTLE DETAIL...
THAT GIRL...
...DIED TOGETHER WITH THE GUY SHE LOVED.

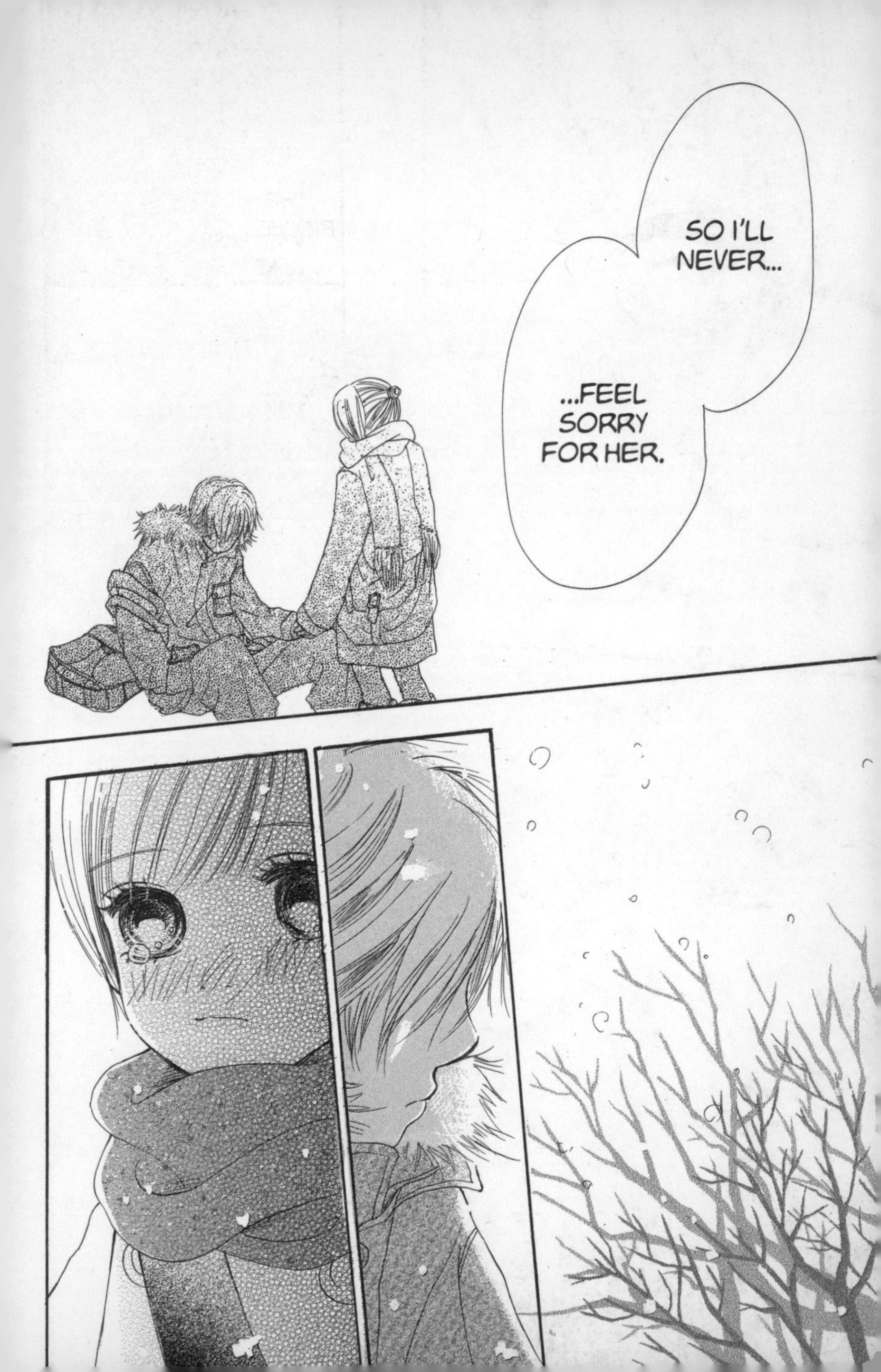
SO I'LL NEVER...
...FEEL SORRY FOR HER.

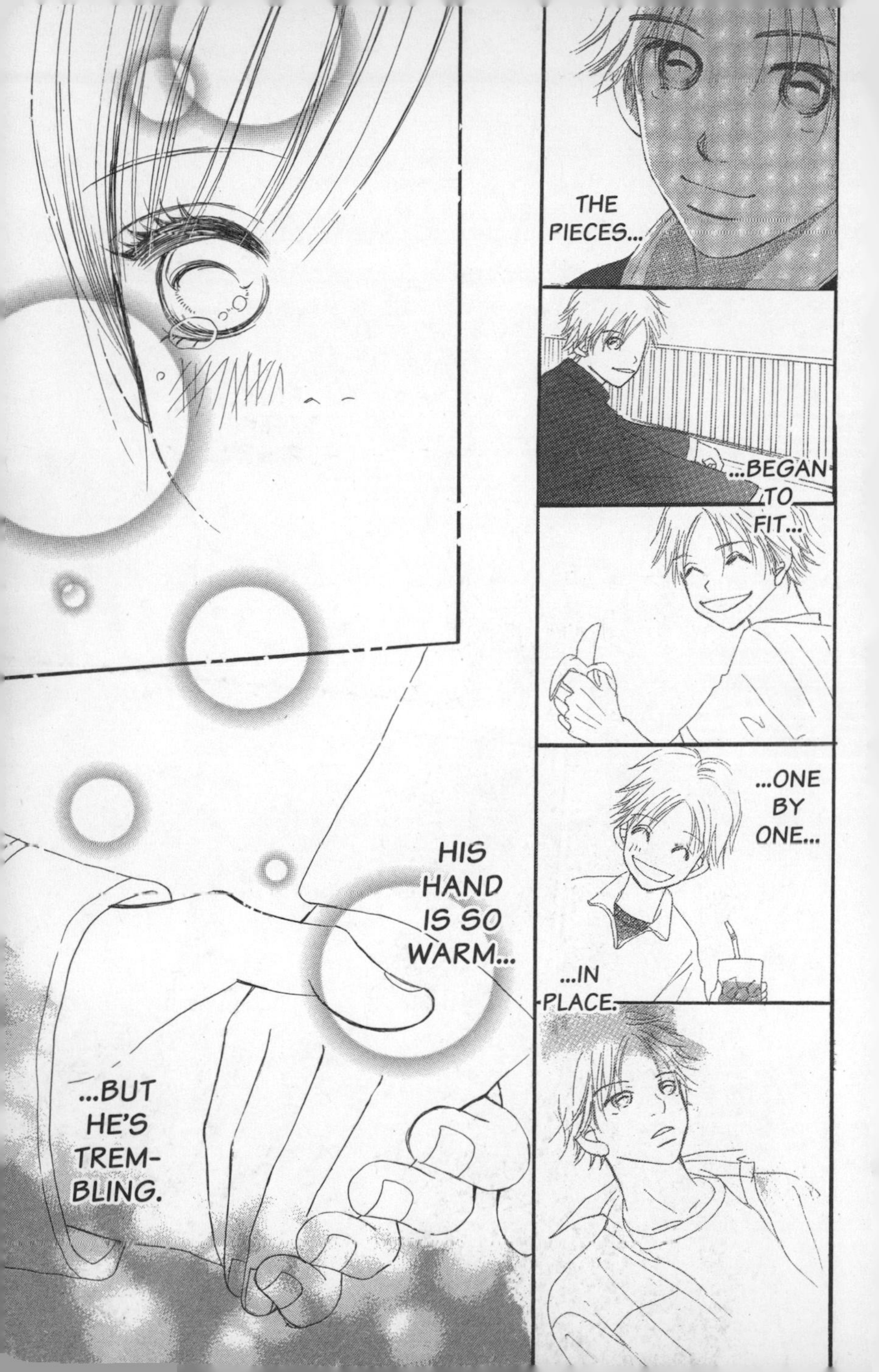
THE PIECES...
...BEGAN TO FIT...
...ONE BY ONE...
...IN PLACE.
HIS HAND IS SO WARM...
...BUT HE'S TREMBLING.

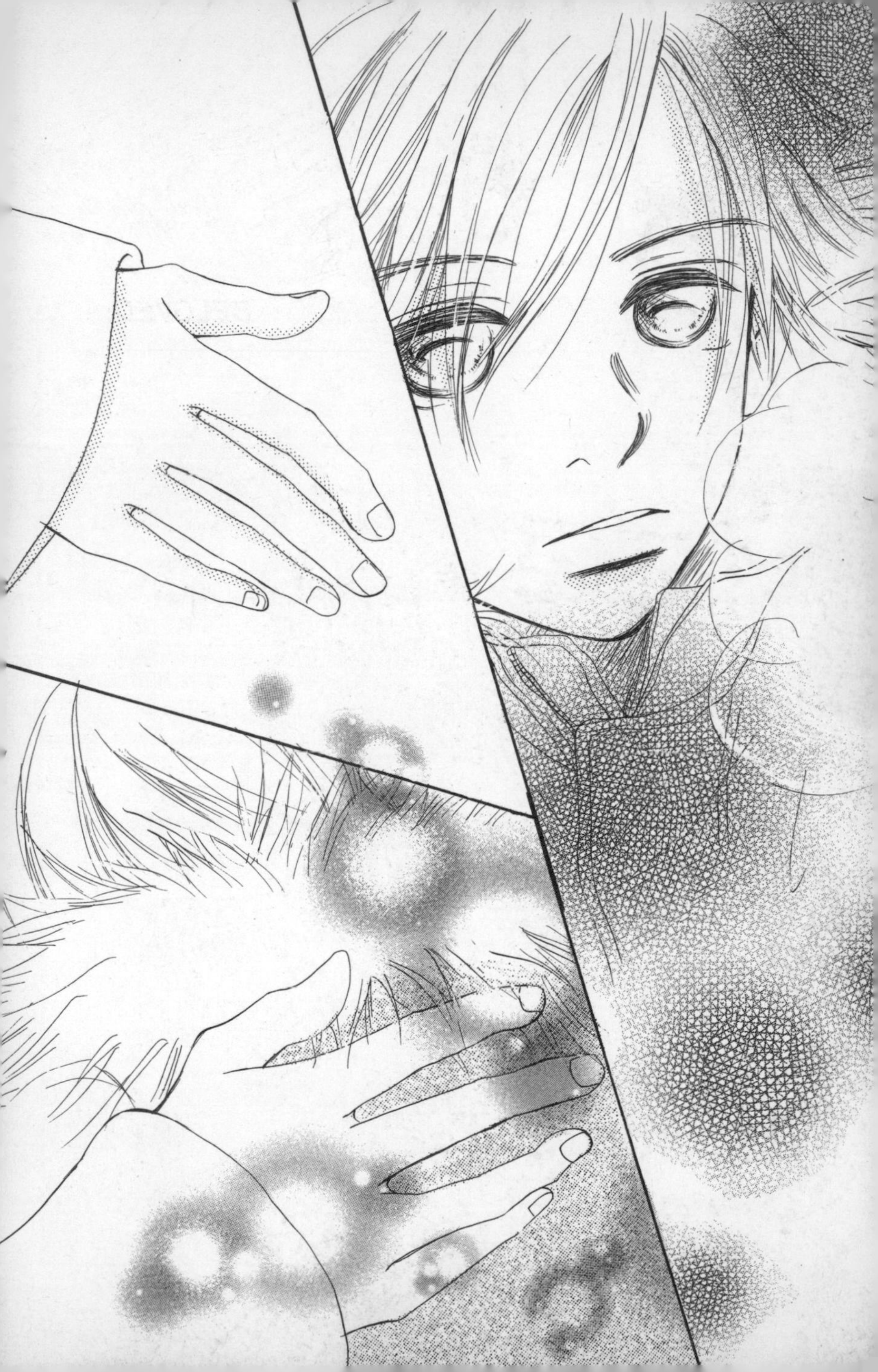

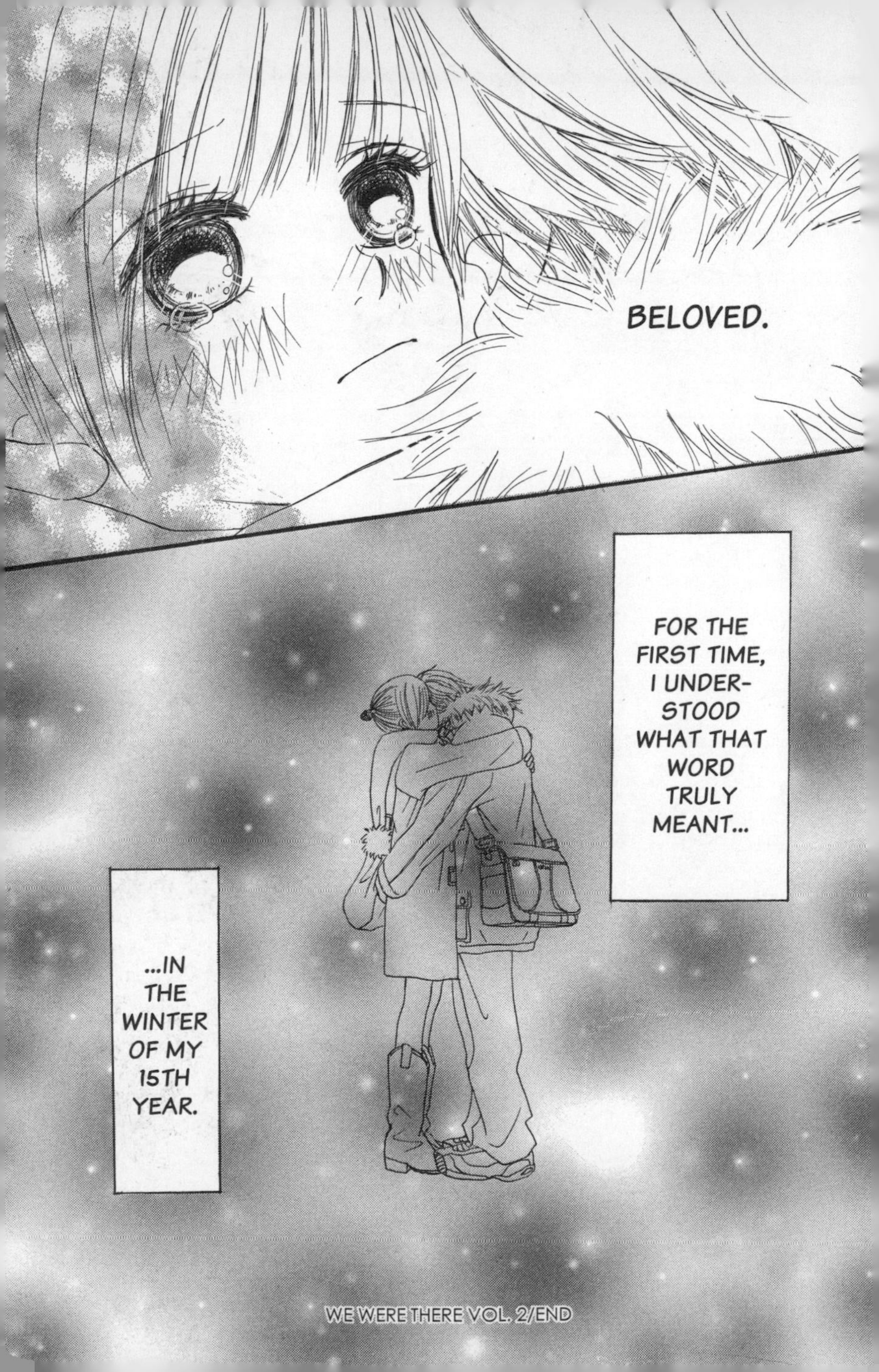
BELOVED.
FOR THE FIRST TIME, I UNDER-STOOD WHAT THAT WORD TRULY MEANT...
...IN THE WINTER OF MY 15TH YEAR.
WE WERE THERE VOL. 2/END

Notes

Honorifics

In Japan, people are usually addressed by their name followed by a suffix. The suffix shows familiarity or respect, depending on the relationship.

Male (familiar): first or last name + kun
Female (familiar): first or last name + chan
Adult (polite): last name + san
Upperclassman (polite): last name + senpai
Teacher or professional: last name + sensei
Close friends or lovers: first name only, no suffix

Nana-chan vs. Nana-san

Nanami's nickname is "Nana-chan." Yano's ex-girlfriend was a year older, so she was known as "Nana-san."

Terms

Yukata is a type of kimono worn in the summer.
Sunday refers to *Shonen Sunday*, a manga magazine for boys.
Nopopon is a line of fluffy, cushion-like objects used for arm and elbow rests.
Mizu-chin is Mizuguchi's nickname.
Wasshoi is a cheer often heard during festivals when a *mikoshi*, or portable shrine, is being carried.

Yuki Obata's birthday is January 9. Her debut manga, *Raindrops*, won the Shogakukan Shinjin Comics Taisho Kasaku Award in 1998. Her current series, *We Were There* (*Bokura ga Ita*), won the 50th Shogakukan Manga Award and was adapted into an animated television series. She likes sweets, coffee, drinking with friends, and scary stories. Her hobby is browsing in bookshops.

We Were There
Vol. 2
The Shojo Beat Manga Edition

STORY & ART BY
YUKI OBATA

Adaptation/Nancy Thistlethwaite
Translation/Tetsuichiro Miyaki
Touch-up Art & Lettering/Inori Fukuda Trant
Design/Izumi Hirayama
Editor/Nancy Thistlethwaite

Editor in Chief, Books/Alvin Lu
Editor in Chief, Magazines/Marc Weidenbaum
VP, Publishing Licensing/Rika Inouye
VP, Sales & Product Marketing/Gonzalo Ferreyra
VP, Creative/Linda Espinosa
Publisher/Hyoe Narita

BOKURA GA ITA 2 by Yuuki OBATA © 2003 Yuuki OBATA
All rights reserved. Original Japanese edition published in
2003 by Shogakukan Inc., Tokyo. The stories, characters and
incidents mentioned in this publication are entirely fictional.

No portion of this book may be reproduced or transmitted in any form
or by any means without written permission from the copyright holders.

Printed in Canada

Published by VIZ Media, LLC
P.O. Box 77010
San Francisco, CA 94107

Shojo Beat Manga Edition
10 9 8 7 6 5 4 3 2 1
First printing, January 2009

www.viz.com

store.viz.com

PARENTAL ADVISORY
WE WERE THERE is rated T+ for Older
Teen and is recommended for ages 16 and
up. This volume contains sexual themes.
ratings.viz.com